# Globalization and Armed Conflict

# Globalization and Armed Conflict

EDITED BY
GERALD SCHNEIDER, KATHERINE BARBIERI,
AND NILS PETTER GLEDITSCH

ROWMAN & LITTLEFIELD PUBLISHERS, INC.
*Lanham • Boulder • New York • Toronto • Oxford*

ROWMAN & LITTLEFIELD PUBLISHERS, INC.

Published in the United States of America
by Rowman & Littlefield Publishers, Inc.
A wholly owned subsidiary of The Rowman & Littlefield Publishing Group, Inc.
4501 Forbes Boulevard, Suite 200, Lanham, Maryland 20706
www.rowmanlittlefield.com

P.O. Box 317, Oxford OX2 9RU, United Kingdom

British Library Cataloguing in Publication Information Available

**Library of Congress Cataloging-in-Publication Data**

Globalization and armed conflict / edited by Gerald Schneider, Katherine Barbieri, and
Nils Petter Gleditsch.
p. cm.
Includes bibliographical references and index.
ISBN 0-7425-1831-0 (cl. : alk. paper) — ISBN 0-7425-1832-9 (pbk. : alk. paper)
1. Peace. 2. Security, International. 3. International trade. 4. Globalization. I.
Schneider, Gerald, 1962– II. Barbieri, Katherine, 1965– III. Gleditsch, Nils Petter,
1942–

JZ5538.G58 2003
303.6—dc21                                                                    2003043177

Printed in the United States of America

∞™ The paper used in this publication meets the minimum requirements of American
National Standard for Information Sciences—Permanence of Paper for Printed Library
Materials, ANSI/NISO Z39.48-1992.

# Contents

## Part II: Empirical Contributions

# Figures and Tables

## Figures

# Tables

# Preface

The rising level of economic integration around the globe has raised many fears and hopes. One of them is the expectation that economic interdependence is somehow causally related to armed conflict. The opponents of what we nowadays call 'globalization' belong to the skeptical camp. Some of these critics believe that increasing economic interaction between states increases the risk of militarized conflict. Others simply believe that globalization will do little to prevent armed conflict, rejecting the notion that a globalized world will necessarily be a more peaceful one. They also argue that growing interdependence has dangerous side effects such as increasing income inequality and environmental degradation. Most proponents of economic integration do not reject the idea that economic activities create such externalities. They firmly believe, however, that the positive effects of a globalizing world economy clearly outweigh these negative aspects. According to the optimists, reducing the risk of armed conflict is among the most important benefits of globalization.

Many politicians have come to share the view of globalization's pacifying effect and regularly contend that increasing trade is one of the most secure means to lower the likelihood of violent conflict. This hope has also received the attention of some influential newspaper commentators. To take the best known example, *New York Times* columnist Thomas L. Friedman has advanced the so-called Big Mac Theory: 'No two countries that both have a McDonald's have ever fought a war against each other' (*NYT*, 8 December 1996). One can easily dismiss the casual empiricism behind this 'law' and point out apparent deficiencies in Friedman's argument. Yet, the lack of theoretical sophistication and empirical rigor in testing the Big Mac Theory does not necessarily disqualify the hypothesis. Similar projections abound in the theory of international relations.

The conjecture that globalization pacifies state leaders dates back at least to the seventeenth century, and has inspired such eminent philosophers as Montesquieu and Kant. Yet, the peace-through-trade hypothesis has gone through several academic cycles. It generally enjoys popularity when the pace of economic integration accelerates. Trade was expanding before World War I when Norman Angell (1910) contended that increasing trade bonds would render war a 'great illusion'. Yet this vision typically loses some of its intellectual appeal in times of increasing protectionism. During such eras mercantilist policies gain ground and with them the aspiration to rely on domestic resources to shield the state against foreign aggression. In part, the rise and decline of protectionism may be traced to periods in which the global economy is expanding or shrinking. Perceptions about globalization's positive and negative effects may be tied to the health of the economy and the perceived benefits and costs.

When the pace of integration accelerated in the 1990s, the link between economic interdependence and militarized conflict experienced an intellectual renaissance. Scholars have offered innovative theories and sophisticated methodologies to address this central policy issue. Although they have made many impressive advances, the case for free trade is far from being closed. On the contrary, the possible nexus between globalization and armed conflict has become a major debate in international relations. This volume provides readers with a representative sample of the most recent advances in trade-conflict research and includes a diversity of views and approaches, as well as active discussion among scholars engaged in the relevant debates. Although a clear differentiation between theory and empirical work becomes increasingly obsolete, we have divided the book into two conceptual segments. The first part starts out with our own introduction and continues with some of the theoretical work done in the field. The second part contains the more empirically oriented chapters and includes some discussions about appropriate estimation techniques.

Each chapter provides an example of cutting-edge research in this area. While some contributions make significant advances on the theoretical side, others mainly break new ground on the empirical frontier. The book grew out of a special issue of *Journal of Peace Research* for which two of us served as guest editors. We would like to thank the editorial committee of *JPR* for its enthusiastic support for the proposal. This volume, though, moves beyond the special issue. It includes several additional articles and allows some authors to respond to criticism of their earlier work. These additions and changes illustrate the rapid growth of our knowledge on the interrelationship between economic interdependence and armed conflict.

Katherine Barbieri and Gerald Schneider would like to thank the International Studies Association for a workshop grant that provided the means for several colleagues to participate in a double panel held at the ISA Annual Convention in Minneapolis in March 1998. Several of the articles collected in this volume were presented for the first time at that meeting. Gerald Schneider would like to extend his gratitude for a scholarship under the German-Norwegian cultural agreement enabling him to present some of the ideas contained in the introductory chapter during lectures at PRIO in April and August 1998, and to the Research Council of Norway for travel support for his second visit. A second academic conference in which some of the authors and editors of this volume participated was the workshop on 'Globalization and Armed Conflict' that Nils Petter Gleditsch and Gerald Schneider organized in Copenhagen in April 2000 under the auspices of the European Consortium for Political Research. Nils Petter Gleditsch would like to thank the World Society Foundation and the Research Council of Norway for funding his own work and that of his colleagues at PRIO.

We would like to thank Jutta Link, Renée Rummel, and Lars Wilhelmsen, who helped in the preparation of the final manuscript.


—Gerald Schneider, Katherine Barbieri, Nils Petter Gleditsch

# PART I

# Competing Models of the Peace-Through-Globalization Hypothesis

# CHAPTER 1

# Does Globalization Contribute to Peace?
# A Critical Survey of the Literature

*Gerald Schneider, Katherine Barbieri, and Nils Petter Gleditsch*

The contemporary surge in economic interdependence referred to as globalization has provoked speculation about its impact on international relations. Many political leaders hold the long-standing belief that economic openness helps to pacify both international and domestic relations, a view typically associated with commercial liberalism. This conjecture has played a key role in international relations thinking in recent decades, but it can be traced back to the writings of liberal thinkers such as Montesquieu or Kant.

In contrast, realist and Marxist critics reject this perspective with the same vigor as internationalization skeptics challenge the allegedly beneficial or neutral effects that globalization has on the environment or social equality. Critics of the 'peace-through-trade'-hypothesis argue that economic interdependence may have either a negligible or amplifying effect on international conflict. Although this position is rare in government circles, it enjoys considerable support among those groups that rally against globalization. The skeptical hypothesis has as long a history as that of commercial liberalism. Hamilton (1791/1966), List (1842), and Hirschman (1945/1980) were among those who showed that economic openness might not always be beneficial. Such doubts gained ground in development economics after World War II and influenced policy makers in international organizations and governments. While en vogue in Western academic circles in the 1960s and 1970s, the skeptical view finds less support in leading universities and think tanks today. Yet, the conjecture that economic interdependence might increase the level of instability both within and between states still emerges in the journalistic work of globalization critics. One example is the best-selling polemic *Jihad vs. McWorld* in which Benjamin R. Barber argues that ethnic fractionalization and globalization feed on each other in a dialectic fashion. Commenting upon the civil war in Bosnia, he writes about the tragic fate of two murdered lovers: 'Before they could cross the magical border that separates their impoverished land from the seeming sanctuary of McWorld, Jihad caught up to them. Their bodies lay along the riverbank, riddled with bullets from anonymous snipers' (Barber, 1996: 19).

This introductory chapter addresses this debate between the opponents and proponents of globalization. To this end we review contributions from the scientific study of war and peace. In particular, we try to bridge the gap between theoretical and empirical research. While much recent empirical work supports the general hypothesis of a positive influence on peace of some facets of globalization, proponents of noncooperative game theory show that this is contingent upon a set of other factors such as enforcement and monitoring mechanisms, the size of the international system, or the distribution of power within states (Skaperdas and Syropoulos, 1996; Dorussen and Hegre, Morrow, Schneider and Schulze, this volume). This new work qualifies the assertion that extensive commercial bonds between nations create a deterrent to conflict. While the peace-through-globalization hypothesis may be accurate at times, it may also be wrong on some occasions. We need to carefully delineate the conditions of our theoretical argument and empirical specifications. Empirical evidence presented in this chapter indeed points out some exceptions to the conjecture that economic integration pacifies states.

More fine-grained theories could result from attempts to establish more solid microfoundations of commercial liberalism. Krugman's (1996) assertion that firms and not states trade, for instance, suggests that recent contributions to the globalization-conflict debate are incomplete. At the moment, most formal and statistical models rely on the much-criticized unitary actor assumption commonly associated with realist thinking. Although trade theorists have disaggregated the state for a long time, extant work in international relations on the trade-conflict question, with the exception of Weede (1995), ignores this trend. Although many studies support the liberal claim, the empirical evidence is hardly as conclusive as that presented in favor of another strand of liberal thought—the Democratic Peace. A series of empirical findings and increasingly sophisticated models have established that democracies do not fight each other (e.g., Russett and Oneal, 2001; Schulze, 2000).

Before moving to a critical discussion of the underlying assumption and unquestioned practices of interdependence-conflict researchers, we first trace the history of the competing claims. Next, we compare the contributions of three different formal modeling traditions—decision theory as well as cooperative and noncooperative game theory. We then assess the empirical work and conclude with the suggestion that future work specifies more clearly the conditions under which interdependent states become more peaceful. We also discuss ways in which empirical work on trade and conflict might be improved and advocate that the next generation of studies in this domain analyzes the impact of economic integration on domestic stability.

## Theoretical Work on Trade and Conflict

The relationship between economic interdependence and conflict has received considerable theoretical attention. Much controversy remains, however, and there are a number of competing propositions: (1) the liberal argument that trade generally promotes peace; (2) the argument advanced by neo-Marxists and some neorealists that symmetrical ties may promote peace while asymmetrical trade leads to conflict; (3) the suggestion that trade increases conflict; and (4) the belief held by many realists that trade is irrelevant to conflict.

Similar hypotheses are increasingly advocated to assess the possible impact that other dimensions of global economic integration have on war. Globalization has undoubtedly been more pronounced in capital markets than in trade during the past two decades (see, e.g., Plümper, 2001). Although the globalization of capital played an important role in the development debate in the 1970s and 1980s, the impact of foreign direct investment and similar facets of globalization on the likelihood of conflict has almost disappeared from the research agenda.[1] This is the reason why we focus almost exclusively on the possible nexus between trade and conflict in the remainder of this review.

The trade-promotes-peace proposition can be traced to ancient writings, but it is most commonly associated with the liberal school of thought (Angell, 1910; Blainey, 1988, ch. 2; de Wilde, 1991; Doyle, 1997, ch. 7; Selfridge, 1918; Viner, 1937). While proponents of this conviction traditionally link the pacifying elements of trade to both economic and social factors, contemporary liberals rely more heavily on economic variables in explaining their argument. However, there is also an implicit, and at times explicit, assumption that the increased social contact that results from trade ties promotes peace and unifies states. This line of reasoning is commonly associated with the writings of Karl W. Deutsch and his associates (Deutsch et al., 1957). This research group maintained that trade and other forms of intercultural exchange would help foster the development of a sense of community that would make the resort to arms unthinkable. Here, we focus our attention primarily on economic arguments, since they have received the most scholarly attention. The starting point of these models is that states are deterred from initiating conflict against a trading partner for fear of losing the welfare gains associated with the trading relationship (Polachek, 1980).

Scholars often cite Kant (1795/1970) or Montesquieu (1748/1991) in tracing the roots of the liberal tradition in the research on interdependence and conflict (e.g., Russett and Oneal, 2001.) Yet, arguments about the benefits of trade can be found in a declaration by Libanius, a fourth-century pagan: 'And so they called commerce into being, that all men might be able to have common enjoyment of the fruits of earth, no matter where produced' (quoted in Irwin, 1996:

16). Although some scholars have disapproved, others like Hugo Grotius have argued for the benefits of trade: 'No one, in fact, has the right to hinder any nation from carrying on commerce with any other nation at a distance' (ibid: 23). One of Grotius's contemporaries, Alberico Gentili, justified a *iustus bellum* if a country refused to trade (ibid.: 22). Both Luther and Calvin, by contrast, were rather skeptical, but their libertarian outlook contributed to the emergence of a capitalist climate in middle and northern Europe.

In the twentieth century, Norman Angell's *The Great Illusion* (1910) provides the most prominent and infamous attempt to conceive of war in times of high economic interdependence as a highly unlikely event of collective irrationality. The well-known short-term irony of this book was that the outbreak of World War I seemingly contradicted Angell's bold predictions. While Angell obtained the image of being an almost pathological idealist, he was more scientific in his writings than some of his critics. He wrote in retrospect that 'To discover why ... nations persisted in methods of security which condemned them to insecurity so great that the end must be destruction', was the purpose of *The Great Illusion* (Angell, 1938: 75, quoted in de Wilde, 1991: 66).

The blow that World War I gave to the liberal school was temporary. After 1945 'embedded liberalism' (Ruggie, 1982), with its promotion of a multilateral order of the world trading system, became the dominant ideology in the Western world. The intensive discussion about integration and globalization gave the peace-through-trade hypothesis another boost. Today, numerous politicians in both the developed and the developing worlds have, in some way or another, claimed that expanding economic ties benefit societies and decrease the risk of social conflict. Rosecrance (1986) developed this idea fully, in asserting that the time is ripe for the 'trading state'.

This liberal conviction is so deeply entrenched in mainstream economics that those who dare question it are portrayed as heretics from the radical fringes. Yet, critics of economic interdependence enjoy an equally long tradition as do the advocates of free trade. Ancient Greece and Rome held a low regard for commerce and those who engaged in it. Most early Christian theologians questioned the legitimacy of commerce. St. Augustine went as far as saying that 'For they are active traders ... they attain not the grace of God' (quoted in Irwin, 1996: 17). To justify protectionism on the grounds of security rather than a higher morality became common during mercantilism. This led, for instance, to the adoption of a set of Navigation Acts that the British Parliament passed in the 1650s and 1660s. These measures included the provision that foreign-built or -owned ships were forbidden to trade with the British colonies. In practice, mercantilism was close to the 'aggressive unilateralism' that Bhagwati and Patrick (1991) attributed to the United States of the Reagan era. Long before the introduction of powerful instruments such as the ones that can be derived from the infamous section 301 of the U.S. Trade Act of 1974, Colbert, for instance, wrote to the town of Marseille in 1664 that 'we are giving orders to all our ambassadors or residents at the courts of the princes, our allies, to make, in our name, all proper efforts to cause justice to be rendered in all cases involving our merchants, and to assure for them entire commercial freedom'.[2] He also feared that 'trade causes a perpetual battle, both in peace and war, between the nations of Europe' (quoted in Niehans, 1990: 20).

Similar considerations motivated Hamilton (1791/1966) and List (1842) to guard against what they considered to be premature liberalization. Their early 'infant industry' argument borrowed from the mercantilist conviction that adequate government intervention could prevent the destabilization of states.[3] Hamilton (1791/1966: 301) wrote that 'there is no purpose, to which public money can be more beneficially applied, than to the acquisition of a new and useful branch of industry ... [that results in] a permanent addition to the general stock of productive labor.' These critical points of view played an important role in the development discussions after World War II. Another major impetus to the critical strand in development economics came from Hirschman (1945/1980), who elaborated 'how relations of influence, dependence and domination arise right out of mutually beneficial trade' (vii). Although not explicitly concerned with the trade-conflict relationship, Hirschman proved influential in the literature by highlighting the negative consequences of asymmetrical dependence. Hirschman's vivid portrayal of the use or abuse of power in asymmetrical relations stood in sharp contrast to the harmonious trading relationships portrayed by liberal scholars.

Dependency theorists further articulated the negative consequences of asymmetrical trade relations for the more dependent state. According to this view, trade and economic dependence tend to benefit powerful states and elite interests within developing societies, while those actors and states lacking power endure the costs of dependence. Dependency theorists reject the liberal portrayal of trade as universally voluntary exchange and mutually beneficial. The existence of trade ties between states may simply reflect an absence of latitude on the part of some states to break free from undesirable trade relations. Unsurprisingly, dependency theorists followed List and Hamilton in advocating temporary protectionist measures in the form of import substitution.

While the dependency argument that foreign penetration was detrimental to the developing world was the source of several disputes between sociologists (see Weede, 1996 for a summary), other theorists went a step further and claimed that trade in general is harmful for world peace. Interestingly, Marxists and neorealists found some common ground in their skepticism toward economic interdependence. Waltz offered the most succinct critique. In his view, 'close interdependence nears closeness of contact and raises the prospects of occasional conflict' (Waltz, 1979: 138). Ten years later Grieco (1988) invoked the relative-gains argument to assess the possibility of cooperation between trading partners. According to this hypothesis, the fear of feeding a potential enemy through the intensification of trade is the major impediment to any attempt to create lasting institutions and trade relations between nonallied states. Although this hypothesis did not survive more advanced formal statements, it has had a lasting impact on the current trade-conflict debate (Morrow, this volume).

Some scholars engaged in trade-conflict research have built upon Hirschman's theme and the issues covered by neo-Marxists and dependency theorists, all of whom cite the adverse consequences of dependence, by arguing that the trade promotes peace-hypothesis is contingent upon the type of dependence that exists in a given economic relationship. Symmetrical ties may promote peace, but asymmetrical dependence creates tensions that may manifest themselves in conflict. Prominent examples of the critical view are the writings of Wallensteen (1972), Gasiorowski (1986), and Barbieri (1995, 2002).

In general, the early work on the nexus between trade and conflict was more open to the possibility that the impact of economic integration might not be universally beneficial. Critics of commercial liberalism asserted that economic relations were not all equal; some trading relationships provided net benefits, while others entailed disproportionate costs for the more dependent state that might result in conflict or at least fail to deter it. A similar argument refers to the distributional effects of increased interdependence. As modern trade theory suggests, growing trade bonds increase general welfare, but have adverse effects for domestic groups. As these constituents strive for compensation, the risk of instability might increase.

In the early decades after World War II scholars appeared more mindful of the legacy of colonialism, imperialism, and neocolonialism, in which trade and conflict seemingly went hand in hand. In contrast, scholarship in the post–Cold War period has largely ignored radical critiques of economic exchange. Few scholars today question the belief that economic integration generally brings economic benefits and peace, although modern political economy discusses the redistributive effects of foreign economic openness. Most policymakers also appear to view the contributions of the early globalization skeptics as largely irrelevant to the new liberal order. Just as Hirschman's influence in the literature reflected a broader skepticism about trade relations, the economic prosperity of the 1980s and the collapse of communism corresponded to the emergence of a new way of looking at trading relationships.

The controversies over the impact of interdependence were not resolved in the empirical studies of the 1970s and 1980s, but commercial liberalism received relatively little attention until the early 1990s. At that time, some scholars began linking issues of economic liberalism to republican liberalism as addressed in the popular democratic-peace literature. As a result, interest in the trade-conflict question grew. This extension included the belief that democracy and trade are strongly interconnected in the construction of a peaceful world, an idea two contributors to this volume trace back to Kant (Oneal and Russett, 2001a).

The debate about the security effects of global economic integration has significantly intensified since the mid-1990s. This increasing scholarly attention was accompanied by a growing public awareness that global integration might influence the stability of states and interstate relationships in profound ways. In the 1990s, the liberal view finally made it into a leading textbook in international economics. Obstfeld and Rogoff (1996: 25–27) used the impact of war on the economy as a test case and argued that during war belligerents wish to borrow abroad to finance their military effort while nonparticipants will run large current account deficits. This means that the consequences of war on capital markets might often be much more immediate than the effects of militarized disputes on trade. An important intervening factor is, however, the expectations that economic agents build about the possible outcome of a war. In the case of the Russo-Japanese war, Obstfeld and Rogoff convincingly argue that the global financial reaction was limited as it was fairly easy to predict the winner.

During the 1990s, critics of globalization asserted that foreign economic liberalization and other measures advocated by the International Monetary Fund and the World Bank undermine the stability of societies and, ultimately, might increase the risk of civil war. In a careful evaluation of such claims, Quinn (2000) argues that capital-account liberalization might have led to constitutional shifts from democracy to autocracy in some countries. Based on the available empirical evidence, it is, however, impossible to say firmly whether such disruptive effects of foreign economic openness are exceptions or indications of a more general trend.

This ambiguity is also still reflected in the current debate on how global economic integration affects the likelihood of militarized conflict. Despite the growth in interest and related research, cumulativeness in the interdependence-conflict literature is still hampered by divergent definitions of basic concepts, inconclusive insights from the theoretical side, and data ambiguities. Yet, as the contributions to this volume demonstrate, much progress has been made on a number of fronts. The following two sections review the state of the art in the most prominent theoretical and empirical studies, and compare these findings with the arguments advanced in this book.

## From Expected Utility Models to Strategic Game Forms

Theoretical models on the relationship between economic integration and conflict are based on some assumptions about the number of relevant actors and their perception of the benefits that increased levels of interdependence might offer. Another category for the classification of the theoretical work is whether a contribution assumes that the nexus between globalization and militarized conflict is unconditional and thus not contingent upon the influence of some intervening variables. We will start the evaluation of the extant theoretical work with the decision-theoretic literature, briefly discuss some cooperative game models, and conclude with a presentation of recent noncooperative work in this area. Table 1.1 summarizes some of the most important contributions that have been made in the three competing subfields in formal theory. The vast majority of the theoretical work focuses on the relationship between trade and conflict, rather than on other forms of economic interdependence.

### Table 1.1. Formal Work on Trade and Conflict

| Type of model/Author(s) | Number of actors | Intervening variables/ Type of model | Effect of trade on peace |
|---|---|---|---|
| *Expected utility models* | | | |
| Polachek (1980) | 1 | – | Positive |
| Copeland (1996) | 1 | Expectations | Positive/negative |
| Polachek (1997) | 1 | Democracy | Positive |
| Polachek, Robst, Chang (1997) | 1 | Distance (Transportation costs) | Positive |
| Polachek, Chang, Robst (1999) | 1 | Foreign aid, contiguity, country size, market power | Positive |
| *Cooperative game models* | | | |
| Grieco (1990) | 2 | Relative-gains reasoning | Negative |
| Snidal (1991a)[a] | 2 | Relative-gains reasoning | Positive |
| Powell (1991, 1993)[a] | | Resource allocation | Positive |
| *Noncooperative game models* | | | |
| Gowa (1994) | 2 | Polarity, relative gains | None |
| Skaperdas and Syropoulos (1996) | ≥2 | Arming | Positive/negative in two/ multiactor cases |
| Morrow (1997) | 2 | Resource allocation, sanctions | Negligible/positive |
| Dorussen (2001) | 3 | Balance of power | Mixed |
| Dorussen and Hegre (this volume) | >2 | Balance of power | Positive, but dependent upon system size |
| Schneider and Schulze (2002a) | 2 | Sector-specific approach | Positive, but dependent on the strength of the military |

[a] Includes noncooperative considerations.

## Expected Utility Models

The proponents of the early expected utility models contend that the peace-through-trade hypothesis is unconditional. This is largely a consequence of the unquestioned assumption that the eventual destruction of trade is costly to all parties concerned. In Polachek's (1980: 61, italics suppressed) classic statement:

> the price of being belligerent is an implicit price that increases with the level of trade. Ceteris paribus, the greater the amount of trade, the higher the price of conflict, and the less the amount of conflict that is demanded.

This unilateral perspective is derived from a country's welfare function w=w (c, z) where c stands for desired consumption and z for existing hostility. The equation c=q+m-x defines that consumption equals total production (q) plus imports (m) minus exports (x). Optimizing behavior then leads to the insight that countries with comparatively high export and import levels will face higher costs of conflict ($\partial z/\partial x < 0$ and $\partial z/\partial m < 0$ respectively). Straightforward cost-benefit reasoning leads Polachek to conclude that such states are less conflict-prone than less interdependent states. A country reaches its optimal levels of conflict at the point where the benefits of more hostility ($\partial w/\partial x$) equal the costs of additional hostility ($x\partial P_x/\partial z - m\partial P_m/\partial z$). Figure 1.1 depicts the interrelationship between the costs and benefits of conflict, based on Polachek's (1980) argument.

**Figure 1.1. The Optimal Level of Conflict**

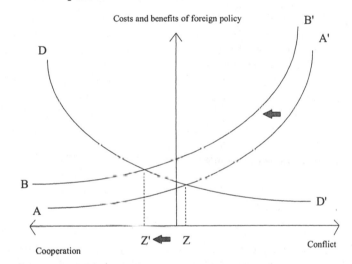

Figure 1.1 shows that if the costs of conflict increase due to a rise in imports or exports, the cost curve shifts upwards from AA' to BB'. Since the new intersection with the demand curve is to the left of the former equilibrium, the optimal level of conflict moves from Z to Z'. The same reasoning underlies extensions of this framework which consider the impact of foreign aid, contiguity, democracy, transportation costs, country size, and market power (e.g., Polachek, 1997).[4]

While expected-utility models offer a straightforward foundation of the unconditional peace-through-trade hypothesis, they neglect the strategic interdependence between nations. A further weakness is the almost tautological reasoning that higher costs of conflict imply lower levels of conflict. Finally, the framework does not distinguish between different forms of conflict and assumes that the net level of conflict or cooperation can be measured on a single scale, that is, derived from events data. War is seen as a continuous variable rather than a discrete event. In his contribution to this volume, Polachek addresses some of these criticisms, arguing that they do not constitute a devastating blow to the liberal model. Hegre (2001) shows that extensions of the expected utility model will allow theorists to go to the very heart of the conflict between liberals and dependency theorists and demonstrates that trade works most efficiently in symmetric dyads. His statistical results reinforce this conclusion and lend support to Hirschman's (1945) claim that the degree of evenness in trading relationships crucially matters. Because trade symmetry and the military balance of power are closely associated, Hegre warns that realist variables contaminate the pacifying impact of economic interdependence.

## Cooperative Models

The cooperative models that address the interrelationship between trade and conflict have largely been constructed by realist scholars. The tradition started with Grieco's (1988, 1990) refutation of some claims made by liberal scholars. He tried to show, in line with the relative-gains hypothesis by Waltz (1979), that a state's utility function should include not only the individual payoff Y, but also integrate the gap between their own payoff and the one of a partner. In the resulting utility function $U=V-k(W-V)$, W stands for the other state's payoff and k measures the sensitivity toward relative gains. This definition is then used in the analysis of two of the most commonly known normal form games, a Prisoner's Dilemma game and a Deadlock game.

Grieco stresses that relative gains concerns might override in the long term the short-term benefits of cooperation. Since states anticipate the externality that cooperation would create, they avoid any long-term agreement that benefits another state disproportionally.

> [M]ost states concentrate on the danger that relative gains from joint action may advantage partners and may thus foster the emergence of what at best might be a potentially more domineering friend and at worst could be a potentially more powerful future adversary. (Grieco, 1988: 44–45)

Another realist, Joanne Gowa (1994, see also Gowa and Mansfield, 1993), asserts that the impact of trade on conflict is an epiphenomenon, which is caused by other factors. She maintains that trade increases economic efficiency, enabling states to devote resources to military purposes. Yet, the anarchy of the international system counteracts this trend by rendering potential adversaries more powerful. Assuming that polarity is the root cause of international behavior, Gowa (1994) lays the theoretical foundations for the popular adage that 'trade follows the flag' and leaves us to expect that free trade is only probable between like-minded states.

In a cooperative setting, orthodox relative-gains arguments are, however, based on the implicit assumption that the size of k is so large as necessarily to prevent any kind of lasting cooperation. Since zero-sum interactions are not the only form of state interaction (Snidal, 1991a, b), creating and maintaining trade partnerships is possible even if states care about the distribution of the eventual benefits that interdependence creates. If growing trade represents higher absolute gains, increasing levels of economic interdependence would foster the likelihood of cooperation. It should further be noted that the games Grieco developed fail to capture the subtleties of the international political economy, since the dichotomous choice between cooperation and conflict is misleading. Even Powell's (1991) admittedly simplistic optimal-tariff model that yields states three options is more realistic since it includes the possibility of avoiding a direct confrontation with a state. This leeway is neglected in conventional games that try to buttress the relative-gains argument.

The empirical question that realists have raised is a typical chicken-and-egg problem. It is not completely clear why polarity should be the root cause of both trade and conflict. On the contrary, one could simply surmise that alliances are expressions of economic or social interdependence and that 'trade' or other forms of societal cooperation predate the 'flag'. Some recent research accordingly suggests that the effect of such security externalities is negligible (Morrow, 1997, this volume) and that states continue to interact economically even in times of war (Morrow et al., 1998; Barbieri and Levy, this volume; see also Anderton and Carter, 2001a, b, this volume). The fascinating evidence assembled by Frey and Kucher (2000) of the recuperations that war events have on government bonds is especially revealing in this regard. Although the most dramatic and well-known events burn a lot of money, the impact is not uniform and sometimes even negligible. The current-account model sketched by Obstfeld and Rogoff (1996) could be a starting point for systematically assessing when and how war events affect capital markets.

## Noncooperative Games

The argument about the security externalities of trade was influential insofar as it inspired other researchers to probe its limitations from the vantage point of noncooperative game theory. These critical studies were a major stimulus for the new debate on trade and conflict that started in the early 1990s. The modern noncooperative tradition starts largely with Powell's (1991, 1993) refutation of Grieco from which a Markov perfect equilibrium of peaceful allocations was deduced. Morrow (1997, this volume) subsequently added trade to Powell's (1993) model, showing that economic exchange is feasible between foes. This eventuality even exists if a distinction between different types of traded goods is made—goods which increase capabilities through increasing wealth; goods which offer an immediate benefit and are thus immune against the eventual retaliatory actions of another state; and finally military goods. Unsurprisingly, the benchmark for a peaceful outcome is the highest when states trade in military goods. Trade maintains a deterrent value in this context only if the short-run costs of arming outweigh the eventual long-term gain that attacking the trading partner might entail.

Morrow's model highlights the effect that the distribution of benefits and enforcement considerations have on interstate relations. These comparative statics results demonstrate that the conflict propensity of a trading state depends to a great extent on the size of intervening factors: 'Both sides' discount factors, their attitudes toward risk, the costs of war, the postwar distribution of resources, and the magnitude of the first-strike advantage all affect equilibrium military allocations' (Morrow, this volume). Enforcement concerns mainly loom large if states trade military goods or goods with an easily capturable surplus. In the event that trade between two states is, however, dominated by normal goods, the incentive to cheat is not so great. Since such goods only increase the security externalities of trade in an indirect fashion, both states might largely gain through the direct growth in national welfare.

Gartzke and Li (this volume) offer an informational rationale for the relative peacefulness of trading dyads. In collaborative work with Boehmer, they have shown independently of Morrow (1999) that governments face a severe trade--off between the political goals and the wish to appease market forces (Gartzke, Li, and Boehmer, 2001; Gartzke and Li, this volume). As the level of globalization increases, the wish for economic stability becomes more important. In game-theoretic terms, the nexus between the state and the market can be used as a device to signal resolve. In opposition to the globalization skeptics, Gartzke, Li, and Boehmer contend that increasing economic interdependence increases government autonomy and allows states to choose among more options than in a situation of autarchy. In their view, global integration decreases the relative attractiveness of using armed force for reaching certain goals.

Their model is thus in some sense a strategic reformulation of the expected-utility argument that Polachek introduced to the literature some twenty years ago. In his contribution to the volume, Polachek presents the extended version of his model and shows that the basic insight is fairly robust. He also discusses several alternative models that try to qualify his major deduction. In an article surveying his contributions to this field, Reuveny (this volume) comes to a similar conclusion. Weede furthermore points out in his sweeping overview that the capitalist peace is a major stabilizing force. Although the rationale he develops is not formal, he carefully discusses alternative models and ultimately dismisses them or integrates them into his own argument. In his view, the security benefits of globalization are much more important than the economic effects.

Schneider and Schulze (this volume) is an attempt to probe the expected-utility argument from the vantage point of political economy. Their model shows some conditions under which the resort to militarized conflict becomes an attractive option for opportunistic governments. They reject the widespread notion that domestic instability creates such incentives (see also Davies, 2001).

According to the diversionary theory of war, the incentive to use force looms larger in the head of the chief executive if a country undergoes a severe crisis and if the population attempts to punish the rulers. This hypothesis has, however, no clear microfoundations. If we distinguish the sectoral interests within a country, only the military has an interest in increasing hostilities with other states. The productive sectors, by contrast, are fearful of such tendencies. The government tends in this perspective only to increase the level of hostility if its popularity depends sufficiently on the military sector. As the two authors show, such an incentive structure can also exist in times of expanding trade ties and, thus, in times of economic expansion, rather than contraction. In other words, the resort to arms is not necessarily linked to the presence of an economic crisis.

Recent work by Skaperdas and Syropoulos (1996) adds another condition to the peace-through-trade hypothesis. They show that conflict might become more likely between a multitude rather than two trading states, if the benefits of a contested territory increase with the number of trading states. In a multiactor world, growing difficulties to win supersede this incentive. Consequently, the smaller the number of countries in a nontrading world, the higher the amount of conflict. Dorussen and Hegre (this volume) deal with the issue of a multiactor world differently. They show, in an extension of Dorussen (1999), that the risks of conflict decrease as the number of states increases. The exchange between these two authors, which led to their joint article published in this volume, also demonstrates that the impact of system size on conflict depends considerably on the proper choice of indicator (Hegre, 2001; Dorussen, 2002).

A further and not yet fully studied boundary condition of the possible nexus between trade and conflict is the effect of alliances. Dorussen (2001) explores this issue. Drawing on the relative gains debate, he concludes that 'allies can use coalition trade that excludes a common adversary to increase their security' (Dorussen 2001: 173). A further intervening factor is the price of the contested resource. The opportunity costs of arming rise if the good is internationally cheaper than under a situation of autarchy. If the contrary is the case, the competition for a resource intensifies. An increased level of armament should be the consequence (Skaperdas and Syropoulos, 2001).

Although these recent results again support the peace-through-trade hypothesis in general, they qualify the initial argument by Polachek substantially. Therefore, we have ample reason to believe that increasing trade has a pacifying impact on some interstate relations, but we have to point out the conditions under which this expectation is likely to be confirmed. At the empirical level, we should not expect that all trading states, commercially interdependent pairs of nations and globalizing eras are more peaceful. The peace-through-globalization hypothesis will probably never be characterized in the strong terms that Levy (1988: 662) used about the democratic peace: 'as close as anything we have to an empirical law in international relations'.

The balance of power, the size of the interstate system, and the relative importance of the military sector are most likely important intervening factors. A further note of caution is that most models, with the important exception of the crisis bargaining models advocated by Morrow (1999) and Gartzke, Li, and Boehmer (2001), do not directly study the decision to use armed force. Hence, most models are still built on the plausible, but implicit assumption that increased arming or a more aggressive foreign policy stance translates into a higher likelihood of conflict. At the moment, no causal mechanism has been developed which directly links economic decisionmaking and conflict initiation. Morrow (1999) proposes that we should rely on the crisis bargaining literature. Yet, to borrow from this side is, in our view, not enough because future models need also to be firmly grounded in international economics and to motivate economic and political decisions simultaneously.

As this volume shows, most models on the trade-war hypothesis still fail to incorporate major insights from modern trade theory. Yet, the models reviewed in this section have successfully dealt with the realist challenge that was formulated in the 1980s. They have also demonstrated that the liberal vision is often right, but does not hold across all cases. Some important game-theoretic reformulations of commercial liberalism are under way. There is thus ample reason to expect the development of microfoundations for the claims made by Kant and other philosophers. The interim achievements are nevertheless considerable.

## Empirical Studies

A rising number of studies assess the interdependence-conflict relationship in a systematic fashion. Table 1.2 presents a summary of empirical studies focused directly on the question of the impact of trade on conflict.[5] As this summary reveals, the literature has expanded rapidly in a relatively short period of time. The table includes only published works and therefore excludes a large number of unpublished conference papers that have spurred further debate and later have become the focus of published work, including Oneal and Russett's (1999b, this volume) response to Barbieri (1996b, 1998). In addition, the table includes only research whose central focus is on the trade-conflict question, rather than pieces that might include findings relevant to the trade-conflict relationship, but whose attention to this link is secondary. As we see from the summary, the growth in scholarship has not yet led to unambiguous support for the liberal cause.

Two of the editors (Schneider, Gleditsch) see the results reported in table 1.2 by and large in support of commercial liberalism. In their view, the original liberal claim seems to hold across different research designs. The earlier studies that find mixed or contrary results (Russett, 1967; Wallensteen, 1972; Domke, 1988) fail to correct systematically for geographical distance, and their results are therefore misleading. However, these editors recognize that there are exceptions and agree that future work has to specify the boundary conditions of the liberal claim more explicitly. They also believe that we need to move away from the ad hoc specification of statistical models by integrating the theoretical and empirical research on economic integration and conflict.

**Table 1.2. Statistical Studies of the Trade-Conflict Relationship**

| Author(s) | Temporal domain and unit of analysis | Methodological techniques | Control variables | Main findings |
|---|---|---|---|---|
| Russett (1967) | 1946–1965 41 warring dyads | Factor analysis Contingency tables | | Trade→War [+] |
| Wallensteen (1972) | 1920–1968 144 warring dyads | Contingency tables | | Trade→War [+] |
| Polachek (1980) | 1958–1967 dyads (30 states) | Regression, two-stage LS | 14 NAs | Trade→Net conflict [-] |
| Gasiorowski and Polachek (1982) | 1967–1978 US–Warsaw Pact | Regression, Granger causality | | Trade→Net conflict [-] |
| Gasiorowski (1986) | 1948–1977 dyads (130 states) | Regression | PE, GDP | Mixed |
| Domke (1988) | 1871–1975 states | Probit | | Mixed |
| Polachek and McDonald (1992) | 1973 dyads (14 OECD states) | Regression | PE, GDP | Trade→Net conflict [-] |
| Polachek (1992) | 1948–1978 dyads | Regression | DE, NA | Trade→Net conflict [-] |
| Polachek (1997) | 1948–1978 dyads (11 states) | Regression, three-stage LS | 17 NAs | Trade→Net conflict [-] |
| | 1958–1967 dyads (30 states) | | RT | Trade→Democratic peace [+] |
| Polachek, Robst, and Chang (1999) | 1958–1967 dyads (30 states) | Regression | Vector of NAs | Trade→Net conflict [-] Tariffs→Net conflict [+] |
| Barbieri (1995,1997) | 1870–1885 dyads | Logit | A, C, RT, RP | Interdependence→MIDs [+] |
| Barbieri (1996a) | 1870–1938 dyads | Logit | A, C, RT, RP | Interdependence→MIDs [+] |
| Barbieri (2002) | 1870–1992 dyads/states | Logit, negative binomial regression | A, C, RT, RP,TD | Interdependence→MIDs [+] for dyads, mixed for states |
| Oneal, Oneal, Maoz, and Russett (1996) | 1950–1985 PRD | Logit | A. EG, C, G,RT | Interdependence→MIDs [-] |
| Oneal and Ray (1997) | 1950–1985 PRD | Logit | A, C, EG, GP, RP, RT | Interdependence→MIDs [-] |
| Oneal and Russett (1997) | 1950–1985 PRD | Logit | A, C, EG, GP, PC, RT, RP | Interdependence→MIDs [-] |
| Oneal and Russett (1999b) | 1950–1992 dyads | General estimating equation (GEE) | A, C, GP, MP, RP, RT, TD | Interdependence→MIDs [-] |
| Oneal and Russett (1999a)[6] | 1885–1992 dyads | GEE | A, C, GP, II, HDE, IGOs, MinP, RP, RT, SSQ, TD | Interdependence→MIDs [-] |

**Table 1.2. Continued**

| Author(s) | Temporal domain and unit of analysis | Methodological techniques | Control variables | Main findings |
|---|---|---|---|---|
| Oneal and Russett (this volume) | 1950–1992 dyads | GEE | A, C, GP, MP, RT, RP,TD | Interdependence→MIDs [-] for PRD, [+] for non–PRD |
| Mansfield (1994) | 1850–1964 system | Regression | Con, EO, H | Trade→MP war [-] Openness→War [+] |
| Mansfield, Pevehouse, and Bearce (1999) | 1950–1985 PRD | Logit, random effects probit | A, C, EG, PTA, RP, RT, TD | Trade→Conflict [I] PTAs→Conflict [-] |
| Mansfield and Pevehouse (2000, this volume) | 1950–1985 PRD | Logit | A, C, EG, GDP, H, PTA, RP, RT, TD | Trade→MIDS [-] for PTA Members, [I] for non-PTA Members |
| Reuveny and Kang (1996a) | 1960–1990s 16 dyads | Granger causality, distributed lag model | | Mixed |
| Reuveny and Kang (1998) | 1960–1990s 16 dyads | Granger causality, distributed lag model | | Mixed |
| Reuveny (1999a, b) | 1990–1999 Israel–Palestine dyad | Descriptive time series | | Interdependence→ Conflict [+] |
| Kang and Reuveny (2001) | 1963–1991 US–USSR– Germany triangle | Vector autoregression (VAR) | | Mixed |
| Crescenzi (2000) | 1966–1992 40 dyads | Logit | | Interdependence→ Low-level Conflict [+]; Interdependence→ High-level Conflict [-] |
| Hegre (this volume) | 1950–1992 extended PRD | Cox regression | A, BP, C, MP, PR, RT, SA | Trade→Conflict [-] for developed dyads, [+/I] for poor dyads |
| Hegre et al. (this volume) | 1960–1997 172 states | Cox regression | BP, EH, GNP pc, Pop, RT, War | Trade→Civil War [I] |
| Gartzke, Li, and Boehmer (2001) | 1951–1985 PRD | Probit | A, AF, C, EG, RP, TD | Interdependence→MIDs [-] |
| Gelpi and Grieco (2003) | 1950–1992 dyads | Logit | A, C, GP, MP, RP, RT, TD | Interdependence→MIDs [-] for democratic dyads, [+] for autocratic dyads |

*Note:* A=Alliance Ties; AF=Affinity; BP=Brevity of Peace; C=Contiguity; Con=Concentration of power; D=Development; DE=Defense Expenditure; EG=Economic growth; EH=Ethnic Heterogeneity; EO=Economic openness; GP=Geographic Proximity; H=Hegemony/ Hegemonic Power; I=Insignificant; MP=Major Power; MinP=Minor Power; NA=National Attributes (social-economic and demographic variables); P=Polarity; PC=Political Change; PE=Price Elasticities; Pop=Population; PR=Political Relevance; PRD='Politically Relevant' Dyads; PTA=Preferential Trade Arrangement; RP=Relative Power; RT=Regime Type; SA=Size Asymmetry; SSQ=Satisfaction with Status Quo; TD=Temporal Dependence

One editor (Barbieri) contends that the exceptions to the liberal view are so strong that no reformulation of the peace-through-trade hypothesis can reinstate commercial liberalism. In her view, critical approaches have greater promise in this research area. She points out that many independently conducted analyses have come up with a host of contradictory findings.

All editors agree that the mixed set of findings pose a considerable, but exciting puzzle. If we consider the conditional nature of the trade-conflict-nexus discussed earlier, the apparent inconsistencies in empirical findings may not be surprising. Yet, as one editor (Barbieri) contends, it might also be possible to attribute the discrepancies to scholars' tendency to focus their attention on different spatial and temporal domains, to adopt varying measures of trade and conflict, and to employ various sets of control variables. The differences in findings that arise from alternative research strategies may, in her view, be highlighting the variations in the trade-conflict relationship that exist under alternative conditions (see Barbieri, 2003). The two other editors (Schneider, Gleditsch), by contrast, believe that some of the recent findings in support of commercial liberalism have received so much scrutiny that we have ample reason to trust their robustness (see, e.g., Beck, this volume; Bennett and Stam, 2000). These independent replications have, however, not yet solved all of the outstanding theoretical and empirical problems that have characterized the scientific study on globalization and conflict since its very beginning.

The earliest empirical studies that considered the impact of trade on international relations identified a positive relationship between trade and war. Russett (1967) found that pairs of states united in clusters of high trade were more likely to engage in war than those not so linked. Wallensteen (1972: 104–105) further demonstrated the conflictual nature of some trading relationships. His work highlights the distinction between symmetrical and asymmetrical relations, by designating states as top dogs or underdogs in the international system. He finds that wars are most likely between structurally unequal states and finds that top dogs (the most important trading states in the system) are more likely to intervene militarily in nations that are dependent upon them economically. This finding may not be surprising in light of the high correlation between major power status, the capacity to trade, and the ability to wage war. At the same time, it calls into question the monadic hypothesis popularized by Rosecrance (1986) and rigorously examined by Domke (1988) that trading states are more peaceful or that trade partners will refrain from conflict.

These early studies failed to control for the potentially confounding influence of variables such as proximity, which is now known to be associated with both trade and conflict. The majority of subsequent research in this area incorporates control variables, although scholars differ as to which control variables should be included.

Polachek's (1980) move to the dyadic level of analysis provided assurance to the liberal cause and influenced all subsequent studies in the trade–conflict literature. His work has consistently revealed an inverse relationship between trade and conflict. Interestingly, the evidence provided in his initial study is based on a very limited sample of relationships. This again raises the question of whether the impact of trade is indeed universal. Moreover, Polachek's early study contains evidence that contradicts some of the basic conclusions we might reach from a superficial reading. Polachek's research agenda, for the most part, assesses the impact of trade on the overall dyadic relationship, where conflictual and cooperative events are evaluated in a combined measure of net conflict (the frequency of conflictual events minus cooperative events). In this respect, it differs from the scholarly efforts to address the question of whether trade inhibits the most serious forms of military conflict. Polachek concludes that trade promotes peace, based on the inverse relationship between trade and his net conflict indicator. Yet, if we take a closer look at Polachek's (1980) initial study, where he disaggregates his net conflict score to determine the impact of trade on different categories of conflict and cooperation, we see that trade has a positive effect on the highest level of conflict and then limited acts of war—as well as the lowest level of conflict. The aggregate measure appears to mask the fact that high trade could be positively associated with the most conflictual acts. In defense of Polachek, we must recognize that his intent is to assess the impact of trade on the overall relationship between states. At the same time, the question arises over whether trade does serve to prevent the most serious forms of conflict.

Polachek has continued to refine his basic model and has provided further empirical support to substantiate his claims (Polachek, 1992, 1997; Gasiorowski and Polachek, 1982; Polachek, Chang, and Robst, 1997; Polachek and McDonald, 1992; Polachek, Robst, and Chiang, 1999). Moreover, his finding that trade might increase some forms of cooperative and some forms of conflictual interactions is in itself a subject deserving of further attention. In fact, de Vries (1990) employs event data to assess the impact of interdependence on conflict and cooperation and finds that interdependence increases the intensity of interactions—both cooperative and conflictual events.

Gasiorowski (1986) provides an early critique of Polachek's work, pointing to the inadequacies of his measure of conflict. Interestingly, Gasiorowski (1986) also criticizes his own study with Polachek (Gasiorowski and Polachek, 1982). He advances an adjusted measure of conflict that deals with some of the problems posed by event data and introduces additional measures of dependence. From this, he provides evidence that leads him to conclude that the previous finding that trade reduces conflict does not hold up under further scrutiny. Although the absolute volume of trade does appear to be inversely related to conflict, other allegedly more reliable indicators of trade and economic dependence are positively related to conflict. Gasiorowski concludes that the beneficial aspects of trade may promote peace, but that the costly aspects appear to be positively associated with conflict. Gasiorowski emphasizes the conditional nature of the trade-promotes-peace proposition.

Gasiorowski's work is indicative of several trends in the trade-conflict literature. First, as his research progresses, he refines his measures of trade dependence and conflict. Second, he offers multiple measures of trade dependence within the same analysis. Finally, he suggests that the relationship of trade to conflict is not straightforward; different factors associated with trade may have different relationships to conflict. Although the lack of consensus in the literature on the appropriate measures of dependence and conflict make it difficult to make comparisons across studies (even those by the same researcher), the positive side of this heterogeneity is that each study contributes additional information about what has been a relatively unexplored puzzle. It may be the case that different dimensions of dependence have different effects on conflict and that scholars who employ alternative measures are actually capturing these variations. This is a theme that has been explored by Barbieri (2002, 2003), one of Polachek's students.

Barbieri's (1995, 1996a, b, 1997, 2002) work focuses on whether trade inhibits the most violent forms of conflict—militarized disputes and wars. Moreover, her research program seeks to incorporate a more diverse set of relationships than had previously been considered and to treat liberal and radical economic theories of trade on an equal footing. In part, she seeks to explain Polachek's finding that the relationship between trade and conflict is positive for some dyads, but negative for others.[7] She assumes that the explanation for the difference resides in whether the relationship is symmetrically or asymmetrically dependent, although she finds only limited empirical support for this assumption. Her examination has expanded by refining measures, expanding her database to incorporate more states, relying on new statistical techniques, and focusing on the impact of trade on various phases of the conflict process and various characteristics of conflict. Her findings, in general, reveal a positive relationship between trade and conflict, both disputes and wars. However, as her research shifts to alternative levels of analysis, she finds some evidence of a pacifying effect of trade at the national level (Barbieri, 2002), consistent with Rosecrance (1986) and Domke (1988).

The work of Oneal and his colleagues (Oneal et al., 1996; Oneal and Ray, 1997; Oneal and Russett, 1997, 1999b, this volume; Russett and Oneal 2001; Russett, Oneal, and Davis, 1998) represents another multistage research project designed to identify the relationship between trade and militarized disputes. Like Barbieri, the group of authors led by Oneal and Russett focus on the relationship between trade and militarized conflict. This research team consistently finds an inverse relationship between trade and conflict. The agenda of this group also differs from Barbieri's in that it seeks to incorporate trade within the broader context of what has been referred to as 'the Kantian tripod for peace' (Russett, Oneal, Davis, 1998, see also Russett and Oneal, 2001; Ward, 2002), which entails a broader conception of the liberal vision of peace beyond commercial liberal prescriptions. In fact, the democratic peace was the central focus of this team's early research efforts, with trade being treated as a control variable (Oneal et al., 1996; Oneal and Ray, 1997). As the importance of trade became apparent, it appears to have taken a more central role in this group's research.

The research conducted by Oneal and his colleagues has progressed by refining measures and data, expanding the domain of inquiry, and incorporating new statistical techniques. Their latest results, for instance, incorporate a control for temporal dependence in logit models. While the influential study of Beck, Katz and Tucker (1998) did not reveal a significant impact of trade on conflict after the introduction of such controls, more recent work by Oneal and Russett (1999a, this volume) does. Beck (this volume) raises another problem, namely, the reliance on a technique that does not seem completely appropriate for the data under examination. Oneal and Russett argue, however, that their results remain robust when a newer statistical tool is used. They (Oneal and Russett, 2001a) make a similar claim in response to a methodological challenge raised by Greene, Kim, and Yoon (2001). Here again, Oneal's and Russett's research has been subject to scrutiny as part of a more general criticism of the methodological techniques employed by international relations scholars. Greene, Kim, and Yoon (2001), like Beck, Katz, and Tucker (1998), find that the adoption of new methodological techniques (in this case, fixed effects logit) renders the impact of trade on conflict insignificant. Greene, Kim, and Yoon (2001) initiated a fruitful debate over the problems that the omission of key variables such as rivalries in some dyads create (Beck and Katz, 2001; Oneal and Russett, 2001a; King 2001). Yet, the proposed remedy to this problem—fixed effects logit—did not solve the problem. One of the main conclusions was that this technique, while certainly appropriate in other contexts, does not seem ideal for binary dependent variables whose one outcome represents a rare event. As King (2001: 505) suggests, conflict researchers can minimize the problem by introducing convincing measures of appropriate control variables. The article by Oneal and Russett (this volume) also prompted some methodological refinements by Beck (this volume). Although applying a different technique, Beck comes up with a finding at least partially in support of the Kantian peace that Russett and Oneal (2001) analyze in a monograph summarizing their joint research effort. Some of Oneal's and Russett's newer work expands the empirical scope and shows by using a Heckman-type selection model that the pacifying impact of trade also relates to less violent forms of interstate interactions than war or militarized interstate disputes (Kinsella and Russett, 2002).

In addition to methodological advancements found in the literature, recent empirical studies have sought to capture the conditional nature of the trade-conflict relationship. Mansfield and Pevehouse (2000, this volume), for example, find that dyads composed of states with preferential trading arrangements (PTAs) enjoy the pacifying effect of trade, while trade has little impact on conflict for nonmembers to PTAs. Gelpi and Grieco (2003) find that trade reduces conflict for jointly democratic dyads, but increases conflict in autocratic dyads. Hegre (this volume) finds that jointly developed dyads experience the pacifying influence of trade, while trade may either increase or have a negligible impact on conflict for poor dyads. Crescenzi's (2000) unpublished dissertation adds to these qualifications by showing that trade dampens the amount of high-level disputes, but seems to increase the likelihood of less violent forms of conflict. This double finding lends some support to the assertion that interdependence serves at least indirectly as a deterrent (Morrow, 1999; Gartzke, Li, and Boehmer, 2001). This finding also bolsters the argument that reducing the risk of war should increase the risk of disputes because the costs of initiating a dispute are reduced in this fashion.[8]

The empirical work of Reuveny reveals similar ambiguities. Using sophisticated times series techniques, he and Kang repeatedly show that commercial liberalism does not seem to hold across all dyads (Kang and Reuveny, 2001; Reuveny and Kang, 1996a, 1998; Reuveny, 1999a, b). Reuveny argues in his contribution to this volume that future theoretical work has to account for these differences and the simultaneity problem that frequently plagues empirical studies on the trade-conflict nexus. A further ambiguity arises in his view because the nature of the goods traded differs considerably across dyads.

If we broaden the perspective of interdependence, the results may become more clear-cut, however. Gartzke, Boemer, and Li (2001), for example, find support for the pacifying effect of economic interdependence, when we conceive of interdependence more generally, to include more than just trade ties, namely, to include financial and monetary ties as well. The most recent empirical studies reveal a more nuanced picture of the trade-conflict relationship. A more complete picture will also require us to understand more fully the impact of trade on conflict at alternative levels of analysis.

While the majority of studies focus on the dyadic level, several scholars have focused on either the national or the systemic level of analysis. As indicated, Domke (1988), Barbieri (2002), and Schneider and Schulze (this volume) provide some evidence that trade-dependent states are less war prone. Surprisingly, there has been little empirical research on the relationship between trade and conflict at the system level, despite the prominent position this level of analysis has had in theoretical discussions about interdependence. The main example is Mansfield (1994) who finds that major power wars are less likely during periods of high trade, but that they are more likely during periods of economic openness. The view that an open economy will be beneficial for peace appears to be contradicted, while that of high trade being more peaceful appears to be supported. He goes on to report that variations in results arise from employing alternative data sets and measures, which raises questions about the robustness of the relationships identified.

A related research question is obviously whether militarized conflicts impinge on the level of trade. In an initial study, Barbieri and Levy (1999, this volume) came to the conclusion that the effect is rather negligible. They argued that this poses problems to both liberal and realist scholarship. Using a larger sample of dyads, Anderton and Carter (2001a, b, this volume) came to the opposite conclusion. Because the samples used in both studies are still fairly limited, no final judgment is possible in this important side debate. Future work on both possible analytical nexuses—the one leading from economic integration to war and the one working in the opposite direction—might, however, profit from addressing the simultaneity problem more explicitly (see also Reuveny, this volume).

## Challenges Ahead

What are the origins of the exceptions to the general rule that growing interdependence fosters peace? The theoretical literature has started to address this issue by proposing theories that specify the boundary conditions of the hypotheses propagated by commercial liberalism. Within the empirical literature on the trade-war nexus, scholars have attempted to identify the factors giving rise to the inconsistent findings (Barbieri, 1996b, 1998, 2002; Beck, this volume; Oneal and Russett, this volume). To date, no compelling rationale has been offered for why empirical findings differ, other than the fact that scholars pursue very different inquiries, with different samples, data, measures or modeling techniques. One obvious consequence of these discrepancies is that defenders of commercial liberalism should strive to specify the conditions under which economic ties among states and other political entities foster peace. We will outline in the following section what we perceive to be the main challenges we face when exploring a more differentiated view of the relationship between economic activities and the decision to wage war.

## Theoretical Challenges

A major theoretical challenge is to embed the trade-conflict relationship within trade theory. As Schneider and Schulze (this volume) argue, the formal models on the nexus between interdependence and conflict are mercantilist in the sense that they model the government as a Leviathan who maximizes social welfare. This neoclassical assumption was acceptable as long as these models were developed to refute the neorealist claim that relative gains reasoning may entice enemies to refrain from trading with each other. The unitary actor assumption is, however, no longer viable if we acknowledge that both the decision to wage war and to liberalize an economy have important domestic repercussions. Although a unilateral move toward free trade might be socially preferable, the losers of such a move might try to prevent it. The same holds true for warfare. While a vast majority might oppose the use of force, small segments of a society might benefit from a more hostile foreign policy. A full defense of commercial liberalism has to show how the two policy variables—openness and hostility—interact.

If we take these redistributional effects of economic openness and war seriously, we have to move away from the mercantilist perspective and adopt an explicit political-economy framework. The Ricardo-Viner model—often referred to as the factor-specific model—provides a particularly promising avenue of research. This type of model assumes that factors are specific for particular industries and are thus not able to move easily across industries in cases of changing market conditions. Such a shortened time horizon is especially compelling if we have to link political to economic decisionmaking. Harold Wilson's dictum that 'a week is a long time in politics' seems to be especially relevant in crisis bargaining. Ricardo-Viner models typically imply that political constituencies in trade policy will build up along the division between the export- and the import-competing sectors. This is in prominent contrast to the Stolper-Samuelson model in which lobbies rally along a factor cleavage (for a discussion of these models see also Mansfield and Pollins, 2001). As Magee (1980) has shown (see also Magee et al., 1989), the factor-specific model seems empirically to be much more relevant although there is still some controversy over the usability of the Stolper-Samuelson theorem (e.g., Deardorff, 1994).

A formidable challenge for this sort of political-economy model is the necessity to include possible reactions by other political entities to the decision to change the trade policy, manipulate the level of hostility, or use both policy instruments simultaneously. Although the refutation of the relative-gains argument is based on two games with two or more actors, we are still far from a dyadic or even multilateral variant of commercial liberalism. If we want to follow in the footsteps of Russett and Oneal (2001) and strive towards a convincing Kantian model of peace, we also need to see how political institutions affect the calculus by opportunist governments in times of growing trade. A possible starting point could be the political contribution model of trade policymaking pioneered by Grossman and Helpman (1994). These authors show, as do Hillman and Ursprung (1988), how political leaders maximize contributions from competing industries. Political institutions play a role insofar as autocratic and democratic governments have to be concerned to different extents about the interest of the general population. While in democracies the median voter is generally the pivotal actor, a less representative individual is able to cast the decisive vote in autocracies. Aggregate social welfare, which is most often represented through the interests of the median voter, matters, thus, differently in the optimization calculus of governments. As it can be easily expected, democratization will shift the balance between the lobbies representing the import-competing and the export sector in the direction of free trade. But we do not yet know how foreign policy choices, like the decision to wage war, affect lobby behavior. Some recent models, though, might help to build a more encompassing view of commercial liberalism. The Grossman and Helpman (1994) model has some striking similarities to the institutionalist model of the democratic peace developed by Bueno de Mesquita et al. (1999). The main advantage of the political-economy model is, however, that it includes decisions by economic agents with specific trade policy orientations. The latter analytical framework only deals with political actors and leaves unspecified the nature of the public and private goods for which rulers are striving.

Besides the interests of actors, their information level is also important. Papers by Gartzke, Li, and Boehmer are among the first to deal with this crucial aspect of policymaking. As the first two of these authors argue in this volume, the information contained in markets provides an important signal to government leaders. Countries that embark on a course of foreign economic liberalization, and especially those that open their capital markets to foreign investors, send important signals to the outside world about how likely a foreign policy confrontation may become. These decisions are important for our understanding of commercial liberalism. However, we do not yet know much about the political economy of capital controls and their possible linkage with other policy decisions, despite the recent advances made by Schulze (2000) and others.

## Empirical Challenges

One key issue in empirical research on commercial liberalism is whether we are capturing the complex phenomenon that we hope to illuminate. The majority of trade-conflict studies have focused their attention on the impact of trade ties on interstate conflict. Yet, trade is only one form of economic interdependence; although an important one, other forms of economic interaction now take on added importance. Integrating information from stock and capital markets is especially necessary. This is, of course, easier said than done, but relevant time-series data are becoming available. For example, Kucher and Frey (2000) demonstrate how historical series can be profitably used for the analysis of how war events affect the economy. Such data might help to solve the dispute on the disruptive effect of war on trade (Barbieri and Levy, 1999, this volume; Anderton and Carter, 2000a, b, this volume).

If we move beyond trade other analytical problems emerge. The catchword globalization has been applied to a host of activities in the economic, social, political, and ecological realm. Researchers investigating globalization have yet to resolve the basic issue of what we mean by globalization and whether or not globalization has changed over time. The field is divided between those who believe that our world today is qualitatively different than that of the past and those who believe we are simply experiencing quantitative variation in the same types of ties that have always existed among peoples of the world. Establishing a consensus about what we mean by globalization is the first, but also the most important, step to pursuing a research program that enables us to understand its impact on the relations between states and competing domestic constituents (see, e.g., Plümper, 2001).

Similarly, our focus on conflict has been narrow, by considering almost exclusively the impact of trade on interstate conflict. In the future we also have to focus on how trade affects the likelihood of civil war. The empirical evidence here is limited despite the growing importance that economists attach to the economic causes of violent disputes (e.g., Collier and Hoeffler, 2002). The U.S. government-sponsored State Failure Task Force has shown that trade openness reduces the risk of internal conflict in the form of revolutionary war, genocide, or severe regime instability (Esty et al., 1999). Their analysis has been criticized on methodological grounds. However, the findings relating to trade openness proved robust to a more sophisticated reanalysis, although most of the negative effect on state failure occurs at very high levels of trade openness (King and Zeng, 2001: 653). De Soysa (2002) demonstrates that trade openness, as measured through trade volume divided by GDP, reduces the likelihood of civil war significantly.

Hegre, Gissinger, and Gleditsch (this volume), on the other hand, find that trade has no significant impact on civil war. Clearly, many questions are still unresolved. It might, for instance, be possible that the impact of economic openness on domestic stability is only beneficial in the long run, but negative in the short run. Furthermore, the positive impact may be conditioned by other factors, such as income distribution. The next generation of studies on economic interdependence will hopefully address some of these issues.

Yet, even when scholars expand the empirical domain of commercial liberalism, there is need for caution. The way in which we often operationalize economic openness is highly problematic. The typical research strategy is to use some trade aggregate divided by GDP. As Leamer (1988) pointed out a long time ago, these measurements are problematic, because they do not reflect government choices and they are typically outcome indicators. One way around the latter problem is to use more sophisticated strategies to capture our variables of interest, such as gravity models (Morrow et al., 1998; Hegre, this volume). However, these models are purely inductive. Political crises should be included if one sets out to measure residuals. The former problem—the lack of data on government choices—is much harder to solve. One measure of economic openness has been introduced in the literature by Sachs and Warner (1995). Summarizing information from five criteria, they create a dummy variable to gauge on a yearly basis whether a country is open or not. Unfortunately, one of these criteria, whether a country is socialist or not, drives the explanatory power of the variable in growth regressions (Harrison, 1996). Martin, Plümper, and Schneider (2001) develop indicators of economic openness that move beyond such simple dichotomies. Following Quinn (2000), they use annual IMF reports to classify the foreign economic openness of a country on four dimensions. Whether these alternative measures better capture the idea of economic openness remains to be seen.

Researchers confront a number of problems when relying upon trade statistics. Economists have long questioned the accuracy and reliability of official trade statistics as an indicator of real trade ties (Bhagwati, 1964, 1967, 1987; Morgenstern, 1963; Ely, 1961; Sheikh, 1974; Yeats, 1978, 1990; de Wulf, 1981). Trade-conflict researchers tend to focus on differences in the elaborate measurement constructions of interdependence. But even before these measures are constructed, trade researchers might differ dramatically in what decision rules they adopt for dealing with trade statistics. Scholars select different sources for trade and exchange rate figures, rely on different country reports for dyadic figures, and treat missing data and reports of no trade differently. This might explain part of the story behind discrepant findings in the trade-conflict literature. Yet, the more important issue is the extent to which official trade statistics serve as an accurate indicator of real transactional flows (see Yeats, 1990). States may have political or economic reasons to undervalue or overvalue their trade reports with a given country.[9] Data limitations may determine the manner in which scholars conceptualize and operationalize economic interdependence. Thus, our measures may not accurately reflect the economic bonds whose impact we seek to explain. A researcher might paint a very different picture of a given relationship, depending upon which country's statistics they used. At a minimum, researchers must maintain a healthy degree of skepticism about the accuracy of trade statistics and must seek other ways of supplementing our measures of economic interdependence. Moreover, we must resist the tendency to speak about our findings with a degree of certainty that is not realistic given the degree of error in our data. We cannot expect data to resolve controversies, when the data themselves contain their own inherent controversy.

We have only just begun to unravel the mysteries of this important relationship. More work is needed in this important area of research if we are to identify the conditions under which globalization promotes peace and those in which it appears to exacerbate tensions.

## Conclusion

This overview has discussed the ways in which recent research has dealt with the interrelationship between economic interdependence and conflict. Reexaminations of old claims have led to an upsurge in the theoretical and empirical work on this issue. Although no consensus on the effects of globalization has been reached, most of the recent theoretical work is much more skeptical with regard to the pacific effects of economic interdependence. This is in some contrast to the empirical literature.

More attention is needed to assessing the factors responsible for variations in the impact of trade under different conditions and with different forms of dependence. If the relationship between trade and conflict is truly robust, it should hold up using seemingly related concepts of interdependence and under different conditions captured by our choice of domain and control variables. This is what we experience in the democratic peace debate. In addition, there are several possible explanations for discrepant findings that have not been adequately addressed. Finally, some important extensions of the current debate have remained surprisingly underexplored in recent years, such as the impact of forms of interdependence other than trade ties. For example, an examination of globalization should include some consideration of the explosive growth in foreign direct investment and international capital markets. Whether the ensuing monetarization of international relations pacifies states or contributes to internal and external instability is an open question. We hope that the next generation of formal and statistical research will address these points.

# Notes

This introductory chapter extends the analysis presented in Barbieri and Schneider (1999). Mansfield and Pollins (2001) and Reuveny (2000) offer other surveys of the literature on trade and conflict. The authors would like to thank Thomas Plümper and a number of the authors in this volume for their comments on earlier versions. As it becomes evident throughout the text, the editors do not always agree on how we should interpret the most recent research on the topic. We have decided to make these different viewpoints explicit rather than to opt for compromise formulations that neither satisfy us nor enlighten our readers.

1. Gartzke et al. (2001) is an important exception. Weede (1996) offers a useful summary of the earlier literature on this topic.

2. The quote was found on the following web page: http://history.hanover.edu/early/colbert.htm (consulted on 24 January 2002).

3. The classic formulation that protection might be a second-best option is due to Johnson (1953/4, 1987).

4. The same reasoning as in Polachek's pathbreaking article can implicitly be found in Copeland's (1996) contribution in which a distinction between optimistic and pessimistic trade expectations is made (see also Davies 2001). Morrow (1999) discusses some empirical problems that might arise if one conceives of trade within a typical crisis bargaining context. See also Gartzke et al. (2001) and Gartzke and Li (this volume) for a similar argument and an original empirical contribution.

5. Here, we consider those studies that focus on the impact of trade on conflict. Most scholars recognize that conflict also affects trade, but differ over whether they believe the trade to conflict or conflict to trade relationship is dominant. Several scholars view causation as flowing from politics to trade relations and find an inverse relationship between trade and conflictual political relations at the dyadic level (Dixon and Moon, 1993; Gowa, 1994; Pollins, 1989a, b). Studies examining the mutual influence of trade and conflict include Polachek (1992) and Reuveny and Kang (1996). Barbieri and Levy (1999) examine the impact of war on trade and find variations across dyadic relationships (see also Anderton and Carter 2001a,b). At the system level, Mansfield (1994) suggests that war reduces trade.

6. Russett and Oneal (2001) report similar results.

7. This finding was conveyed in personal communications in 1992, but it is also discussed in Polachek (2001).

8. We owe this observation to Jim Morrow.

9. Although they might still carry some of the disadvantages of the official trade statistics, Barbieri's (http://pss.la.psu.edu/datares.htm) and Gleditsch's (2002a) trade data sets have raised the standard for accuracy.

# CHAPTER 2

# Multilateral Interactions in the Trade-Conflict Model

*Solomon W. Polachek*

## Critiques of the Liberal Hypothesis

A number of articles in economics as well as in political science examine how economic variables affect political activities. The trade-conflict model considers the extent to which international trade strengthens political relations among trading partners. Although the potential role of trade in fostering international cooperation emanates from ideas at least as early as Crucé (1623), research especially in the last couple of decades presents a cogent theory along with empirical tests. The logic is simple: If conflict leads to a cessation or at least a diminution of trade through tariffs, quotas, embargoes, or other means, then countries with the greatest gains from trade face the highest costs of conflict. As a result they engage in the least conflict and most cooperation. Thus, trading nations cooperate more and fight less. In a number of empirical analyses, I have used the Cooperation and Peace Data Bank (COPDAB) and the World Events Interaction Survey (WEIS) to support this contention (Polachek, 1978, 1980, 1992; Polachek, et al. 1999). Others use the Correlates of War (COW), Militarized Interstate Dispute (MID), and other data (Kim, 1995; Mansfield, 1994, 1995; Oneal et al., 1996; Oneal and Ray, 1997; Oneal and Russett, 1997; and Wallensteen, 1973). This inverse relation between trade and conflict is often denoted as the 'liberal peace' because liberal philosophers such as Kant and others following him advocated the importance of democratic institutions as a means to enhance trade as a path toward peace. Often the trade-conflict relationship is referred to as the 'interdependence-conflict' relationship or simply the 'liberal hypothesis'. In this chapter I use these terms interchangeably.

Since the late 1980s, the trade-conflict relationship has been subject to much empirical testing, with the most recent work using sophisticated econometric techniques. Whereas most studies find that trade reduces conflict, others suggest the opposite, namely, that trade partners fight more. The editors of this volume summarize the relevant findings (chapter 1).

Taken at face value, the nonuniformity of results suggests something possibly askew with liberal theory, leading some to pose alternative theories. My read of the literature yields three alternatives, each with implications seemingly different from the inverse trade-conflict relationship. One theory is Marxist-based, of late advocated by Barbieri (1996a, 1997). The second, espoused by Smith (1980), Seiglie (1998), and Findlay (2001), stems from implications of Ricardian international trade theory. Finally, the third represents an application of game theory adopted by Morrow (1997, 1999) and Gartzke and Li (2001). I contend that these theories neither contradict the liberal approach nor do they yield implications that differ from the inverse trade-conflict relationship. However, to understand the contradictory results, it is important to show why these three theories fail to rectify the paradoxical empirical results. Instead of coming up with alternative theories, I believe the appropriate strategy is to refine the expected-utility model upon which the liberal theory is based. As such, in this chapter, I go beyond the current conflict-trade model by expanding the theory to incorporate multilateral considerations. Thus I obtain new empirical implications, which can be tested in future research.

The chapter is divided into two parts. The first defends the liberal theory's inverse conflict-trade prediction against the three alternative approaches mentioned above. The second presents a graphical generalization of the bilateral trade-conflict model incorporating multilateral consideration. Implications regarding how trade as well as factors related to trade, such as tariffs, foreign aid, and contiguity, affect third-party interactions are obtained.

## Marxist-based Theories of Trade and Conflict

Marxist-based theories contend that colonialism and imperialism go hand in hand with trade, and that countries essentially use military force to expand trade. Trade, viewed in this framework, implies an oppressor nation and an oppressed nation, with the powerful oppressor exploiting the weaker nation. In this case, not only does trade lead to asymmetric trade gains, but trade is involuntary with the gains strictly one-sided. One side wins all, and as such, the other side actually suffers major losses from trade.

Clearly a nation losing resources based on involuntary exploitative trade is far different from a nation engaged in mutually beneficial bilateral trade, where both sides gain. Both types of nations face far different circumstances. One gains from trade, and the other loses. But were trade gains to be negative, even a liberal theorist would find it reasonable for a nation to fight exploitation. In such a situation neither Marxist nor liberal theories contradict each other. The real questions become whether trade is involuntary, and so exploits a nation thus rendering negative gains from trade, as Marxists claim; or whether trade is mutually beneficial, as certainly most economists now believe. Only if the former exploitation scenario is true can trade lead to conflict, but this circumstance is an empirical question—*not* a counterexample to the liberal hypothesis. Thus there is no contradiction, only the need for researchers to evaluate trade gains.

But, according to some, even in the context of Ricardian neoclassical economic models, positive gains from trade can lead to conflict.

## Ricardian-based Theories of Trade and Conflict

Whereas the conflict-trade model uses a Ricardian (1817) framework to show how countries engage in cooperation to protect trade gains, another approach (Smith, 1980; Seiglie, 1998; and Findlay, 2001) adopts the Ricardian gains-from-trade framework to show how conflict can *rise* with trade. In these latter models, rather than trade partners acting cooperatively to protect trade gains, each trading partner utilizes newly acquired gains-from-trade wealth to purchase more of *all* goods and services, including military equipment.

For a state, augmenting its overall domestic well-being makes sense, as does purchasing more military equipment. Indeed, historically nations used their navy to protect themselves from pirates, which probably was the navy's prime raison d'être. On the other hand, it is not clear that augmenting military expenditure to protect trade, or even to augment other aspects of a nation's security, implies more dyadic conflict.

Military expenditure, addressed by these theories, does not necessarily have to be equated with conflict. Although military equipment resulting from military expenditures often is used in combat, it can be employed for other purposes, such as augmenting national security. However, even if used for conflictive purposes, the resulting conflict most likely would *not* be directed toward trading partners, but more likely directed at third parties from whom protecting trade gains is not an issue. As such, gains-from-trade induced military expenditure would not contradict the liberal trade-conflict model that more trade increases cooperation, since any belligerence, if it even occurs, most likely would not be directed toward trading partners. Simply put, military expenditure is an aggregate measure encompassing far more than dyadic conflict. Indeed, bilateral interaction among trading partners should improve to protect the trade gains, which enable spending some of the gains from trade on higher military expenditure to ensure greater security. Thus theories propounding trade to induce higher military expenditures do not contradict the trade-conflict model.[1] As will be illustrated next, the same is true for game theoretic-models.

## Game-theoretic Models Relating Trade to Conflict

In the typical game-theory model, parties vie to split contested resources. As already indicated, trade produces gains, which must be divided between two (or more) trading partners. Accordingly, trade gains become the contested resource, and game theory is invoked to determine how each party behaves to determine the division. But, in the process of dividing a given resource, it becomes obvious that what one party gains, the other loses, so that the process itself is conflictive. To game theorists the logic is simple: first, trade creates trade gains; second, trade gains must be divided; finally, dividing trade gains leads to conflict. Following the logic through, trade leads to conflict.

Again there is no contradiction with the liberal trade-conflict model which states that trade yields more cooperation than conflict. Two issues are involved: (1) whether dividing trade gains necessarily yields conflict as game theoretic models imply, and (2) whether the conflict emanating from splitting trade gains outweighs the necessary cooperation needed to protect the trade, which created the gains in the first place.

Take the first issue. The output of a country can be visualized by a production-possibilities frontier representing all goods and services a country can produce under autarky. Comparative advantage occurs when one country's production-possibilities frontier differs from another's. Under such circumstances it pays for each country to trade by exporting what it produces most efficiently and importing what it produces less efficiently. That way neither country need devote resources to inefficient production. Thus if country A has a comparative advantage in agriculture and country B in manufacturing, each can specialize; and both can be made better off. The amount of trade is determined by maximizing both countries' joint welfare, and the terms of trade are set accordingly. Clearly each country gains, but the extent of the gains are determined by relative prices. With only two countries it might pay for each to posture their social welfare in a way to mislead the other in order to eke out a better terms of trade. Such gamesmanship can lead to conflict; nevertheless, it does not pay to have so much conflict so as to deter trade, since such action eliminating trade would eradicate trade gains completely. This is essentially the conclusion reached by Krugman (1995). Thus even if (1) above is correct, dividing trade gains need not imply an amount of conflict that exceeds the amount of cooperation necessary to protect trade in the first place. But it is not obvious that game theory is even always relevant in splitting trade gains.

Trade gains are determined by prices. Clearly the higher the export price, the greater a country's revenues from selling its products; and as a result, the greater the trade gains, all else constant. In a global world, prices are usually set in the market. Market determined prices mean that posturing for the best price is not a viable option for the typical (small) country, because the typical country must simply take prices as given. In this case there are no contested resources. Gains from trade are fixed, since each trading partner cannot change world prices. Indeed the only option is to take one's trade elsewhere, but here too the market basically sets the price. So game theory is essentially irrelevant, because except for countries with monopolistic power the market determines price.

Essentially there is no real contradiction between the above three approaches and the conflict-trade model itself. As such, because there is no contradiction, these three models cannot serve as an alternative explanation for the nontrivial instances of a positive trade-conflict relationship. For this reason, one needs to better understand the conflict-trade model and its implications, in order to better understand the seemingly contradictory findings relating trade and conflict. Accordingly, the remainder of this chapter reexamines the conflict-trade model. I adopt a graphical, rather than the purely mathematical approach used in past articles. Further, I explore implications regarding multilateral rather than solely bilateral relations.

## The Analytics of the Trade-Conflict Model

### The Basic Model

A world system encompasses numerous countries. Many of these trade with each other because the virtues of trade make each better off economically. This trade results in a system of interdependent countries, which if based on competitive free-market conditions, maximizes world output. Any country breaking off trade not only decreases its own economic well-being but that of its trading partners as well. Tangentially, as will be illustrated, other nontrade partner nations can also be affected. As such, reneging on a trade relationship could be costly from a private as well as global perspective.

Perhaps, for this reason Hirschman (1980: v, xvi) emphasizes 'the politics of foreign trade' by which he spells out 'the possibility of using trade as a means of political pressure ... in the pursuit of power'. Decreasing trade reduces the gains from trade though these losses can be somewhat mitigated if other trading partners can be found. But even here, finding other trading partners is costly.

The formal model initially focuses on one country behaving in isolation with an internal political process governed by the median voter. Depict either the country's or the country's median voter's social welfare function as

(2.1)   $W = W(C)$

where $C$ denotes a set of goods consumed by its citizens. The number of consumer goods produced depends on the autarky's resources, and is depicted by a production possibility frontier (Q). Standard theory dictates that the country's leaders maximize a welfare function, subject to the production possibility frontier. This yields an optimal production ($Q^*$) equal to consumption ($C^*$).

The country's optimization process can be illustrated graphically for the two-commodity case (figure 2.1). Curve AB depicts the production possibility frontier giving the amounts of goods $C_1$ and $C_2$ that can be produced. Curves $U_i$

are iso-welfare curves. Point C\* indicates the optimal production for the country
to maximize well-being.

**Figure 2.1. An Autarky's Equilibrium Consumption**

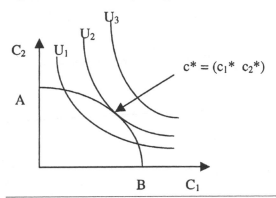

Allowing other countries implies the actor can boost welfare by engaging in
trade. Rather than consuming all its own production, it can sell some production
in order to finance imports. Consumption C, is defined as

$$C = Q + M - X$$

where M = imports and X = exports. Exports and imports are chosen by maximizing welfare subject to the countries production-possibility frontier, and a
balanced-budget constraint depicting its ability to trade. As such,

(2.2)    Max W(C), where
(2.3)    $C = Q = M - X$ and $\Sigma P_x X = \Sigma P_m M$,

where $P_x \equiv$ export prices and $P_m \equiv$ import prices. This yields a new production
Q\*\* that exploits comparative advantage along with optimal imports and exports. Figure 2.2 illustrates the new equilibrium, given terms of trade depicted
by line $p_x/p_m$. As can be seen, trade increases country welfare by $U_3 - U_2$.

Terms of trade $p_x/p_m$ are determined in the international market place, that is,
for competitive markets they are simply determined by equating supply and demand curves for each commodity traded. Without much loss of generality, one
can summarize all these market interactions by representing the market for all
an actor's exports in one supply and demand diagram, which is given in figure
2.3. Similarly one can depict the market for imports in figure 2.4.

Figures 2.3 and 2.4 are not as simplistic as they might first appear. First, note
that in each diagram two different sets of countries are represented. It is important to mention that the vertical axes represent relative prices—the price of exports relative to imports in the export market, and the price of imports relative to
exports in the import market. In figure 2.3, actor's exports are depicted by the
upward sloping supply of exports curve indicating that more exports will be

supplied to the market as the export-relative-to-import price rises. This supply curve is designated by $S_x^A(P)$ where A denotes the exporting 'actor' country and P is the relative price. The demand curve is depicted as $D_x^T(P, Z_i = 0)$ where T signifies the importing target country. ($Z_i$ will be defined later.) The down-ward- sloping demand curve depicts target countries' demands for the actor's exports. In contrast, the demand in the import market (figure 2.4) reflects the actor country's demand while the supply curve reflects target countries' supply. The equilibria in each figure are depicted by points $(P^*, X^*)$ and $(P'^*, M^*)$, respectively, meaning that in the export market X* units are traded at relative price $P_x/P_m$, and in the import market M* units are traded at relative price $P_m/P_x$.

**Figure 2.2. The Equilibrium Allowing for Trade**

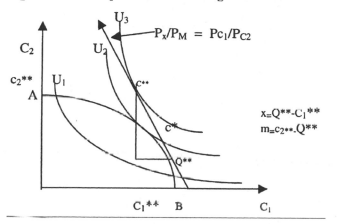

Now suppose that the actor country can interact with target countries *not* only through economic trade *but* also via political behavior. Assume political interactions can be either cooperative or conflictive. Indeed such political be-havior can be represented by a number of possible indices denoting the overall degree of cooperation or conflict. Such indices are consistent with the type be-havior exhibited in events data such as the Cooperation and Peace Data Bank, (COBDAB) the World Events Interaction Survey (WEIS), or the Kansas Events Data Study (KEDS), which include measures of cooperation and conflict. They are also consistent with the Militarized Interstate Dispute data, (MIDs) and the other Correlates of War (COW) data that only get at the degree of conflict. Also assume such political behavior affects a country's social welfare and has exter-nal effects on other countries. To simplify, for now, I concentrate on conflictive behavior, but note that cooperative behavior is really the opposite of conflict—each simply being reverse ends of the political spectrum.

**Figure 2.3. The Export Market from Actor i's Vantage**

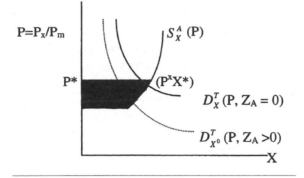

**Figure 2.4. The Import Market from Actor i's Vantage**

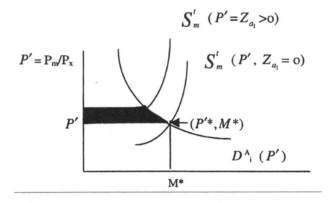

Not unreasonably, assume an actor's conflict instigates a target to respond by shifting its demand and supply curves. Consider two cases: one the target country's reaction to the exporting actor's conflict, and second the target country's response to the importing actor's conflict. In the export market, the target facing an exporter's conflict cuts its demand for the actor's exports. In the import market the target cuts its supply to the actor. Both outcomes can be illustrated graphically in figures 2.3 and 2.4, respectively. In figure 2.3, the target's response to actor conflict is to cut demand for exports. This implies a demand-curve shift for the actor's products resulting in lower actor exports and lower export prices. The new demand is $D_{x^o}^T(P, Z_A > 0)$, where $Z_{A_i} > 0$ denotes actor i conflict vented toward target j. Of course, the magnitude of the effect depends on the extent of the shift, which depends on a number of factors including actor and target country size, as well as other economic factors to be addressed later.

This export-price change is illustrated by the new export equilibrium found by equating demand and supply in figure 2.3.

Similarly, in the import market, it makes sense for a target country to respond to belligerence by cutting its exports to an aggressive actor. Decreasing exports shifts inward the import-supply curve an actor faces, and results in lower import quantities and higher import prices. This scenario is illustrated in figure 2.4. Import-supply curve $S'_m(P', Z_{A_i} = 0)$ shifts to $S'_m(P', Z_{A_i} > 0)$ as targets reduce the supply of exports to the offending actor, yielding a new equilibrium ($P'^*, M^*$).

In short, conflict lowers the price a perpetrator receives for exports and raises the price a perpetrator must pay for imports. Thus

(2.4)     $P_x = P_x(Z)$ s.t. $P'_x(Z_i) < 0$ and

(2.5)     $P_m = P_m(Z)$ s.t. $P'_m(Z_i) > 0$,

where Z represents conflict and i denotes the target country.

Clearly conflict is more costly the greater the rise in import prices and the greater the decline in export prices. But, as can be seen in figures 2.3 and 2.4, the cost of conflict to actor country i is the shaded area depicting the welfare losses from conflict. These welfare losses are the producer or consumer surplus attributable to conflict depicted by the shaded areas under the demand and supply curves. The larger these shaded areas, the higher the costs of conflict, so factors determining the changes in consumer and producer surplus are crucial to understanding conflict. Unmistakably these factors consist of the elasticity of import demand and the elasticity of export supply, and any related economic variables shaping these bilateral elasticities. Given the paucity of bilateral elasticity measures especially for particular products, this chapter concentrates on the impact of antecedent factors affecting these elasticities.

One can obtain the above conclusion regarding the role of import demand and supply elasticities via more formal analysis. But first take a simple case. Maximizing welfare function (2.1) subject to equations (2.2) to (2.5) shows that the budget constraint incorporating the impact of conflict on import and export prices will result in conflict being inversely related to trade. This is illustrated as follows:

Max $W_i(C)$ subject to: $C = Q + M - X$ and $X P_x(Z) - M P_m(Z) = 0$ implies maximizing the Lagrangian multiplier equation

(2.6) $L = W(Q + M - X) + \lambda (X P_x(Z) - M P_m(Z))$.

The resulting equilibrium condition is:

(2.7) $X \dfrac{dPx}{dz} + M \dfrac{dPm}{dz} = 0$

which has an interesting interpretation regarding the optimal amount of conflict. The term, $X\frac{dPx}{dz}$ represents the level of exports multiplied by the lower price an actor receives when engaging in an extra unit of conflict. As such, it depicts the lower revenues a country obtains by engaging in conflict. The term $M\frac{dPm}{dz}$, represents the amount of imports multiplied by the higher import price an actor must pay when engaging in an extra unit of conflict. It depicts the extra cost a country faces when increasing conflict. The sum of the two is the marginal cost of each extra unit of conflict. If this curve is upward-sloping (like most marginal cost curves), then optimal conflict occurs when this curve intersects the horizontal axis. Simply put, a country cuts back on conflict until the point where conflict no longer pays. 'One turns one's cheek', at least until the point it gets slapped. This optimality condition is illustrated in figure 2.5 by point Z*.

**Figure 2.5. Optimal Actor Conflict**

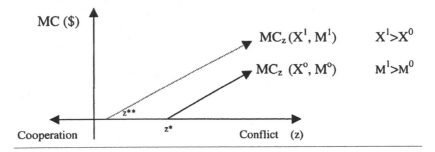

It is easy to show that the marginal cost of conflict shifts upward as a country engages in more foreign trade. Clearly, $\partial MC(Z,X,M)/\partial X>0$ and $\partial MC(Z,X,M)/\partial M>0$ so that a larger X or M implies greater marginal costs of conflict and hence less conflict. This is depicted by the dotted marginal cost curve in figure 2.5. Equilibrium conflict is lower, Z** instead of Z*.

The above result is based purely on economics. Countries minimize the costs of conflict by cutting any conflict to the point at which they will not be taken advantage of; they are nice, but not too nice. However, not everyone would agree that conflict is completely an economic decision. Realist theory, which emphasizes the importance of national security, might motivate one to incorporate conflict directly into a country's social welfare function, especially if policymakers perceive directed conflict to actually protect a nation. Further, although one would hope a country's voters have no desire for conflict, there remains the possibility that leaders act belligerently to appear strong internationally. Such leadership may stimulate a nation to rally around the flag as a means of deflecting important issues, but alternatively it could cause a nation to acquire more territory and impose political, religious, or ethnic agendas worldwide. To account for such innate conflictive desires entails adding Z directly to the actor's social-welfare function (or in our case, the median voter's social-welfare function). Modifying W(C) to incorporate conflict entails adding conflict to the social welfare function so that the median voter gets added utility directly from conflict. This is achieved by rewriting (2.1) as follows:

(2.1′) W(C,Z) where $\partial W/\partial Z > 0$

Maximizing (2.1′) introduces an extra term in (2.7) so that now

(2.7′) $\partial W/\partial Z + \lambda (X\, dP_x/dZ + M dP_m/dZ) = 0$

where $\partial W/\partial Z$ is the marginal social benefit of an extra unit of conflict. In equilibrium a country now equates the marginal benefit of conflict with conflict's marginal cost. Given a typically downward sloping marginal benefit curve (figure 2.6), this implies an equilibrium Z* at the intersection of curves $MC_Z(X^0,M^0)$ and $MB_Z$ when trade is $(X_O,M_O)$; or Z** at the intersection of $MC_Z(X^1,M^1)$ when trade is $(X_1,M_1)$.

**Figure 2.6. Optimal Actor Conflict**
**Incorporating Noneconomic Motives for Conflict**

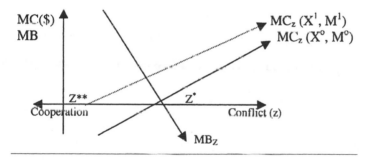

## Extending the Basic Model

### Multilateral International Interactions

One limiting feature is the failure of equation (2.1′) to distinguish specific target countries. Specifying conflict without regard to a specific target, results in conclusions based on bilateral interactions, but does not yield insights regarding multilateral relations. Yet multilateral relations are important both politically and economically. How alliances form and how third parties intervene in ongoing conflicts form a large political science literature (e.g., Altfield and Bueno de Mesquita, 1979; Holsti et al., 1973; Kim 1991; Sabrosky, 1980; Singer and

Small, 1966a, b; Siverson and King, 1979, 1980). In this vein, Altfield (1984), Morrow (1991), and Simon and Gartzke (1996) among others base alliances on security gains from joining a coalition. Altfield and Bueno de Mesquita (1979) use an expected-utility model to predict that intervention depends on the utility gained from one or the other party winning. As such intervention is more likely if a third party gains considerable utility from country i winning, instead of country j.

Many alliances contain both large and small countries. Small countries might have an incentive to join such an alliance due to the security a large country offers. On the other hand, rather than substantial security, a large country possibly gains an export market from allying with a small country. Larger export markets yield gains from trade and as a result increased wealth.

Economic trade also increases multilateral relations more directly. For example, Feng (1994) finds that the United States' trade with allies depends on its relations with adversaries. Thus extending the conflict-trade model to consider multilateral interactions is important.

To incorporate multilateral considerations, one must distinguish the specific target countries with which an actor interacts. Denote these targets as $i=1, ..., n$. In this framework, the social welfare function (2.1′) is further modified so that now the actor country's social welfare function is

$$(2.1'')\quad W_A = W\ (C, Z_1, Z_2, ..., Z_n; W_1, W_2, ..., W_n)$$

where $i=1,...n$ denotes each of the world's n countries actor A faces. The variable $Z_i$ reflects conflict with each country i. The variable $W_i$ depicts each other country's welfare level. As before, $\partial W_A/\partial Z_i{>}0$ depicts the welfare gain from conflict with country i. But now, $\partial W_A/\partial W_i$ designates how country i's welfare affects the actor. If the country is a friend, then $\partial W_A/\partial W_i{>}0$, but $\partial W_A/\partial W_i{<}0$ if the country is an enemy. Simply put, friends revel in each other's welfare being high. On the other hand, an actor's welfare is smaller the higher the welfare of a foe. In principle, one can define the welfare relationship more generally: $\partial W_i/\partial W_j{>}0$ imples i and j are friends and $\partial W_i/\partial W_j{<}0$ implies i and j are enemies.

Whereas an actor's conflict toward country i can increase actor welfare $\partial W_A/\partial Z_i \geq 0$, it most certainly decreases the target's welfare since no country likes to be the recipient of conflict. Thus, $\partial W_i/\partial Z_i{<}0$. Making use of these inequalities, it makes sense that friendship with a target mitigates conflict whereas rivalry increases conflict. To show this result, recall that the marginal benefit of conflict is $\partial W_A/\partial Z_i$; but this term is equal to ($\partial W_A/\partial W_i \cdot \partial W_i/\partial Z_i$). This term is negative if actor A and target i are friends (because $\partial W_A/\partial W_i{>}0$ and $\partial W_i/\partial Z_i{<}0$ so the product is negative). Thus as illustrated in figure 2.7 the marginal benefit curve shifts down implying less conflict between friends. Conversely, the curve shifts up when i is a rival (because $\partial W_A/\partial W_i{<}0$ and $\partial W_i/\partial Z_i{<}0$ so the product is positive) leading to more conflict (figure 2.8). Thus friendships and rivalries affect dyadic relations.

## Multilateral Considerations and Trade

But friendships and rivalries also affect multilateral interactions. Consider three countries: (1) an actor A, (2) a target i, and (3) a country j that can either be a friend or foe of i. Ask how an actor's conflict with country i changes when its trade with country j rises. As will be shown, an actor's conflict with country i declines if country j is a friend of i; and an actor's conflict with country i increases if countries i and j are rivaling foes. Thus trade with a friend-of-a-friend decreases conflict, while trade with a foe-of-a-friend increases conflict.

**Figure 2.7. Interaction with a Friend**

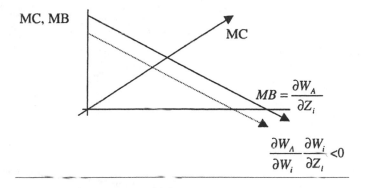

$$MB = \frac{\partial W_A}{\partial Z_i}$$

$$\frac{\partial W_A}{\partial W_i}\frac{\partial W_i}{\partial Z_i} < 0$$

**Figure 2.8. Interaction with a Rival**

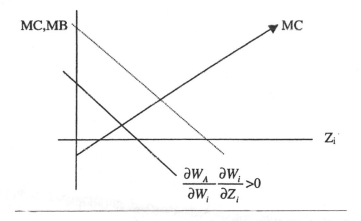

$$\frac{\partial W_A}{\partial W_i}\frac{\partial W_i}{\partial Z_i} > 0$$

To see this, recall that trade gains imply that bilateral trade increases cooperation and decreases conflict. Thus an actor's conflict with j would decrease were its trade with j to increase. As such, $\partial Z_j/\partial x_j < 0$. Decreased conflict with j raises country j's welfare because $\partial W_j/\partial Z_j < 0$. But increased country j's welfare raises country i's welfare, when countries i and j are friends. Finally, an increase in country i's welfare raises the actor's welfare, thereby implying that conflict with country i decreases. As such, trade with a friend-of-a-friend decreases conflict. This is illustrated in figure 2.9 by the downward shift in conflict's marginal benefit curve, thereby decreasing conflict from $Z^*$ to $Z^{***}$. The scenario for a foe-of-a-friend is the opposite.

**Figure 2.9. Conflict Given Multinational Considerations**

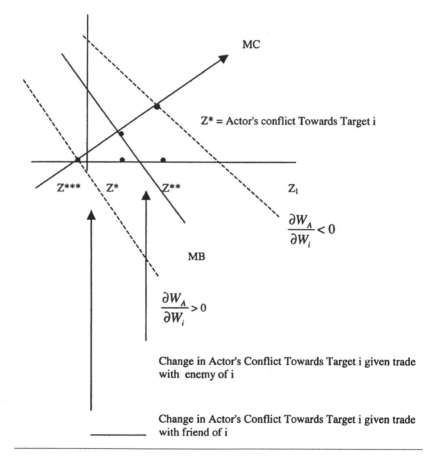

Change in Actor's Conflict Towards Target i given trade with enemy of i

Change in Actor's Conflict Towards Target i given trade with friend of i

Trade with an enemy-of-a-friend raises conflict. To see this, follow the same logic as above. An actor's conflict with j decreases as its trade with j increases. Thus $\partial Z_j / \partial x_j < 0$. Decreased conflict with j raises country j's welfare because $\partial W_j / \partial Z_j < 0$. But increased country j's welfare decreases country i's welfare, when countries i and j are enemies. Because of this decreased welfare the actor country increases conflict with i. This phenomena is illustrated in figure 2.9. For a friend-of-a-foe the marginal benefit curve shifts up, thereby yielding $Z^{**}$ conflict, and thus implying that conflict with country i increases. One can apply the above notions about how trading with a third party affects bilateral political interactions to other situations.

## An Application to Tariffs

Consider the impact of tariffs. Tariffs are an import duty country i imposes on an actor's exports. As such, gross export prices increase, although the price the actor actually gets decreases since extra revenues accrue to the importing nation. As a result, trade decreases because of the higher prices paid by importers. Based on the previous gains from trade analysis, decreased trade means increased conflict. This is easily seen in figure 2.5 or figure 2.6 by higher conflict $Z^{**}$ among trading partners compared to nontrading partner's conflict $Z^*$. But it is possible that tariffs can also affect third party conflict.

Whereas most literature deals with multilateral sanctions in the sense that several countries impose a tariff (Mansfield, 1995; Martin, 1992; Mastanduno, 1992), the analysis used here assesses how a tariff affects conflict even on countries that don't impose a tariff. As shown above, trade between an actor and target can alter conflict between the actor and third parties. Since tariffs alter actor-target trade, they may also influence an actor's conflict with third parties. According to the theory illustrated in figure 2.9, actor-target conflict depends on the relationship between the target and the third party. Recall that trade with a foe-of-a-friend increases conflict while trade with a friend-of-a-friend diminishes conflict. As such, a third-party imposed tariff can decrease conflict if the target and third party are enemies, whereas conflict can increase if the target and third party are friends.

## An Application to Foreign Aid

How foreign aid influences political relations is a topic often considered by political scientists (e.g., Abegunrin, 1990; Holsti, 1882; Orr, 1889/1990; Richardson, 1978). Most view foreign aid in a bilateral setting, a framework in which foreign aid is simply considered a transfer payment from one country to another but often with requirements to purchase imports from the aid provider. To the extent that foreign aid simply becomes a subsidy to purchase a beneficiary's products, one can analyze foreign aid through its impact augmenting trade. Again, applying the analysis behind figures 2.5 and 2.6, increased trade implies decreased conflict (movement from $Z^*$ to $Z^{**}$). But just like with tariffs, it is possible that foreign aid can alter third party political interactions.

Again refer to the theory behind figure 2.9. Actor-target conflict depends on the relationship between the target and the third party. Trade with a foe-of-a-friend increases conflict while trade with a friend-of-a-friend diminishes conflict. As such, third party foreign aid can increase conflict if the target and third party are enemies, whereas conflict can decrease if the target and third party are friends. The extent depends on the gains from trade and degree of friendship.

## An Application to Contiguity

Many find that contiguity increases war proneness (Barbieri, 1996a; Bremer, 1992; Diehl, 1985; Gleditsch, 1995; Gochman, 1991; Goertz and Diehl, 1992). Indeed, one would be hard pressed to find noncontiguous countries that engaged in militarized dispute prior to the 18th century. The relationship is so well established that some current research addresses *why* neighbors fight, rather than *whether* they fight (i.e., Vazquez (1995). On the other hand, it is well known that neighboring nations take advantage of small transportation costs to engage in more bilateral trade (Anderson, 1979; Arad and Hirsch, 1981; Deardorff, 1984; Gowa, 1994; Tinbergen, 1962). According to the trade-conflict model, greater trade induces less conflict, thus appearing to contradict the empirical findings regarding contiguity and war. However, rather than contradicting each other, the two models may be complementary.

Analyzing the effects of contiguity is difficult because ignoring the effects of trade can lead to an omitted variable bias. One must isolate each effect, otherwise one runs the risk of underestimating conflict between neighboring countries. Despite appearing high to begin with, current conflict measures might underestimate true conflict among neighboring states because they ignore the mitigating effects of trade. Thus while neighbors fight, they might engage in even more conflict were it not for the greater trade levels induced by their proximity to each other. But greater trade between neighboring countries can affect relations with more distant countries, as well.

Again refer back to the analysis regarding third parties. Trade with a friend-of-a-friend fosters less conflict than otherwise, while trade with a foe-of-a-friend brings greater conflict. As such, given the greater trade exhibited between neighbors, an actor should display less conflict toward friends of neighboring countries and more conflict toward a neighbor's rivals.

## Conclusion

A number of recent articles have presented theory and evidence that apparently contradict the liberal conflict-trade hypothesis. Each article appears to fall in one of three genres: Marxist-based theory, Ricardian-based theory, and finally game theory. This chapter shows that neither genre contradicts the liberal conflict-trade model. Ricardian-based trade models emphasize how countries utilize trade gains to enhance internal security, but have no propositions regarding protecting trade gains through international cooperation. As such, these models address defense expenditures as a means toward achieving internal security, but they do not take up conflict and cooperation. Game-theoretic models deal with dividing the gains-from-trade bounty, but these models become inappropriate when competitive markets divide gains-from-trade through the international price system. Even in noncompetitive international markets governed by negotiated prices, countries still have the incentive to protect trade gains through cooperation. Finally the Marxist model assumes strongly asymmetric trade gains, so much so that one exploited nation receives *negative* gains. But the magnitude of trade gains, whether they are negative or positive, is an empirical question. Either econometric estimation to measure trade gains is required, or the Marxist theory must be expanded to get at other corroborative implications. It is in this vein, namely, to expand the conflict-trade model to get at corroborative evidence that motivates this article.

Instead of merely examining the simple conflict-trade relationship, this chapter gets at the model's underlying foundation by moving from a purely mathematical formulation used in Polachek et al. (1999) to a graphical approach with propositions regarding how high gains-from-trade retard political conflict and enhance cooperation. In addition, this chapter extends the model by considering how such factors as tariffs, foreign aid, and contiguity affect international interactions. Finally, this chapter considers multilateral interactions. The approach yields several implications. First, trade with friends yields lower levels of conflict than trade with rivals. Second, when a nation trades with a third party friend-of-a-friend, lower bilateral conflict tends to result with the nation's friend than before. Third, when a nation trades with a third party enemy-of-a-friend, higher bilateral conflict tends to result with the nation's friend than before.

Whereas these propositions have empirical implications, they are difficult to test because measures of friendship rely on assumptions about how one country's welfare affects another, which are unavailable. However, this problem can be overcome. First, data on *relative* levels of conflict contain information on friendship. If, holding constant trade, France is less conflictive with England than the United States; one can infer that England and France are friendlier than the United States and France. Second, alliance data and United Nations voting data specify other ways to define friendship. Hopefully by extending these notions, future work will test some of the model's propositions.

## Notes

This chapter is motivated by findings contradictory to the conflict-trade hypothesis presented in *Journal of Peace Research*, 1999, 36(4). It attempts to put those results in perspective as well as present results from Polachek et al. (1999) in a graphical format. The author wishes to thank Katherine Barbieri, Yuan-Ching Chang, John Robst, and J. David Singer for discussion and important insights, as well as Gerald Schneider and two anonymous referees for their comments.

1. Schneider and Schulze (2002b) present empirical results consistent with these notions. The negative military expenditure trade interaction term coefficient presented in their table 5.2 supports this hypothesis since it implies that military expenditures for trading countries are associated with less actual conflict (war initiation).

# CHAPTER 3

# When Do Relative Gains Impede Trade?

*James D. Morrow*

Neorealists argue that states may refuse to engage in mutually profitable trade because of concern about 'relative gains'. However, this argument ignores the ability of states to respond to external threats by arming. As long as a state does not spend its entire gain from trade on the military, it is better off with trade than without it. Concern with relative gains then should not block trade even between rivals.

I present a formal model that addresses the enforceability of agreements to trade. It examines three types of goods that vary in how quickly the gains of cheating can be turned into a military advantage. The more quickly this can be done, the more difficult the enforcement of a trade agreement is. For most trade goods, the gain cannot be turned into a military advantage quickly, and so this problem is not likely to be important. Trade in goods with direct military applications can be exploited, and so trade in those goods is likely to be blocked.

Neorealists claim that states may refuse to engage in mutually profitable international trade because of concerns with 'relative gains' (Grieco, 1988, 1990). Trade brings economic benefits that states can devote to produce a military advantage. States must be concerned with the distribution of the benefits of trade as well as its profitability. If the benefits of trade accrue disproportionately to one side, the other side has to fear that the first will gain an advantage in military capabilities. The first state could use that advantage against its trading partner. The disadvantaged side should refuse to trade under these conditions, according to the relative-gains argument. Neorealists claim that others miss this concern because they focus on the 'absolute gains' from trade instead of the relative gains.

The crudest version of the relative-gains argument asserts that states not only gain value as their own economic capabilities increase, but they also gain value as other states' economic capabilities decrease.[1] But as Powell (1991, 1999: 53–55) has argued, states do not place value on others' capabilities in and of themselves; they care about others' capabilities out of the fear of what those capabilities could do to them. States value 'absolute gains', but they must be concerned with their relative position because other states could use a relative advantage to take what they have.

The sophisticated version of the relative-gains argument asserts that states must be concerned about the distribution of the benefits of trade even though they only care about their own economic size. If a state gains disproportionately from a trade agreement, it might turn that economic advantage into a military advantage. Its prospective trading partner might choose autarky over trade even though it would gain economic benefits from the trade. States are, as Grieco says, 'defensive positionalists'. They must be concerned about their relative position to protect their absolute benefits.

This chapter examines the relative-gains argument regarding trade. I present a formal model of trade between two rival states. Each state seeks greater economic consumption but must also worry that the other may attack and conquer it, which leads each to allocate some of its income to the military to protect itself, and perhaps attack the other if it gains a military advantage. Trade provides an opportunity for both to increase their income with a fixed distribution of the gains from trade, but trade occurs only if both sides agree to allow it. Additionally, either side can cheat on a trade agreement and use its ill-gotten gains to create a military advantage. If states are 'defensive positionalists', they must be concerned with both the distribution of gains from and the enforcement of a possible trade agreement. I analyze both these concerns. In general, both states will agree to trade unless the benefits are highly skewed toward one of them or either side can turn any temporary advantage from cheating into a military advantage before the other can respond. The latter problem increases the incentive to cheat on an agreement, making the enforcement of a trade agreement more difficult.

The essential point here is that states can raise their military allocations to protect themselves against threats (Choi, 1994 makes a similar point). If one state spends some of its gain from trade on its military, the other can reduce that threat by spending more on its own military. Military allocation rates are typically below 10 percent of national income, so it is unlikely that either side would spend all of its gain from trade on the military. Each nation's consumption is higher then with trade than without it. Even defensive positionalists prefer trade.

However, this argument depends on each state having the opportunity to build weapons to defend itself. Unilateral trade barriers can shift the benefits of trade to one side. The side cheating on the agreement could turn its ill-gotten economic advantage into a military advantage before the other side could arm in response. Further, such cheating can convey an additional economic advantage on the cheater. It can reduce its military allocation in the short run because the cheated state's economic resources are reduced by the shift in trade in favor of the cheater. If so, both parties might prefer not to sign a trade agreement out of fear of their vulnerability to such cheating.

This vulnerability depends on how quickly states can realize an economic and military advantage from cheating on their agreement. I address three possibilities in this chapter, representing the speed with which barriers work at shifting advantage in favor of the cheater. First, a state could raise counterbarriers before any economic gain is realized by the cheater; most trade goods fall into this category. Comparative advantage works sufficiently slowly that barriers are likely to be discovered before the cheater gains substantially. Second, a state might have the opportunity to raise its military spending after learning of the trade barriers but before an attack. This second case covers situations where the economic gain from cheating takes time to turn into a military advantage. The side disadvantaged by the cheating has the opportunity to rearm but cannot recover the loss in national income from the unilateral barriers. Third, the cheater can turn its gain into a military advantage and attack before the other side has any chance to respond. Some goods are militarily sensitive. The side selling them cannot prevent the buyer from putting them to use in its military once trade has been established. Only the third case undermines the willingness to trade.

The relevance of this paper for the debate about trade and conflict lies in the careful elaboration of how security motivations affect trade. This relationship is more complicated than many arguments make it out to be. For example, the argument here suggests why war can disrupt trade, a key assumption of the argument that trade reduces the motivation for war. Further, it also suggests why large wars are more likely to disrupt trade than small wars, a discrepancy in the results of Barbieri and Levy (1999) and Anderton and Carter (2001a). Security concerns in peacetime are not likely to have much effect on trade flows except for the cases of goods that are militarily useful.

## The Plan of the Argument

My model draws on two existing models, one by Robert Powell (1993; also see Powell, 1999: 40–81) and a second by Joanne Gowa (1989, 1994; Gowa and Mansfield 1993). Powell's model analyzes military allocation in dyadic competition, and Gowa's model addresses the dynamics of a trade agreement with a concern for security.

In this section, I informally review both models and how I combine them in this article. Powell's model assumes that both nations receive a set income each period as long as they exist. The two states alternate making decisions on military allocations and war. In its turn, a nation divides its income into consumption and military spending. After this allocation decision is made, it can choose to begin a war. In a war, a side's relative military allocation determines its chance of winning. If a side wins a war, both sides' income is fixed in the future with the winner getting the lion's share. Both nations wish to maximize the discounted sum of their consumption over time. Higher military allocations reduce current consumption but raise the chance of victory in a war. Powell (1993) finds a perfect Markov equilibrium of the game. Neither side initiates war in that equilibrium, and both sides allocate a fixed proportion of their income to the military from period to period. In short, neither war nor arms races occur in Powells' model.

Gowa's model provides the assumptions about the consequences of a trade agreement. It is also the most sophisticated relative-gains argument (Gowa, 1989, 1994; Gowa and Mansfield, 1993). She begins with the common argument that the setting of trade barriers between two nations has the form of a Prisoners' Dilemma game. Each nations' optimal tariff is its dominant strategy, but both would be better off if both adopted lower barriers to trade than their optimal tariffs. States that could benefit from trade can police defections from agreements to lower barriers when discount factors are sufficiently high. Because gains from trade can be diverted to the military, Gowa argues that trade produces security externalities that make the enforcement of agreements to lower barriers more difficult. Each nation must weigh its gains from trade to that of its trading partner. Each state fears that the other's gains will increase the other's military capabilities and so reduce the state's security.

Powell's model provides a way to introduce an endogenous security externality into Gowa's model. Rather than assuming that trade must produce a security externality, the sides adjust their armaments and decisions about whether to go to war in response to a trade agreement. In this way, the model analyzes the relative-gains argument that security concerns impede trade.

I add to Powell's model the possibility of a trade agreement between the two sides. At the beginning of the game, the sides can agree to trade. If they trade, both sides' income for that period rises by a fixed and known amount. The benefits of trade could be unequal; the sides do not have to receive the same amount from a trade agreement. Once the game begins, both sides have the opportunity to cheat on the agreement. Such cheating represents adopting barriers that shift the terms of trade, and the benefits of the trading relationship, in favor of the cheating nation. After cheating, if any, occurs, the other state can retaliate by raising barriers of its own.

When nations learn about cheating is the critical element in their decision whether to continue trade with each other. I model three possibilities here. First, both sides could be informed of cheating instantaneously. They would then have the option of raising retaliatory barriers to trade against cheating, which I assume would eliminate any benefit from cheating. Second, they could be informed of cheating after any possibility of retaliatory sanctions but before military allocations. They then could increase their own military allocation to protect themselves. Third, cheating could be hidden until after war is declared.

The sequence of when nations acquire knowledge of cheating should not be thought of as literal. Rather, it reflects the difficulty of gaining sufficient economic advantage from cheating to substantially increase a nation's income and of turning an economic advantage into military capability.

In equilibrium, states honor trade agreements except under the following special conditions:

1. The benefits of trade might be distributed very unequally. The side that receives lesser benefits might have to increase its military allocation by more than its gains from trade to counter the higher allocation that the side receiving greater benefits would make with trade. The former side would reduce its consumption if it agreed to trade.
2. Trade could produce a situation where at least one side would spend all of its added income from trade on the military because of a quirk in technology such that military allocations rise rapidly with added resources.
3. Cheating could be hidden until after war is declared. Both sides may then have an incentive to cheat, gain the benefits of cheating, raise their military expenditures, and hope to attack the other side.
4. Cheating could be revealed before military allocations are made but after retaliatory sanctions could be enforced. Both sides would have an incentive to cheat to raise their income even if they did not plan to attack the other side. This requires large benefits of cheating relative to the level of trade under mutual optimal tariffs.

The next section reviews Powell's model of military allocation by rivals. I then describe how trade is added to the model. Three different sequences are introduced to represent the different ways violations of trade agreements could be monitored. I present three propositions describing when peaceful trade occurs for each game. I conclude with a discussion of the results of the model and the relative-gains argument. That discussion addresses Gowa's model of security externalities in detail. The appendix contains complete statements of the propositions and proofs.

## Powell's Model

This section summarizes Powell's model of the trade-off between guns and butter. I use Powell's notation wherever possible. Two states, $S_1$ and $S_2$, play an infinite-horizon game, with the rounds indexed by $t$ and first period $t = 0$. At the beginning of each even-numbered period, $S_1$ allocates its resources, $r_1$, between consumption and its military. Let $m_1(t)$ be its military allocation in period $t$; $S_1$'s consumption is $r_1 - m_1(t)$ in period $t$. $S_2$ allocates its resources, $r_2$, in odd-indexed periods. A state's military allocations are fixed during the periods when the other state chooses its allocation. After a state allocates resources to its military, it can attack the other state.

States' payoffs depend on whether there is a war. If neither state ever starts a war, then both receive the discounted sum of the consumption over all periods. The utility that $S_1$ attaches to its stream of consumption, $P_1(m_1)$, is

$$\sum_{t=0}^{\infty} \delta_1^t \left( r_1 - m_1(t) \right)^{\rho_1}$$

where $\delta_1$ is $S_1$'s discount factor and $\rho_1$ is $S_1$'s attitude toward risk. $S_2$'s utility function is analogous. If $S_1$ attacks $S_2$ in period $t_0$, it enjoys its consumption in the periods before and including $t_0$. $S_1$ defeats $S_2$ with probability $\pi(m_1(t), m_2(t), \omega)$ in a war in period $t_0$ that $S_1$ begins, and is defeated with the complementary probability. The probability of winning a war depends on both sides' military allocations and the size of the first-strike advantage, $\omega$. War eliminates the loser as a rival of the winner. Both sides then receive set levels of consumption for all periods after the war, and neither need commit any resources to its military. The postwar levels of consumption for $S_1$ are $v_1$ after a victory and $d_1$ after a defeat. $S_1$'s utility for going to war in period $t_0$, $W_1(m_1, m_2, t_0)$, is

$$\sum_{t=0}^{t_0} \delta_1^t (r_1 - m_1)^{\rho_1} + \pi(m_1(t_0), m_2(t_0), \omega) \sum_{t_0+1}^{\infty} \delta_1^t v_1^{\rho_1} +$$
$$(1 - \pi(m_1(t_0), m_2(t_0), \omega)) \left( \sum_{t_0+1}^{\infty} \delta_1^t d_1^{\rho_1} \right)$$

where the first term gives $S_1$'s consumption before and during the war, the second term its consumption after the war if it wins times the probability of victory, and the third term its consumption after the war if it loses times the probability of defeat.

Powell characterizes the peaceful Markov perfect equilibria of his model. In a peaceful equilibrium, neither side attacks, and both sides commit the minimal expenditures necessary for deterrence of attempts to 'breakout' with higher expenditures and then go to war. Perfect Markov equilibrium ensures that both actors would carry out the threats implicit in their strategy but not realized in equilibrium. To characterize a peaceful equilibrium, I introduce two sets of functions that Powell employs. The first, $\overline{W}_1(m_2)$, is

$$\overline{W}_1(m_2) = \max_{m_1} W_1(m_1, m_2, 0).$$

This function gives the maximum utility that $S_1$ can receive if it attacks when $S_2$'s military allocation is $m_2$. It need not be the case that $S_1$ allocates all of $r_1$ to the military in the round it attacks. It may be that additional military expenditures do not raise the probability of victory sufficiently to compensate for the loss of the current consumption.

We can compare $\overline{W}_1(m_2)$ to $P_1(m_1)$ to determine the pairs of both sides' allocations where $S_1$ prefers war to peace. The second function, $\tilde{m}_1(m_2)$, specifies the level of military allocation that makes $S_1$ indifferent between war and peace for each level $m_2$ of military allocation by $S_2$. This function $\tilde{m}_1(m_2)$ satisfies:

$$\overline{W}_1(m_2) = P_1(\tilde{m}_1(m_2))$$

and is given by:

$$\tilde{m}_1(m_2) = r_1 - \left( (1 - \delta_1)(\overline{W}_1(m_2)) \right)^{\frac{1}{\rho_1}}$$

Figure 3.1 illustrates this function and the analogous function for $S_2$. $S_1$ prefers war for all combinations of both sides' military allocations that lie below the curve and prefers peace for all combinations above the curve. On the curve, $S_1$ is indifferent between remaining at peace with $S_2$ and consuming $r_1 - \tilde{m}_1(m_2)$ per period and increasing its expenditures to the optimal level and attacking $S_2$. The function $\tilde{m}_1(m_2)$ characterizes whether $S_1$ goes to war for each pair of military allocations. The function $\tilde{m}_2(m_1)$ does the same for $S_2$, with $S_2$ preferring war for allocations above $\tilde{m}_2(m_1)$ and peace for allocations below $\tilde{m}_2(m_1)$.

**Figure 3.1. Military Allocations and Preferences for Attacking in the Powell Model**

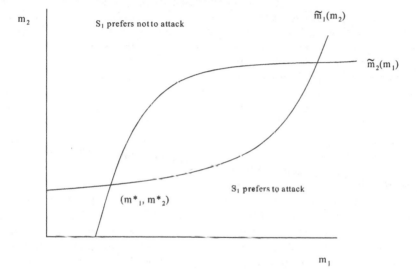

Figure 3.1 also illustrates the conditions for a peaceful equilibrium in Powell's model. A peaceful equilibrium is possible only if the curves $\tilde{m}_1(m_2)$ and $\tilde{m}_2(m_1)$ overlap, as they do in figure 3.1. Both $S_1$ and $S_2$ prefer peace for allocations inside the lens where the curves overlap. Out of this set of all pairs of allocations where neither side wishes to attack, the pair of allocations at the bottom tip of the lens is the peaceful Markov equilibrium. This pair of allocations, labeled $(m^*_1, m^*_2)$ in figure 3.1, Pareto dominates all other peaceful equilibria. No higher allocations can form a peaceful Markov equilibrium. If $(m_1, m_2)$ is a pair of military allocations inside the lens with $m_j > m^*_i$, at least one player has an incentive to lower its military allocation to $\tilde{m}_i(m_j)$. In words, at least one player is spending more on defense than is necessary to deter an attack by the other player. At $(m^*_1, m^*_2)$, both players are allocating the minimal resources needed

to deter the other. If either allocates less than its equilibrium allocation, the other will attack in the next round after setting its military allocation to the optimal level for attacking. In equilibrium then, neither side responds to increases in the other's military allocation. Each side knows it can deter the other, and the excess allocation is merely a temporary deviation, not a signal that the other side is preparing for war. After all, it could have attacked after making the excess allocation but chose not to.

## Adding Trade to the Powell Model

The Powell guns-versus-butter model provides a way to represent military allocation decisions. I examine the security consequences of a trade agreement between rivals. $S_1$ and $S_2$ can agree to lower trade barriers before the first round of the game. Trade raises both nations' resources above their level under mutual optimal tariffs, although not necessarily by the same amount. A trade agreement must also be enforced against violations. A state can shift income to itself by imposing its optimal tariff. This tariff shifts the terms of trade in its favor, raising the price of its exports relative to its imports. The state imposing the tariff increases its income above its income under a trade agreement, while the victim of the tariff loses income relative to its position under mutual optimal tariffs. The victim can respond by adopting its optimal tariff itself.

There are four possible outcomes after a trade agreement. In the first outcome, both sides could honor the agreement. In the second and third outcomes, one state could defect from the agreement while the other does not retaliate (there are two outcomes here because $S_1$ defecting while $S_2$ honors their agreement is different from $S_2$ defecting without retaliation from $S_1$). In the fourth outcome, the victim could retaliate against a defection, leaving both sides with less income than under the trade agreement. Each state's income is highest when it raises its optimal tariff without retaliation, followed by free trade, mutual optimal tariffs, and no retaliation against an optimal tariff by the other state. These levels of income lead to the common notion that trade between two states forms a Prisoners' Dilemma game.[2] Prisoners' Dilemma has a dominant-strategy equilibrium; both sides prefer cheating, and both retaliate when the other cheats. Free trade Pareto dominates the outcome of this dominant-strategy equilibrium, mutual optimal tariffs.

But trade is a dynamic problem; any possible trade agreement persists over time. The players can use the future of the game to police the present. We can represent the future by having the players play Prisoners' Dilemma repeatedly without end, in the same way that the Powell model is repeated infinitely. The players discount future payoffs with their discount factors. According to the folk theorem, a range of agreements to support free trade can be enforced. Any division of the payoffs where each player receives at least as high a payoff per round as it does when both adopt mutual optimal tariffs can be supported in equilibrium. Such divisions are enforced by a 'grim trigger' strategy; if one player defects from the agreement, the other player employs its optimal tariff for all future rounds.

The model represents both the four possible outcomes of trade and the dynamic nature of violations and retaliations. The state of the game, represented by $\sigma$, represents the current status of a trade agreement between the two nations as given in table 3.1. The amount of resources that each nation has to allocate depends on the current state of the game. Let $r_i(\sigma)$ be the resources that $S_i$ can allocate if the current state of the game is $\sigma$ for $i = 1,2$. Then the following inequalities represent the notion that the enforcement of trade produces the preferences of Prisoners' Dilemma:

$$r_1(3) > r_1(2) > r_1(1) > r_1(4)$$

$$r_2(4) > r_2(2) > r_2(1) > r_2(3)$$

Similarly, I also index expectations from war, $\overline{W}_i(m_j, \sigma)$, and military allocations, $\tilde{m}_i(m_j, \sigma)$, by the current state of the game. If a peaceful equilibrium exists in a state $\sigma$, I call the equilibrium military allocations to be: $(m^*_1(\sigma), m^*_2(\sigma))$.

**Table 3.1. States of the Game with a Trade Agreement**

| | |
|---|---|
| $\sigma=1$ | Trade agreement has collapsed after a defection and retaliation. |
| $\sigma=2$ | Trade agreement is in force; no defection has occurred. |
| $\sigma=3$ | $S_1$ has defected from the trade agreement, but $S_2$ has not yet retaliated. |
| $\sigma=4$ | $S_2$ has defected from the trade agreement, but $S_1$ has not yet retaliated. |

I make the following assumptions about the military competition that results from the four possible states of a trade agreement.

1. There is a conflict of interest in all four states.

Powell defines a conflict of interest to exist when each side prefers attacking a disarmed opponent to simply devoting all its resources to consumption. Obviously, the model will not capture the strategic problem of trade in the face of a security dilemma if there is no security dilemma in the model.

2. There is a peaceful Markov equilibrium for subgames with fixed $\sigma = 1,2$.

This assumption produces unique equilibrium levels of military allocations in the Powell model. In figure 3.1, there are two pairs of levels of military allocations that could be supported in equilibrium, corresponding to the lower and upper intersections of the two curves that form the lens. Only the allocations corresponding to the lower intersection can be supported in equilibrium. Each state prefers lowering its military allocations and being attacked in the next round to maintaining its allocation corresponding to the upper tip of the lens.

Such allocations cannot be supported in equilibrium precisely because of such defections.

Assumption 2 places two restrictions on the model. First, it asserts, as in Powell's model, that the sides will not wish to reduce their military expenditures in the face of an attack they could deter. It is possible that sides might wish to engage in a strategy of 'eat, drink, and be merry, for tomorrow we die' in the face of an attack. Assumption 2 eliminates the possibility that sides will not resist attacks in order to consume more now.

Second, assumption 2 asserts that peaceful equilibria exist under both a stable trade agreement and the absence of a trade agreement. However, it does allow the possibility that there does not exist a peaceful equilibrium if one state cheats on the trade agreement and the other does not retaliate. This facet of assumption 2 focuses the analysis on the security externalities of trade directly. In the relative-gains argument, trade does not lead to war. Rather, security concerns reduce the value of trade, and so less trade occurs than one might expect. This assumption models the relative-gains argument then. If trade cannot lead to peace, then obviously the sides will avoid trade. But that is not the question; it is whether security concerns impede trade.

3. The payoffs from war, $v_i$ and $d_i$, are fixed and independent of $\sigma$.

Assumption 3 asserts that the consequences of war are independent of whether a trade agreement is in place before a war. Given Powell's assumption that war eliminates the loser as a power (but not necessarily all of its income), I assume that the winner could also force the loser to accept a trade deal after the war. The consequences of victory and defeat do not depend on the prewar state of trade.

The sequence of actions in each round of the game completes the model. I allow for three different sequences of a round to model different abilities to monitor and respond to violations of a trade agreement. I assume the sides begin the game with a trade agreement and examine when at least one side has an incentive to defect from that agreement. The speed with which the victim of a defection can detect and respond is critical. Tables 3.2, 3.3, and 3.4 give the three different sequences of actions in a round of the model. Each table gives one round of the game where $S_i$ allocates resources during the round. $S_i$ is $S_1$ during even-numbered rounds beginning with round 0 (the first round of the game) and $S_i$ is $S_2$ during odd-numbered rounds. $S_j$ is the state that does not allocate resources during a given round.

The game is repeated indefinitely. The three different sequences of opportunities to cheat on a trade agreement, retaliate against such cheating, and allocate to the military and attack represent how fast nations can take advantage of a violation of a trade agreement. In all three games, $S_1$ and $S_2$ are assumed to begin the game with an agreement to trade ($\sigma = 2$ initially).

If one party violates the agreement, when does the other learn of that violation and have the opportunity to respond? Two factors determine the speed of response. The first is how long it takes a country to turn its economic advantage into a military advantage. Barriers to trade can shift the terms of trade and thus the benefits of trade quickly. But nations must tax the added income and turn it into military capability to take advantage of it. Military build-ups take years to produce new equipment and trained soldiers. Most traded goods add to a state's military capability only indirectly by raising the wealth of a country. In general then, cheating on a trade agreement should not lead to immediate military advantages. The second factor is how long it takes to detect unilateral trade barriers. The speed with which such barriers shift the terms of trade is critical here. Those barriers that create big, immediate shifts in national income should be easy to detect; those that work slowly are more difficult to discern. Cheating that leads to quick income gains should lead to quick responses.

Table 3.2 represents the situation for most traded goods. The victim of unilateral barriers learns of the violation before any significant shift in either nations' militaries have occurred. It has time both to raise counterbarriers and build up its own military. I refer to this case as 'typical trade goods'. Most goods add to a nation's military capabilities only indirectly by raising its wealth. Any increase in the military from trade in these goods arises only because wealthier nations can afford larger, more expensive militaries.

## Table 3.2. One Round of the Game with Typical Trade Goods

1. $S_i$ can raise barriers to trade. If $\sigma = 2$, $S_i$ can shift $\sigma$ to 3 if $i = 1$ or 4 if $i = 2$ in this round.
2. $S_j$ can retaliate if $S_i$ has raised barriers to trade. If $i = 1$ and $\sigma = 3$, $S_j$ can shift $\sigma$ to 1; if $i = 2$ and $\sigma = 4$, $S_j$ can shift $\sigma$ to 1.
3. $S_i$ allocates resources $r_i(\sigma)$ (as in the Powell model).
4. $S_i$ can attack $S_j$ (as in the Powell model).

The gains from trade can be captured more easily for some goods. In table 3.3, the victim learns of the violation in sufficient time to shift resources to the military to protect itself but after the predatory tariff has shifted the benefits of trade toward the violator. The victim can rectify the trade imbalance in future rounds by retaliating two rounds later. In the short run, it must worry about the security consequences of its economic exploitation. This case occurs when a side can capture the surplus generated by trade quickly before countervailing duties can eliminate the unfair advantage. I refer to this case as having a 'capturable trade surplus'. The chance to arm in response to trade barriers occurs because it takes time to turn the economic gain into a military advantage.

## Table 3.3. One Round of the Game with a Capturable Trade Surplus

1. $S_i$ can retaliate if $S_j$ has raised barriers to trade. If $i = 1$ and $\sigma = 3$, $S_i$ can shift $\sigma$ to 1; if $i = 2$ and $\sigma = 4$, $S_i$ can shift $\sigma$ to 1.
2. $S_j$ can raise barriers to trade. If $\sigma = 2$, $S_j$ can shift $\sigma$ to 3 if $j = 1$ or 4 if $j = 2$ in this round.
3. $S_i$ allocates resources $r_i(\sigma)$ (as in the Powell model).
4. $S_i$ can attack $S_j$ (as in the Powell model).

Some traded goods have immediate military value. Armaments are the extreme example, but other goods can also be applied directly to the military once acquired. The United States restricted trade to the Soviet Bloc in a variety of technological products during the Cold War because the technology had immediate military applications. In table 3.4, the violator can turn the ill-gotten gains of an optimal tariff into military might before the victim realizes the violation has occurred. Goods with immediate military application fall into this case. I refer to it as 'trade in military goods'.

**Table 3.4. One Round of the Game with Trade in Military Goods**

1. $S_j$ can retaliate if $S_j$ has raised barriers to trade. If $i = 1$ and $\sigma = 3$, $S_j$ can shift $\sigma$ to 1; if $i = 2$ and $\sigma = 4$, $S_j$ can shift $\sigma$ to 1.

2. $S_j$ can raise barriers to trade. If $\sigma = 2$, $S_j$ can shift $\sigma$ to 3 if $i = 1$ or 4 if $i = 2$ in this round.

3. $S_j$ allocates resources $r_i(\sigma)$ (as in the Powell model).

4. $S_j$ can attack $S_j$ (as in the Powell model).

These sequences of play also assume that a 'grim trigger' strategy is used to enforce trade. All three games begin with a trade agreement in place ($\sigma = 2$). I analyze whether such an agreement is stable. If not, the players would not sign the trade agreement in the first place. Once one player raises trade barriers ($\sigma = 3$ or 4), the state cannot move back to free trade ($\sigma = 2$). Once the other player retaliates after one raises barriers ($\sigma = 1$), the players cannot sign another trade agreement. Mutual optimal tariffs are an absorbing state in these games. Once one player violates the initial agreement, the eternal punishment of the 'grim trigger' is the only form of enforcement available. I adopt this assumption to parallel Gowa's (Gowa and Mansfield, 1993; Gowa, 1994) use of the 'grim trigger' in her modified Prisoners' Dilemma models of trade under security externalities.

## Trade and Peaceful Equilibrium in the Models

We wish to know when trade can be sustained in each of the three games. If trade cannot be sustained, then the parties would not sign a trade agreement at the beginning of the game. I characterize the peaceful Markov perfect equilibrium of each game. I specify an equilibrium by giving both sides complete best replies for each state they can face in each game. Powell's notation for the Markov perfect equilibrium of his model is useful here.

*Proposition* (Powell, 1993): The equilibrium of the Powell model is:

$$R_1(m_2) = \begin{cases} (m_1^*, not\ A)\ if\ m_2 \geq m_2^* \\ (m_1^a(m_2), A)\ if\ m_2 < m_2^* \end{cases}$$

$$R_1(m_2) = \begin{cases} (m_1^*, not\ A)\ if\ m_2 \geq m_2^* \\ (m_1^a(m_2), A)\ if\ m_2 < m_2^* \end{cases}$$

where

$$m_i^a(m_j) = \arg\max_{m_i} W_i(m_1, m_2)$$

These best replies support equilibrium allocations of $(m^*_1, m^*_2)$ and payoffs $(r_1 - m_1^*)^{\rho_1} / (1 - \delta_1)$ and $(r_2 - m_2^*)^{\rho_2} / (1 - \delta_2)$, for $S_1$ and $S_2$, respectively.

In other words, the equilibrium allocations are supported by strategies that punish lower allocations and ignore higher allocations. If either side allocates less than its equilibrium allocation, the other side allocates the optimal amount to attack and then attacks in the next round. If either side allocates more than its equilibrium allocation, the other side ignores that excessive allocation and continues to allocate its equilibrium level; that amount is sufficient to deter an attack. The $m_i^a(m_j)$ function gives state $i$'s optimal military allocation in response to $m_j$ if state $i$ is going to attack. The $R_i$ functions specify state $i$'s best reply given $m_j$.

For ease of exposition in stating the proposition, I will continue to use these terms and index them by the state of the game. For example, $R_i(m_j, \sigma)$ gives state $i$'s best reply for its allocation and decision to attack given that the current state is $\sigma$. Similarly, $m^*_1(\sigma)$ gives $S_1$'s equilibrium military allocation when the current state is $\sigma$.

Trade occurs in the model under peaceful equilibria where neither party raises trade barriers, when $\sigma = 2$ for all rounds of the game. The following proposition gives the conditions under which neither actor wishes to raise barriers to trade with typical trade goods:

*Proposition 3.1*: The game with typical trade goods has trade in a peaceful equilibrium when:

(a) $\overline{W}_i(m_i^*(2), 2) \geq \overline{W}_i(m_i^*(1), 1)$ for $i = 1, 2$.

See the appendix for a complete statement of the proposition and a proof. Both sides can respond to defections from free trade before those defections produce significant economic effects. Trade in typical goods occurs except when one side's expectation for war under free trade is less than under mutual optimal tariffs. This condition is common to all three equilibria. In the next section, I discuss what this condition and the added conditions of the next two propositions imply about when trade occurs in a rivalry.

The second proposition addresses trade with a capturable surplus. In that game, the victim cannot retaliate to a defection for two rounds after the defection occurs, but it does learn of the defection in time to raise its military allocation against a possible attack. Defection then is more tempting in this game than before. Proposition 3.2 gives the conditions for peaceful trade.

*Proposition 3.2* The game with a capturable trade surplus has trade in a peaceful equilibrium when:

(a) $\overline{W}_i(m_i^*(2),2) \geq \overline{W}_i(m_i^*(1),1)$ for $i = 1,2$.

and (b) for $\sigma = 3,4$, one of the following two conditions is true (the conditions are written for $\sigma = 3$; for $\sigma = 4$, replace 3 with 4 and reverse 1 and 2 in subscripts):

(i)    there exists a peaceful equilibrium for $\sigma$ and
$$P_1(m_2^*(2),2) \geq r_1(2) - m_1^*(3) + \delta_1\left(r_1(3) - m_1^*(3)\right)$$
$$+ \delta_1^2\left(r_1(3) - m_1^*(3)\right) + \delta_1^3 P_1(m_1^*(3),3) \text{ , or}$$

(ii)   there does not exist a peaceful equilibrium for $\sigma$ and
$$P_1(m_2^*(2),2) \geq r_1(2) - m_1^a(m_2^a(3),3) + \delta_1\left(\overline{W}_1(m_2^d(3),3)\right),\text{where}$$
$$m_2^d(3) = \arg\max_{m_2 \leq r_2(3)}\left[(1 + \delta_2)\left(r_2(3) - m_2\right) + \delta_2^2\left(W_2(m_1^a(3),m_2)\right)\right]$$

Deterring defection from free trade is more difficult with a capturable trade surplus. One possibility is that exploitation–trade barriers that have not yet been met with retaliatory sanctions–is peaceful (condition i). The payoff for defection can be substantial here. The defector can lower its military allocation in the round before it raises the trade barriers, knowing that the victim cannot attack before the trade barriers reduce its income and so its military allocation. It collects the extra income from exploitation for two rounds before the victim can retaliate. Those short-run benefits could outweigh the long-run loss from the loss of trade under autarky. The second possibility is that defection might not have a peaceful equilibrium. However, the victim of the trade barriers does have time to raise its military allocation after the defection but before the attack. It sets its military allocation in anticipation of the coming attack, making that attack more difficult and less profitable for the state defecting from free trade. Then trade can occur with a capturable surplus even if there is not a peaceful equilibrium when a state defects. The victim may be able to make war after a defection sufficiently costly to deter defection.

The third and final proposition addresses trade in military goods. Here the defector can attack before the victim even has a chance to raise its military in response.

*Proposition 3.3*: The game with trade in military goods has trade in a peaceful equilibrium when (a) $\overline{W}_i(m_i^*(2),2) \geq \overline{W}_i(m_i^*(1),1)$ for $i = 1,2$. and (b) for $\sigma =$

3,4, one of the following two conditions are true (the conditions are written for $\sigma$ = 3; for $\sigma$ = 4, replace 3 with 4 and reverse 1 and 2 in subscripts):

(i)  there exists a peaceful equilibrium for $\sigma$ and
$$P_1(m_2^*(2),2) \geq r_1(3) - m_1^*(3) + \delta_1\left(r_1(3) - m_1^*(3)\right) + \delta_1^2 P_1(m_1^*(1),1) , \text{ or}$$

(ii)  there does not exist a peaceful equilibrium for $\sigma$ and
$$P_1(m_2^*(2),2) \geq r_1(3) - m_1^a(m_2^*(2),3) + \delta_1\left(\overline{W}_1(m_2^*(2),3)\right)$$

As with a capturable surplus, there are two possibilities to consider. First, if defection does not necessarily lead to war, condition (i) ensures that the long-run costs of retaliation exceed the short-run benefits of defection. Second, condition (ii) states when defection as a preparation for war is deterred. This condition is probably the most difficult to satisfy of all the conditions in the three propositions. The defector can catch its victim with a peacetime military allocation. In addition, the defector gains the benefits of exploitation to raise its military allocation in preparation for its attack. Consequently, its expectation from war ($\overline{W}_1(m_2^*(2),3)$ is likely to be much higher than its expectation from peaceful trade ($P_1(m*_2(2),2)$). In equilibrium, $\overline{W}_1(m_2^*(2),2) = P_1(m*_2(2),2)$. After defecting, its resources are higher, so $\overline{W}_1(m_2^*(2),3) > \overline{W}_1(m_2^*(2),2)$. The only chance of deterrence here is for the short-run cost of arming to be so high that defectors will not suffer those costs to gain the long-run benefits of victory. A peaceful equilibrium after defection is the best chance for peaceful trade in military goods.

## Discussion

When is peaceful trade possible under military competition according to these propositions? The conditions of each of the propositions must be satisfied for trade to be stable and so for the sides to agree to trade. I break these conditions into two groups: the distribution of benefits and concerns with enforcement.

## Marginal Military Allocations and Gains from Trade

Begin with the fundamental condition in all three propositions, $\overline{W}_i(m_j^*(2),2) \geq$ $\overline{W}_i(m_j^*(1),1)$; both states' expectation from war must be higher with trade *than* without it. This condition is easier to satisfy than it seems at first glance. In equilibrium, these expectations equal discounted consumption from peace in each state, $P_i(m*_j(\sigma),\sigma)$. In peace, consumption is just resources minus military allocation. Then a state's expectation from war is higher with trade than without if it does not allocate *all* of the gain from trade to the military.

In two possible situations a state might allocate all of its gain from trade to the military. First, the gains from trade could be distributed very unequally. The state receiving the lesser gains might be forced to allocate all of its gains to the military just to balance the increased spending of the state gaining the lion's share of the benefits from trade. This possibility is one careful statement of the relative-gains argument. An insufficient relative gain in the trade deal induces an absolute loss in consumption.

Second, even if the benefits from trade are distributed relatively equally, there could be a quirk in the technology of war such that military allocations rise very steeply with resources. Imagine, for example, that both sides are $10 short of building nuclear weapons under mutual optimal tariffs. Trade raises their income, making both states now able to afford nuclear weapons. Now, both sides might require much higher levels of military spending to deter one another in equilibrium. In both situations, the exact amount of additional military allocation that trade produces depends on the complex interaction of the variables in the Powell model. Both sides' discount factors, their attitudes toward risk, the costs of war, the postwar distribution of resources, and the magnitude of the first-strike advantage all affect equilibrium military allocations.

In any case, it is unlikely under normal circumstances that the benefits of trade are totally consumed by the additional military allocations that greater wealth allows. The key question is the size of the marginal increase in military allocations as a function of resources. A reasonable first assumption is that such marginal increases are of the magnitude of total military allocations relative to total national product. Table 3.5 presents both the average and range of military expenditures as a percentage of gross national product (GNP) for a selection of countries during the Cold War. In peacetime—even during the Cold War—very few nations allocate over 15 percent of their GNP to the military, and most fall below 5 percent. I have omitted the former Soviet Union because their military allocations as a percentage of GNP are still unknown. SIPRI estimated them around 10 percent during the 1970s, but the real figure may have been as high as 25 percent of GNP. Even countries locked in long-term rivalries, such as Pakistan and India, do not allocate large fractions of their economy to defense. The Pakistan and India case also illustrates the main argument here. Defense preparations are endogenous; Pakistan compensates for its smaller economy by spending more than India. Of course, marginal increases may not be the same magnitude as total allocations are. It is hard to believe that trade could produce marginal allocations over 100 percent of the gain from trade. Security externalities should not block trade between rivals during peacetime.

Wartime is a different story. Military allocations rise dramatically during war, particularly world war. Table 3.6 presents Organski and Kugler's (1980) estimates of military allocations as a percentage of GNP during World War II. Given the nature of the military struggle, these countries spent every penny they could on their militaries during the war. It appears then that states cannot spend significantly more than 50 percent of their GNP on the military even under the greatest of threats. These levels are high enough to suggest that states would

**Table 3.5. Military Allocations as a Percentage of GNP for a Selection of Countries, 1972–90**

| Country | Average allocation | Highest allocation | Lowest allocation |
|---|---|---|---|
| United States* | 6.0 | 6.7 | 5.1 |
| Great Britain | 4.8 | 5.3 | 3.9 |
| France | 3.9 | 4.2 | 3.6 |
| Japan | 0.9 | 1.0 | 0.8 |
| West Germany | 3.3 | 3.6 | 2.8 |
| Israel* | 17.7 | 27.2 | 8.4 |
| Egypt* | 14.0 | 36.5 | 4.6 |
| Syria* | 14.3 | 21.1 | 8.9 |
| South Korea | 5.1 | 6.2 | 3.8 |
| Austria | 1.2 | 1.3 | 1.0 |
| Brazil | 1.2 | 1.7 | 0.5 |
| India* | 3.2 | 3.9 | 2.8 |
| Pakistan* | 6.2 | 7.1 | 5.0 |

*Source:* All figures are from SIPRI (1982, 1992).
\* Includes years the country was involved in an interstate war.

wish to cut off trade out of fear of security externalities. But not always. In 1806, during the Napoleonic Wars, the Victualling Board of the Royal Navy bought far more brandy (625,000 gallons) than rum (250,000 gallons)—even though France was the source of brandy and rum was produced in the British West Indies (Parkinson, 1948: 169). The British navy appears to have not cared whether it put money in Napoleon's pocket. I return to this point after discussing trade and security externalities.

**Table 3.6. Military Allocations during World War II for Selected Major Powers**

| Year | Percentage of Gross National Product allocated to the military | | | |
|---|---|---|---|---|
| | United States | Japan | Germany | United Kingdom |
| 1938 | 1 | 17 | 30 | 7 |
| 1940 | 2 | 17 | 37 | 43 |
| 1941 | 11 | 23 | 41 | 52 |
| 1942 | 33 | 30 | 44 | 52 |
| 1943 | 45 | 42 | 45 | 55 |
| 1944 | 46 | 51 | 50 | 54 |

*Source:* Taken from Organski and Kugler (1980: 218).

The relative-gains problem in peacetime is not large enough to give states a reason to break off mutually profitable trade, except under unusual circumstances. Both states will agree to trade if they do not spend all of their gain from trade on the military. If states have marginal military allocation rates of 5 percent or less, then the gains from trade must be divided about 20-to-1 for the side receiving less to consume all of its gain from the trade in added military spending. Wartime is a different matter. Because military allocations are much higher during wartime, the distribution of benefits from trade does not need to be so skewed for one side to be a net loser from trade.

Furthermore, the model and this argument assume that the division of the benefits of trade is fixed. But they are not. The trading states can agree to divide the benefits differently. Imagine that state $A$ gains the lion's share of the benefits, such that state $B$ would rather not trade. State $A$ could offer a greater share of the benefits to $B$ in order to provide $B$ with some net benefit. $A$ would be better off because $B$ will block trade without that adjustment of the distribution of benefits. Indeed, Grieco (1990: 222–223, 231; also see Keck, 1993) mentions this point himself. The problem of relative gains then does not block trade, but it might lead states to ask for a redistribution of the benefits of trade.

Of course, actors without any concern about relative gains would also ask for such redistributions of the benefits. If trade places the parties on the Pareto frontier, then the only way either can get more is at the expense of the other. The only way to force such a redistribution is to threaten to break off the deal. This threat is more likely to be credible when one side receives little of the gain from trade relative to the other. Concern about relative gains is not needed to explain why parties seek more equal distributions of benefits from trade.

## Enforcement Concerns

The other conditions in propositions 3.2 and 3.3 address enforcement concerns. Proposition 3.1 assumes that defections from free trade can be monitored and that victims can respond to such defections before the defector can take military advantage of its gain. Enforcement is less of a concern under those conditions. The picture for trade between rivals is not so nice for trade in goods with a capturable surplus and in military goods. Again, the sequence of each game should be thought of as representing how trade barriers affect the accumulation of wealth and the application of wealth to the military. Some goods, such as computer technology and underwater propeller designs during the Cold War, could be applied quickly to the military once obtained. These technologies were uncontrollable; once they had been obtained through trade, their application to the military could not be blocked. Not surprisingly, technologies with immediate military value were not traded during the Cold War.

The game for trade in military goods mirrors this logic. Neither side can prevent the other from stealing the technology and using it to their military advantage if they agree to trade. Trade is still possible in this game if the goods traded do not have a decisive military effect, that is, cause the breakdown of a peaceful equilibrium if either side cheats on the trade agreement. The problem then is the deterrence of defection from a trade agreement for the short-run advantage of shifting trade in the defector's favor.

With a capturable trade surplus, the primary problem is the deterrence of defections for short-run profit. This game represents goods where detection of cheating is sufficiently slow that the defector can gain an advantage over some time. But the victim of such cheating can prepare to defend itself if the cheating lays the ground for an attack. Trade in some capital goods may fall into this class. Their possession alone provides a substantial and lasting economic advantage for states that do not have them already. But their application to military ends may take sufficient time to allow a possible target the opportunity to arm itself in defense. Cheating for short-run economic advantage is attractive here precisely because retaliation takes longer. More short-run benefits can be taken before the punishment of autarky begins.

But most goods do not fall into either of these classes. The logic of comparative advantage works slowly. National incomes do rise as a consequence of trade, but the rise is gradual and slow. Furthermore, most traded goods have little direct military significance. The only way they produce security externalities is by raising the overall wealth of a trading nation. Richer societies can afford higher military allocations and so do produce some greater threat to their trading partners. But trade raises both sides' income, and it is unlikely that the rise in military spending is so great that it consumes all of the benefits of trade for either nation.

## Allies, Adversaries, and Trade

The propositions show that concerns about relative gains are unlikely to block trade between rivals. They also cast light on the most sophisticated neorealist argument about security and international trade. Gowa (1989, 1994; Gowa and Mansfield, 1993) combines both the security consequences of trade and the enforceability of trade agreements against short-run defections. Trade creates a security externality, according to her argument. Between allies, this externality is positive; higher national income means higher military spending, and both allies benefit from each other's spending. Between adversaries, the externality is negative. Higher military allocations by one state make the other less secure.

These externalities alter the value of trade making the enforcement of trade agreements easier when they are positive and harder when they are negative. Both sides will live up to their agreement when the long-run value of continuing the agreement exceeds the short-run advantage of defecting from it. The positive externality raises the long-run value of trade, making defection less likely and enforcement easier. The negative externality between adversaries reduces the value of trade, making it more likely that states will defect on trading arrangements for their own short-run gain. States should manage their trade when they can anticipate which states will be their allies and adversaries in the future. They should seek to expand trade with their prospective allies and reduce trade with their projected adversaries.

Gowa continues by adding the effect of polarity. Neorealists assert that alliances in bipolar systems are more likely to persist than alliances in multipolar systems. We should expect then that bipolar systems should foster trade inside each bloc but not across blocs. Within a bloc, all states anticipate that their alliance will persist and so expect to benefit from the positive security externalities of trade. Across blocs, trade is difficult because both sides fear the negative security externalities. In multipolar systems, even allies that trade must fear that their alliances may break in the future, turning their current ally into their future enemy. Gowa then concludes that free trade should flourish within alliances in a bipolar system but not within alliances in a multipolar system.

The critical question here is the size of the security externality. Security externalities change the value of trade by forcing adversaries to spend more on the military and allowing allies to spend less. But if the marginal increases in military allocations as a function of resources are comparable to overall military allocations as a proportion of total resources, these effects are small–in the neighborhood of 5 percent. Further, it is not clear that allies' military allocations are always substitutes (Murdoch and Sandler, 1982; Theis, 1987; for an explanation why, see Morrow, 1991). Indeed, a state may raise its military expenditures in response to an increase by its ally. Trade may produce security externalities, but only under unusual conditions are those externalities large enough to change the willingness to trade.

A simple example may illustrate this point and demonstrate the limits of the security externalities argument. Figure 3.2 gives a Prisoners' Dilemma game with specific payoffs for illustrative purposes. Security externalities change these payoffs. When enemies play the game, both must spend more as their incomes rise; allies spend less as their incomes rise. Gowa (1989) represents these effects by subtracting or adding, for enemies and allies, respectively, a fraction W of the other player's payoff in each cell of the game. She then calculates the discount factor needed to support cooperation in each case and shows that a larger range of discount factors supports cooperation between allies than between enemies.

**Figure 3.2. A Sample Prisoners' Dilemma**

*Player 2*

|  |  | C | D |
|---|---|---|---|
| *Player 1* | C | (1,1) | (-1,2) |
|  | D | (2,-1) | (0,0) |

$$\delta \geq (2-1)/(2-0) \geq .5$$

How wide is the range of discount factors where allies cooperate but enemies do not? The empirical evidence suggests that states typically spend no more than 5 percent of their GNP on the military in peacetime and no more than 50 percent in wartime. I use these values for illustrative effect in figure 3.3. This figure displays four modified Prisoners' Dilemmas–one pair for peacetime when $W = .05$ and one pair for wartime when $W = .5$. Each pair includes a game between enemies and a game between allies. Below each game I have calculated the minimal discount factor needed to support cooperation in that game. In both pairs, allies have a wider range of discount factors that support cooperation than enemies. The wartime example has a range from 0 to .8; any discount factor in this range produces cooperation between allies but not between enemies. If all discount factors are equally likely, then in wartime allies are much more likely to trade than enemies. The peacetime example produces a very narrow range of discount factors where allies cooperate but enemies do not, .462 to .537 to be precise. It is unlikely that this precise interval occurs. Of course, these figures should be taken illustratively, rather than literally. Security externalities matter much more during wartime than during peace.

**Figure 3.3. Comparison of When Trade Can Be Supported in Peace and War**

During Wartime

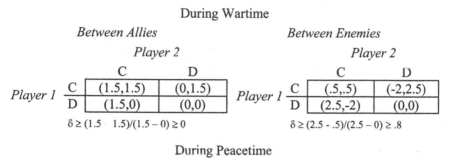

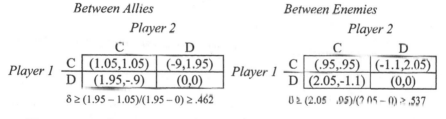

The argument here may explain a puzzle about whether war reduces trade. Barbieri and Levy (1999) and Anderton and Carter (2001a) use interrupted time series to examine the effects of war on trade flows between warring states. However, they find inconsistent results; Barbieri and Levy find that war has no discernable effect on trade, while Anderton and Carter find the opposite. The difference may lie in the cases they examine. The rise in military allocations during war corresponds to a change in the value of $W$ underlying the calculations in figure 3.3. War leads to a disruption of trade when the critical discount factor $\delta$ necessary to support trade in the face of security externalities shifts above the discount factors of the states. This shift corresponds to a movement in figure 3.3 from the game in the lower right corner to the game in the upper right corner. An increase in $W$ always raises this critical $\delta$, but the size of that change depends on the importance of the war to both sides. Minor wars do not require either side to raise their military allocations substantially to fight effectively, meaning the increase in $W$ caused by a minor war is small. Major wars, on the other hand, lead to large increases in both military allocations and the resulting

*W*. Major wars then are more likely to disrupt trade than minor wars. This is exactly the pattern across the results of Barbieri and Levy (1999) and Anderton and Carter (2001a). Barbieri and Levy analyzed minor wars, such as the Boxer Rebellion, while Anderton and Carter tested major wars, such as the World Wars. The former find that war has little discernible effect on trade, and the latter find substantial effects of war on trade.

The security externalities argument is logically correct but likely to be empirically insignificant. Security externalities exist, but they are unlikely to be large enough to lead adversaries to suspend trade during peacetime. If security externalities blocked trade, we should not observe trade between divided nations, like the Germanies—but those nations do trade (Dorussen and Mo, 1995).

Still, trade during the Cold War prospered within, but not across, the ideological blocs. If security concerns do not explain this pattern, what other factors might? States may direct trade for other political benefits, such as supporting friendly regimes (Dixon and Moon, 1993). Ideologically similar systems can foster trade between themselves. Economic actors respond to the risk of political disruptions of trade (Morrow, Siverson, and Tabares, 1998, 1999; Pollins, 1989a, b). Such risks are larger between rivals than between states with good relations.

## Conclusion

The relative-gains argument asserts that trade will not occur because states are concerned about the security consequences of trade. This article shows that such security concerns are unlikely to undermine trade. States can allocate more to their militaries to compensate for any enlarged threat to their security. Such additional allocations are likely to be smaller than the gain from trade. Consequently, trade increases national consumption even in the face of such security concerns.

Why might states be unwilling to trade according to the model here? First, it could be that trade leads to war; the model rules this possibility out by assumption. If added resources eliminated the possibility of any peaceful outcome, then at least one side is better off not trading. Second, the benefits of trade could be distributed very unequally. The side receiving the much smaller share could be forced to spend more than its gain from the trade to compensate for the added military spending of the side that received the lion's share of the benefits from trade. The former would refuse to trade under those conditions. However, the side receiving the majority of the benefits would be better off negotiating a more even division of the benefits in this case. It could offer enough so that the other side would prefer trade to autarky.

Third, the goods traded could have direct military applications or a capturable surplus. Then a side might be able to violate the agreement to shift the benefits of the trade in its favor and gain a military advantage before the other could erect retaliatory barriers or prepare to defend itself. The latter would refuse to trade out of the fear of such a surprise defection. But the problem here is the enforcement of the agreement, not a concern about the consequences of an agreement that is honored by both sides.

I conclude by discussing three limitations the model inherits from the Powell and Gowa models. First, the Powell model does not make a distinction between stocks and flows (Powell, 1993: 122). Military allocations are treated as the equivalent of stocks that depreciate to zero in every round. Current military allocation always gives current military strength. The timing issues about detection and retaliation are likely to be more significant in a model that distinguishes between stocks and flows. Short-run defection could lead to a military advantage over several rounds. Defection from trade could be the start of a breakout strategy designed to end in war. States could compensate for this threat by building higher military stocks in peacetime, but such buffering strategies reduce the value of trade by increasing peacetime military allocations.

Second, the model is played under complete information. As a consequence, there are no arms races in the Powell model; both states can perfectly anticipate one another's future actions. If there were private information, it is possible that the sides could interpret one another's actions as signals of future intentions (cf. Kydd, 1997). If so, higher expenditures could trigger reactions and arms races. In my model, defections from free trade could be signals of future increases in military allocations. This possibility could make trade agreements easier to enforce by increasing the costs of cheating on an agreement.

Third, the model assumes that there are definite benefits from trading with another specific country because Gowa's model makes this assumption. If there are alternative trading partners, then such definite benefits may not exist. A nation can gain the comparative advantage of trade from the world market if a particular trade partner blocks trade. Further, the optimal tariff for a nation may be zero instead of the positive tariff assumed in Gowa's model. Unilateral free trade could produce a higher national income than any level of protection.

If relative gains concerns do not explain the inability of states to reach mutually beneficial reductions in trade barriers, what could account for these failures? First, there is always a question of the distribution of the benefits of trade at the state level. Many different agreements to reduce barriers could be reached, all with different distributions of the gains between the parties. Any deal which can be enforced and where both sides benefit over the status quo is an equilibrium of the negotiation game to reduce trade barriers. Negotiations over which deal to adopt may fail simply because negotiations over distributional issues in the face of uncertainty cannot be ex post efficient (Myerson and Satterthwaite, 1983). States then may fail to reduce trade barriers because they argue over the distribution of the benefit (even though both only care about their own absolute gain).

Second, opening trade produces winners and losers domestically in addition to raising national income (Rogowski, 1989; Hiscox, 2001). The losers from trade openness may organize to seek protection from their government (Grossman and Helpman, 1994). This argument is well known but operates below the state level. The sources of difficulty in increasing openness to trade lie more in distributional issues at both the international and domestic level than in the security consequences of the increased income trade produces.

# Appendix

This appendix contains complete statements and proofs of the equilibria of the three trade games. I begin with a lemma that shows that $S_i$'s expectation from war increases with its resources and declines with the other side's resources.

*Lemma*: $\overline{W}_1(m_2)$ is increasing in $r_1$ and decreasing in $r_2$.

*Proof*: Let $r'_1 > r_1$ and $m*_1(r_1)$ be $S_1$'s equilibrium military allocation with resources $r_1$. Then:

$$\overline{W}_1(m_2(r'_1)) = \max_{m_1 \leq r_1} W_1(m_1, m_2, 0)$$

$$= \max_{m_1 \leq r_1} \left[ \delta(r'_1 - m_1)^{\rho_1} + \pi(m_1, m_2(m_1), \omega) \sum_{i=1}^{\infty} \delta^i v_1^{\rho_1} + \left(1 - \pi(m_1, m_2(m_1), \omega)\right) \sum_{i=1}^{\infty} \delta^i d_1^{\rho_1} \right]$$

$$\geq \delta(r'_1 - m_1^*(r_1))^{\rho_1} + \pi(m_1^*(r_1), m_2(m_1^*(r_1)), \omega) \sum_{i=1}^{\infty} \delta^i v_1^{\rho_1}$$

$$+ \left(1 - \pi(m_1^*(r_1), m_2(m_1^*(r_1)), \omega)\right) \sum_{i=1}^{\infty} \delta^i d_1^{\rho_1}$$

$$> \delta(r_1 - m_1^*(r_1))^{\rho_1} + \pi(m_1^*(r_1), m_2(m_1^*(r_1)), \omega) \sum_{i=1}^{\infty} \delta^i v_1^{\rho_1}$$

$$+ \left(1 - \pi(m_1^*(r_1), m_2(m_1^*(r_1)), \omega)\right) \sum_{i=1}^{\infty} \delta^i d_1^{\rho_1}$$

$$= \overline{W}_1(m_2^*(r_1))$$

Powell (1993) shows that $m*_1(r_1)$ is increasing in $\overline{W}_1(m_2)$ and so must also be increasing in $r_1$. By a similar argument, $m*_2(r_2)$ is increasing in $\overline{W}_2(m_1)$ and so also increasing in $r_2$. Powell also shows that $\overline{W}_1(m_2)$ is decreasing in $m_2$. Then $\overline{W}_1(m_2)$ is decreasing in $r_2$.

Similar arguments show that $\overline{W}_2(m_1)$ is increasing in $r_2$ and decreasing in $r_1$. The next lemma demonstrates that retaliation is strictly dominant.

*Lemma*: If $\sigma = 4$, $S_1$ strictly prefers shifting to $\sigma = 1$ when it has an opportunity to retaliate.

*Proof:* If $\sigma = 1$, $S_1$'s continuation value is $P_1(m*_1, 1) = \overline{W}_1(m_2^*, 1)$ because a peaceful equilibrium exists for $\sigma = 1$ by assumption. If $\sigma = 4$, $S_1$'s continuation value is $\overline{W}_1(m_2, 4)$ regardless of whether a peaceful equilibrium exists for $\sigma = 4$. $\overline{W}_1(m_2)$ is increasing in $r_1$ and decreasing in $r_2$, $r_1(1) > r_1(4)$, and $r_2(4) > r_2(1)$; therefore, $\overline{W}_1(m_2^*, 1) > \overline{W}_1(m_2^*, 4)$.

*Definition:* The following strategy pair is peaceful competition with trade:
(a) If $\sigma = 2$, do not change the state.
(b) For $S_1$ and $\sigma = 4$, change state to $\sigma = 1$. For $S_2$ and $\sigma = 3$, change state to $\sigma = 1$.
(c) Play $R_i(m_j, \sigma)$ in allocation and attack moves if there is a peaceful equilibrium for state $\sigma$.
(d) Play $(m_i(m_j, \sigma), A)$ in allocation and attack moves if there is not a peaceful equilibrium for state $\sigma$.

The following propositions specify when peaceful competition with trade is a Markov perfect equilibrium of each of the three games.

*Proposition:* Peaceful competition with trade is the unique Markov perfect equilibrium of the game with typical trade goods if $\overline{W}_i(m_j^*(2), 2) > \overline{W}_i(m_j^*(1), 1)$ for $i = 1, 2$.

*Proof:* The previous lemma shows that part b must be part of any best reply. Powell shows that part c gives best replies for each state with a peaceful equilibrium. By definition, $(\tilde{m}_i(m_j, \sigma), A)$ is a best reply if there is no peaceful equilibrium. Then if either nation shifts the state from $\sigma = 2$, the other will shift the state to $\sigma = 1$ before any new allocations are made. Then neither side prefers shifting the state away from $\sigma = 2$ if their continuation values with trade are greater than those without trade. Because $P_i(m*_j(\sigma), \sigma) = \overline{W}_i(m_j^*(\sigma), \sigma)$

for $i = 1, 2$ and $\sigma = 1, 2$, $\overline{W}_i(m_j^*(2), 2) > \overline{W}_i(m_j^*(1), 1)$ for $i = 1, 2$ shows that continuation values are greater with trade than without it.

*Proposition:* Peaceful competition with trade is the unique Markov perfect equilibrium of the game with a capturable trade surplus if:
(a) $\overline{W}_i(m_j^*(2), 2) > \overline{W}_i(m_j^*(1), 1)$ for $i = 1, 2$, and
(b) for $\sigma = 3, 4$, one of the following two conditions is true (the conditions are written for $\sigma = 3$; for $\sigma = 4$, replace 3 with 4 and reverse 1 and 2 in subscripts):

(i) There exists a peaceful equilibrium for $\sigma$ and

$$P_1(m_2^*(2),2) \geq r_1(2) - m_1^*(3) + \delta_1(r_1(3) - m_1^*(3))$$
$$+ \delta_1^2(r_1(3) - m_1^*(3)) + \delta_1^3 P_1(m_1^*(3),3), \text{ or}$$

(ii)    there does not exist a peaceful equilibrium for $\sigma$ and

$$P_1(m_2^*(2),2) \geq r_1(2) - m_1^a(m_2^a(3),3) + \delta_1(\overline{W}_1(m_2^d(3),3)), \text{ where}$$

$$m_2^d(3) = \arg\max_{m_2 \leq r_2(3)} [(1 + \delta_2)(r_2(3) - m_2) + \delta_2^2(W_2(m_1^a(3),m_2))]$$

*Proof:* The first condition merely asserts that both states prefer $\sigma = 2$ (trade) to $\sigma = 1$ (mutual optimal tariffs). The second condition addresses the other possible defections from trade depending on whether there is a peaceful equilibrium when $\sigma = 3,4$ (after trade barriers go up but before retaliation). If there is a peaceful equilibrium, condition i asserts that the potential defecting side (say $S_1$) prefers $\sigma = 2$ to defecting to gain $\sigma = 3$ for two rounds and then $\sigma = 1$ thereafter. Note that the potential defector can reduce its military allocation in the round before it defects to $\sigma = 3$. If there is no peaceful equilibrium, condition ii asserts that $\sigma = 1$ (peaceful trade) is preferred to an attack after a defection from trade. Note that the victim (say $S_2$) can raise its military allocation in anticipation of the coming attack.

*Proposition:* Peaceful competition with trade is the unique Markov perfect equilibrium of the game with trade in military goods if:

(a)   $\overline{W}_i(m_j^*(2),2) > \overline{W}_i(m_j^*(1),1)$ for i = 1,2, and

(b)   for $\sigma = 3,4$, one of the following two conditions is true (the conditions are written for $\sigma = 3$; for $\sigma = 4$, replace 3 with 4 and reverse 1 and 2 in subscripts):

    (i)     there exists a peaceful equilibrium for $\sigma$ and

$$P_1(m_2^*(2),2) \geq r_1(3) - m_1^*(3) + \delta_1(r_1(3) - m_1^*(3)) + \delta_1^2 P_1(m_1^*(1),1), \text{ or}$$

    (ii)    there does not exist a peaceful equilibrium for $\sigma$ and

$$P_1(m_2^*(2),2) \geq r_1(3) - m_1^a(m_2^*(2),3) + \delta_1(\overline{W}_1(m_2^*(2),3))$$

*Proof:* Directly parallels the previous proposition. Note that the defecting state can now attack in the same round and that retaliation cannot occur for two rounds if the defection is peaceful.

# Notes

An earlier version of this article appeared in *Journal of Conflict Resolution* (Morrow, 1997). Reprinted by permission of the publisher.

    1. Grieco (1988, 1990) has states with utility functions that increase in their own 'payoffs' and the difference between its own 'payoff' and the other state's 'payoff'. Ignoring Grieco's confusion about the term 'payoff' and treating economic capability as

'payoff', his utility function reduces to one where a state's utility increases in its own capabilities and declines in the other state's capabilities.

2. I ignore for now obvious problems with sequence in this story. Retaliation suggests that the states do not move simultaneously. In this case, the question of sequence is irrelevant; adding sequence would lead to the same outcome.

# CHAPTER 4

# Extending the Multicountry Model of Trade and Conflict

*Han Dorussen and Håvard Hegre*

## The Peaceful Trading State?

The hope that over time economic interdependence will replace national strife as the dominant force in interstate relations has been repeatedly expressed throughout this century. To provide a recent example, the trading state in Rosecrance's (1986) theory replaces territorial conquest with commerce. Historical reality, however, gives cause for sober reassessment. Extensive trade failed to stop Germany and Great Britain from fighting World War I. Lenin (1916/1985) argued consequently that the imperialist trade strategies pursued by the main powers had caused the war. From an entirely different perspective, following World War II, Hirschman (1945/1980) analyzed the ways in which Nazi Germany had put trade in service of its war aims. Gowa (1994) also argues that in the first place security concerns determine trade relations. Barbieri (1996a) shows that theoretical arguments have been advanced for all possible positions in this debate: trade leads either to less conflict, or to more conflict, or has no effect on the likelihood of conflict at all.

This chapter addresses the disagreement concerning the link between trade and conflict by analyzing how trade affects expectations about gains from the use of force. Clearly, trade and conflict are related in an intricate and simultaneous way, which goes a long way in explaining the existing confusion in the literature. The use of formal models forces us to specify our assumptions and it provides clear criteria to assess the validity of our deductions. We find that the effect of trade on conflict depends on specific assumptions about the nature of conflict and the number of countries in the international system. Dorussen (1997, 2001) has pointed out the problem that much of the current research in political science relies implicitly on two-country models. We first outline a multicountry model of trade and conflict which is essentially a revised balance-of-power model based on expected utility. The model was previously presented in Dorussen (1999). We examine if and how a larger number of countries change the effect of trade under various assumptions about conflict.

The number of countries in the international system is not necessarily constant. Their number may increase because of incorporation of 'new' countries in the system. An appropriate analogy is the discovery of land hitherto 'terra incognita'. In this way, the total amount of resources in the international system may increase. Second, a larger number of countries may share an already existing amount of resources, making the international system more fragmented. In the twentieth century, the latter conceptual pattern has been predominant. Following World War II, independence movements dismantled the nineteenth-century colonial empires, and the end of the Cold War ushered in a new period of state building mainly at the expense of the former Soviet Union.

Both conceptions of an increasing number of countries can be linked to current discussions about globalization. Väyrynen (1997: 3) holds globalization to mean 'the expansion and deepening of market relations within and especially between the dominant political units, usually states, in such a manner that these relations attain an increasing amount of autonomy'. One possible interpretation of the expansion of market relations is the inclusion of more and more countries into a global economic order. The consequences of globalization for international relations are thought to be benign, fostering economic growth and international cooperation, as well as malign, increasing inequalities between nations and destabilizing international politics. Scholars have, however, only recently begun to directly address the issue of globalization, trade, and international conflict (Hegre, 2000, 2001; Oneal and Russett, 1999b; Polachek et al., 1999)

Furthermore, multicountry models analyzing the effect of trade on conflict are still rare. The study of balance of power makes use of multicountry models, but deals exclusively with security concerns (Niou and Ordeshook, 1990; Powell, 1999; Riker, 1962; Smith, 1995; Wagner, 1986). Some scholars have studied the effect of conflict on trade with the help of multicountry models. For example, Gowa (1994) and Werner (1997) both argue that cooperation on security issues and trade go together. Snidal (1991a, b) finds that security concerns are less likely to affect trade given an increasing number of countries. Dorussen (1996, 1997, 2001) analyzes models in which two allies have to decide about trade facing a common enemy (see also Niou and Ordeshook, 1994; Papayoanou, 1997). Finally, work by Skaperdas (1992) and Skaperdas and Syropoulos (1996) demonstrates that the incentives to use resources for armament differ given many, instead of two, countries.

In this chapter, we analyze an important aspect of the much larger issue of globalization, trade, and conflict; namely, we consider how an increasing number of countries changes the effect of trade on the incentives to initiate conflict. For this purpose, we outline a model of trade and conflict in the next section. The model is based in part on work by Snidal (1991a: 714ff). In the subsequent two sections, the model is used to study the implications of trade restrictions on state security. First, we consider the effect of trade assuming that conflict eventually will lead to the complete elimination of the losing side—in this case, the conflict is 'total'. In addition, the effect of trade is analyzed when conflict does *not* lead to the elimination of the losing side—such conflict is called 'limited'. In both sections, we pay particular interest to the implication of a larger number of countries for the effect of trade. Furthermore, we present and discuss various indicators to evaluate the effect of trade on conflict and evaluate their appropriateness for multicountry situations. Section five focuses on balance-of-power concerns and considers explicitly the effect of alliances on the relation between trade and conflict.

Revisiting the model of balance of power and trade provides an apt framework to derive comparative static results for the number of countries and the number of countries choosing free trade. We find that trade in general reduces the incentives for conflict. Moreover, the pacifying effect of trade on conflict strengthens if the number of countries increases.[1] Given 'limited' conflict, trade has the largest impact if countries trade freely before conflict but halt trade following conflict. An important finding is that if countries expect trade to resume following conflict, under certain circumstances such 'ex post' trade makes the initial conquest of resources more attractive. In the final section, we relate these results to security in a balance-of-power perspective. The credibility of a commitment not to trade with an adversary following conflict depends on the distribution of resources, the number of allies, and the efficiency of intra-alliance trade.

## Modeling Trade and Conflict

We outline a basic model of trade and conflict following Dorussen (1999) and Snidal (1991a: 714ff). In this model, the international system consists of a number of countries, all of which control resources. Resources stand for economic productivity, that is, wealth, but also for military strength. As an aid to memory, think of resources as factories and of political leaders as maximizing the industrial potential of their country. We study the effect of two independent variables: a state's openness to international trade and the number of states in the system. The analysis focuses on how choices with respect to trade in a given period affect incentives for conflict in the next period. It is necessary to introduce some notation: $S = \{S_1, S_2, ..., S_n\}$ is the set of countries, and $r = \{r_1, r_2, ..., r_n\}$ the distribution of resources across $S$. Countries aim at maximizing expected gains from resources minus the costs of conflict, whenever they take part in a conflict.[2]

Countries may benefit from their resources in basically two ways. First, production and trade are a peaceful means for countries to gain. Second, countries can use their resources to conquer other countries' resources, which can then also be used in production and trade. However, resources can only be won by way of risky and costly conflict.

A *production and trade function* (PTF) models the peaceful gains from resources.[3] In this part of the model, the efficiency of trade and the distributions of its gains is of central importance. The parameter $\lambda$ measures the benefits from trade since it depends on the level at which barriers to trade exist. It is equal for all states and pairs of states in the system.[4] The PTF determines the gains from production and trade on the basis of the number of resource units that can be paired. For any country, total benefits can be discerned as based on pairs of domestic resources only (i.e., production or $P$), and on pairs of domestic and foreign resources (i.e., trade or $T$). In other words, if $S_i$ has $r_i$-resource units, each unit is matched with $(r_i - 1)$ domestic units and possibly all foreign units (cf. Snidal, 1991a: 714ff). Consider the following PTF:

$$2\binom{r_i}{2} + \sum_{Sj \neq Si} \lambda r_i r_j = r_i(r_i - 1) + \sum_{Sj \neq Si} \lambda r_i r_j = P + T \tag{1}$$

Throughout the chapter, we standardize the gains from *unrestricted* trade as equal to gains from domestic production (and set this value at 1). The range of gains from restricted trade falls between zero and one, or $0 \leq \lambda \leq 1$. In other words, any difference between domestic production and foreign trade is caused by restrictions on trade, and these restrictions are always a loss. Total expected gains from production and trade are:

$$(P+T) + \phi(P+T) + \phi^2(P+T) + \phi^3(P+T) + \Lambda = \frac{P+T}{1-\phi} \equiv B \tag{2}$$

We denote these gains with $B$. The parameter $\phi$ is the discount factor and reflects the rate of time preference. The expected benefits from production and trade thus depend on the number of countries and the distribution of resources.[5]

A *contest success function* (CSF) models explicitly the relationship between trade and conflict. Conflict results from strategic choices that aim at obtaining direct control over the resources of other countries. Within the confines of the model, the demand on the resources of another country needs to be backed with a credible threat to use force.[6] It is relatively easy to find examples of military conflict motivated by a desire to control raw materials or centers of industrial productivity such as France's occupation of the Rhineland in 1923 or Japan's annexation of Manchuria in 1931. We use a security model linking the distribution of resources with the outcome of military conflict.

The CSF links the relative amount of the resources committed to conflict with the probability of victory.[7] It is a commonly known function which maps the resource ratio between combatants into a probability distribution over victory ($p_v$), defeat ($p_d$), and stalemate ($p_s$). We make the reasonable assumptions that countries are more likely to be victorious if their resources increase relative to the opponent's amount of resources, and that stalemate is most likely if warring countries are evenly matched.[8]

The CSF is useful to determine the expected gains from conflict. In any period, the conflict is either decided or the outcome is a stalemate. If the conflict is decided, the expected outcome for a given country $S_i$ equals $p_v V_i + p_d D_i - c$, where $V_i$ and $D_i$ are the one-period benefits from resources a victory or defeat implies, and $c$ is the one-period cost of conflict (excluding the trade-related costs). The probability of stalemate determines the duration of a conflict. The model further assumes that as long as conflict continues there are no gains from trade or production. Once a conflict is decided (by victory or defeat), the gains from trade are a discounted stream of payoffs in perpetuity. Based on these assumptions, the resources expected from conflict are:

$$p_v V_i + p_d D_i - c + p_s \{ p_v V_i + p_d D_i - c + p_s ( \Lambda ) \} \tag{3}$$

Since countries expect gains *in future periods* from the resources won (or forfeited), the expected utility from conflict is a discounted sequence. Appendix 4.1 shows that the expected gains from conflict for $S_i$ can be represented as:

$$\frac{p_v V_i + p_d D_i - c}{(1 - p_s)(1 - \phi)^2} \equiv W \tag{4}$$

The threat to initiate a conflict is credible when a country expects to benefit more from conflict than from maintaining the status quo, that is:

$$W \geq B = \frac{P + T}{1 - \phi}$$

This requires a sufficient power advantage. As long as conflict is costly ($c > 0$), there is also an upper limit to the power advantage: when a large country considers attacking a much smaller one, the expected gains are too small compared to unlikely but still possible losses.

Whether the condition for conflict is satisfied thus depends on the gains and losses from conflict, $V_i$ and $D_i$, which may be affected by trade. Further, the costs of conflict, $c$, and the initial distribution of resources also matter. Trade and (the absence of) conflict are related in the model. However, because the effects of trade on the parameters as well as the effects of changes of parametric values are complicated, it is not surprising that the overall effect of trade on conflict is complex.

It is useful to compare the effect of trade on conflict in the model outlined above with the effect in classical expected utility models (Polachek, 1980). The latter assume that trade directly effects the parameter $c$. If conflict leads to the interruption of trade, the foregone gains from trade are added to the costs of conflict. Higher costs of conflict make it less attractive to upset the status quo.[9]

In the model presented in this chapter, higher costs of conflict also make conflict less likely. However, the costs of interruption of trade enter the model by way of the parameter $p_s$, the probability of stalemate. Trade also affects the value of victory and defeat, $V_i$ and $D_i$, respectively.[10] The remainder of the chapter traces these more intricate effects of trade on the expected gains and losses from conflict.

## Trade and the Gains from Conflict under Total Conflict

In what way does trade affect the conditions under which countries expect to gain by using force? Answering this question will allow considerable progress in establishing the relationship between trade and conflict. Conflict should be extremely unlikely if no country expects to gain from the use of force. Trade basically enables countries to benefit from resources over which they have no direct control. However, countries do value direct control over resources, partly (as we will demonstrate) to avoid costly barriers to trade. Conflict will be inevitable if a state desires direct control. Conflict is risky and costly, in part because it stops countries from benefiting from trade and production. There is an expanding literature which analyzes the impact of these factors on the choice between productive and appropriative economic activities (Brito and Intriligator, 1985; Grossman and Kim, 1996; Powell, 1993; Skaperdas, 1992). Of particular interest is the study by Skaperdas and Syropoulos (1996), who use a multicountry model to analyze whether countries allocate less resources to conflict when they have the opportunity to trade.

In the argument presented here, we assume that countries are not equally free to maneuver in the international system. We distinguish between two aspects of constraint. First, a country may be 'small' relative to other countries, because of its relative lack of resources. Second, it may be impossible for a country to capture the full gains from trade, because of the existence of trade barriers. For now, we focus on the effect of trade efficiency constraints—and leave size to a later section.

A theoretical justification for tariffs is that they are the result of interest groups successfully lobbying for protection against imports, and politicians agreeing to trade restrictions that benefit the few at the expense of the many (Magee et al., 1989). From a public-choice perspective, economic sanctions, which are examples of other costly barriers to trade, result from interest-group pressure as well. Economic sanctions are politically efficient, even though they are economically inefficient (Kaempfer and Lowenberg, 1992).

Barriers to trade influence the incentives to use force. A threat with the use of force is only credible if a country expects to gain from its use; in other words, conflict requires a credible threat to use force. Recall that the parameter $\lambda$ indicates the remaining efficiency of trade with a constrained country.[11] In this section, moreover, we make the important additional assumption that all countries control the same amount of resources: $r_i = r_j = r$.[12]

Below we list the expected payoffs which depend on the efficiency of trade and whether or not there is conflict. First, equation (5) gives the benefits from autarky, that is, production on the basis of domestic resources in the absence of trade, and in the absence of conflict. Equation (5a) contains the gains from production *and* trade. The gains from trade depend on trade efficiency—indicated by the parameter $\lambda$.

$$B^0 = \frac{(r)(r-1)}{(1-\phi)} \qquad\qquad \text{No conflict, no trade} \qquad\qquad (5)$$

$$B^\lambda = \frac{(r)(r-1)+\lambda r^2(n-1)}{(1-\phi)} \qquad\qquad \text{No conflict, trade} \qquad\qquad (5a)$$

Equation (5b) evaluates the expected benefits from conflict, assuming that all resources are at stake. In this case, by definition, there is no opportunity for trade following conflict. If a country wins, it appropriates the full benefits from the production with all resources. If a country is defeated, it has no resources left with which to produce. The conflict is thus total or absolute, rather than limited in its aims.[13] We previously introduced $V_i$ and $D_i$, measuring the one-period gains from resources a country controls following conflict: $V_i$ in case of a victory and $D_i$ in case of defeat. The victor appropriates the gains from production with all resources, $(nr)(nr - 1)$. Since there are no resources left for trade, $V_i$ equals $(nr)(nr - 1)$. A defeated country loses all resources, therefore $D_i = 0$. In any given period, a country has to choose between the gains from trade and conflict, where the latter is a risky lottery over $V_i$ and $D_i$.

$$W = \frac{p_v(nr)(nr-1)+p_d(0)-c}{(1-p_s)(1-\varphi)^2} \qquad\qquad \text{Conflict, no secure resources} \qquad\qquad (5b)$$

The threat with force is credible, if it is preferable to the status quo without conflict and with trade. First, we analyze the effect of trade on the *incentives* to initiate conflict. Further, we determine how an increase in the number of countries taking part in conflict influences the effect of trade on these incentives. Hence, we determine the minimum probability of victory which makes conflict preferable to trade, or for which $p_v$ is $W \geq B^\lambda$ (or (5b) $\geq$ (5a)). We denote this minimum probability of victory as $\underline{p}_v^\lambda$. We set the minimum probability of victory required to make conflict credible in case of autarky equal to $\underline{p}_v^0$; that is, for which $p_v$ is $W \geq B^0$ (or (5b) $\geq$ (5)).

## The Difference Indicator Given Total Conflict

The difference between $\underline{p}_v^{\tilde{\lambda}}$ and $\underline{p}_v^0$ becomes one way to measure the effect of trade on the incentives for conflict. Clearly, whenever $\lambda = 0$, $\underline{p}_v^{\tilde{\lambda}} = \underline{p}_v^0$, and if $\lambda > 0$, $\underline{p}_v^{\tilde{\lambda}} > \underline{p}_v^0$. It is straightforward to express the difference between $\underline{p}_v^{\tilde{\lambda}}$ and $\underline{p}_v^0$ as a function of $\lambda$, $n$, and $p_s$:

$$\underline{p}_v^{\tilde{\lambda}} - \underline{p}_v^0 = \left(\frac{n-1}{n}\right)\left(\frac{\lambda r(1 - p_s)(1 - \phi)}{nr - 1}\right) \tag{6}[14]$$

We call this the *difference indicator given total conflict*. Since by assumption $n \geq 2$ and $0 \leq p_s, \phi \leq 1$, all elements in equation (6) are positive, and the difference between $\underline{p}_v^{\tilde{\lambda}}$ and $\underline{p}_v^0$ thus increases if $\lambda$ increases. This reduces the incentives for conflict since it becomes less likely that the actual probability of victory exceeds the minimum probability of victory. It follows that countries need a higher minimum probability of victory to initiate a conflict with a country with which they trade, and more efficient trade increases the required minimum probability. The finding can also be rephrased as follows: countries that are more constrained, that is, less open to trade, are more exposed to the use of force. It follows that, contrary to popular perception, leaders who limit the openness of their country to international trade actually decrease its security.

Proposition 4.1 summarizes this basic relationship between trade and the incentive for conflict in the model:

*Proposition 4.1 Trade always reduces the incentive for conflict.*

## The Ratio Indicator Given Total Conflict

Clearly, the two minimum probabilities of winning, $\underline{p}_v^0$ and $\underline{p}_v^{\tilde{\lambda}}$, decrease if there are more countries in the international system. Since there is more to be gained by military conflict, the minimum probabilities of victory necessary for a credible threat go down. Since both functions of the minimum probability of victory are always larger then zero, their difference also has to be decreasing (Hegre, 2002). To assess the pacifying effect of an increasing number of potential trading partners, it is necessary to compare the slopes of the minimum probability of victory given trade ($\underline{p}_v^{\tilde{\lambda}}$) with the minimum probability without trade ($\underline{p}_v^0$) as functions of increasing $n$. In other words, for the pacifying effect of trade to decrease (increase) with a larger number of countries, $\underline{p}_v^{\tilde{\lambda}}$ needs to decrease faster (slower) than $\underline{p}_v^0$. A negative partial derivative of the difference indicator, $\underline{p}_v^{\tilde{\lambda}} - \underline{p}_v^0$, with respect to the number of countries does not suffice to demonstrate this point.

As a direct alternative, Hegre (2002) proposes to analyze the ratio of the two minimum probabilities of victory, $\dfrac{\underline{p}_v^{\tilde{\lambda}}}{\underline{p}_v^0}$, which takes the following form:

$$\frac{\underline{p}_v^{\tilde{\lambda}}}{\underline{p}_v^0} = 1 + \tilde{\lambda}(n-1)z , \tag{7}$$

where $z = \dfrac{r^2(1-p_s)(1-\phi)}{r(r-1)(1-p_s)(1-\phi)+c}$ .

This is the *ratio indicator given total conflict*. Note that $z$ is always positive. It is straightforward to determine the derivatives of the ratio indicator (7) with respect to $\tilde{\lambda}$ and $n$:

$$\frac{\partial\left[\dfrac{\underline{p}_v^{\tilde{\lambda}}}{\underline{p}_v^0}\right]}{\partial\tilde{\lambda}} = (n-1)z , \text{ and } \frac{\partial\left[\dfrac{\underline{p}_v^{\tilde{\lambda}}}{\underline{p}_v^0}\right]}{\partial n} = \tilde{\lambda}z .$$

The partial derivative of the ratio indicator with respect to $\lambda$ is always larger than 1, implying that increased trade efficiency always increases the minimum probability of victory required, and hence reduces the incentives for conflict. This is consistent with Proposition 4.1.

The partial derivative of the ratio indicator with respect to $n$ provides an accurate test for the effect of an increasing number of countries on the relation between trade and conflict. Since $z$ is always larger than zero, the partial derivative of the ratio indicator is positive. It follows that trade *increases* the pacifying effect of trade when the number of states increases. We state this in Proposition 4.2:

*Proposition 4.2 The effect of trade on the incentive for conflict increases with more states in the system.*

## The War-Cost Threshold Indicator Given Total Conflict

So far, we have discussed the impact of changes in trade efficiency on the minimum probability of winning a militarized conflict. It is also fruitful to gauge the effect of trade by investigating how increasing trade affects the cost-benefit

benefit calculations of war. The inequality $W \geq B^\lambda$ may be stated in terms of the per-period cost parameter $c$. We want to determine the minimum cost level $\underline{c}$ over which conflict is determined to be too costly to pay. This is equivalent to comparing the minimum probability of victory with the *actual* probability of victory. We label the third indicator the *'war-cost threshold' indicator given total conflict.*[15]

The indicator requires us to add an explicit model of the actual probability of victory ($p_v$). It is reasonable to assume that the actual probability of winning is proportional to the amount of resources controlled by the countries. A simple CSF (contest success function) models the probability of victory as proportional to the fighting effort by that country divided by the total fighting effort in the conflict. In case of a two-country conflict, the probability of conflict for country 1 thus becomes:

$$p_v = \frac{(b_1 F_1)^m}{(b_1 F_1)^m + (b_2 F_2)^m}$$

where $b_1$ and $b_2$ are measures of per-unit battle efficiency; and $m$ is a decisiveness parameter (cf. Hirshleifer, 2000: 775). For simplicity, we make a number of additional assumption allowing us to apply the CSF to our multicountry model; namely, $b_1 = b_2 = 1$, $m = 1$, and each country's fighting effort is a fixed share $f$ of the resources they control. Furthermore, we assume that the probability of stalemate is zero ($p_s = 0$) and that all countries control an equal amount of resources $r$. The actual probability of winning of a war of one country against all others then becomes:

$$p_v = \frac{fr_i}{fr_i + \sum_{j \neq i} fr_j} = \frac{r}{r + (n-1)r} = \frac{r}{nr} = \frac{1}{n}.$$

The war-cost threshold indicator is derived by solving $W \geq B^\lambda$ for $c$:

$$W \geq B^\lambda \Leftrightarrow c < -\lambda r^2 (n-1)(1-\phi) + r^2 (nr-1) + \phi r(r-1) \equiv \underline{c} \tag{8}$$

If the actual costs exceeds this threshold, war will not pay. Accordingly, the higher the threshold is, the higher are the chances that the country has an incentive to initiate a conflict. The derivative of $\underline{c}$ with respect to $\lambda$ is $-r^2 (n-1)(1-\phi)$. This derivative is always negative, such that the cost threshold over which war does not pay is always decreasing in $\lambda$. It follows that an increase in trade efficiency may transform a situation where the costs are just below the threshold values into a situation where they are above the threshold. In other words, trade can turn situations in which war is an actual possibility into situations in which countries are no longer interested in initiating a military confrontation. This is consistent with Proposition 4.1. Moreover, the $(n-1)$ term in the derivative shows that the effect of trade efficiency on the cost threshold is stronger when the number of countries in the system increases, as stated in Proposition 4.2. So far, the war-cost threshold indicator yields the same conclusions as the difference and ratio indicators: more efficient trade renders the war option less attractive, and the pacifying effect of trade becomes stronger with a larger number of countries.

Even though these findings are important, they need to be interpreted with caution because some very strict assumptions underlie the model. First of all, we assumed that all countries initially control the same amount of resources and second, that victory or defeat is absolute. Consequently, only the effect of trade on conflict matters, and not vice versa. Conflict cannot have any effect on trade, because following conflict, there is no opportunity for trade.

The dynamics of empire building by the early modern European merchant states, such as Holland and England, may serve as a useful illustration of the model outlined so far. The merchant states possessed advanced warfare technology and conquered large areas of recently discovered land. For them, the actual probability of victory was high, and there were many resources to be appropriated. Moreover, the maximization of the gains from the newly discovered resources required direct control in many cases. On the one hand, the model suggests that better trade opportunities would have made the merchant states more 'peaceful'. However, the model also shows that the possible effect of trade opportunities should not be exaggerated, because of the sheer amount of resources that were open to conquest.

## Gains from Trade and Limited Conflict

The assumptions made so far are less appropriate to analyze conflict in which countries have more limited aims. Countries may try to acquire only part of other countries' territory or to gain control of contested land outside the homeland. The nineteenth-century competition between the colonial powers illustrates the latter form of conflict. In these conflicts, defeat generally did not imply that an independent country was eliminated from the international system, but instead defeat meant loss of some resources, that is, part of that country's colonial empire. If not all resources are contested, defeated countries will also participate in future trade. However, they may be reluctant to trade with 'aggressor states'. In other words, the expectation of reduced trade after conflict also affects the likelihood of conflict. In this section, we maintain the assumption that all countries initially control the same amount of resources.

In the equations (9) and (9a) below, we modify the expected gains from conflict originally given in equation (5b), to encompass the existence of secure resources. Trade matters for the value of $V_i$ and $D_i$, if countries control resources after conflict and if they are still willing to trade. Geographic barriers or international norms of conflict can justify the assumption of secure resources. In the equations below, the parameter $\sigma$ indicates the proportion of resources that is contested. As long as $\sigma < 1$, countries are left with resources even after defeat; to be precise, with $(1 - \sigma)r$ resources. In this sense, we can say that conflict is limited. In equation (9a), we further allow for the possibility of trade following conflict. In appendix 4.2, we deduce equations (9) and (9a) step by step.

$$W_2^0 = \frac{p_v r(1 + n\sigma - \sigma)(r + nr\sigma - r\sigma - 1) + p_d r(1 - \sigma)(r - r\sigma - 1) - c}{(1 - p_s)(1 - \phi)^2} \tag{9}$$

conflict, secure resources, and no trade after conflict

$$W_2^\lambda = W_2^0 +$$
$$\frac{p_v \lambda(n-1)r^2(1 + n\sigma - \sigma)(1 - \sigma) + p_d \lambda r^2(1 - \sigma)(1 + n\sigma - \sigma) + p_d \lambda(n-2)(r - r\sigma)^2}{(1 - p_s)(1 - \phi)^2} \tag{9a}$$

conflict, secure resources, and trade after conflict

## Difference Indicators and the Pacifying Effect of Trade

It is straightforward to derive the various indicators for the effect of trade on conflict. We will consider in detail the difference indicators—measuring the effect of trade on the incentives for conflict—and the 'war-cost threshold' indicators—measuring the maximum costs at which war remains an actual option, that is, at which a country finds the *actual* probability above the *minimum* probability of victory.[16] The existence of secure resources does not affect how to proceed in the analysis of the relationship between trade and conflict. Given secure resources, $\underline{p}_{v2}^0$ now describes the minimum probability of victory making conflict credible in the absence of trade; that is, $\underline{p}_{v2}^0$ is the minimum probability of victory such that $W_2^0 \geq B^0$ (or (9) > (5)). We compare $\underline{p}_{v2}^0$ with the minimum probability of victory making conflict preferable to trade, called $\underline{p}_{v2}^\lambda$, derived from $W_2^0 \geq B^\lambda$ (or (9) > (5a)).

$$\underline{p}_{v2}^\lambda - \underline{p}_{v2}^0 = \left(\frac{n-1}{n}\right)\left(\frac{\lambda r(1 - p_s)(1 - \phi)}{\sigma(2r - 1 + n\sigma r - 2\sigma r)}\right) \tag{10}$$

Also when part of the resources are secure, trade increases the minimum probability of victory required to make conflict credible. Equation (10) provides this information in a straightforward way, because the effect of trade, that is, $\underline{p}_{v2}^\lambda - \underline{p}_{v2}^0$, increases with the value of $\lambda$ for all appropriate values of n, $\sigma$, r, $\phi$, and ps. A country that is less open to trade (with lower $\lambda$) is therefore more vulnerable to conflict.

As long as countries have not experienced conflict, security provides a reason for remaining as open to trade as possible. The more efficient international trade is, the less incentives a country has to use force. From equation (9a) follows directly that countries want to commit to not trading (i.e., using economic sanctions) following conflict. The minimum probability of victory derived from equation (9a) will be lower because the second part of the equation is positive given all appropriate parameter values. 'Ex ante', countries minimize the risk of conflict if they trade freely and, at the same time, refuse to trade with any country that initiated conflict. Unfortunately, the commitment not to trade following conflict is not credible. 'Ex post' conflict, as long as a country is left with resources, it has an incentive to trade. The outcome of conflict does not matter for the 'ex post'-incentives to trade.

A country can thus expect that the gains from conflict equal $W_2^\lambda$ (equation (9a)). The implication is that a country's minimum probability of victory is determined by the condition that $W_2^\lambda \geq B^\lambda$ (or (9a) > (5a)). To determine the effect of trade on the incentives for conflict, we compare the minimum probabilities of victory with and without trade—in this case denoted by $\underline{p}_{v3}^{\tilde{\lambda}} - \underline{p}_{v3}^0$.[17]

$$\underline{p}_{v3}^{\tilde{\lambda}} - \underline{p}_{v3}^0 = \left(\frac{n-1}{n}\right)\left(\frac{\lambda r(1-p_s)(1-\phi)}{\sigma(2r-1+nr(\sigma+\lambda-\lambda\sigma)-2r(\sigma+\lambda-\lambda\sigma))}\right) \tag{11}$$

So far we have determined difference indicators for the effect of trade given three different sets of assumptions. First, $\underline{p}_v^{\tilde{\lambda}} - \underline{p}_w^0$ (6) which measures the effect of trade assuming conflict is total. Second, $\underline{p}_{v2}^{\tilde{\lambda}} - \underline{p}_{v2}^0$ (10) measuring the effect of trade assuming limited conflict with no trade 'ex post'. Third, $\underline{p}_{v3}^{\tilde{\lambda}} - \underline{p}_{v3}^0$ (11) which gives the effect of trade under limited conflict and with trade 'ex post'. Proposition 4.3 compares the effect of trade on conflict under these three sets of assumptions:

*Proposition 4.3 The deterrent effect of trade is*
  (a) *larger under limited conflict if there is no trade 'ex post' than if there is trade 'ex post', that is, that it is possible to credibly commit to not trading with the adversary after the conflict*
  (b) *larger under limited conflict given no trade after conflict than under total conflict*
  (c) *larger under limited conflict if there is trade 'ex post' than under total conflict*

Trade after conflict thus reduces the pacifying effect of trade on conflict, but at worst it undoes the favorable effect if conflict is limited instead of total. The proof of Proposition 4.3 requires that for all appropriate parameter values

$\underline{p}_v^{\bar\lambda} - \underline{p}_v^0 \leq \underline{p}_{v3}^{\bar\lambda} - \underline{p}_{v3}^0 \leq \underline{p}_{v2}^{\bar\lambda} - \underline{p}_{v2}^0$ and is given in appendix 4.3. As discussed below, 4.3(a) and 4.3(b) also holds for the war-cost threshold indicator.

## War-Cost Threshold Indicators Given Limited Conflict

Assuming the same CSF as above, 'war-cost threshold' indicators can be derived for the situation of limited conflict. Furthermore, by setting $r = 1$, the war-cost threshold indicator analogue to (8) for the case of limited conflict and no trade 'ex post' becomes:

$$\underline{c}_2 = -\lambda r^2(n-1)(1-\phi) + \sigma^2 r^2(n-1) + \phi r(r-1). \tag{12}$$

The partial derivative of $\underline{c}_2$ with respect to $\sigma$ (the proportion of resources that are contested) is $2\sigma r^2(n-1)$. The positive partial derivative indicates that if more resources are contested, the cost threshold is higher. If we think of the *actual* costs of conflict as distributed randomly, a higher cost threshold implies that it is more likely that the actual costs are below the threshold. In other words, when a larger share of a country's resources is contested, the actual probability of victory more easily exceeds the minimum probability. War is thus more likely to be an attractive option when the stakes are higher.

The derivative of $\underline{c}_2$ with respect to $\lambda$ equals $-r^2(n-1)(1-\phi)$, which is the same as the derivative of $\underline{c}$ with respect to $\lambda$. In the absence of trade 'ex post', the existence of secure resources does not modify the effect of trade. The war-cost threshold indicator yields the same conclusions under limited conflict without trade 'ex post' as under total conflict: more efficient trade renders the war option less attractive (Proposition 4.1), and the pacifying effect of trade is stronger given a larger number of countries (Proposition 4.2).

Under the assumption of limited conflict, losing countries can still engage in production and trade following conflict. Moreover, as long as a country is left with resources, the incentives to trade 'ex post' conflict are not affected by the outcome of the conflict. It is still fairly straightforward to derive a third war-cost threshold indicator based on the minimum probabilities of victory with 'ex post' trade compared to the actual probability of victory:

$$\underline{c}_3 = -\lambda r^2(n-1)(\sigma^2 - \phi) + \sigma^2 r^2(n-1) + \phi r(r-1). \tag{13}[18]$$

The partial derivative of $\underline{c}_3$ with respect to $\sigma$ is $2\sigma r^2(n-1)(1-\lambda)$. As before, the partial derivative is positive. Consequently, if a larger share of a country's resources is contested, the cost threshold is higher and conflict is thus more likely. The partial derivative also reveals that the effects of limited conflict and trade 'ex post' interact. If states are willing to trade following conflict, the effect of the share of contested, or insecure, resources decreases.

The interaction between limited conflict and trade 'ex post' becomes even more notable, if we consider the partial derivative of $c_3$ with respect to $\lambda$: $-r^2(n-1)(\sigma^2 - \phi)$. By definition $\sigma^2 \leq 1$. A comparison of the partial derivatives of $c$, $c_2$ and $c_3$ with respect to $\lambda$ show that the pacifying effect of trade is always smaller given limited conflict with trade 'ex post' than under the two other conflict scenarios.

Furthermore, trade only makes conflict less likely if $\frac{\partial c_3}{\partial \lambda} < 0$, or $(\sigma^2 - \phi) > 0 \Leftrightarrow \sigma^2 > \phi$. Trade reduces the incentives for conflict if the square of the proportion of resources that is contested exceeds the discount factor. If a small proportion of the resources is contested and the potential aggressor is sufficiently patient, trade may actually *increase* the likelihood of conflict. Finally, the effect of trade, be it conflict increasing or reducing, is stronger the more states there are in the system.

The intuition is straightforward because the value of 'ex post' trade efficiency increases after a successful conquest. When trade is possible 'ex post', conquest increases both the value of domestic production and international trade. 'Ex post' trade may thus offset any pacifying effects of trade due to trade as an alternative means to gain from 'foreign' resources and the short-term costs of trade losses during war.[19] Since more states also means that there is more to gain from trade after conflict, a larger number of states makes it also more attractive to conquer resources that subsequently can be used in trade. Proposition 4.4 summarizes these findings.

*Proposition 4.4*

    (a) *Conflict is more likely the higher the proportion of resources that are contested*

    (b) *The effect of trade on the incentives for conflict increases with the number of countries in the system*

    (c) *If there is no trade 'ex post', the deterrent effect of trade is independent of the amount of secure resources*

    (d) *If there is trade 'ex post', the deterrent effect of trade decreases with the proportion of resources that are secure*

    (e) *If states value future gains sufficiently, and there is a sufficient share of secure resources, more efficient trade following conflict makes the option of war more attractive.*

Note that there are a couple of discrepancies between the findings of the difference indicator, summarized in Proposition 4.3, and those of the war-cost threshold indicator in Proposition 4.4. First, Proposition 4.3(b) states that the deterrent effect is larger under limited conflict given no trade 'ex post' than under total conflict, whereas 4.4(c) says that the effect of trade is independent of the extent to which the conflict is limited. Moreover, Proposition 4.3(c) states that the deterrent effect is larger under limited conflict if there is trade 'ex post' than under total conflict, and 4.4(d) postulates that if there is trade 'ex post', the deterrent effect of trade decreases with the proportion of resources that are secure, which is the very opposite.

These differences are due to the fact that, in the absence of trade, increasing the share of resources that are secure decreases the probability that the states have incentives for conflict—the minimum probability of winning increases in $\sigma$. The difference indicator measures the effect of trade on the minimum probability of victory in absolute terms, which may be larger if the minimum probability of victory is higher (cf. Hegre, 2002: 111–112). The war-cost threshold indicator, on the other hand, is more closely related to the ratio indicator, and estimates the effect of trade in relative terms. Proposition 4.4(d) captures the aspect that when the proportion of secure resources is high, the probability of conflict is low (Proposition 4.4(a)), and there is not much room for trade to make a difference. Proposition 4.3(c) does not control for this change in the baseline risk.

We set out to answer two questions. First, in what way does trade affect the incentives for conflict? Second, does it matter if we are dealing with a larger number of countries? We have found that the answer to the first question is that trade generally *reduces* the incentives for conflict. If countries have better opportunities to trade, they have less need for the use of force. The answer to the second question is that a larger number of countries strengthen the effect of trade. Better opportunities from trade can result from lower barriers to trade or from the availability of more countries as potential trade partners. The straightforward implication is that a more open international system is more peaceful.

However, if we assume that conflict is limited rather than total, these conclusions ask for an important modification. The anticipation of the resumption of 'ex post' trade may undo the pacifying effects of trade. If countries expect to be able to use the resources acquired in conflict in future trade, trade may make conflict more rather than less attractive. An important condition is that the risks of war are relatively minor; that is, only few of a country's resources should be at stake.

In light of the often insurmountable difficulties to sustain economic sanctions, it is reasonable to expect the resumption of trade. The problems surrounding the UN sanctions against Iraq come to mind here. Potential targets of conflict therefore want to commit themselves to abstaining from trade after conflict. Policies to this effect vary from legal restrictions on trading with the enemy to the imposition of economic sanctions on countries breaking norms of peaceful international coexistence, even when their actions do not affect one's national security directly. Compliance with such strategies is, however, often notably imperfect. The current sanctions imposed against Iraq provide an example of how countries may disagree about the appropriate trade strategy after conflict. The USA and the United Kingdom appear to have abandoned the idea of future trade or are gambling on a new Iraqi regime. Other countries, such as France and Russia, are clearly unwilling to commit themselves to a specific trade strategy.

Countries can also adopt military strategies which destroy the industrial potential of an enemy during conflict—thereby eliminating a country as a valuable trading partner after the conflict—alternatively, they can demand unconditional surrender. Both strategies make conflict total. During World War II, the military strategy of the Allied Forces against Germany emphasized both aspects. Such strategies are, however, also far from foolproof. As a case in point, the postwar balance of power forced a rapid rebuilding of the German—in particular West German—economy. In the next section, we consider in more detail the importance of such balance-of-power concerns for the effect of trade on conflict.

## Balance of Power, Conflict, and Intra-Alliance Trade

Any study of the relationship between trade and conflict given more than two countries has to consider explicitly alliances. Recently, several scholars have observed that allies trade more than adversaries (Gowa and Mansfield, 1993; Gowa, 1994). This suggests the need to distinguish between trade among allies and trade among adversaries. In this section, we analyze the gains from discriminatory trade. In the previous section, we demonstrated that the refusal to trade following conflict increases the deterrent effect of trade. We also argued that such a strategy is not subgame perfect. Here, we take a somewhat different approach and analyze the effect of barriers to alliance trade assuming that a commitment not to trade with a common adversary is credible.

In this case, a larger number of countries refers to a more fragmented alliance. We can observe that, historically, large conflicts did actually lead to further fragmentation of the international system. After World War I, several smaller countries replaced the Austrian Habsburg empire in Central Europe. Following World War II, independence movements dismantled the nineteenth-century colonial empires, and the end of the Cold War ushered in a new period of state building mainly at the expense of the former Soviet Union and Yugoslavia.

If we include balance-of-power considerations into the general model of trade and conflict, we are faced with a bewildering array of possible distributions of resources. The problem gets worse if the number of countries increases. But to maintain the assumption made in previous sections that all countries have the same amount of resources is clearly overly restrictive. To keep the analysis as simple as possible, we assume that allies have equal resources and face a single adversary that controls a larger amount of resources. In terms of the balance-of-power literature the adversary is a 'hegemon' or 'near-predominant', able to threaten any combination of other countries (Niou and Ordeshook, 1990; Wagner, 1993).

In terms of the model introduced previously, the international system is a set of countries, $S = \{S_1,..., S_{n-1}, S_n\}$, where $r_1 = ... = r_{n-1} < r_n$. The countries $S_1$

through $S_{n-1}$ are allies, and the adversary, $S_n$, is a single country. We need two new parameters: the parameter $r$ stands for the combined resources of the alliance, and the parameter $\rho$ indicates the resources of the adversary relative to the alliance, where $0 < \rho \leq 1$.[20] The model now allows the allies to discriminate in trade, which calls for a redefinition of the trade parameter $\lambda$. For example, if $S_1$ and $S_2$ are allies, we need to distinguish trade barriers between $S_1$ and $S_2$ from trade barriers between $\{S_1, S_2\}$ versus $S_n$, the adversary. The standardized gains from trade with the adversary $S_n$ are set to zero. The gains from alliance trade (between $S_1$ and $S_2$) are represented as $\lambda_a$, where $0 \leq \lambda_a \leq 1$. The standardization allows us to focus on the effects of just one parameter, $\lambda_a$, which gives the difference between domestic production, trade among allies, and trade between allies and the adversary.[21] Rewriting equation (2), the one-period gains from production and trade become:

$$r_i(r_i - 1) + \sum_{Sj \neq Si} \lambda_a r_i r_j + 0 r_i r_n = P_i + T_i \tag{14}$$

$$r_n(r_n - 1) + 0 r_n r_i = P_n \tag{14a}$$

where $i = 1 \ldots n - 1$ and $i \neq j$

We are now ready to determine the effect of discriminatory trade on allies' gains from production and trade versus the gains from production of the adversary.[22] The efficiency of discriminatory alliance trade determines whether allies gain or lose versus the adversary. The efficiency of alliance trade necessary to avoid losing relative to the adversary depends on the number of allies and their combined resources. The minimum efficiency of alliance trade can be expressed as:

$$\underline{\lambda}_a = \frac{(n-1)\rho^2 r - n\rho + n - 1 + \rho - r}{r(n-2)} \tag{15}$$

If the efficiency of discriminatory alliance trade falls below $\underline{\lambda}_a$, the exclusion of the adversary causes the allies to sustain a relative loss each period. In other words, the adversary gains more from production alone than the allies from production and trade. It is easy to show that a more fragmented alliance needs more efficient alliance trade. The limit of equation (15) with respect to the total resources of the alliance equals:

$$\lim_{r \to \infty}(\underline{\lambda}_a) = \frac{(n-1)\rho^2 - 1}{n - 2}$$

which is an increasing function of the number of allies. If the number of allies becomes very large, equation (15) approaches the value $\rho^2$. It follows that allies are less dependent on efficient trade if their combined strength increases relative to the adversary, that is, if $\rho$ is small.

Thus we have shown that discriminatory trade affects the distribution of gains from resources. Gains from trade allow countries to realize higher economic productivity that may underlie increased military strength. It is beyond the scope of this chapter to fully explore the implications of changes in the balance of power. However, the comparison of allies and adversary's gains is clearly relevant: If allies fail to trade efficiently, all investments in military strength derived from trade can be matched or even surpassed by the adversary. A more fragmented or relatively weaker alliance has a greater need to trade efficiently.[23]

In the previous section, we demonstrated that the deterrent effect of trade is maximized if countries trade before conflict and, at the same time, can commit to not trading following conflict. However, countries want to renege on their commitment not to trade following conflict. It is now possible to be more precise about the incentives to renege, because the commitment problems are twofold. First, countries stand to gain from resuming trade regardless. Second, discriminatory trade causes allies to lose relative to the adversary if they fail to trade efficiently. Inefficient alliance trade thus increases the commitment problems of refusing to trade with an adversary.

The security situation after World War II is closest to the logic outlined in this section, because the Western alliance clearly perceived one common enemy, namely, the Soviet Union. The alliance was relatively fragmented. The United States tried simultaneously to promote trade among its allies and to limit their trade with the Soviet Union. The model outlined above explains this strategy as based on the logic of power politics, where relative position is all-important. The efforts to impede trade with the Soviet Union made the promotion of intra-alliance trade more urgent. Moreover, the model draws attention to two factors that increased the need for efficient intra-alliance trade: the relative strength of the Soviet Union and the fragmentation of the Western alliance.[24]

## Conclusion

Possibly contrary to first appearances, the size of the international system is not constant. Until the close of the nineteenth century, parts of the world were still being incorporated into the modern world. In the twentieth century, decolonization and quest for national independence dramatically increased the number of countries. Currently, the debate on globalization draws attention to the rapidly increasing speed at which countries are integrated into the global economy. Nevertheless, most analyses of trade and conflict do not just insist on treating the number of countries as a constant, but are limited to two-country models.

This chapter has outlined an explicit multicountry model of trade and conflict. The model shows in what way decisions concerning trade affect decisions to initiate conflict. Interstate conflict is explained as the consequence of rational choices made by political leaders. Expected gains determine whether they find trade or conflict more attractive. The model makes strong assumptions about the nature of conflict; these assumptions are strictly 'realist'. Specific functions describe the gains from trade and conflict: the production and trade function and the conflict success function. The analyses explore various ways in which the *number* of countries can become a relevant variable in the relation between trade and conflict.

In summary, it is useful to relate the main findings of this model to the current interest in globalization. Expectations about the effect of globalization on interstate conflict have not yet been clearly specified. The pessimistic view is that globalization, of which trade is only a part, leads to inequality and instability. The optimistic neoliberal expectation is that globalization will reduce international conflict because political leaders will realize that the costs of conflict have become prohibitive. The latter argument is basically an extension of the traditional argument about the pacifying effect of trade: If trade reduces conflict, trade among more countries would reduce conflict even more.[25] To a large extent, our analysis confirms this argument.

We observe, however, an important exception to the generally pacifying effect of trade. If conflict is limited and states expect trade to be resumed after conflict, trade may actually make the conquest of additional resources a more attractive option. It is important that conflict does not become a low-risk adventure. If the gains from trade are also extended to 'aggressive' political regimes, globalization may well lead to an increase of conflict on the fringes of the international system.

Furthermore, the analysis has shown that any commitment to abstain from trade following conflict is problematic, because it is in a country's interest to resume trade following conflict. This commitment problem becomes even more serious if a country is part of a relatively weak and fragmented alliance. We have used a simple model to demonstrate that in such circumstances, efficient intra-alliance trade becomes more important. Consequently, if globalization leads to a further fragmentation of the international system, any commitment to exclude 'aggressors' from the gains from trade requires the other states to lower their barriers of trade toward each other as much as possible.

## Appendix 4.1 Derivation of the Expected Gains from Conflict, Equation 4

We start with some preliminary observations. It is generally easier to treat the probability distribution over victory, defeat, and stalemate as a compounded distribution. First, stalemate occurs with probability $p_s$ or a conflict is decided with probability $1 - p_s$. Next, conditional on a conflict being decided, a state is either victorious $p_v'$ or defeated $p_d'$. Observe that:

$$p_v = (1 - p_s)p_v' => p_v' = p_v / (1 - p_s), \text{ and}$$
$$p_d = (1 - p_s)p_d' => p_d' = p_d / (1 - p_s). \qquad [I]$$

Consider the following series: If at any period a conflict is decided a country obtains payoff $x$ with probability $(1 - p_s)$. Else with probability $p_s$, the game continues into the next period. The expected gain of a conflict that ends no later than time $t$ is:

$$(1 - p_s)x + p_s(1 - p_s)x + p_s^2(1 - p_s)x + \ldots + p_s^{t-1}(1 - p_s)x =$$
$$(1 - p_s)x(1 + p_s + p_s^2 + \ldots + p_s^{t-1}) =$$
$$x(1 - p_s + p_s - p_s^2 + p_s^2 - \ldots - p_s^{t-1} + p_s^{t-1} - p_s^t) = x(1 - p_s^t) \qquad [II]$$

Next, we consider that the payoff obtained at the end of conflict is a stream. If $\phi$ is the discount factor, the expected stream of payoffs up to period $t$ equals:

$$\frac{x}{1-\phi} + \frac{\phi x}{1-\phi} + \frac{\phi^2 x}{1-\phi} + \Lambda + \frac{\phi^{t-1} x}{1-\phi} =$$
$$\frac{x}{1-\phi}\left(1 + \phi + \phi^2 + \Lambda + \phi^{t-1}\right) = \frac{x}{1-\phi}\left(\frac{1-\phi^t}{1-\phi}\right) \qquad [III]$$

Wagner (2000: 473) considers a series in which there is a constant per period cost associated with conflict. The expected cost of a conflict ending at time $t$ equal:

$$(1 - p_s)c + p_s(1 - p_s)2c + p_s^2(1 - p_s)3c + \ldots + p_s^{t-1}(1 - p_s)tc =$$
$$(1 - p_s)c(1 + 2p_s + 3p_s^2 + \ldots + tp_s^{t-1}) =$$
$$c(1 - p_s + 2p_s - 2p_s^2 + 3p_s^2 - \ldots - (t-1)p_s^{t-1} + tp_s^{t-1} - tp_s^t) = \qquad [IV]$$
$$c(1 + p_s + p_s^2 + \ldots + p_s^{t-1} - tp_s^t) = c\left(\frac{1 - p_s^t}{1 - p_s} - tp_s^t\right)$$

Applying [II] through [IV] to the following stream of payoffs minus costs from conflict:

$$(1 - p_s)\left(\frac{x-c}{1-\phi}\right) + p_s(1 - p_s)\left(\frac{\phi(x-2c)}{1-\phi}\right) + \Lambda + p_s^{t-1}(1 - p_s)\left(\frac{\phi^{t-1}(x-tc)}{1-\phi}\right) =$$
$$\frac{1-\phi^t}{(1-\phi)^2}x(1 - p_s^t) - \frac{1-\phi^t}{(1-\phi)^2}c\left(\frac{1 - p_s^t}{1 - p_s} - tp_s^t\right) \equiv (X - C)_{t,\phi}$$

The total expected gains minus costs from conflict equal therefore:

$$\lim_{t \to \infty}(X - C)_{t,\phi} = \frac{x}{(1-\phi)^2} - \frac{c}{(1 - p_s)(1-\phi)^2} \qquad [V]$$

In equation [V], we can replace $x$ with the *conditional* probabilities of victory, $p_v'$, and defeat, $p_d'$, and the expected per period payoff, respectively $V_i$ and $D_i$:

$$\frac{x}{(1-\phi)^2} - \frac{c}{(1-p_s)(1-\phi)^2} \Rightarrow \frac{p_v'V_i + p_d'D_i}{(1-\phi)^2} - \frac{c}{(1-p_s)(1-\phi)^2}$$

We apply [I] to express the last equation in *unconditional* probabilities of victory, $p_v$, and defeat, $p_d$:

$$\frac{p_v'V + p_d'D}{(1-\phi)^2} - \frac{c}{(1-p_s)(1-\phi)^2} \Rightarrow \frac{p_v'V_i + p_d'D_i}{(1-p_s)(1-\phi)^2} - \frac{c}{(1-p_s)(1-\phi)^2}$$

The final equation can be simplified to equation 4:

$$\frac{p_v V_i + p_d D_i - c}{(1-p_s)(1-\phi)^2}$$

## Appendix 4.2 Derivation of Gains from Limited Conflict, Equations (9)–(9a)

In both equations, we need to demonstrate in what way the existence of secure resources alters the value of victory ($V_i$) and defeat ($D_i$) in equations (4) and (5b). By assumption, all countries initially control $r$ resources. The parameter $\sigma$ indicates the share of contested resources of any country which partakes in conflict. Thus, loss implies that a country retains control of $(1 - \sigma)r$ resources. The amount of resources a country controls after defeat depends on the number of countries that took part in the conflict. If $n$ countries are in conflict, $n - 1$ countries each lose $\sigma r$ resources, and the victorious country attains control over $(1 + n\sigma - \sigma)r$ resources.

Equation (9) assumes that there are no benefits from trade ($\lambda = 0$) after conflict. Thus only the gains from production matter. If a country is defeated, it has $(1-\sigma)r$ resources left to produce with, or $D_i = ((1-\sigma)r)((1-\sigma)r - 1) = (r - r\sigma)$ $(r - r\sigma - 1)$. If a country wins, it has $(1 + n\sigma - \sigma)r$ resources to produce with, or $V_i = ((1 + n\sigma - \sigma)r)( (1 + n\sigma - \sigma)r - 1) = (r + nr\sigma - r\sigma)(r + nr\sigma -r\sigma - 1)$. Equation (9) is found by plugging the appropriate values for $V_i$ and $D_i$ into (4), which gives:

$$W_2^0 = \frac{p_v(r + nr\sigma - r\sigma)(r + nr\sigma - r\sigma - 1) + p_d(r - r\sigma)(r - r\sigma - 1) - c}{(1-p_s)(1-\phi)^2}$$

Equation (9a) describes the expected gains if countries trade following conflict. Since the gains from trade and conflict are separable, equation (4) can also be expressed as:

$$\frac{p_v(P+T \mid victory) + p_d(P+T \mid defeat) - c}{(1-p_s)(1-\phi)^2}$$

$$= \frac{p_v(P \mid victory) + p_d(P \mid defeat) - c}{(1-p_s)(1-\phi)^2} + \frac{p_v(T \mid victory) + p_d(T \mid defeat)}{(1-p_s)(1-\phi)^2}.$$

We can thus concentrate on the gains from trade and use equation (9) to describe the gains from production. A victorious country can use the expanded resource base to trade with $n-1$ countries each having lost $\sigma r$ resources. Focusing solely on the gains from trade, the victorious country expects: $\lambda(n-1)(r + nr\sigma - r\sigma)(r - r\sigma)$, where $\lambda$ stands for the expected level of trade *following* conflict. In case of defeat, trade with the other $(n-2)$ defeated countries needs to be distinguished from trade with the single victorious country. The gains of trade with the latter are: $\lambda(r - r\sigma)(r + nr\sigma - r\sigma)$. The total gains of trade with the defeated countries equal: $\lambda(n-2)(r - r\sigma)^2$. This allows us to express the expected gains from conflict with secure resources in the presence of trade following conflict as:

$$W_2^\lambda = W_2^0 +$$

$$\frac{p_v\lambda(n-1)(r + nr\sigma - r\sigma)(r - r\sigma) + p_d\lambda(r - r\sigma)(r + nr\sigma - r\sigma) + p_d\lambda(n-2)(r - r\sigma)^2}{(1-p_s)(1-\phi)^2}$$

## Appendix 4.3 Proof of Proposition 4.3

Note that $\underline{p}_v^\lambda - \underline{p}_v^0$ is given in equation (6), $\underline{p}_{v2}^\lambda - \underline{p}_{v2}^0$ in (10), and $\underline{p}_{v3}^\lambda - \underline{p}_{v3}^0$ in (11). Proposition 4.3 holds that, for all appropriate values of $\sigma$, $\lambda$, $\phi$, $p_s$, $n$, and $r$, (6) $\leq$ (11) $\leq$ (10). Observe that these equations have several elements in common, namely, $\frac{n-1}{n}$, and their numerator $\lambda r(1 - p_s)(1 - \phi)$. Only their denominators differ. Demonstrating that equation (6) $\leq$ (11) $\leq$ (10) is equal to demonstrating that the denominator of (6) $\geq$ the denominator of (11) $\geq$ the denominator of (10).

First, we focus on the denominators of (11) and (10). The condition becomes, $\sigma(2r - 1 + nr(\sigma + \lambda - \lambda\sigma) - 2r(\sigma + \lambda - \lambda\sigma)) \geq \sigma(2r - 1 + nr\sigma - 2r\sigma)$. Again canceling out terms that are the same as well as evaluating at the smallest usable number of countries, $n = 3$, this reduces to: $\sigma + \lambda - \lambda\sigma \geq \sigma \Rightarrow \lambda(1 - \sigma) \geq 0$. Because $0 \leq \lambda, \sigma \leq 1$, this is true.

Second, we consider the denominators of (11) and (6). The condition that needs to be satisfied is: $nr - 1 \geq \sigma(2r - 1 + nr(\sigma + \lambda - \lambda\sigma) - 2r(\sigma + \lambda - \lambda\sigma))$. Observe that if $\sigma$ and $\lambda$ are equal to 1, the denominator of (11) equals $nr - 1$. To prove that the inequality holds for all parametric values, we evaluate:

$$(nr - 1) - (\sigma(2r - 1 + nr(\sigma + \lambda - \lambda\sigma) - 2r(\sigma + \lambda - \lambda\sigma))) =$$
$$(1 - \sigma)(nr(1 + \sigma - \lambda\sigma) + 2r(\lambda\sigma - \sigma) - 1)$$

Clearly the first part $(1 - \sigma)$ is always positive given appropriate values of $\sigma$. The second part is not immediately obvious. we consider three possible extreme cases:

$\sigma = 1$, $\lambda = 1$. The second part equals $nr - 1$, which is larger than zero.

$\sigma = 1$, $\lambda = 0$. This gives $2nr - 2r - 1$, which is positive given $n \geq 2$.

$\sigma = 0$. The second part again equals $nr - 1$, which is larger than zero.

Since the denominator of (6) is larger or equal to the denominator of (11), it is also larger than the denominator of (10). It follows that $(6) \leq (11) \leq (10)$.

# Notes

This article is largely based on Dorussen (1999), Hegre (2002), and Dorussen (2002).

1. The conclusion that the effect of trade becomes stronger corrects a contrasting finding in Dorussen (1999). Hegre (2002) points out the shortcomings of the so-called difference indicators and proposes to use ratio indicators instead. Dorussen (2002) admits that his original findings need to be amended, but also argues that various indicators are very sensitive to the specific assumptions made about conflict in multicountry models.

2. Countries are assumed to be either risk-neutral or risk-averse. All conditions are derived using risk-neutrality.

3. Grossman and Kim (1996), Hirshleifer (1996), and Skaperdas and Syropoulos (1996) use production functions to model the allocation of resources between an economic and military sector.

4. The parameter $\lambda$ is best seen either as determined exogenously or as the outcome of domestic politics not modeled explicitly.

5. Restrictions on trade do not enable countries to gain directly in relative terms. The model assumes that barriers to trade are always costly. Any relative gain occurs because either a country is bigger than other countries (i.e., it depends less on trade) or because a country varies in its openness to trade across other states (i.e., it distinguishes between allies and adversaries). We only allow for such strategies in the final section. We assume that trade restrictions impose the same costs on the restricting country and target.

6. In the complete information model presented here, a necessary condition for conflict is that the threat to use force is credible. However, the threat may go unopposed if a target chooses to avoid the costs of a military confrontation. Accordingly, a threat to conflict need not imply the actual use of force, namely, war. Misrepresentation of private information about the expected outcome of conflict is a possible explanation for the actual occurrence of war. The incomplete information explanation is central in deterrence models. Multicountry models with incomplete information are, however, notoriously intractable, see Fearon (1995), Powell (1996, 1997), and Wagner (1994a, 2000).

7. For examples of different CSF functions, see Dorussen (1996), Hirshleifer (1996, 2000), Skaperdas and Syropoulos (1996), Tullock (1980), Wagner (1994b), and espe-

cially Fearon (1997). If the outcome depends on the difference between the resources of combatants, the CSF generally has the logistic functional form.

8. Technically, the CSF is defined over $\{p_v, p_d, p_s\}$ such that $\partial p_v/\partial r_i > 0$, $\partial p_d/\partial r_i < 0$, $p_v = 1$ if and only if $r_j = 0$, $p_d = 1$ if and only if $r_i = 0$, and $p_s$ is maximal if $r_i = r_j$. Further restrictions to the probability distribution are reasonable. In case of any two countries (or opposing alliances), $S_i$ and $S_j$, $p_{vi} = p_{dj}$, $p_{di} = p_{vj}$, $p_{si} = p_{sj}$. These restrictions are, however, not needed for the argument presented in this chapter.

9. Higher costs, however, make it also less worthwhile to resist in case such a redistributive demand is made anyway. But the latter observation is made only rarely. Higher costs of conflict either have no effect on the occurrence of war, or make it less likely. Yet, even without war the eventual distribution of resources may differ radically (Wittman, 1979).

10. The model may understate the costs of conflict. Clearly, if conflict involves physical warfare, then the gains of victory and defeat should also reflect the expected destruction of capital and loss of lives. Such costs are more permanent and last well beyond the time of conflict. Including such reasoning would complicate the model significantly, but it would increase the deterrent effect of trade. However, in the current specification trade has already a deterrent effect. Most important for the argument presented here, a different model specification would not change the effect of the number of countries.

11. Recall that we do not assume that a country gains directly from restricting trade. The argument is therefore not based on strategic trade or optimal tariffs as relative gains arguments commonly are (see, Morrow, 1997; Powell, 1991). Instead, in accordance with most models in international economics, all barriers to trade are costly.

12. Thus the probability of victory of one country over another is exclusively a function of military technology and not of relative size. Evidently, this does not apply for a conflict between differently sized alliances. An obvious consequence of the assumption that all countries have the same amount of resources is that if the number of countries increases, the relative strength of any particular country decreases. Consequently, the actual probability of victory of one country against all others also decreases. At the same time the amount of resources to be won in case of victory over all other countries increases. In order to focus the analysis we study the effect of trade on the minimum probability of winning.

13. For an insightful discussion of the distinction between absolute (or total) and 'real' (or limited) war, see Wagner (2000: 479-481).

14. Equations (5), (9), and (10) need a simplification which only holds under the assumption that $n \geq 2$.

15. The difference between the incentive and war-cost threshold indicators is important and an illustration helps to clarify the distinction. Consider for example, Cuba and the United States with nearly complete barriers to trade ($\lambda \approx 0$). Since Cuba would appropriate a lot of resources in case of a victory over the United States and would lose only relatively few in case of defeat, its minimum probability of victory is very small. If trade becomes possible, the minimum probability of victory will be larger, but still a very small number. The effect of trade on the *incentives* for conflict is the change of these two minimum probability of victory. Clearly, a Cuban victory over the United States, especially a victory that would imply the appropriation of resources, is extremely unlikely. Arguably, the *actual* probability of victory is even smaller than the minimum probability of victory (with or without trade). From the perspective of the United States,

the minimum probability of victory—based on incentives—is probably quite large, because the United States would lose a lot in case of defeat and only appropriate relatively few resources in case of victory. Trade would not change these minimum probabilities very much either, because for the United States the potential gains from trade with Cuba are relatively small. However, most likely the *actual* probability of a U.S. victory over Cuba, although probably also quite large, is still smaller than the minimum probability of victory.

16. It is also possible to derive ratio indicators for the case of limited conflict. However, these ratio indicators have only a few of the nice analytical properties of the ratio indicator given total conflict, see Dorussen (2002).

17. The definition of $\underline{p}_{v3}^{\lambda}$ is the minimum $p_v$ such that $W_2^{\lambda} \geq B^{\lambda}$ (or (9a) > (5a)), and $\underline{p}_{v3}^{0}$ is defined as the minimum $p_v$ such that $W_2^{\lambda} \geq B^0$ (or (9a) > (5)).

18. In order to facilitate comparison, equation (13) assumes the same CSF as (12) and (8).

19. Although the models are clearly not directly comparable, it is interesting that Powell (1999, 72-3) makes a similar observation in the case of a 'guns-versus-butter' model. Moreover, this result provides an explanation of why extensive trade cannot prevent incidents as the 'cod war' disputes. The chance that these disputes between close allies escalate beyond shooting cold grenades is negligible—in effect, the proportion of resources that are contested is very, very low. Simultaneously, increasing national control over fishing resources is made very valuable precisely because of the efficient international market for fish.

20. If $\rho > 1$, the adversary controls more resources than the allies combined. In this case, the allies can only lose from restricting trade with the adversary.

21. Note the difference between the parameters $\lambda$ (given nondiscriminatory trade) and $\lambda_a$ (given trade discrimination). If trade between allied countries is less efficient than their trade with the adversary, the allies lose relative to the adversary.

22. The comparison involves one-period gains, which are payoffs instead of utilities.

23. Other studies relevant for this topic are Dorussen (2001), Papayoanou (1997), and Powell (1999).

24. Gowa (1994) presents an alternative model for how power politics may determine trade. Her model relies on an optimal tariffs or strategic trade explanation for relative gains. Alliances are a more important determinant of trade if the balance of power clearly prescribes their existence. The balance of power makes the deterrence of optimal tariffs or strategic trade more credible. In my model, there is a direct link between the balance of power and the need for efficient alliance trade.

25. The liberal literature on trade and conflict is vast. For an historically important work see Angell (1910). For more recent studies, see Bhagwati and Srinivasan (1986), Polachek (1980), and Rosecrance (1986).

# CHAPTER 5

# The Domestic Roots of Commercial Liberalism: A Sector-Specific Approach

*Gerald Schneider and Günther G. Schulze*

Proponents of the commercial variant of liberal thinking forcefully advocate that increasing levels of economic interdependence inhibit militarized conflict. Although this hypothesis receives convincing empirical support at the aggregate level (e.g., Oneal and Russett, this volume), other tests point out that the hypothesis does not hold across all dyads (Barbieri, 2003a; Beck, this volume). In this chapter, we present a domestic politics specification of the peace-through-trade hypothesis to account for these inconsistencies in commercial liberalism. We particularly introduce conditions under which governments may embark on a conflictive course of action in periods of increasing economic interdependence.

The formal argument we sketch here especially takes issue with the unitary-actor assumption that underlies most empirical studies on the nexus between economic integration and war. Quite ironically, most liberal studies on the democratic peace question this cornerstone of realist studies on war and peace and point out the necessity to disaggregate the state. The extant literature on economic interdependence, however, implicitly adopts a mercantilist perspective that has completely vanished in modern trade theory. In particular, the authors of statistical studies on commercial liberalism assume that governments act as welfare-maximizing, benevolent actors. This argument necessitates, however, that neither trade liberalization nor war redistribute income among domestic constituents significantly and that governments do not have to care about the reactions to these shifts by affected interest groups. In short, the standard version of the peace-through-trade hypothesis assumes away domestic politics and considers sectoral interests to be irrelevant in the constitution of trade preferences.

This chapter takes a different stance and introduces a political-economy variant of commercial liberalism. We particularly argue that expanding trade ties do not necessarily appease a government. Our analytical framework is based on a political-economy model fully fleshed out in Schneider and Schulze (2002). The starting point of our political-economy version of commercial liberalism is a situation in which an import-competing export sector tries to influence the bilateral tariff with which a government regulates the commercial interactions with another state. We add to this basic setting a military sector and stress—in line with the literature on diversionary foreign policy (Levy 1989b, Davies 2001)—that domestic economic motives can be a key to our understanding of war. The chapter moves, however, beyond the scapegoat arguments typically offered in this theoretical strand and shows that the military sector has a simultaneous interest in increasing aggregate income and in enhancing hostility toward another state. The likelihood that a government initiates a militarized conflict, an increase in the level of trade notwithstanding, builds on this contradictory relationship. Armed conflict in an integrated world is possible if the military sector's conflict-generated income grows more quickly than the income from trade shrinks as a consequence of the costly hostilities. A further precondition of our qualification is that government survival sufficiently hinges upon the support of the praetorian sector. Conversely, if a country is able to control the impact of the military sector or other war profiteers, the unilateral incentives to wage conflict in an interdependent world vanish.

We test the implications of this domestic politics specification of commercial liberalism at the proper monadic level of analysis in a reexamination of Rosecrance's (1986) influential claim that trading states are less likely to wage war than protectionist states. Our longitudinal event-count models show that an increased level of interdependence appeases a state, while military expenditure does not matter in the aggregate. In partial confirmation of our conditional argument, however, these findings do not hold for those states that invest above the average in the military sector. Our negative binomial regression results also indicate—in contrast to Domke (1988) and Benoit (1996)—that democracies are not less likely to be involved in militarized disputes than other states. We illustrate our basic claim that the pacifying impact of trade on conflict depends on the relative power of the military sector with case study evidence from states that pursued a strategy of economic opening and simultaneously pursued a relatively aggressive foreign policy stance.

The chapter is structured as follows: The next section presents some recent innovations in the theoretical literature and explains why a political-economy perspective is appropriate for the study on trade and conflict. Next, we present the analytical framework and deduce some hypotheses from it. The presentation of the research design leads to the bivariate and multivariate statistical analysis. The chapter concludes with some illustrative case study evidence and the outline of future avenues of research.

## The Theoretical Debate

In the current trade-conflict debate—as in the early research on the democratic peace—empirical findings rather than theoretical innovations dominate the research agenda. This onesidedness has contributed to the proliferation of sophisticated studies that explore the relevance of commercial liberalism statistically, but are built on causal mechanisms that a scholar like Kant introduced to the literature some 200 years ago. The theoretical stalemate becomes obvious when we take a closer look at the rhetoric that some contemporary researchers use to justify the peace-through-trade hypothesis. A typical publication strategy is to embellish the main hypothesis with frequent allusions to the history of ideas. To take one prominent example, Oncal and Russett (1999b: 4) forcefully reinvigorate the vision of the Königsberg philosopher:

> Liberalism, that is, sees democratic governance, economic interdependence, and international law as the means by which to supersede the security dilemma rooted in the anarchy of the international system. For states not much linked by these ties, however, the threat of violence remains. In addition, liberal states must fear those illiberal states that remain outside the Kantian confederation.

Oneal and Russett (1999b: 5) sketch two explanations for the optimistic expectation that liberal states do not wage war against each other. While a constructivist account might refer to the cross-national sentiments of shared identity, the rational-choice argument assumes that governments engage in cost-benefit calculations when they decide on peace and war:

> Fearful of the domestic political consequences of losing the benefits of trade, policymakers avoid the use of force against states with which they engage in economically important trade.

This second justification of the peace-through-trade hypothesis is in line with the traditional explanation discussed in the introduction to this volume, most notably Angell's (1910) famous prophecy that war in an age of economic interdependence is an act of collective madness.[1]

The frequent reference to the history of ideas is, however, problematic. Although the peace-through-trade hypothesis is straightforward, it does not stem from a convincing causal mechanism. Since the underlying justification of commercial liberalism narrowly focuses on the decisions made by a personalized state, the current explanation is decision-theoretic rather than strategic. In addition to the lack of sound theoretical foundations, the opportunity-cost argument typically employed in empirical studies suffers from three main shortcomings: Problems relating to *tautology, added value,* and *the choice of unit of analysis.*

## The Tautology Problem

The standard expected-utility explanation borders on the tautological because the conclusion seems to flow directly from the assumption. According to the expected-utility adage, trading dyads have a lower probability of engaging into armed conflict than nontrading dyads because their governments recognize that using force would be harmful. Polachek's classic treatise offers a nice version of this opportunity-cost argument. In his perspective, conflict 'raises the costs of trade, thereby making at least one of the countries worse off (in a welfare sense). The implicit price of being hostile is the diminution of welfare associated with potential trade losses'. He deduces from this that 'countries involved in *more* trade have on balance higher costs of conflict, and hence *ceteris paribus* are hypothesized to engage in less conflict' (Polachek, 1980: 78, italics in original).

Although belligerents probably learn ex post in most cases that waging war and thereby disrupting trade ties are costly endeavors, it remains unclear why a welfare-maximizing government should ever increase the level of hostility when it knows ex ante that doing so will be harmful. Consequently, the standard expected-utility argument cannot explain why governments make nonoptimal decisions like engaging in armed conflict or increasing the level of protection.[2] In short, if we take the classic formulation of commercial liberalism at face value, we should not see armed conflict at all once states start to trade.

An easy way out of this deterministic deadlock would be to assume that states only opt for war if they are uncertain about the nature of their adversary or if severe commitment problems hamper the conclusion of a truce (Fearon, 1995; Wagner, 2000). The standard realist model explains war along these lines as the consequence of a costly lottery. However, this escape route, which is typically chosen in other expected-utility arguments on war and peace (Bueno de Mesquita, 1981), does not change the basic peace-through-trade hypothesis. Adding uncertainty to the opportunity-cost argument simply implies that the likelihood of engaging into conflict diminishes with increasing levels of trade because economic interdependence influences the relative attractiveness of war negatively.

Persuasive explanations of the peace-through-trade conjecture have to offer a causal mechanism that motivates both trade and conflict and does not exclude one action by assumption. We believe that conflict researchers can easily avoid the triviality problem by abandoning the unitary-actor assumption and assuming instead that a diverse set of actors shapes a country's trade policy. The unitary-actor assumption no longer makes much sense, and almost all advanced political-economy models in trade theory avoid the mercantilist tradition on which the proponents of the peace-through-trade-hypothesis rely (e.g., Hillman, 1989; Plümper, 2001). The main reason for this change is that domestic interests take part in the policy-formation process. If we do not consider the various lobbies, we cannot satisfactorily explain the very phenomenon that the peace-through-trade literature looks at.

If we disaggregate the state and assume that governments depend on different economic interests, an incentive to wage war can arise. Although warfare might be socially detrimental and hurt the interests of most economic sectors, some political groups believe that they may profit from an increasing level of hostility toward another state. Obviously, the impact of the military sector varies across political regimes and is mitigated by political institutions. The influence of the trade regime on the hostility proneness cannot be expected to be uniform for all countries. It is therefore imperative that we look at the institutional setting in general and the role of the military in particular when analyzing the influence of trade on the likelihood of peace.

## The Added-value Problem

A convincing explanation of the trade-conflict nexus has to move beyond those theories on war and conflict that have been developed for other purposes. Relying on an explanatory mechanism that has proven to be useful in one context is not a commendable research strategy as long as we deal with another, distinctive problem. A typical example of thinking by analogy is the analytical sketch by Morrow (1999; see also Gartzke, Li, and Boehmer, 2001), which relies on the crisis-bargaining literature to show what the absence or presence of trade signals. Signaling games have been successfully used to explain the democratic peace (e.g., Schultz, 1998, 1999; Fearon, 1994) or, more generally, to explore the possibility of deterrence in an anarchic world (Fearon, 1995). The main problem in using the signaling-games analogy is theoretical, and not only limited to a specification problem in the regression analysis (Morrow, 1999). If the impact of trade and democratic institutions on the likelihood of armed conflict were to follow the same logic, an additional explanation would ultimately be unnecessary. In this perspective, the institutional setting of a country could then simultaneously determine the foreign economic and the security policy that its government adopts. This conclusion would, however, contradict those empirical findings showing that both variables exert an independent influence (Oneal and Russett, 1999a, c).

Gartzke, Li, and Boehmer (2001) offer a formal model that moves the conception of commercial interactions as signals beyond the purely analogical. They contend that 'leaders willing to endanger domestic prosperity distinguish themselves from the less determined ones via the rational market response' (Gartzke and Li, this volume: 132). In their view, the market indirectly serves as a signpost that informs about the true intentions of a government. Although such a strategic interpretation of the standard opportunity-cost argument moves the debate significantly forward, using signaling games in this context raises the problem that signals are not really moves by governments but rather by market players.

If we want to offer nontautological and independent explanations of the relationship between levels of trade and the possibility of armed conflict, we have to present a causal mechanism that offers additional analytical leverage over the extant theories of war and peace. One possibility is to interpret increasing trade as a good that offers both absolute and relative gains. Models built on this assumption are widespread and have initially fostered the neorealist belief that conflict between trading states is largely due to the fear of helping a potential enemy. Evaluations of this literature (Morrow, this volume) have, however, shown that this argument does not always hold and that trade is possible even between hostile nations. The first alternative to the standard expected-utility model is also not convincing because it assumes interpersonal utility comparisons and, more importantly, because it sticks to the mercantilist perspective of unitary states.

## The Unit-of-Analysis Problem

A last challenge to current scholarship on the peace-through-trade hypothesis is empirical and concerns the discrepancy between the level of analysis used in the baseline model and the statistical tests. Polachek's and other expected-utility models justify in line with classical reasoning in economics why a unilateral move toward free trade is beneficial and why it should work as a sufficient deterrent against the use of armed force. If we take this argument seriously, statistical tests should be done at the monadic level. In contrast, most empirical studies use dyads—usually undirected dyads—to uncover a negative link between levels of trade and the likelihood of conflict. Such a discrepancy between units of analysis is unfortunate in tests of hypotheses derived from formal models (Morton, 1999).

The way out of this threefold dilemma is obviously to use the correct unit of analysis in the empirical tests and to rely on a strategic rather than decision-theoretic framework. Strategic studies have already contributed significantly to the debate, most obviously showing the error in some neorealist generalizations (Schneider, Barbieri, and Gleditsch, this volume). They are, however, unable to yield an endogenous explanation of conflict as long as they stick to the unitary-actor assumption.

We believe that a political-economy approach is able to meet the threefold challenge of avoiding tautological reasoning, adding analytical leverage to the literature and sticking to the same unit of analysis throughout the examination. However, explaining armed conflict merely as a consequence of the protectionist inclinations of the import-competing industry would be misguided. If we analyze the interrelationship between trade and conflict simply by using a standard political-economy model, we cannot gain the mileage needed to solve the peace-through-trade puzzle. Our framework tries to overcome this problem by enlarging the setup public-choice theorists have introduced to explain protection.

## The Analytical Framework

This section presents a political-economy framework that helps to understand how trade and foreign policymaking interact. As we have spelled out the complete model in Schneider and Schulze (2002), we give here only the gist of the argument. The starting point of our theoretical analysis is the observation that the domestic political process that leads to a certain combination of trade regime and foreign policy is influenced by those interest groups that have a stake in the policy outcomes.

We employ a Ricardo–Viner model of international trade that assumes one factor specific to each sector (a factor that remains immobile between industries even as market conditions change), and one factor that varies across sectors. As owners of the specific factors are residual claimants, they will be affected by trade liberalization according to the trade orientation of their sectors. While capital owners in the export industry will gain from trade liberalization, their equivalents in the import-competing industries will lose (cf. Jones, 1971). The society as a whole receives gains from trade.[3] The specific-factors model that we apply has been used widely in political-economy modeling because it portrays a short-term situation of sector-specific interest. This is the relevant time horizon for governments which seek to stay in power, regardless whether they need to be reelected or need to prevent being overthrown.

The political-economy version of the specific-factors model we use follows the logic pioneered by Stigler (1971) and Peltzman (1976). They showed in their models of regulatory policymaking how governments are able to maximize the support of relevant interest groups through the manipulation of policy instruments. Building on this rich tradition, Hillman (1989) and other have demarcated the conditions under which governments embark on a protectionist course although unilateral moves toward free trade would be socially beneficial. The idea behind these models is that self-interested governments maximize their political support and not social welfare, as most unitary-actor models suggest. As a consequence, if political support offered by protectionist interests exceeds the one offered by pro-free-trade interests, trade protection will result although it is not in the interest of the society at large. The interests of the general population are expressed through the effect that policy choices have on the national income.

In accordance with the problem at hand our innovations are (i) that we add the military as an additional and politically influential sector to the economy and (ii) that we model the impact of hostility on the production process. The military sector is not productive as such; it draws resources from the productive sectors to build up its capacities; in other words, the economy is taxed at a rate $\tau$ to finance military expenditures. This taxation needs to be justified to the general public as well as to the owners of the industry-specific factors and the chief justification is the military's role to defend the country against foreign aggressors. Thus, we assume—much in line with the literature on arms races—that the threat of foreign aggression or invasion is larger, the higher the level of hostility.[4] In short, $\tau$ increases with the current level of hostility. We consider the level of hostility to be a policy instrument at the government's disposal.[5] Hostility hurts productive activities not only through a higher tax in favor of the military sector (which includes the weapons industry, etc.), but it also reduces productivity directly. This technical regress has a number of reasons, such as destruction of production facilities by the enemy, reduced availability of (imported) inputs, and longer and more costly supply routes. These two effects explain the policy stance of the owners of the specific factors and the general public—they oppose hostilities because foreign-policy aggressiveness reduces the national product and also their share in it as the military receives a larger portion. In short, business flourishes best in peaceful times.

The military sector seeks to maximize the resources it has control over, an assumption which is in accordance with the theory of bureaucracy pioneered by Niskanen (1971) and corroborated by the ubiquitous complaints of the military of being understaffed, underequipped, and underpaid. As Richardson showed already in 1919 in his unpublished study *The Mathematical Psychology of War*, this rhetoric increases funding at least sometimes. As a consequence the military sector favors hostilities to a certain point, as they increase the military's *share* of the national product. At the same time, hostilities reduce the national product on which the military can draw at increasing rates so that the positive tax-rate effect described earlier is countervailed by a negative tax-base effect. Unlimited escalation is not in the interest of the military it kills the cow it seeks to milk. The described rationale also explains the military's stance toward trade policy. As trade liberalization increases the national product through gains from trade, it increases ceteris paribus the pool of resources of which the military gets a certain cut.[6] Table 5.1 summarizes the preferences of the relevant interest groups with respect to the two policy instruments at hand.

We model the political process in a very general and flexible form that is able to portray different political systems. The government seeks to maximize political support it can receive from the relevant domestic actors by setting the politically optimal policy mix. It acts as a purely opportunistic player as its primary goal is to stay in power and enjoy the benefits thereof.[7] Interest groups reward the government for policies in their interest by offering political support in various forms (money, lucrative posts for politicians after retirement, rallies, military might, votes, information, campaign contributions, bribes, etc.). We assume similar to standard assumptions in utility theory that the marginal political support of an interest group is positive. Conversely, marginal opposition is an increasing function of the deviation from the interest group's ideal policy. Under these circumstances, the government will set a policy mix that balances marginal political support and marginal political opposition from the relevant interest groups.

**Table 5.1. Preferences of Domestic Interest Groups**

| Group | Level of tariff | Hostility level |
|---|---|---|
| Export sector | - | - |
| Import-competing sector | + | - |
| Military sector | - | + |
| General public/national income | - | - |

*Note:* A positive (negative) sign implies that an actor benefits (suffers) from an increasing tariff or hostility level.

Our model thus allows us to deduce ex-ante motivations for war. If the government chooses a more aggressive foreign-policy stance, it garners support from the military but will evoke opposition from both the export- and import-competing sectors as they suffer from the growing friction. We do not consider the reactions by another state to increasing levels of tariffs and hostility and assume that the policy choices by a government are simply a function of the relative weight of contending domestic interest groups. Our theory is, in short, purely monadic.

The quite realistic preference assumptions depicted in table 5.1 allow us to derive several hypotheses that qualify the liberal hypotheses on the relationship between trade and conflict. The first insight is that a government *may* under certain circumstances possess unilateral incentives to wage war in times of growing interdependence.[8] The mechanism that leads to this counter-intuitive result is based on the tax effect of increasing economic integration. If a government decides to embark on a course of foreign economic liberalization, it increases the tax base and thus also the income of the military sector. Cutting tariffs simultaneously profits the export sector at the expense of the import-competing sector. The export sector will thus tolerate an increasing level of hostility as long as the income lost through the aggressive course of interactions does not exceed the gains it can concurrently reap from economic integration. The same may be true for the public at large as the net-of-tax national product may increase in the course of trade liberalization by more than the military will additionally gain through a higher tax rate, that is, the tax-base effect exceeds the tax-rate effect. The export sector, the public at large, and the military will support the government as long as they can expect a net gain from trade and foreign policymaking.

The import sector, however, will never support a government that simultaneously opts for economic openness *and* an aggressive foreign policy. These contrasting reactions mean for the government that it can pursue such a policy mix up to the point where the countervailing influence of the two instruments on its popularity starts to hurt. Strictly speaking, it is not necessary for a policy of trade liberalization cum increased hostility to be optimal so that all three groups (military, export sector, general public) favor this policy mix. All that is required is that the total marginal support exceeds the marginal opposition from all groups opposing this policy move. The *relative* domestic strength of the military (at the margin) condition whether the incentive to become more aggressive in times of expanding trade ties is positive or negative. Figure 5.1 summarizes these insights and shows how our reformulation of commercial liberalism differs from the traditional version of this important hypothesis. We distinguish between two conditional impacts of trade on war and the original, unconditional one.

If the military sector is not relevant as a political power, it easily follows from our preference assumptions that governments do not possess a unilateral incentive to increase the level of hostility in the event of growing economic interdependence. This is in line with the classic statement of Polachek and other proponents of the opportunity costs argument developed to bolster commercial liberalism. It is a special case of our model setup, which is more general than previous works. In figure 5.1, the line dubbed 'unconditional impact', stands for this simple case.

If the military plays a significant role domestically, a country's level of hostility in interactions with other states will generally be larger than in a country with a strong civil society. However, our argument that the interaction between the domestic power of the military and economic interdependence can increase the level of conflict up to a certain point does not pertain to all states. The two lines—depicted as Conditional impact I and Conditional impact II—show two possible cases. In the first case the military is able to influence the political support calculations of the government to some extent, but never so much that the

**Figure 5.1. Commercial Liberalism: Conditional and Unconditional Impact on Conflict**

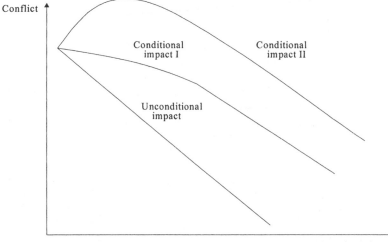

hostility level in the case of growing interdependence exceeds the one observable under autarchy. We experience the second conditional case only if the government's net gain in political support from increased interdependence is lower at some point than the one from hostility.

Another implication of the model is that we should expect an alliance between the military and the export sector at the expense of the import-competing industry in times of moderate hostility and expanding trade ties. Obviously it is not an alliance in the traditional sense, that both groups have common interests. The export sector would certainly prefer a zero-hostility level, but if the hostility-trade policy mix was suitably packaged both groups could agree to the package as a whole.[9] This observation somehow runs against the main tenet in the diversionary theory of war (for a summary see Levy, 1989b). This important theoretical strand expects the likelihood of an international conflict to grow during economic turmoil or other forms of domestic crisis. We contend, however, that this conventional conjecture is at odds with the insights we can gain from a factor-specific model of trade policymaking. We believe from our interest-based perspective that an increasing hostility level should be more common in periods of foreign economic liberalization, which, according to most econometric tests, is positively associated with growth (e.g., Plümper, 2001).

A third and final implication that we would like to address is the influence of the general public that we can derive from our model. Our model implies that the more democratic a government, that is, the more weight the general public has in the political optimization calculus, the more important will be the national income net of taxes for military. Because trade and peace contribute to economic growth, we should expect democratic countries to trade more and to engage less in hostilities. There is some evidence that democracies trade more (e.g., Russett and Bliss, 1998), although this result has recently been challenged (Penubarti and Ward, 2000). More importantly, our model suggests that the level of hostility will decrease as a consequence of increasing democracy. Our analytical framework thus adds to the existing monadic versions of the democratic peace (Schultz, 2001).

To sum up, our domestic-politics variant of commercial liberalism demonstrates that unconditional opportunity-cost arguments that link increased levels of trade to a decreased level of hostility are incomplete at best. Our sector-specific argument does not reject the optimistic conjecture of enlightenment philosophers like Kant and their contemporary adherents. However, it qualifies their optimism in important ways and shows that the peacefulness of trading states crucially hinges on the importance opportunistic governments have to attribute to their military sector.

Because we believe that the influence of trade is contingent upon a set of domestic preconditions, we will test the conditional version of commercial liberalism in a multivariate setting. Before we move to the quantitative and qualitative assessment we will present the research design for these empirical tests.

## The Foreign Policy Course of Protectionist and Liberal States

The nontrivial theoretical result that the relative political strength of the military crucially affects the pacifying effect of growing interdependence begs the question of whether or not it is of any empirical relevance. This section offers some empirical evidence and shows that some of the regimes that have opened their economies during the last decades have been involved in militarized disputes and war. In line with our basic hypotheses but in contrast to most extant tests, we examine the basic peace-through-trade hypothesis in a monadic setting.

Previous tests that rely on the state or the state year as units of analysis have been inconclusive. Domke (1988) reports a significant impact while the multivariate event-count regressions by Benoit (1996) lead to nonsignificant results for the impact of economic interdependence on the war involvement of around 100 nation states between 1960 and 1980.[10] The results reported in Barbieri (2003a) are equally mixed. These mixed results alone cast serious doubts on the empirical validity of the *simple* peace-through-trade hypothesis.

We will test the hypothesis that the impact of the trade orientation of a country depends on the relative importance of the military sector in a multivariate analysis covering the time period from 1961 to 1992. We will use longitudinal event-count models to estimate the incidence of militarized disputes and wars in a nation state in a given year. Our unit of analysis is the country-year, in contrast to most extant studies in the field. This is appropriate given our claim that most theoretical justifications of the peace-through-trade hypothesis are monadic by nature. Because we want to control for overdispersion, we choose a cautious empirical strategy and employ negative-binomial random models (Cameron and Trivedi, 1998: 275–300).[11] We have opted for a random-effect model because in the fixed-effect models we lose countries that did not experience MIDs or wars in the time period under consideration. However, random-effect models require individual specific unobservables to be uncorrelated with individual specific observables.[12]

## Operationalization of Variables

We use two indicators to measure a country's orientation in foreign economic policy. The first one is the dummy variable developed by Sachs and Warner (1995) that distinguish between open and closed economies. Although it suffers from some severe drawbacks (Harrison, 1996), this variable reflects the political choices better than the second indicator, the sum of exports and imports as a ratio of the GNP.[13] This latter variable, strongly criticized by Leamer (1988), was for instance employed by Benoit (1996) and also customarily appears in the most recent dyadic examinations of the peace-through-trade hypothesis (e.g., Oneal and Russett, 1999b, c, this volume). Data from the Penn World Tables were used for the latter openness indicator. The Sachs and Warner measure is 0 (closed) if a country fulfills at least one of five conditions. The first requirement is the application of nontariff barriers to trade on more than 40 percent of imported goods, and a second criterion is an average tariff exceeding 40 percent. Third, a country also qualifies as closed if the black market exchange rate is more than 20 percent below the official rate. A fourth indication is the existence of a state monopoly for the most important export goods. The fifth and final benchmark is whether or not the economic system of a country is socialist. Sachs and Warner (1995: 22) classify a state as open if it meets none of the above conditions. We will use the Sachs and Warner criteria for classification purposes only while the Trade/GDP ratio will be employed in the statistical tests as an explanatory variable.

We measure the influence of the military as defense expenditure in million U.S. dollars (current value) divided by the GNP. We use information from various data sets that were collected by the United States Arms Control and Disarmament Agency (US ACDA, 1992). Conflict involvement is measured by the number of war and MID onsets a country experienced in a given year. We obtained the data through the Correlates of War project (Jones, Bremer, and Singer, 1996). Our controls include a dummy variable measuring whether or not a country enjoys a major power status. We coded all permanent members of the UN Security Council as 1, other states as 0. We used the Polity III data set to establish how democratic a country was in a given year by subtracting the autocracy from the democracy score. A further variable that we used is country size that we measure with the population variable obtainable from the Penn World Tables. The gross domestic product per capita which we gathered from the same source serves as our wealth indicator.

We start the analysis with some bivariate evidence. Table 5.2 reports how often protectionist and liberal states have made part of interstate militarized disputes in the time period under consideration. We use the Sachs and Warner (1995) and U.S. ACDA datasets to classify the Correlates of War (COW) nation states along these and some related dimensions. A country was overspending (underspending) in a given year if its military expenditures belonged to the top (bottom) quartile on this crucial category.

The evidence reported in table 5.2 suggests that both military spending and the foreign economic policy of a country seem to make a difference. Interestingly, overspenders seem to have a much higher likelihood to experience both war or militarized disputes than underspenders, which never initiated a war in the time period under consideration. Contrary to conventional wisdom, free-trade states were more belligerent than protectionist states, but the difference is not as clear as for high spenders. Our argument that the pacifying nature of

**Table 5.2. Average Number of Dispute and War Onsets in Various Categories of States, 1961–92 (Nation-years)**

|  | Average number of new MIDs (Standard deviation) | | | Average number of new wars (Standard deviation) | | |
|---|---|---|---|---|---|---|
|  | Initiator | Target | Aggregate | Initiator | Target | Aggregate |
| Free trader (n=1,052) | 0.205 (0.558) | 0.229 (0.592) | 0.434 (1.140) | 0.010 (0.097) | 0.024 (0.152) | 0.033 (0.179) |
| Protectionist (n=2,192) | 0.286 (1.016) | 0.302 (1.059) | 0.589 (2.072) | 0.013 (0.114) | 0.016 (0.124) | 0.029 (0.167) |
| Overspender (n=806) | 0.460 (1.504) | 0.491 (1.575) | 0.952 (3.075) | 0.029 (0.167) | 0.031 (0.173) | 0.060 (0.237) |
| Underspender (n=806) | 0.071 (0.288) | 0.084 (0.331) | 0.155 (0.610) | 0.000 | 0.014 (0.112) | 0.014 (0.112) |
| Overspending free trader (n=333) | 0.306 (0.729) | 0.330 (0.764) | 0.637 (1.486) | 0.027 (0.162) | 0.024 (0.153) | 0.051 (0.220) |
| Underspending free trader (n=115) | 0.087 (0.339) | 0.104 (0.406) | 0.191 (0.736) | 0.00 | 0.017 (0.131) | 0.017 (0.131) |
| Overspending protectionist (n=319) | 0.805 (2.218) | 0.856 (2.321) | 1.661 (4.535) | 0.044 (0.205) | 0.050 (0.219) | 0.094 (0.292) |
| Underspending protectionist (n=596) | 0.070 (0.287) | 0.086 (0.330) | 0.156 (0.606) | 0.00 | 0.015 (0.122) | 0.015 (0.122) |
| All states (n=4,297) | 0.235 (0.805) | 0.260 (0.850) | 0.495 (1.647) | 0.010 (0.097) | 0.026 (0.159) | 0.035 (0.187) |

interdependence depends on the size of the military sector finds, however, its best expression in the standard deviations. Hence, the variance in the behavior of overspending free-traders and of overspending protectionists is considerably larger than the variance in the corresponding categories for underspending states.

We should not exaggerate the significance of such findings because we do not control for realist variables such as former dispute involvement or the power status of a country. But we can show with two examples that government choices can differ to a considerable extent across increasingly interdependent states. A telling example for a militaristic country which embarked on a course of foreign economic liberalization is Chile under General Pinochet: After successfully mounting a coup against the democratically elected government of Salvador Allende, the capitalist autocrat radically replaced the traditional import-substitution regime with a rather radical free-market orientation. According

**Table 5.3. Longitudinal Random-Effect Negative-Binomial Analysis of the Number of War Onsets by Nation, 1961–91**

|  | (1) | (2) | (3) | (4) | (5) |
|---|---|---|---|---|---|
| War t-1 | -0.42 | -0. 31 | -0.31 | -0.18 | -18.68 |
|  | (0.33) | (0.331) | (0.33) | (0. 62) | (411,956.1) |
| MilExp/GDP |  | 15,237.18** | 14,761.62** | 25,808.49** | -1,263,487.0 |
|  |  | (6,084.43) | (6,188.12) | (12,139.49) | (3,164,687) |
| Trade/GDP | -0.02* | -0.03*** | -0.03*** | -0.03*** | .01 |
|  | (0.010) | (0.008) | (0.009) | (0.010) | (0.08) |
| MilExp*Trade/GDP |  | -166.65** | -161.44** | -19,504.41 | 1,420,036.0 |
|  |  | (67.18) | (68.21) | (11,947.2) | (2,688,842) |
| Democracy |  |  | -0.010* |  |  |
|  |  |  | (0.006) |  |  |
| GDP per capita |  |  | 2.75e-06 |  |  |
|  |  |  | (0.00005) |  |  |
| Population |  |  | -1.51e-06 |  |  |
|  |  |  | (1.78e-06) |  |  |
| Council |  |  | 0.96 |  |  |
|  |  |  | (1.25) |  |  |
| Constant | 14.71 | 15.47 | 16.10*** | 16.20 | 12.93 |
|  | (457.41) | (388.31) | (0.620) | (435.43) | (391.25) |
| N | 3,424 | 3,219 | 3,219 | 651 | 711 |
| Log likelihood | -345.43 | -330.36 | -328.84 | -131.58 | -32.60 |
| Wald (d.f.) | 5.46* | 24.84(4)*** | 27.33(7)*** | 18.45(4)*** | 0.68 |
| Likelihood ratio test | 148.45*** | 127.90*** | 114.90*** | 41.79*** | 41.51*** |

*Note:* Entries are unstandardized parameter estimates and standard errors.
*p< 0.10, **p<0.05, ***p<0.01.

to Sachs and Warner (1995), the move toward economic openness happened in 1976. In the five years before this transition the Latin American country experienced no MIDs, as opposed to eight in the five following years.[14] Pinochet strengthened the role of the military systematically during this period. Scheetz (1992: 180) notes that defense outlay was more volatile than police expenditure in the period from 1969 to 1987, but that it grew faster than any other expenditure category, most notably social spending. A symbolic expression of this change of priorities was that Pinochet simultaneously acted as president and commander in chief of the armed forces. Chile is thus a prime example of a free trader engaging in military conflict and simultaneously experiencing an increasing power of the praetorian sector.

The evidence from the second case study is not as conclusive, indicating that the choices of opportunistic governments can indeed differ considerably in times of increasing interdependence. Indonesia already moved toward a capitalist orientation in 1971 according to Sachs and Warner and experienced two MIDs in each of the five-year periods before and after this transition. If we enlarge the time span to ten years, covering obviously the turmoil in the aftermath of the independence struggle, we capture eight additional MIDs for the protectionist period of the country.[15]

Our multivariate analysis will show whether we can account for such differences between countries in a systematic fashion. As mentioned before, we test our main hypotheses by estimating how many conflict onsets occurred in a country-year for both war and MID onsets. We focus on the aggregate number of MIDs and wars; tables reporting the incidence of war and MIDs initiations are available upon request. Table 5.3 includes the estimation results for five different tests that we conducted for the aggregate war onsets while table 5.4 reports the equivalent for MIDs. Model 1 takes the Trade/GDP ratio to measure the impact of economic interdependence on war, while model 2 adds military spending to this equation. Once again, we are not fully convinced of this indicator of economic openness, but we believe that its alternative—the dummy variable that Sachs and Warner advocate—suffers from a lack of variance. Model 2 also introduces an interaction term between the Trade/GDP ratio and the military spending variable. We also use the interaction term together with the controls and the Trade/GDP measure in the full model 3. Models 5 offers tests of the main hypotheses for the subsample of those state years in which government allocated below-the average resources to the military sector. Model 4 is based on the counterpart subsample of overspenders.

The results reported in tables 5.3 and 5.4 suggest that the peace-through-trade hypothesis receives support in the aggregate, after we have controlled for other important influences, notably the role of the military sector. The estimations we run for models 1 to 3 show first that higher military expenditure per capita is associated with a higher incidence of war while the trade ratio has the opposite effect. The pacifying impact of economic interdependence becomes stronger once we control for the impact of the military. We believe that this is strong evidence in favor of our hypothesis that the domestic power distribution crucially influences the foreign-trade and foreign-policy decisions of opportunistic governments. Model 5 also suggests that the peace-through-trade hypothesis is not necessarily supported for the subsample of the states that spend a disproportional sum on the military sector. This evidence, however, is contradicted to some extent by the effect of the interaction variable. The significantly negative coefficient for this indicator lends some support to the conviction that open economies are less frequently involved in wars especially if the military spending is growing. Yet, it could also be the case that interdependent states have more spending possibilities and invest more heavily into the military. Since the model involving the underspending variable is not very revealing, we cannot make further inferences on the conditionality conjecture at this point.

**Table 5.4. Longitudinal Random-Effect Negative-Binomial Analysis of the Number of MID Onsets by Nation, 1961–91**

|  | (1) | (2) | (3) | (4) | (5) |
|---|---|---|---|---|---|
| MID t-1 | 0.08*** | 0.03*** | 0.04*** | 0.02* | 0.15 |
|  | (0.02) | (0.01) | (0.01) | (0.01) | (0.11) |
| MilExp/GDP | -.022** | 14,340.12*** | 10,998.26*** | -9.39 | 16546.12 |
|  | (0.004) | (3,027.84) | (3,452.42) | (147.45) | (175,698.6) |
| Trade/GDP |  | -0.02*** | -0.02*** | -0.02*** | -0.04*** |
|  |  | (0.003) | (0.002) | (0.004) | (0.01) |
| MilExp*Trade/GDP |  | -157.67*** | -120.97*** |  |  |
|  |  | (33.38) | (38.03) |  |  |
| Democracy |  |  | -0.003 |  |  |
|  |  |  | (0.003) |  |  |
| GDP per capita |  |  | 0.00003 |  |  |
|  |  |  | (0.00002) |  |  |
| Population |  |  | -7.67e-07* |  |  |
|  |  |  | (4.10e-07) |  |  |
| Council |  |  | 0.13 |  |  |
|  |  |  | (0.33) |  |  |
| Constant | -0.30** | -0.43*** | -0.64*** | 0.38* | 0.87 |
|  | (0.13) | (0.16) | (0.18) | (0.23) | (0.83) |
| N | 3424 | 3219 | 3219 | 805 | 806 |
| Log likelihood | -2,690.50 | -2,191.75 | -2,187.30 | -758.64 | -253.73 |
| Wald (d.f.) | 56.50(2)*** | 109.49(4)*** | 117.36(8)*** | 42.93(3)*** | 22.26(3)*** |
| Likelihood ratio test | 383.23*** | 298.17*** | 268.92*** | 106.93*** | 48.74*** |

*Note*: Entries are unstandardized parameter estimates and standard errors.
*p< 0.10, **p<0.05, ***p<0.01.

Table 5.3, however, provides only very limited support for the monadic version of the democratic-peace hypothesis, namely, the notion that democracies are inherently more peaceful than autocracies. It is, however, the only control variable that proves to be influential in the multivariate test. Table 5.4 reports, by and large, similar results. The longitudinal analysis of the yearly number of MIDs in a country shows furthermore that democracy no longer pacifies the nation-states under examination.

The event-count models for the number of MIDs show particularly clearly that military expenditure restrains the pacifying impact of trade on state behavior. This becomes clear if we compare the incidence rate ratio of the Trade/GDP ratios for both overspending and underspending countries. This measure allows one to estimate how the incidence of MIDs per year change as a consequence of a unit change in the interdependence variable. While the IRR amounted to 0.98 for overspenders, it was 0.88 for the underspenders. The spending variables reported for models 4 and 5 also differ in their sign. If we accept this qualification of the peace-through-trade hypothesis, we can conclude that the initial expectation of Kant and his current adherents is certainly right that free-trading states are inclined to move toward a more cautious approach in their interactions with other states. Yet, our tests of the political-economy hypothesis suggest that we should be equally careful in how we interpret multivariate models of commercial liberalism. There is ample evidence, illustrative as well as systematical, that the pacifying impact of trade depends on the role military interests are allowed to play in the domestic arena.

## Conclusion

This chapter has taken issue with one of the analytical cornerstones in the growing literature on the nexus between interdependence and conflict. The political-economy model we have outlined establishes domestic foundations of what is often referred to as commercial liberalism (Nye, 1988). We argue, based on Schneider and Schulze (2002) that not all trading states possess unilateral incentives to refrain from using force.

We challenge the mercantilist line of argument that most empirical contributions to this debate have implicitly adopted until now. They argue that governments more or less automatically shy away from relying on military force if the threat of commercial losses looms more and more in their calculations. Introducing domestic politics especially helps us to uncover an important and nontrivial missing link in the opportunity-cost argument underlying this popular hypothesis. Our argument is based on the expectation that intensifying commercial links strengthens the military sector. If the government depends on the support of the 'military-industrial complex', it can optimize its political support through the effective manipulation of the level of hostility even in a situation of growing trade. An increased level of hostility allows the military sector to control a larger share of the national product. This increases its support of the government at the expense of reduced support by the productive import-competing and export sectors, which are put at the receiving end. An optimizing government will set the hostility level such that the marginal gain of political support from the praetorian sector is equal to the marginal loss of political support from the productive sectors. Increased openness enhances the national product through gains from trade and thereby the tax base for the military sector. This increases the military's interest in further raising the hostility level, and thus the rate at which the economy is taxed, and will also be in the government's interest if the military wields enough power in the political process. In such a situation the export sector is compensated for the detrimental effects of higher hostility through larger gross sales as a consequence of liberalized trade regime while the import-competing sector suffers from both policies.

This result shows that the motivation as to why we should expect states to refrain from using force in an interdependent world depends very much on the underlying conceptualization of the decisions governments make in the realm of trade policy. The opportunity-cost interpretation critically hinges upon the assumption that a government can be modeled as a benevolent dictator who maximizes overall welfare. If we abandon this assumption and treat a government as an opportunistic actor conflict becomes a viable option. The general precondition for this result is the existence of a praetorian sector that is interested in increasing levels of hostility because its power within a state crucially depends on the income generated in a conflict. To include the military as an independent sector is especially relevant for the countries in which the military is not subjugated to democratic control and in which many political leaders are recruited from the top echelon of the armed forces.

The empirical tests suggest that the role of the military sector does matter. Admittedly, data on the strength of the military sector suffer from many gaps, especially in military regimes. Our quantitative and qualitative tests nevertheless suggest that overspending on security to some extent dampens the pacifying impact of trade.

Future political-economy work should incorporate the reactions of another state to increasing levels of hostility and protection. Only such work will give the frequent dyadic tests the much-needed analytical foundations. Although our model treats some important political variables in an exogenous manner and although other trade models, such as, for instance, the corruption approach pioneered by Grossman and Helpman (1994), could be used, we believe that such possible extensions will not necessarily undermine our domestic politics qualification of the monadic peace-though-trade hypothesis.

Whatever the possible extensions or improvements may be, our analysis already shows that the simple peace-through-trade hypothesis is inadequate as it lacks a sound analytical foundation: it neglects the domestic political process that leads governments to engage in both trade liberalization and military conflicts. In particular, it seems an unjustified oversimplification to disregard the role that the military plays in the political process when analyzing the very justification for its existence, a possible war. When we incorporate these ideas in the theoretical and the empirical analyses we can demonstrate not only the consistency and empirical relevance of our arguments; in the end our critique and qualifications will put the peace-through-trade hypothesis on a much more solid theoretical *and* empirical foundation than it currently enjoys.

## Notes

Previous versions of this chapter have been presented at the ECPR Joint Sessions of Workshops, Copenhagen, 15–19 April 2000, the 'Identifying Wars' workshop at the University of Uppsala, 8-9 June 2001, at the Annual Meeting of the American Political Science Association, 2001, San Francisco, CA, 30 August–2 September, and at the Universities of Essex and Konstanz. We would like to thank participants for their comments. Travel assistance from the European Union and the European Consortium for Political

Research is gratefully acknowledged. This chapter builds on Schneider and Schulze (2002), which offers a full exposition of the formal model sketched here.

1. Russett and Oneal's (2001) book-length study on the triple impact of democracy, interdependence, and international organization on state behavior offers a fuller justification of the visions Immanuel Kant developed during the reign of Napoleon. The theoretical argument offered in *Triangulating Peace* does, however, not move beyond the decision-theoretic framework that the Königsberg philosopher and some of his contemporaries introduced two centuries ago.

2. To be sure, there are (rare) occasions in which countries can expect to win the military conflict without incurring great losses, so that the net gain can be expected to be significantly positive. Most conflicts, however, do not fall in this category.

3. The change in the real wage rate is less obvious, a result also known as the neoclassical ambiguity. Yet, if we assume that workers have a consumption pattern similar to the society as a whole, we can expect workers to profit from liberal trade policies, cf. Ruffin and Jones (1977).

4. This reasoning follows the same logic as the peace dividend realized after the end of the Cold War and is in accordance with the observation that in many developing countries the military pursues an active role in engaging in military disputes to increase its grip on the society.

5. This concept is relatively close to the continuous variable introduced in Polachek (1980).

6. We assume that the government can tax the economy effectively and that external liberalization will not open further significant channels for tax evasion; hence, liberalization will lead to a positive tax-base effect. For an analysis of tax avoidance through external transactions and an extensive literature review see Schulze (2000), part II.

7. This is why the government does not appear in table 5.1 as a player with a specific policy preference. It could, however, be implemented in our setup as long as political support maximization remains a goal of the government. (See Ursprung, 2000, for models that include the ideological preferences of the government.)

8. For a derivation of the conditions see Schneider and Schulze (2002). Basically the marginal political support of the military needs to exceed the marginal political opposition from the import-competing sector and possibly from the general public and the export sector. The latter two groups may not oppose the increase of hostility in the course of trade liberalization as they may be fully compensated by gains from trade.

9. It would be a second-best solution for the export sector. Its first best would be complete liberalization and zero hostility.

10. Benoit (1996) employs a purely cross-sectional design and counts the number of war involvements over the whole period.

11. This modeling choice seems appropriate because the Poisson regression results clearly indicate strong overdispersion in the data.

12. We would like to thank Wilfried Pohlmeier for a discussion on the relative merits of different longitudinal models.

13. The Sachs–Warner index is—in contrast to the Trade/GDP indicator—a direct expression of government choices in the area of foreign economic policymaking. Although it serves the purposes of this paper well, this dummy variable has several problems as for instance its dependence on a dichotomous planned/nonplanned economies subcategory (e.g., Harrison, 1996; Martin, Plümper, and Schneider, 2001). The Trade/GNP ratio is widely used in empirical analyses; this is why we use it here as well. However, it does not measure openness (how easy it is to trade), but rather actual trade. Since larger countries tend to have larger internal and smaller external trade relative to their size other things being equal, this measure is systematically biased.

14. To be fair, two MIDs were reported in 1965 as well as in 1967. No MIDs occurred in the time period under investigation after 1982.

15. That the foreign economic liberalization Sachs and Warner (1995) report for this country is not reflected in changes in the trade ratio, which more or less remained stable throughout the 1960s and 1970s.

# CHAPTER 6

# How Globalization Can Reduce International Conflict

*Erik Gartzke and Quan Li*

> I used to think that if there was reincarnation, I wanted to come back as the president or the pope. But now I want to be the bond market: you can intimidate everyone.
>
> Clinton administration political strategist James Carville (1995: 3).

The collapse of the bipolar world order in the early years of the last decade encouraged students of world politics to broaden their conceptions of the fundamental precipitants and processes of international relations. Rejecting traditional claims about imperatives imposed by international anarchy, researchers have increasingly come to regard domestic political variables as major determinants of variation in the foreign policies of states. Similarly, distinguishing the high politics of diplomats from the low politics of merchants appears hackneyed in light of the rising political salience of global markets. Efforts to divine political consequences of global economic integration are now a cottage industry. Advocates from a diverse spectrum of perspectives seem largely to agree that globalization matters, that economic integration is bound to influence state behavior.[1] Yet, there remains profound disagreement about the nature and significance of global economic change.

Our focus here is on the consequences of economic integration for world peace. We argue that globalization can reduce dispute behavior for reasons that have been largely missed in the current debate. To influence interstate conflict, changes in global economics must alter the incentives that impel states to fight. Existing arguments pose diametrically opposed claims about the effect of globalization on peace. Liberals argue integration makes war more costly and less likely whereas realists and radicals believe it can make war more frequent. Though existing claims bracket the realm of possible consequences, we argue that contrasting conventional accounts fail to speak to a coherent logic of war. States fight over distributional issues, but this is not the same as saying that wars result from the distribution of power, threat, or interests. Instead, wars and other contests can best be said to result from disagreements over the status of distributional issues. Beginning with the growing literature on the informational nature of international disputes, we argue that globalization creates an alternative to military violence as a means for states to unravel the uncertainty surrounding global political competition. In addition to better responding to a coherent theory of war, our argument emphasizes intuitive and dynamic features of the interaction of state and market.

We briefly review existing debates about globalization and peace below. We then offer an interpretation of globalization that seems to us to be more consistent both with basic insights of the theory of economic markets and with new thinking about the causes of international contests. After presenting the argument, we offer as an illustration a case study of the 2000 Taiwan Strait crisis. We then conclude with an extensive discussion of some of the theory's implications.

## Defining Our Terms

Economic globalization implies an international market of goods and factors of production, financial capital moving across national borders with relatively little friction, production networks spread over several states, and elaborate communication networks linking people around the globe.[2] We define globalization for the purposes of this chapter as the increasing integration of cross-border markets, as well as the increasing ease with which a variety of nonstate economic actors can intervene in the national economic markets of integrated states. Researchers are interested in globalization for many reasons, but of particular interest is the impact of globalization on the conflict (dispute) behavior of states. Can global integration promote world peace, if only modestly? For many, peace is not simply the absence of war. Wars and lesser military contests constitute a small portion of the frequent and widespread contentious interaction of states. Still, wars and disputes are quite reasonably the subject of the keenest normative concern, because of their harm to individuals, groups, and societies. We define 'peace' as the absence of militarized dispute behavior. While one might consider other definitions, it seems most important here to distinguish 'peace' from 'amity'. Peace may be a more reasonable objective if political actors are still expected to disagree, but to more often seek to realize their differences through nonviolent methods of competition. While differences of interest exist to a greater or lesser degree in almost all circumstances, we are most concerned here with why states appear to vary in how differences are managed, with how integration can alter the need for costly and harmful interstate warfare.

## The Literature on Economic Globalization

Globalization involves the interaction of states and markets. It is peculiar, then, that standard treatments of globalization in the security studies community ignore, or at least fail to emphasize, certain basic properties of markets. The fundamental structural change that results from economic globalization concerns the state-market relationship, rather than the state-state relationship. If integration changes politics, it does so because first and foremost the interaction of markets and states is changed by globalization. Yet, it is the interaction of political actors that captures the core of interest in standard approaches to globalization in the security studies literature. Though markets appear as entities that change the rules of interstate politics, researchers are quick to move to the analysis of new political conditions without giving much further attention to how markets and states interact. We are concerned that markets are poorly conceived in security studies of the pacific effect of globalization, and that this inattention to the interaction of states and markets leads to errant claims about the effects of market changes on interstate political interactions.

Inadequate treatment of the nexus linking states and markets can be explained away by the interests of students of international politics, who reasonably care more about their own subject than that of another discipline. Still, while researchers must typically simplify issues, items, or processes based on the proximity of these factors to topics of interest, markets are both proximate and relatively easily described when it comes to the topic of globalization and its consequences for international conflict. The problem appears to be that the significance of markets to states can take several forms and that the form most appropriate to interstate political conflict has yet to be clearly identified. Since a focus on politics is not synonymous with a focus on the political consequences of economic globalization, one needs to use relevant aspects of theory and context to ensure that the aspects of markets that are said to impinge on state behavior do indeed carry some weight.

As even our cursory review of the literature will show, profound differences in conclusions about the impact of globalization for world politics follow in large part from differing views of the relationship of states to markets, not due to differing views of the interaction of states. Paradoxically, we see this consensus about the state-state relationship as the origin of confusion in the literature. Studies fail to carefully assess the nature of the political interaction on which the state-market nexus is said to impinge. For markets to affect violent competition globally, it must be the case that features of economic exchange alter the logic of contests. On the other hand, to correctly identify politically significant implications of the state-market relationship, one must capture critical features of the state-state relationship. Globalization research comes to contrasting conclusions because researchers begin with the same flawed premise, that war is a consequence of material variables. If so, then shifts in material variables lead to shifts in the probability of war and a debate can (and does) occur about how globalization shifts the distribution of power, threat, or interests. Though our reading of the literature suggests that market consequences are more often assumed than demonstrated, consensus about how states interact provides the foundation for confusion about the political consequences of markets. If war is instead a consequence of informational, rather than material, conditions, then research on the effects of globalization on conflict has been looking in the wrong place even as the consequences of globalization for peace are less ambiguous. We extend our discussion of the informational view of state-state and state-market interactions below. First, however, we relate elements of the two main existing debates in the literature.

## Economic Globalization and the State-Market Relationship

The consequences of changes in the state-market relationship are widely debated in the globalization literature. One view claims the death of nation-states as either an economic unit or as sovereign entities (Kindleberger, 1969; Strange, 1996). Accompanying such death notices are assertions about a loss of meaning of state territoriality and the coming of a borderless world (Cohen, 1998; Mathews, 1997; Ohmae 1996; Ruggie 1993). The trend toward an increasing number of states, as well as the apparent desire of many to form new autonomous entities (French Canada, Scotland, etc.) suggests that state sovereignty and the politicization of territory have yet to be reduced to insignificant commodities.

A second view is that, far from being dead, states are simply severely constrained in the scope of their capacity and policy autonomy (Andrews, 1994; Drucker, 1997; Evans, 1997; Reinicke, 1998; Rodrik 1997). The presence of increasing capital mobility, the adoption of flexible exchange rate regimes, and the rise of global trade mean that states have lost their monetary and fiscal policy sovereignty and are left with a heavily eroded ability to provide a domestic social safety net. Authors in this category of argument seem to concede that total state eclipse is unlikely, but that globalization limits state options to repressive methods of avoiding economic collapse (Evans, 1997) or to acquiescing to global policy regimes orchestrated by supranational entities (Drucker, 1997; Reinicke, 1998).

A third view argues that states remain the single most important international actors (Kapstein, 1994; Krasner, 1999; Waltz, 1999, 2000). According to this argument, the market has played a submissive though expanding role in interstate competition. National borders continue to define the boundaries of systems of capital accumulation (Wade, 1996). States created international regulatory structures based on home-country control, within which the world economy develops (Kapstein, 1994). They still retain much room for effective macroeconomic management while limitations on the welfare state are exaggerated (Garrett, 1999).

At the center of the controversy is the status of the market relative to the state, a topic of significant debate even before Adam Smith. In each of these arguments, the state is seen as involved in a competitive relationship vis-à-vis the market. Juxtaposing state and market in this manner ignores key differences in their roles. While each incurs on the other, both have distinguishable functions that encourage cooperation as well as conflict. States require the productive efficiency of markets for their rents and for the political survival of leaders while markets need states for regulation and for addressing market failures. The magnitude of market constraint on the state continues to be debated, but the emerging consensus is that the state is relatively less autonomous than in the past and thus that there has been a transfer of power from the state to markets (Held et al., 1999). Globalization increases financial capital mobility across borders and facilitates the relocation of means of production from country to country. States, in their competition with other states, are more often forced to construct their economic policies to please global investors and transnational firms, ceding de facto state sovereignty and reducing control over trade and capital flows. It is this new structural constraint upon the state that we apply to analyze the impact of economic globalization on interstate political relations.

## Political Consequences: Realists versus Liberals

Traditional interpretations of international relations privilege analysis of sovereign states. The interaction of sovereign entities ('high politics') is said to command the leader's agenda while state-market relationships ('low politics') are merely means to high political ends (Morgenthau, 1958). This perspective continues to be voiced by prominent figures in the study of international relations. As Kenneth Waltz puts it, 'The most important events in international politics are explained by differences in the capabilities of states, not by economic forces operating across states or transcending them' (2000: 52). Globalization is simply not relevant to the conduct of high politics. Other realists are even less sanguine about the pacific consequences of economic integration. Mearsheimer (1990) argues that if globalization creates interdependence between states, it also reduces the ability of states to act as autonomous political agents. States under globalization are no longer free to pursue international politics (through balancing, etc.), and stability in world politics is threatened.[3]

Liberals praise the economic benefits of globalization, but treat the political implications of global integration with suspicion. Kant (1795/1957) argued that commercial interests are naturally inimical to the goals of warfare. Trading states avoid war because fighting is bad for business. Woodrow Wilson was so convinced of the Kantian claim that he made free international markets one of his Fourteen Points (Wilson, 1918).[4] The Great Depression and World War II battered liberal ideas, but the potency of liberalism as an intellectual force revived with peace and prosperity. While acknowledging the power of power politics under anarchy, neoliberals such as Keohane and Nye (1989) returned to the notion that markets inhibit political conflict and emphasized the decreasing divide between 'high' and 'low' politics in international relations. The benefits of economic linkages were thought to deter military violence for fear of lost economic opportunities. Statistical evidence marshaled to support the liberal notion continues to increase the research community's confidence in the correlation of trade interdependence with peace (cf. Oneal and Russett, 1997, 1999b).

Modern advocates of the liberal view are often so convinced of the value of globalization on purely economic grounds, and so concerned about political intervention in markets, that they seek to justify the pursuit of free markets independent of political consequences (Bhagwati, 1998; Krugman, 1996). Indeed, the liberal position is largely normative, rather than positive (a position akin to the U.S. drug policy that pleaded for citizens to 'just say no'). By abstaining from optimistic assertions about the behavior of political actors in the face of growing market power, liberals have effectively acquiesced to the political claims brought by critics of globalization, that the growing power of markets is a net threat to the pursuit of high politics by states. While international liberals continue to argue that integration promotes peace, interaction with realists has affected the liberal view. As Moravcsik (1997) has pointed out, domestic liberals advocate the protection of markets from the encroachment of political institutions while international liberals are willing to advocate the use of institutions to protect states from markets. The liberal position seeks to treat state-market interactions as noninteractive. States and markets do not interact to bring relative international peace. The only direct political value in markets in bringing peace is that they create wealth that in turn is said to deter recourse to political violence.

There is thus nothing inherent in the interaction of states and markets in either realism or liberalism that is thought relevant to state-state relationships. Markets affect state power and states can in turn regulate markets, but markets are not seen as responding to politics any more than politicians are thought to respond to the status of market conditions. We believe this view of globalization is incorrect, that neither realists nor liberals are capable of satisfactorily explaining the impact of economic globalization on interstate violence. The problem with current conceptions is twofold. First, most studies on the topic of globalization and peace ignore key insights about why states fight. Recent thinking about the origins of costly interstate contests has begun to emphasize that an important cause of wars is informational, rather than material conditions (Fearon, 1995; Gartzke, 1999; Morrow, 1999; Wagner 2000). Second, liberals and realists treat markets as exogenous, ignoring strategic interactions between state and market. Our argument differs from the above approaches. For the class of contests that are informational in nature, if markets are valuable to states because of capital and informative to states as aggregators of information, then globalization can change the frequency with which states fight by changing the informational conditions under which states compete. The integration of global markets provides a new venue for states to settle competition short of military violence by allowing states to credibly communicate information about relative resolve through costly but nonviolent means. We extend below our discussion of the argument that war and markets interact informationally to bring peace.

## Our Argument

To accurately gauge the effect of globalization on interstate dispute behavior, one must do two things. First, one must see the state-market relationship as interactive, not merely as a directional process whereby markets develop and threaten states. Market behavior can affect states, but states can also affect markets. It is in the interdependence of state and market that we are most likely to identify behavior that can transform, or at least moderate, global politics. Second, discussion of the impact of the state-market relationship on global conflict must involve an explicit treatment of the process generating interstate disputes. Too often, students of world politics identify modifiers of conflict behavior without mapping a causal logic underlying contests. Accounts of how globalization affects the frequency of interstate contests require a clear enunciation of what can lead states to fight. We explore these two elements below, beginning with the state-state relationship.

## The State–State Relationship: A Logic of Costly Contests

One of the readily discernable features of interstate conflict is its episodic nature. Wars begin, last for some period of time, and then end.[5] A second discernable feature of interstate contests is that they typically terminate in some settlement (tacit or overt). Finally, disputes appear costly. States may profit from war and may even derive psychic benefits from fighting or victory. However, contests, by their very nature, involve positive costs in the form of expenditures of gold, blood, and equipment. These features of warfare lead to the conclusion that disputes result primarily from informational asymmetries (plus incentives to compete).

States that disagree often settle disagreements diplomatically. Indeed, states seem to prefer to settle disagreements when and where settlements seem to offer terms comparable to those that are likely to be obtained from fighting. War is costly. Contests consume resources that are otherwise available for use in furthering other objectives. At the same time, wars almost invariably terminate in some form of settlement. The task in explaining disputes is not, as many have presumed, in identifying conditions under which states may be able and/or willing to fight. Rather, given that some settlement eventuates, a logic of disputes explains why it is that states sometimes settle ex ante and at other times require violence to identify terms.

Disputes most often occur because competitors are unable to arrive at the bargains ex ante that settle contests ex post. To see why this is so, imagine that two states ($A$ and $B$) compete over some disputed issue, territory, etc. Suppose that the states have the option of engaging in some contest at a cost $c$, in which the probability of victory is equal to $a$ for state $A$ and equals $(1 - a)$ for state $B$. If the stakes in the contest equal $x$, and if all the spoils go to the victor, then the expected value of fighting for a state is just the product of a state's odds of victory multiplied by the stakes $[ax - c; (1 - a) x - c]$. If either player (state) is allowed to make a proposal to its opponent, and if we assume that the issue space is infinitely divisible, then there always exists some offer both parties prefer to fighting. The inevitability of some settlement, as well as the positive cost of a contest, mean that obtaining an ex ante settlement is always a Pareto-improving move, if actors can identify the proper bargain.

The most general explanation for why states sometimes disagree on settlements ex ante that resolve contests ex post is that states often differ in their predictions about the consequences of a contest. In order for states to fight, at least one party must be overly optimistic about its own prospects in a dispute. Blainey (1988) argues that states irrationally misperceive, but actors can err simply by being uncertain about strategic variables (capabilities, resolve, etc.). Fearon (1995) notes that uncertainty (and incentives to compete) then constitute the necessary conditions for a rationalist theory of dispute behavior. To see why this is so, imagine that the states discussed above (*A* and *B*) on the brink of a dispute are suddenly able to see into the future and anticipate the terms that will eventually settle a given contest. If we assume that there is some positive cost to fighting, then competitors are always better off accepting the terms that eventuate from a contest prior to the contest itself. In a world of omniscient states, wars would seldom happen.[6] Obviously, states do fight. It follows that states are most often at war because they are unable to anticipate, or at least to agree upon, the settlements that eventually terminate contests prior to the onset or continuation of fighting.

Costly contests involve at least two elements. First, there is a zero-sum competition for excludable goods.[7] Conflict is a difference of interest over issues, territory, etc., that two or more states cannot possess simultaneously. Second, a contest is a negative-sum interaction that may be used as a mechanism to settle a conflict (threat, dispute, sanction, etc.). The transaction costs associated with contests deprive 'winners' of benefits and increase the burden for 'losers' so that all are better off selecting contests that minimize the cost involved in obtaining settlements. Since war is costly, fighting is only efficient if comparable agreements are unobtainable through other, cheaper methods. A theory of contests thus explains, not just why states differ in a manner that sustains a conflict of interest but why states pursue a particular (and particularly costly) method for addressing such differences. Put another way, a theory of disputes explains why ex ante settlements are unobtainable to competitors that will settle ex post.

The bargaining literature on costly contests argues that wars result from uncertainty about conditions likely to influence eventual settlements as well as the incentives states have to misrepresent private knowledge about conditions. States often possess private (asymmetric) information about strategic variables (capabilities, intent, etc.). Efficient ex ante bargains are obtainable if states can credibly share asymmetric information. Unfortunately, asymmetry gives weak or unresolved states an opportunity to conceal weakness even as competition provides weak or unresolved states with the incentives to deceive (to bluff) other competitors. A state can 'pool' with other states, claiming to be resolved or capable regardless of its true status. 'Cheap talk' claims make it difficult to distinguish resolved or capable opponents from weaker types. Only by imposing contests can states 'separate', or distinguish resolute opponents from those seeking to bluff. Thus, states fight in large part because they cannot determine bargains that each prefers to what each expects to obtain from fighting. If states can agree on the content of eventual settlements, then mutually preferred bargains typically exist ex ante. Thus, uncertainty about the allocation of spoils from the contest accounts for the contest itself.

## The State–Market Relationship: Costly Signaling through Markets

Markets are informational devices. The simplest description of a market involves exchanges between buyers and sellers and the price mechanism for market clearing. Markets embody consensus beliefs about factors affecting the value of goods and services. Since political decisions affect the value of goods and services, decision making on the part of political actors influences markets. Similarly, since market behavior increasingly affects the wealth of nations, state actions that threaten market welfare also harm states.

Costly contests occur because states in competition are sometimes thwarted from obtaining efficient ex ante settlements. States have incentives to make self-serving claims about strategic variables (to bluff) and thus competitors have difficulty identifying the true nature of eventual settlements. States must sometimes fight to demonstrate capability or resolve, something that is difficult to credibly communicate through talk alone because of states' incentives to bluff.

The interdependence of state and market makes leaders' talk costly and hence, more credible. Leaders engaged in political competition must choose between making competitive political claims and appeasing market concerns about stability and profitability. Some state leaders will prefer to pacify global markets by moderating their political demands. Other leaders will decide that the value of political issues is too great to ignore, preferring possible political gains to certain economic losses. To the degree that leaders (or states) differ in their subjective valuation of potential political benefits and economic costs, observers learn about the true value of strategic variables from the actions of leaders confronted with globalization. Signals transmitted through global markets distinguish or 'separate' resolved or capable leaders from those less capable and less resolved, the interaction of state and market serves to inform the political process. The rise of global markets offers politicians an opportunity to learn through the interaction of states and markets.

Students of globalization emphasize that economic integration causes a loss of policy autonomy for states. Markets become increasingly able to avoid or counteract attempts by states to impose regulation or restrictions. This structural change in the state-market relationship does limit the ability of states to pursue preferred policies, but only in realms directly relevant to markets. In fact, because states that are confronted by global markets are better able to signal resolve short of military violence, integrated states are also better able to pursue a wider variety of political competition. Under autarkic conditions, states are free to compete over any issue. However, the limited range of mechanisms available to states in seeking to pursue competing interests means that autarchic states must often choose between cheap talk and risking war as the only means available. Many contentious issues are just not of sufficient importance for a state to consider the recourse to military force. Economic integration provides an alternative means of political competition, one that is less costly because of the reduced risk of war. This means that some issues that autarkic states are deterred from pursuing are pursued by economically integrated states. In other words, at least according to some measures, globalization *increases* the ability of states to pursue political competition in some aspects of international interactions.

Global markets thus serve to arbitrage information about strategic variables, enhancing the ability of states to obtain ex ante settlements and reducing the need for military violence. In a world of high capital mobility, profit-driven investors respond to political risk by exiting states at risk or else by imposing higher rents on capital. Leaders who contemplate military threats must consider the economic consequences of contentious politics in a global economy. Globalization makes the otherwise cheap talk by leaders more expensive and thus more credible.

Mobile capital can anticipate and react to political shocks. The resulting economic harm damages rents from office and may even threaten leader tenure. Therefore, leaders who pursue policies harmful to investors reveal a willingness to accept economic burdens in the pursuit of political goals. Those leaders willing to endanger domestic prosperity distinguish themselves from the less determined ones via the rational market response. The strategic economic behavior of the 'invisible hand' of global markets thus informs interstate political interactions by communicating credibly about political variables and reduces the need for military violence.[8]

The globalization of markets allows market actors greater ability and autonomy in their anticipation of and response to political conditions. Because autonomous markets can convey credible information about political variables, economic integration offers states a cheaper means to pursue competing political goals. While state liberalization of restrictions over trade and capital flows is generally interpreted as a loss of state autonomy, more robust markets in turn allow states to exploit markets as efficient and effective instruments of statecraft. States integrated into the world market are actually blessed with a greater degree of freedom to act competitively in the political arena through costly economic signaling. The ominous consequences of seeking to change status quo conditions under autarky can only be interpreted as autonomy in the same way that a starving man on a desert island is 'free' to dream of food. Economic integration feeds the economic needs of states, but it also frees states to pursue a broader set of political objectives. This counterintuitive conclusion contradicts the conventional wisdom of both proponents and critics of economic globalization. Proponents of globalization emphasize economic benefits while critics assert that integration heightens political tensions. In contrast to both, we identify important positive political externalities of globalization, showing that integration can reduce the advent of militarized violence even as it enhances the ability of states to compete. We illustrate our argument with a case study of the crisis of the Taiwan Strait involving China, Taiwan, and the United States.

## A Case Study: The Taiwan Election Crises[9]

In March 2000, the People's Republic of China (PRC) and the Republic of China (ROC) seemed on the verge of converting a war of words into a military contest. A crisis over the previous election in 1995–96 had brought threatening military action in the form of Chinese missile tests. All participants in the previous crisis had learned something of the nature and intensity of the competing demands.[10] Thus, the tensions were not a total surprise. What was surprising was the intensity with which each country held to its conflicting views. China sought concessions intended to cement the future of Taiwan firmly to the mainland while Taiwanese voters contemplated converting de facto autonomy into de jure independence. Yet, the crisis quickly subsided after each side moderated incompatible demands. Why? Had the nations involved been limited in their competition to cheap words or costly war, it is possible, even likely, that China would have resorted to force. While several factors contributed to a tacit settlement, we argue that an important mechanism averting the need for military action to demonstrate resolve was the presence of valuable economic linkages.

When the Communists took power on the mainland in 1949, Nationalists under Chiang Kai-shek fled to Taiwan, where the fiction of a greater Republic of China was maintained, 90 miles off the Fujian coast. A cold war continues between the ROC and the PRC. The PRC considers Taiwan to be a renegade province and has consistently demanded reunification. For decades, Taiwan also sought reunification, though under Nationalist rule. The United States and the PRC adopted the ambiguous 'one China' principle as part of the Sino–U.S. rapprochement in 1972. Leaders in Beijing, recognizing the impracticality of invasion, could bide their time as long as ruling parties on both sides of the Taiwan Strait favored 'eventual' reunification.

Ironically, while conflicting visions of reunification helped in the past to stabilize tensions between the ROC and the PRC, a lessening of political tensions since the 1970s contributed to the crisis. Opening of the mainland to Taiwanese goods and investments in recent years had helped to build Taiwanese prosperity that in turn fostered democracy and nationalism on the island even while KMT legitimacy declined. Many Taiwanese began to contemplate a course independent of the mainland. Independence was a key objective of the main opposition Democratic People's Party (DPP), dominated by majority indigenous Taiwanese (as opposed to KMT mainland ex-patriots). Increasingly, China now perceives a need to stem the ebb tide of enthusiasm for the 'one China' principle. The March 1996 elections in which DPP candidates figured prominently were overshadowed by PRC war games and missile tests intended to intimidate Taiwanese voters.[11] The strategic situation became more complex as the United States rushed two carrier battle groups to the area. The PRC learned that it had under-estimated U.S. intentions, while citizens on Taiwan learned that the issue of the status of the island remained important to leaders in Beijing. The fact that a second crisis occurred in 2000 demonstrates that the parties involved continued to differ in their expectations about the nature of an eventual settlement. The fact that the second crisis did not involve war (only threats of military violence) suggests that the parties had a unique means of competing unavailable to most states throughout history.

During the first few months in 2000, a new crisis broke out with Taiwan scheduled to hold its second direct presidential election on 18 March. The election posed a three-way race among the pro-independence Democratic Progressive Party (DPP) candidate Chen Shui-bian, incumbent Kuomintang (KMT) candidate Vice President Lien Chan, and the independent candidate James Soong. Among the three parties, the DPP most favored independence. As a candidate, Chen Shui-bian symbolized the independence movement, having advocated Taiwan's independence from *both* the KMT and from the mainland throughout his career.

On 21 February, fearing the prospect of Chen's victory in the March election, China's State Council issued a policy white paper warning of a possible military attack if Taiwan declared independence, if outside forces 'meddled' in China's internal affairs (a not-so-veiled threat aimed at the United States), or if Taiwan persisted in dragging its feet over reunification. The first two conditions are consistent with earlier statements by the PRC, but the last condition appears to reflect China's fears that it can no longer afford to bide its time, that China may be 'losing Taiwan'. Finally, just three days before the election, Chinese premier Zhu Rongji raised tensions to a fever pitch by warning that election of a proindependence candidate could bring war.

In spite of PRC intimidation, on 18 March 2000, voters elected pro-independence candidate Chen Shui-bian as the new president of Taiwan. Obviously, an attack never materialized from the mainland. One might offer that PRC military forces remain incapable of mounting an amphibious assault on the island, but this is only a partial explanation.[12] As early as the 1996 crisis, China had prepared plans and equipment for a sustained bombardment of Taiwanese ports with conventionally equipped short-to-medium range missiles.[13] Such an attack would clearly devastate Taiwan's heavily trade-dependent economy. Roughly 70 percent of Taiwan's trade ships through two ports, Kao-hsiung and Chi-lung, both of which were targeted in war games in 1996.

Another reason for limited escalation was that each side learned about its opponent during the crisis. Before March 2000, observers could plausibly downplay Taiwanese enthusiasm for its evolving path. While Taiwanese citizens said they favored autonomy, it was not yet clear how much Chinese pressure they would resist. Issues on Taiwan had evolved since the 1996 crisis. Candidates were no longer debating autonomy but independence. Even while the pace of the independence movement seemed to increase, the real impetus behind the movement was not yet clear. Was Taiwan moving toward rapid independence or was this just a 'fad' that would soon pass? The position of Taiwanese after the 2000 crisis is much less ambiguous.

In large part, the ability of competitors on both sides of the Taiwan Strait to discern intentions short of military violence was due to the prevalence of the new global economy. Resolve was tested, and threats made credible, through currency exchanges rather than through artillery battles. The new availability of an intermediate step between boisterous talk and military violence made it possible to compete short of war. During the crisis, Taiwan's stock market suffered sharp downturns that, along with Chen Shui-bian's victory, signaled Taiwanese resolve. From experience, Taiwanese voters knew that electing Chen Shui-bian was bound to lead to a stock market crash. On 9 February 2000, the market was at a 29-month high, breaking 10,000 points. Yet on 22 February, a day after China's policy white paper, Taiwan's Stock Exchange index plummeted 617.7 points (6.6 percent) to 8,812, the largest drop in Taiwanese history (surpassing a 612.5-point dive on 7 April 1990). The market index continued its decline throughout March, with a 195.6-point drop on 16 March (the day after Zhu Rongji's warning) to 8,473. It is thus not surprising that after Chen Shui-bian won the election on 18 March (Saturday), the Taiwan stock market again fell sharply the following Monday, losing 254.7 points (2.9 percent). Knowing the economic consequences, roughly 83 percent of Taiwan's 15.5 million voters turned out to cast ballots with Chen obtaining 39.3 percent of the votes, leading second-place candidate James Soong by a 2.5 percent margin.[14] The Taiwanese voters traded stock market prosperity for the proindependence candidate, sending an informative signal about their resolve to withstand potential China military attacks and seek independence or at least greater autonomy.

Throughout the crisis, China used various methods to display its opposition to the Chen Shui-bian candidacy. However, China knew that threats, missile tests, and even war games might not appear credible to Taiwan voters. China had attempted to influence Taiwan's first direct presidential election in 1996. But voters still elected Beijing's least preferred candidate (Lee Teng-hui). In a time when China placed high priority on trying to develop economically, conflict with Taiwan is costly and thus undesirable. On the other hand, the PRC needed to make Taiwanese voters understand the seriousness with which it viewed the question of Taiwanese independence. Trade politics with the United States offered an opportunity for credible communication.

China has long sought accession to the WTO (the World Trade Organization). To gain entry, China first needed to obtain permanent normal trade relations with the United States. On 15 November 1999, after extended talks and the direct intervention of Premier Zhu Rongji, U.S. and Chinese negotiators finally reached an agreement whereby China would open its economy to more extensive competition in exchange for WTO membership. As a follow-up to the agreement, President Clinton needed to obtain congressional passage of the trade bill granting permanent normal trade relations with China. The PRC leadership knew that, although the Clinton administration made passage of the China trade bill a priority, its prospect in Congress was not at all certain. Supporters of the bill (Republicans and the business lobby) were opposed by two-thirds of House Democrats together with traditional Democratic constituents (labor, environment, and human rights groups). If China wanted to assure WTO membership, it should have avoided antagonizing a divided U.S. Congress.

Yet, in sharp contrast to their previous relentless efforts at WTO accession, PRC leaders repeatedly provoked the U.S. Congress over Taiwan. In February 2000, China issued the threatening white paper, stiffening opposition to the trade bill even before it reached Congress. On 8 March, President Clinton sent the trade bill to Congress and then launched a major effort to rally congressional support. Once again, on 15 March, with the fate of the bill at a critical juncture in Congress, Premier Zhu Rongji delivered the much publicized threat about the upcoming election in Taiwan, emphasizing that the people of the mainland were willing to 'shed their blood' to prevent Taiwan's secession. Zhu Rongji jeopardized his own considerable efforts on behalf of China's accession to WTO by delivering this heavy-handed threat against Taiwan. Yet, by doing so, the PRC more clearly demonstrated its resolve to whoever eventually came to power in Taiwan. While the bill eventually passed both houses of Congress, the long delay and the willingness of China to risk its WTO status in an attempt to deter Taiwanese independence is telling. Just as the Taiwanese proved resolved in the crisis, the Chinese leadership also was able to demonstrate strong interest without firing a shot.

Credible demonstrations of resolve on both sides of the Taiwan Strait led to a mutual postelection wind-down. After his electoral victory on 18 March, Chen Shui-bian made a series of conciliatory moves, delivering an acceptance speech without inflammatory reference to independence, retaining the current defense minister, and planning to revise the DDP's charter regarding Taiwan independence. Meanwhile, China issued the statement that it would 'observe where [Chen] will lead cross-Strait relations'.[15] The crisis passed without violence, in part because both sides were able to signal through economic rather than military means. The crisis of the Taiwan Strait was a source of tension and concern worldwide, but it also offers hope in an increasingly integrated world. Globalization more often makes it possible for states to avoid military contests.

## Implication

Policymakers acutely feel the presence and impact of global markets. South Korea's former prime minister Lee Hong Koo commented, 'In the old days we used to say, 'History dictated this or that'. Now we say that 'market forces' dictate this and you have to live within [those forces]. It took us time to understand what had happened. We didn't realize that the victory of the Cold War was a victory for market forces above politics' (quoted in Friedman, 2000: 107). That the markets for stocks, bonds, and currencies can profoundly influence national economies overnight is no longer an abstraction after financial crises in Asia and Russia. Economic markets, driven by expectations about economic and political fundamentals, can handle evolving information efficiently, resulting in informative market behaviors. It is these properties of the markets that allow economic globalization to affect interstate political relations. As we discuss here and demonstrate elsewhere formally, it is not the benefits of globalization that deter disputes (Gartzke and Li, 2001). States can too easily use the vulnerability of their counterparts to leverage new political concessions. Rather, the size and presence of global assets make it possible for leaders to credibly demonstrate resolve in ways not traditionally available.

States are still asymmetrically integrated into the world economy. Asymmetric integration is often pointed to as a possible precipitant of conflict. The impact of asymmetry in dispute behavior deserves more careful assessment. We conjecture that asymmetry does not directly increase the probability of disputes. Instead, asymmetrically integrated dyads are asymmetrically able to signal. This suggests a useful refinement of policy actions intended to influence interstate violence. Measures that decrease interstate inequality and asymmetry in integration are normatively desirable and can be justified on this basis alone. However, whether such efforts are justified in terms of war reduction is a different question. The informational argument claims that disputes are not generally a consequence of situational variables. States do not fight due to inequality, but because of different perceptions about dissatisfaction and/or resolve. Even if economic integration leads to slightly greater inequality, the advantages of globalization in terms of costly signaling may be justified. The United States and other major economic powers can encourage peace by promoting global economic ties.

The rise of the autonomous market does not necessarily imply a weakened state. The assumption of many students of globalization is that states and markets are in competition, that the state-market relationship is zero-sum. Realists are pessimistic because they see the rising power of markets as necessarily weakening states while liberals are more optimistic because they see international institutions as a remedy for many of the purported problems of globalization and because they value 'low politics' more than realists. In some cases, increasing market power *does* limit state power. For example, the liberalization of tariffs and capital controls is always associated with some loss of state control. In many areas, however, state and market are not direct competitors, but are more appropriately seen as complementary entities.

One consequence of globalization that is clear but that has been ignored in previous studies is that increasing market autonomy opens up new avenues for competition between states. As Friedman (2000: 12) aptly put it, 'the Cold War was a world of "friends" and "enemies". The globalization world, by contrast, tends to turn all friends and enemies into "competitors"'. It would not be surprising to find that globalization makes states even more aggressive and interventionist, at least in some policy areas. Proponents of globalization typically advocate the formation of supranational institutions to conduct essential functions, and eventually supercede, sovereign states. But such a vision, while sufficient, is certainly not necessary for the pursuit of globalization. Nor is it the case that states require protection from the inherently negative repercussions of markets. Negative repercussions are likely to exist, but the balance of consequences for states from markets has not been properly evaluated and may even be positive, as we suggest here. Thus, the need for global institutions to regulate externalities between state and market is an assumption not derived from the structure of state-market relationships. Further, the nature of market externalities may be such that they benefit, rather than harm, the global political arena. Integration stands to facilitate credible interaction among states, but only if institutional mechanisms designed to protect politics from markets do not interfere.

One of the benefits of the globalization debate has been increasing attention to the linkages between international politics and international political economy. Still, studies of the interconnectedness of the two subjects have yet to progress sufficiently. Political economists emphasize the relationship between state and market. IR scholars are typically concerned with interstate relations. Even when they do appear interested in the effects of economics on international politics, students of international conflict often remain interested only in political consequences of economic change, a preoccupation that has led them to fail to notice how the effect of state behavior affects the state-market relationship, which in turn affects interstate relations. The emergence of greater economic autonomy means that market actors can shift wealth with greater ease, ironically making the global market more sensitive to political behavior. Traditional international relations focus only on interstate political relations, without looking at the emerging role of market actors, a source of criticism from international political economists (Strange, 1996). Keohane and Nye (1979) make a powerful argument for the inclusion of nonstate economic actors, though later research reverts to a more traditional state centrism (Keohane, 1993). In the early stages of globalization, where we appear to be now, the continued reification of the state may not be too problematic. However, if global economic integration continues to affect the world economy structurally, it necessitates additional complexity (or at least new actors) in the conduct and analysis of international politics. As Strange (1996) argued, structural changes in the world economy are changing the nature of diplomacy from solely between states to that between states, between firms and between states and firms. States may continue to play a game of power politics, ignoring the interests of market actors. Yet, increasingly states can do so only at a very great price. Liberals argue that international institutions are needed to thwart such market inefficiencies while realists are concerned that states might bow to market inefficiencies and stop playing as robust a game of politics. We offer a more optimistic 'middle way', one that appears to us to be far more consistent with the logic of how political conflict evolves. We see the inefficiencies of political competition as virtuous because they provide information to political actors in competition. At least one rationale for protecting the state from the market is removed if markets do not increase the probability of conflict. Similarly, protecting markets from states stands to limit the informational value of signaling through the strategic interaction of state and market actors. Making the threats and demands of political competitors more expensive makes such actions more informative and promises to reduce the need of states to resort to militarized violence.

Students of globalization have restricted their attention to one area of interest (state-state or state-market), such that the interactions between state-state and state-market relations under globalization have yet to be fully explored. Also, students of the state-state relationship have just begun to explore informational, rather than distributional, explanations for interstate contests. As a result, participants to the globalization debates have failed to notice one of the most important positive political externalities of economic globalization, that is, its pacifying effect over interstate political contests through the informational properties of markets. The two fields (international conflict and international political economy) can both benefit from a bridge between them. By looking at the emerging power of the market as a third party, students of international conflict can better understand interdependence and go beyond trade ties. By looking at the implications for interstate political contests, students of international political economy can more appropriately assess the ramifications of economic globalization, beyond the usual debate on state-market relations alone.

# Notes

1. Waltz (1999) argues that global economic integration will not much change international politics.

2. Sassen (1996) discusses the shift in relative power between states and markets, but also emphasizes the continuing importance of the symbiotic relationship between states and markets (states need markets for rents while markets need states for enforcement of contracts, public goods provision, etc.).

3. It seems to us perplexing to claim both that globalization reduces state autonomy, leading to war and that anarchy is the cause of international conflict. If anarchy is a permissive condition for war (which we contest, note that guerrilla warfare seeks to *cause* anarchy and that domestic conflicts far outnumber major international disputes), then actions that remove or limit anarchy (such as the promotion of international institutions that are associated with globalization) would appear to remove, or at least reduce, one of the conditions that are claimed to precipitate international conflict. An attempt to sufficiently chronicle inconsistencies in the realist position is, however, beyond the scope of this project.

4. 'The removal, so far as possible, of all economic barriers and the establishment of an equality of trade conditions among all the nations consenting to the peace and associating themselves for its maintenance', Wilson (1918), Point III.

5. Wars need not end by resolving differences between states. Rather, they resolve uncertainty about the likely consequences of pursuing differences through force. Wars may also end because competitors are no longer physically able to sustain combat, though these contests (total wars) appear to be significantly less common.

6. There are exceptions to this argument involving commitment problems and indivisibility of issues that allow disputes to occur among fully informed actors. We omit

discussion of these issues to retain the parsimony of our explanation and because we believe that these other accounts are not modal behavior (see Gartzke, 1999).

7. Excludability implies that property rights are enforceable. There are few incentives to fight for what cannot be denied the loser. Relative gains concerns suggest that non-rival goods can still form the basis for contests.

8. Gartzke, Li, and Boehmer (2001) show that opportunity costs seldom deter disputes directly, which dispels a conventional liberal conviction. Competitors must have beliefs about what opponents will accept in lieu of fighting. If states are less willing to fight, then opponents have incentives to make additional demands so that the pacifying effects of opportunity costs are subsumed in eventual settlements.

9. Lexis-Nexis Academic Universe http://web.lexis-nexis.com/universe/form/academic/s_wires.htm

10. 'The 1996 crisis of the Taiwan Strait came as a shock to people in both capitals. Many in Beijing had convinced themselves that the United States would wash its hands of Taiwan or perhaps already had in order to avoid confrontation with China. Many in Washington thought China would not engage in military adventurism and risk relations across the strait and across the Pacific, upon which its rapid economic development depended. Following the 1996 confrontation, those beliefs were less common'. Garver (1997: 5–6).

11. 'The current tension across the Taiwan Strait has been entirely caused by the perverse acts of some leaders in Taiwan who preach an independent Taiwan'. Shen Guo-Fang, PRC Foreign Ministry spokesman. CNN Interactive, 'China Admits Taiwan Intimidation', 7 March 1996, www-cgi.cnn.com/WORLD/9603/china_Taiwan/07/missiles/index.html.

12. 'Beijing's amphibious lift capability is extremely limited at present and there are no indications that China is devoting resources to improve significantly its amphibious assault capability'. (DOD, 1999). Also see Moore (2000).

13. Taiwanese efforts to obtain two sea-based Aegis missile systems (aboard Arleigh Burke class destroyers made in the United States) are largely motivated by the SRBM and MRBM threat.

14. Chinese leaders seem to have interpreted market signals in line with our argument. In a warning three days prior to the election, Chinese premier Zhu Rongji cited plunging Taiwanese stock market prices as evidence of market anxiety about the possibility of war (Xinhua News Agency Xinhua general news service, 15 March 2000).

15. United Press International. 'Beijing, watching Taiwan, maintains "one China" policy' (Beijing, 19 March 2000).

PART II

**Empirical Contributions**

CHAPTER 7

# Assessing the Liberal Peace with Alternative Specifications: Trade Still Reduces Conflict

*John R. Oneal and Bruce Russett*

## Why Look Again at the Effect of Trade on Conflict?

Many research reports over the last few years have indicated that economically important trade has statistically significant and substantively important benefits for reducing interstate violence (Domke, 1988; Mansfield, 1994; Oneal, Oneal, Maoz, and Russett, 1996; Reuveny and Kang, 1996a; Oneal and Russett, 1997; Oneal and Ray, 1997; Way, 1997; Kim, 1998, Russett, Oneal, and Davis, 1998; Oneal and Russett, 1999a, b; Bennett and Stam, 2000; Hegre, 2000; Mousseau, 2000; Gartzke, Li, and Bochmer, 2001; King and Zeng, 2002; Oneal and Russett, 2001; Russett and Oneal, 2001; Gleditsch, 2002b; Lagazio and Russett, 2003). While finding support for the complementary liberal thesis regarding the conflict-reducing effects of joint democracy, Nathaniel Beck (Beck, Katz, and Tucker, 1998) and Katherine Barbieri (1998a) challenged these results regarding the effects of interdependence. Beck et al. argue that simple logistic regression analysis is inappropriate for cross-sectional and time-series data because observations are not temporally independent. They suggest a method to correct for this problem and show that, with their technique, the beneficial influence of economic interdependence reported in Oneal and Russett (1997) becomes statistically insignificant.[1]

Barbieri (1998a), incorporating Beck et al.'s (1998) correction, surprisingly reports that greater interdependence significantly increases the risk of a militarized dispute. Even among the so-called politically relevant dyads (Maoz and Russett, 1993)—contiguous states and pairs containing at least one major power—she finds that economically important trade is positively associated with conflict, though the relationship for this important group of countries is not statistically significant. Several of Barbieri's analyses are similar to those in Oneal and Russett (1997), but differ in the specific definitions of the dependent and independent variables, the controls included in the regression equation, and the set of cases analyzed. It is important to ascertain whether these differences in specification significantly affect the results.

In this chapter we address the concerns of our colleagues by adopting their suggestions for testing liberal theory, although we do not regard all of their proposed procedures as appropriate. Nevertheless, when we adopt their methods, we find that interdependence did significantly *reduce* the likelihood of conflict during the years 1950–92 among contiguous and major-power pairs. We then undertake a series of analyses for the post–World War II period using all pairs of states to determine if the pacific benefits of trade are confined to politically relevant dyads. Assessing the consequences of trade using all possible dyads requires that special care be taken to control for the influence of geographical distance if spurious findings are to be avoided. We also explore the implications of other key methodological decisions in assessing the liberal peace. Finally, we estimate the effects of interdependence on the likelihood of conflict for the contiguous states, major-power pairs, and all other dyads separately. Our results indicate that economically important trade has large benefits for the contiguous dyads, those most prone to conflict. Interdependence also reduces the probability of militarized disputes among the major-power pairs. It has no substantive effect in the 'non-relevant' subset of cases.

## The Logic of Our Analyses

Barbieri (1998a) reports the results of logistic regression analyses that cover an extended period of time, 1870–1992, and include alternative indicators of the importance of bilateral trade. We limit our attention here to her analyses of the post–World War II period, 1950–92. We have reported support for the benefits of trade in the years before World War II elsewhere (Oneal and Russett, 1999a, b; Russett and Oneal, 2001). Our strategy is to replicate her tests, using the same measurement techniques, sample of cases, and estimation techniques. Importantly, we explicitly take into account duration dependence in the time series data using Beck, Katz, and Tucker's (1998) correction. We then make a series of modifications in step-by-step fashion to reveal more fully the relationship between economic interdependence and the likelihood of militarized disputes. By adopting the methodology of those who suggest that the liberal thesis is debatable, we explore the robustness of our previous findings.

Barbieri (1998a) estimates the effects of interdependence using two basic measures. The first is the concentration of trade, or 'partner dependence', which equals the fraction of a state's total exports and imports accounted for by its trade with a dyadic partner. This measure is available for the entire 1870–1992 period. For the post–World War II period, she also employs a measure of economic dependence, which is calculated by dividing a state's bilateral trade with its partner by its gross domestic product (GDP). This measure of the economic importance of trade, which we have used in all our studies, is preferable because states differ markedly in the degree to which they are autarkic. A state's trade may be concentrated; but as we show elsewhere (Oneal, 2003), that is unlikely to restrain it from using force against a commercial partner if its dependence on trade is limited. On the other hand, a state may have a diversified portfolio of trading partners but be very open to the international economy, so be restrained from threatening military action against any one of them or even against third parties. Consequently, we focus our attention on Barbieri's analyses of economic dependence, 1950–92.

An important feature of Barbieri's (1995, 1996a, 1998a) work is that she analyzes a large sample of dyads. We have often focused on contiguous pairs and dyads containing at least one major power because there is good reason to believe that these pairs engage in meaningful interstate relations that could involve the threat or use of military force. Indeed they account for 83 percent of the militarized disputes, 1950–92. Limiting analyses to the politically relevant subset is also convenient because it reduces the number of observations from over 386,000 to just 38,039, 10 percent of the total. Thus, the incidence of disputes among the politically relevant dyads is 44 times that of the nonrelevant pairs. Barbieri and others argue that we should model the factors that give rise to all interstate conflicts, rather than excluding some dyads as being irrelevant.

Discussion of the relative merits of inclusiveness versus focusing attention on cases for which the theories tested are clearly relevant continues (Gleditsch and Hegre, 1997; Lemke and Reed, 2001). But restricting analyses to dyads for which data are reported in the IMF's *Direction of Trade Statistics* (DOTS) also reduces the sample of cases and can be avoided. Only 46 percent of the disputes occurring between 1950 and 1992 involved dyads with trade reported in the DOTS. Dropping cases for which there are missing trade data is not the best solution to this problem (King et al., 2001); it is certainly inconsistent with the desire to model conflict for the largest number of dyads possible. Indeed it is not necessary to assume that missing trade data are in fact unknown because members of the International Monetary Fund are required to report a variety of economic statistics, including their bilateral exports and imports, to the IMF. Consequently, according to the IMF's Statistics Department (Laveda, 1998), missing data for IMF members indicate zero (or nearly zero) trade. Thus, in several analyses below, we expand the empirical domain of our study by assuming that when data for trade of IMF members are missing there was no (or negligible) bilateral commerce.

If all dyads, not just the politically relevant pairs, are considered, it is especially important to control for the effect of distance on interstate relations. Geographical proximity produces opportunities to fight and issues to fight about (Siverson and Starr, 1991; Goertz and Diehl, 1992; Kocs, 1995); but trade levels (Tinbergen, 1962; Deardorff, 1995; Bliss and Russett, 1998; Russett and Oneal, 2001), shared international organization memberships (Russett, Oneal and Davis, 1998; Russett and Oneal, 2001) and alliances (Bremer, 1992) are also positively related to proximity. Including all possible pairs of states can spuriously indicate that trade (or alliances) increases the risk of conflict. The problem is compounded because the number of peaceful dyads with a low level of interdependence is sharply increased. Many are 'false negatives'; that is, the absence of conflict between Mali and Argentina is surely not a result of their negligible economic ties. Consequently, the influence of distance must be carefully modeled if the danger of spurious findings is to be minimized (Gleditsch, 1995; Lemke, 1995). In most of the analyses reported below, therefore, we include a dichotomous control for contiguity and a continuous measure of the distance between states' capitals (or major ports for the largest countries).

These measures are not redundant as they might first appear. Like Barbieri (1998a), we identify states as contiguous if they share a land boundary or are separated by less than 150 miles of water. More importantly, we both include indirect borders through dependencies. As a result, the United States is contiguous in our data with 21 countries, at one time or another, in the postwar period. In addition to Mexico and Canada, the USA is contiguous with the Netherlands, Great Britain, France, Japan, and New Zealand among others during some years. Consequently, the correlation between our indicator of contiguity and the logarithm of the distance separating states' capitals is only .43. Another way to indicate the difference between these two measures is to note that the average distance separating the major cities of contiguous states is about 750 miles.

To insure that the large number of nonrelevant dyads does not distort our understanding of the effects of interdependence, we also estimate the coefficients of an expanded equation designed to reveal the influence of our theoretical variables within each of three subsets of cases in our sample: the contiguous dyads, the major-power pairs, and other dyads.

We modify Barbieri's (1998a) specification in two other ways in order to clarify the consequences of trade. First, we decompose her measures of interdependence into more basic constituents. Barbieri (1996a, 1998a) has assessed liberal theory using three variables: salience, symmetry, and interdependence. $SALIENCE_{ij,t}$ equals the square root of $DEPEND_{i,t}*DEPEND_{j,t}$, where $DEPEND_{i,t}$ is state i's exports to and imports from state j divided by i's gross domestic product and $DEPEND_{j,t}$ is their trade divided by j's GDP. $SYMMETRY_{ij,t}$ is $1 - | DEPEND_{i,t} - DEPEND_{j,t} |$; and $INTERDEP_{ij,t}$ equals $SALIENCE_{ij,t}*SYMMETRY_{ij,t}$. The construction of these measures was well motivated. It responded to concerns about the effects of asymmetric economic relations on the likelihood of military conflict. Critics of capitalism in particular have argued that relations between developing countries and those economically advanced are characterized by dependency, not interdependence. Patterns of unequal exchange are said to allow the larger, more independent state to exploit its commerce with its smaller trading partner, increasing the risk of military conflict.

In practice, however, Barbieri's measures are problematic because most of the values taken by DEPEND, the bilateral trade-to-GDP ratio, fall in a very narrow range. As a consequence, the mean value of SYMMETRY is 0.997. Because INTERDEP is simply SALIENCE*SYMMETRY, the correlation between SALIENCE and INTERDEP is .99. Thus coefficients estimated for these variables are apt to be sensitive to changes in the sample. We consider, therefore, alternative measures of the character of the trading relations linking states.

Barbieri's three variables can be decomposed into the lower ($DEPEND_L$) and higher ($DEPEND_H$) trade-to-GDP ratios, variables first used in Oneal and Russett (1997). $SALIENCE_{ij}$ can be expressed as the square root of $DEPEND_L*DEPEND_H$; $SYMMETRY_{ij}$ is 1 - ($DEPEND_H$ - $DEPEND_L$); and $INTERDEP_{ij}$ equals $SALIENCE_{ij}*SYMMETRY_{ij}$. $DEPEND_L$ and $DEPEND_H$ have the virtues of being less highly correlated (r = .48), simpler in construction, and fewer in number. They are also easy to interpret and well grounded theoretically. The lower trade-to-GDP ratio indicates the constraints on the use of force experienced by the less constrained state in each dyad (Oneal and Russett, 1997). The probability of a dispute should be primarily a function of the freedom of action of this weak-link in the chain of peace (Dixon, 1994); the estimated coefficient of $DEPEND_L$ will be negative if the liberals are right: The likelihood of conflict falls as trade becomes increasingly important economically for the less constrained state. If asymmetric trade, or dependency, increases the danger of conflict, then the sign of the coefficient of $DEPEND_H$ would be positive.

The last change we make to Barbieri's (1998a) specification is to use an alternative means of correcting for dependence in the time series. Beck, Katz, and Tucker (1998) propose that researchers using logistic regression remedy duration dependence by creating a variable that marks the number of years that have elapsed from the most recent occurrence of a dispute and then generating a spline function of the years of peace. Following their suggestion, we created a curve with three interior knots, which produced four variables (PEACEYRS1 through PEACEYRS4). This solution is problematic, however. Decisions on how to treat dependence in the data involve theoretical questions of model specification as well as methodological ones (Bennett, 1999). Beck et al.'s treatment rests on the assumption that the effects of the theoretical variables and of time are separable (Beck and Tucker, 1996). This is particularly unlikely in the case of trade. Trade falls with the occurrence of a dispute, which is why states are thought to avoid conflict when trade is economically important. It rises over time after a dispute has ended, as traders' confidence in the durability of peaceful relations increases. It is no more surprising, then, that the statistical significance of interdependence declines in the presence of the PEACEYRS variables (Beck, Katz, and Tucker, 1998) than that a measure of inflation will be less significant in a regression that also includes a control for the money supply.

To guard against the danger of wrongly rejecting a true hypothesis, we estimate the coefficients of most of our equations using the General Estimating Equation [GEE] (Liang and Zeger, 1986; StataCorp, 1997) in addition to Beck, Katz, and Tucker's (1998) method. GEE is a quasi-likelihood method developed specifically for pooled time-series, cross-sectional analyses. A great virtue is its flexibility, as Zorn (2001) has stressed. GEE can be used to estimate general linear models, including analyses of dependent variables that are binomial or a count of events as well as those with a normal distribution. Researchers can specify the function linking the covariates to the response variable and the correlational structure of the error terms within groups. We have assumed that our time series exhibit an autoregressive process of the first order (AR1). Thus when using GEE we allow for temporal dependence in the time series but do so in a way that gives the variables in our theoretically specified model primacy in accounting for interstate disputes. Beck et al.'s method introduces the PEACEYRS variables into the estimation process as coequals of the theoretical terms.

## Domain, Definitions, and Sources

Our unit of analysis throughout is the dyad-year. We examine the years 1950–92 and do not limit our study to the politically relevant dyads as we have done in the past. This temporal domain includes several post–Cold War years, extending the generalizability of our previous results.

## Militarized Disputes: Onset and Involvement

To address the concerns of others (Bremer, 1992; Barbieri, 1998a; Beck, Katz, and Tucker, 1998), we focus our attention on the first year, or onset, of a militarized dispute. We use the recently revised data from the Correlates of War (COW) project (Bremer, 1996). A militarized dispute is an international interaction involving threats, displays, or actual uses of military force (Gochman and Maoz, 1984; Jones, Bremer and Singer, 1996). $ONSET_{ij,t}$ is a dichotomous variable that equals 1 when a dispute between states i and j started in year t and 0 otherwise; subsequent years of multiyear disputes are dropped from the analysis. We consider in one set of analyses states' involvement in disputes. Then, the dependent variable ($DISPUTE_{ij,t}$), as in our previously published articles, equals 1 in any year that a dispute was ongoing between i and j and 0 only in years of peace.

Though we concentrate on the onset of disputes, we are convinced that, for several reasons, researchers should be concerned with all years in which states are involved in a conflict. Most importantly, all our theories begin with the assumption that national leaders are rational. This implies that they frequently reevaluate a decision to use force. Unsophisticated decision makers may not review past decisions, and sophisticated people may not reconsider unimportant choices; but the decision to threaten, display, or use force is manifestly consequential, and all nations have established procedures designed to select leaders who are thought to have exceptional decision-making abilities. Consequently,· national leaders should frequently reevaluate their positions: escalating, de-escalating, or maintaining a conflict contingent on changes in domestic politics, the availability of economic and military resources, and international alignments. Smith (1998) models interstate conflict from such an assumption. We agree with Blainey (1988: x):

> the beginning of wars, the prolonging of wars, the ending of wars and the prolonging or shortening of periods of peace all share the same causal framework. The same explanatory framework and the same factors are vital in understanding each stage in the sequel of war and peace.

Moreover, an examination of 166 multiyear disputes during the period of our analyses revealed that slightly more than half either involved a change in the level of force employed from one year to another, or in the second or subsequent years of a dispute a new dispute arose at the same level after the conclusion of the first dispute.[2] This is clear indication that policymakers do not relinquish control of events in times of military conflict.

## Independent Variables

All our independent variables are lagged one year in order to insure that they have not been affected by a dispute to be explained.

*Economic Interdependence.* To assess the effect of interdependence on the likelihood of military conflict, we use the *Direction of Trade Statistics* of the International Monetary Fund [IMF] (1996a). The IMF reports country i's exports to country j ($X_{ij,t}$) and i's imports from j ($M_{ij,t}$). The economic importance of their trade is calculated by assessing the sum of exports and imports relative to their national incomes. We use gross domestic products [GDPs] (Summers and Heston, 1988, 1991; Summers et al., 1995). Thus, country i's dependence on trade with j in year t-1 is: $DEPEND_{i,t-1} = (X_{ij,t-1} + M_{ij,t-1}) / GDP_{i,t-1}$

To be consistent with Barbieri (1998a), we calculated the bilateral trade-to-GDP ratio using trade and GDPs converted to current dollars using exchange rates.[3] This ratio represents the economic importance of trade in national prices, because the exchange rate in the numerator and denominator cancel. In the past, we calculated states' dependence on trade in current international prices following the example of the originators of the Penn World Tables (Summers et al., 1995) and Maddison (1991, 1995).

To ascertain the consequences of trade for interstate relations, we first use the three variables developed by Barbieri (1996a, 1998a). Recall that SALIEN-CE$_{ij, t-1}$ equals the square root of DEPEND$_{i,t-1}$*DEPEND$_{j,t-1}$; SYMMETRY$_{ij,t-1}$ is 1 - |DEPEND$_{i,t-1}$ - DEPEND$_{j,t-1}$|; and INTERDEP$_{ij,t-1}$ equals SALIENCE$_{ij,t-1}$* SYMMETRY$_{ij,t-1}$. As noted earlier, however, SALIENCE and INTERDEP are highly correlated because of the limited range of DEPEND. Therefore, we also conduct analyses using the lower and higher trade-to-GDP ratio for each dyad, as in Oneal and Russett (1997). DEPEND$_{L,t-1}$ equals DEPEND$_{i,t-1}$ if DEPEND$_{i,t-1}$ is less than or equal to DEPEND$_{j,t-1}$; otherwise, it equals DEPEND$_{j,t-1}$. DE-PEND$_{H,t-1}$ is constructed in analogous fashion.

*Joint Democracy.* We estimate the peacefulness of democracies using the most recent Polity III data (Jaggers and Gurr, 1995, 1996). We created a summary measure of the political character of regimes using the autocracy (AUTOC) and democracy (DEMOC) scales: DEM$_{i,t}$ = DEMOC$_{i,t}$ - AUTOC$_{i,t}$. This is preferable to using either component alone, because many governments have both democratic and autocratic characteristics. DEM ranges from -10 for the most autocratic regimes to +10 at the democratic end of the scale. A measure of joint democracy is created using the regime scores of the two members of each dyad. JNTDEM$_{ij,t-1}$ equals [(DEM$_{i,t-1}$ + 10)*(DEM$_{j,t-1}$ + 10)].[4]

*Alliances.* We control for the influence of alliances using a variable (AL-LIED$_{ij,t-1}$) that equals 1 if states were linked by a mutual defense treaty, a neutrality pact, or an entente and 0 otherwise. The source of our data is Singer (1995), which we updated using Rengger (1995).

*Capability Ratio.* We include a measure of the dyadic balance of power. Recent evidence suggests that a preponderance of power inhibits overt conflict (Bremer, 1992; Maoz and Russett, 1993; Kugler and Lemke, 1996; de Soysa, Park and Oneal, 1997). To measure national capabilities, we used the COW military capabilities index composed (in equal weights) of a country's share of the system's total population, urban population, energy consumption, iron and steel production, military manpower, and military expenditures (Singer and Small, 1995). CAPRATIO$_{ij,t-1}$ is the natural logarithm of the ratio of the stronger state's capability index to that of the weaker member in each dyad.

*Contiguity and Distance.* We include in our analyses a variable that identifies contiguous dyads. CONTIG$_{ij,t-1}$ equals 1 if two states are directly or indirectly contiguous via dependencies, either sharing a land boundary or separated by less than 150 miles of water. In analyses of the politically relevant dyads, this indicator distinguishes between the contiguous dyads, which are particularly conflict-prone, and the major-power dyads. In most of the analyses reported below, we also include an explicit measure of the distance separating the homelands of the dyadic members because of the importance of controlling for distance when considering the nonrelevant dyads. DISTANCE$_{ij,t}$ equals the natural logarithm of the great circle distance between i's and j's capitals (or major ports for the United States, the USSR/Russia, and Canada).

# Results

We evaluate the effects of economically important trade and other theoretically interesting variables on the likelihood of military conflict using logistic regression analysis of pooled cross-sectional time-series data. We begin by trying to replicate Barbieri's (1998a) results using our data with her specification. We analyze the onset of militarized disputes, using her measures of salience, symmetry, and interdependence. The economic importance of trade is calculated in terms of national prices, we make no assumption about missing values of trade, and we employ the same controls and lag structure. Finally, we correct for duration dependence using the method suggested by Beck, Katz, and Tucker (1998) and correct for heteroskedasticity using Huber's robust standard errors. We report conservative two-tailed tests of statistical significance.

Then, in order to reveal their implications for the substantive findings, we modify our analyses in four steps. First, we correct for autocorrelation in the time series using the General Estimating Equation. Second, we modify the specification of the regression equation, using the lower and higher trade-to-GDP ratios and introducing better controls for geographical distance. Third, we expand the domain of our analyses to include pairs of states that can reasonably be assumed to have had no bilateral trade. Finally, we consider the consequences of interdependence for three subsets of cases: contiguous states, pairs of states that include a major power, and all other dyads.

First, following Barbieri (1998a), we estimate the following equation:

$$\text{ONSET}_{ij,t} = \beta_1 * \text{SALIENCE}_{ij,t-1} + \beta_2 * \text{SYMMETRY}_{ij,t-1}$$
$$+ \beta_3 * \text{INTERDEP}_{ij,t-1}$$
$$+ \beta_4 * \text{JNTDEM}_{ij,t-1} + \beta_5 * \text{CONTIG}_{ij,t-1} + \beta_6 * \text{MAJPOWR}_{ij,t-1} \qquad (7.1)$$
$$+ \beta_7 * \text{ALLIED}_{ij,t-1} + \beta_8 * \text{CAPRATIO}_{ij,t-1} + \beta_9 * \text{PEACEYRS1}_{ij}$$
$$+ \beta_{10} * \text{PEACEYRS2}_{ij} + \beta_{11} * \text{PEACEYRS3}_{ij} + \beta_{12} * \text{PEACEYRS4}_{ij}$$

The estimated coefficients for equation 7.1 are reported in the first column of table 7.1. We find no evidence with this specification and set of cases that interdependence reduces the likelihood of a militarized dispute. None of the three terms—SALIENCE, SYMMETRY, and INTERDEP—is close to statistical significance; but there is also no evidence that trade increases the danger of interstate conflict, as Barbieri (1998a) reported. Joint democracy, on the other hand, has important pacific benefits (p < .001). As expected, contiguous states and dyads containing at least one major power are more conflictual than other pairs; and a preponderance of power makes conflict less likely. Allied states are not significantly more peaceful; but unlike Barbieri (1998a), we do not find that they are more likely than other dyads to become engaged in conflict. The PEACEYRS variables are very significant jointly, as they are in all our analyses; their coefficients are not reported in this or later tables in order to save space. The pseudo-$R^2$ is .32; without PEACEYRS1 - PEACEYRS4, it is .23.

### Table 7.1. The Barbieri (1998a) Model, MID Onsets, 1950–92

| Variable | | All Dyads with IMF Trade Data | Politically Relevant Dyads with IMF Trade Data | |
|---|---|---|---|---|
| | | PEACEYRS Correction | PEACEYRS Correction | GEE |
| Salience$_{t-1}$ | ß | 10.4 | 33.4 | 28.1 |
| | SE$_ß$ | 30.9 | 24.4 | 25.9 |
| | p | .74 | .17 | .28 |
| Symmetry$_{t-1}$ | | -1.50 | -2.41 | -2.79 |
| | | 2.14 | 2.02 | 2.39 |
| | | .49 | .23 | .24 |
| Interdependence$_{t-1}$ | | -15.9 | -53.5 | -64.9 |
| | | 33.9 | 25.2 | 25.8 |
| | | .64 | .03 | .01 |
| Joint Democracy$_{t-1}$ | | -0.00396 | -0.00257 | -0.00204 |
| | | 0.00078 | 0.00064 | 0.00073 |
| | | <.001 | <.001 | .005 |
| Contiguity$_{t-1}$ | | 2.58 | 0.940 | 1.74 |
| | | 0.22 | 0.206 | 0.25 |
| | | <.001 | <.001 | <.001 |
| Major Power$_{t-1}$ | | 1.21 | | |
| | | 0.23 | | |
| | | <.001 | | |
| Allied$_{t-1}$ | | -0.148 | -0.425 | -0.637 |
| | | 0.198 | 0.188 | 0.243 |
| | | .46 | .02 | .009 |
| Log Capability Ratio$_{t-1}$ | | -0.208 | -0.258 | -0.208 |
| | | 0.050 | .049 | 0.061 |
| | | <.001 | <.001 | <.001 |
| Constant | | -1.92 | 1.13 | -0.750 |
| | | 2.16 | 2.06 | 2.461 |
| | | .37 | .59 | .76 |
| $X^2$ | | 1595.1 | 499.6 | 120.2 |
| $X^2$ d.f. | | 12 | 11 | 7 |
| P of $X^2$ | | <.0001 | <.0001 | <.0001 |
| Pseudo-$R^2$ | | .32 | .24 | – |
| N | | 118,466 | 21,619 | 21,613 |

In column 2, table 7.1, the politically relevant dyads alone are considered. The equation estimated is the same as equation 7.1, except that MAJPOWR has been dropped to avoid collinearity. For this important subset of cases, economic interdependence does significantly reduce the danger of a dispute. INTERDEP is significant at the .03 level. The benefits of trade are masked in the first analysis by the sheer number of the nonrelevant pairs. As shown in table 7.1, there are approximately five times as many of these other pairs as there are dyads that are either contiguous or contain at least one major power. The coefficients of the other variables are similar to what they were in the previous analysis, except that ALLIED is now significant (p < .02). The pseudo-$R^2$ is .24; dropping the PEACEYRS variables, it is .11.

Column 3 in table 7.1 contains the estimated coefficients for the same set of theoretical variables, again for just the politically relevant pairs; but these estimates were obtained by correcting for temporal dependence using the General Estimating Equation (StataCorp, 1997; Liang and Zeger, 1986). Accordingly, the PEACEYRS variables were dropped from equation 1. The results are similar to those produced by Beck, Katz, and Tucker's (1998) correction. The evidence for the benefits of economically important trade among the politically relevant pairs is important because these dyads are particularly prone to conflict. We return to this issue below when we estimate the effects of interdependence on the likelihood of conflict for the contiguous states, major-power pairs, and the non-relevant dyads. First, however, we reconsider two important issues: measuring economic interdependence and controlling for distance.

As noted earlier, SALIENCE, SYMMETRY, and INTERDEP can all be expressed as functions of the lower (DEPEND$_L$) and higher (DEPEND$_H$) trade-to-GDP ratio in each dyad, so, as in Oneal and Russett (1997), we use these variables directly to determine the effect of trade on the likelihood of conflict. We also change the specification of the regression equation to control more fully for the influence of geography. The results we have reported thus far indicate that the likelihood of conflict is a function of contiguity; but as noted earlier, this variable is somewhat misleading because states are 'contiguous' if they share a common border indirectly through dependencies (Maoz and Russett, 1993; Oneal and Russett, 1997; Barbieri, 1998a; cf. Bremer, 1992).

To capture more completely the effects of geographical proximity, we introduce a second control into our analyses: the logarithm of the great circle distance between states' capitals (or major ports for the largest countries). This yields the following equation:

$$ONSET_{ij,t} = \beta_1*DEPEND_{L,t-1} + \beta_2*DEPEND_{H,t-1} + \beta_3*JNTDEM_{ij,t-1}$$
$$+ \beta_4*CONTIG_{ij,t-1} + \beta_5*DISTANCE_{ij,t-1} + \beta_6*MAJPOWR_{ij,t-1} \qquad (7.2)$$
$$+ \beta_7*ALLIED_{ij,t-1} + \beta_8*CAPRATIO_{ij,t-1}$$

This equation is estimated both with Beck, Katz, and Tucker's (1998) correction for duration dependence, in which case PEACEYRS1-PEACEYRS4 is added to the specification, and with the General Estimating Equation.

The results of estimating this second specification for all dyads whose trade is actually reported by the IMF using Beck et al.'s correction are given in column 1, table 7.2. Those from estimating equation 7.2 with GEE, allowing for a first-order autoregressive (AR1) process, are reported in column 2. As expected, the likelihood of a dispute declines as the distance separating the members of a dyad increases (p < .001), whichever correction for temporal dependence is applied; and the indicator of direct or indirect contiguity is still highly significant (p < .001). Controlling better for distance provides more evidence for the pacific effects of both trade and alliances. The estimated coefficients for AL-LIED in the first two columns indicate that allies, as most would expect, are less likely to fight. As Bremer (1992) showed, allies appear more conflictual than other pairs of states if the influence of geographical distance is not taken into account. The lower trade-to-GDP ratio is significant (p < .03) when GEE adjusts for autocorrelation though not with Beck et al.'s correction for duration dependence (p < .15), using a two-tailed test. The higher dependence score is insignificant in both estimations. The influences of joint democracy, the involvement of a major power, and a preponderance of power remain largely unchanged.

The analyses performed thus far include only dyadic trade reported to the IMF. As noted earlier, this eliminates a large number of cases because many states do not report the absence of trade. This may bias the results and is unnecessary because of the IMF's reporting requirements.

Accordingly, we reestimated equation 7.2 assuming that missing trade data for IMF members indicate zero (or virtually zero) trade. The estimated coefficients are reported in the last two columns of table 7.2. The coefficients in column 3 were obtained using Beck et al.'s suggested correction; those in the fourth column are from a GEE estimation in which adjustment is made for an AR1 process. With this more complete set of dyads, there is statistically significant evidence for the pacific benefits of economically important trade using either correction for dependence in the time series. The lower trade-to-GDP ratio is significant at the .03 level using Beck et al.'s approach; it is significant at the .007 level with GEE. Again the higher dependence score is clearly insignificant. Thus, there is no evidence that asymmetric trade leads to conflict. Neither are larger values of $DEPEND_H$ associated with more peaceful interstate relations, but this reveals not so much a weakness in the liberal argument as it suggests that there are declining marginal benefits of interdependence, as we have reported elsewhere (Oneal and Russett, 1999b). The influences of the other variables remain largely unchanged. Note that over 150,000 cases have been added to the analysis; the number of disputes increased by 69 percent.[5]

Finally, we estimate an expanded model designed to reveal the influence of our theoretical variables within each of the three subsets of cases in our sample: the contiguous dyads, the major-power pairs, and other dyads. To do this, we created interactive terms using an indicator variable for the major-power (MA-JPOWR) and so-called nonrelevant (NOTREL) dyads. We multiplied each of these indicators by all the variables in equation 7.2 except for the higher dependence score because, as seen in table 7.2, this variable has a negligible influence on the onset of militarized disputes.[6] Thus, we added a series of interactive terms, for example, $MAJPOWR*DEPEND_L$ and $NOTREL*DEPEND_L$, and the indicators themselves, namely, MAJPOWR and NOTREL, to equation 7.2 and dropped $DEPEND_H$. The specification can be inferred from the list of variables in table 7.3. The influence of any variable, for example, $DEPEND_L$, on the like-

**Table 7.2. The Revised Model, MID Onsets, 1950–92**

| Variable | | All Dyads with IMF Trade Data | | All Dyads with IMF and Imputed Data | |
|---|---|---|---|---|---|
| | | PEACEYRS Correction | GEE | PEACEYRS Correction | GEE |
| Lower Dependence$_{t-1}$ | ß | -25.9 | -67.6 | -51.9 | -115.4 |
| | SE$_ß$ | 17.9 | 30.7 | 23.4 | 42.7 |
| | p | .15 | .03 | .03 | .007 |
| Higher Dependence$_{t-1}$ | | 1.40 | 0.71 | 1.52 | 0.810 |
| | | 1.69 | 2.43 | 1.96 | 2.72 |
| | | .41 | .77 | .44 | .77 |
| Joint Democracy$_{t-1}$ | | -0.00363 | -0.00281 | -0.00322 | -0.00239 |
| | | 0.00077 | 0.00087 | 0.00068 | 0.00075 |
| | | <.001 | <.001 | <.001 | <.001 |
| Contiguity$_{t-1}$ | | 2.14 | 2.80 | 2.46 | 2.46 |
| | | 0.22 | 0.26 | 0.21 | 0.23 |
| | | <.001 | <.001 | <.001 | <.001 |
| Log Distance$_{t-1}$ | | -0.399 | -0.489 | -0.592 | -0.701 |
| | | 0.079 | 0.088 | 0.076 | 0.081 |
| | | <.001 | <.001 | <.001 | <.001 |
| Major Power$_{t-1}$ | | 1.21 | 1.58 | 1.91 | 1.94 |
| | | 0.23 | 0.27 | .23 | 0.25 |
| | | <.001 | <.001 | <.001 | <.001 |
| Allied$_{t-1}$ | | -0.430 | -0.666 | -0.532 | -0.870 |
| | | 0.212 | 0.242 | 0.168 | 0.196 |
| | | .04 | .006 | .002 | <.001 |
| Log Capability Ratio$_{t-1}$ | | -0.188 | -0.168 | -0.231 | -0.224 |
| | | 0.056 | 0.0778 | 0.051 | 0.061 |
| | | <.001 | .034 | <.001 | <.001 |
| Constant | | -0.351 | -1.85 | 0.517 | -0.362 |
| | | 0.623 | 0.678 | 0.626 | 0.656 |
| | | .57 | <.001 | .41 | .58 |
| $X^2$ | | 1481.4 | 970.4 | 2166.8 | 1691.5 |
| $X^2$ d.f. | | 12 | 8 | 12 | 8 |
| P of $X^2$ | | <.0001 | <.0001 | <.0001 | <.0001 |
| Pseudo-$R^2$ | | .33 | | .34 | – |
| N | | 118,466 | 118,382 | 271,262 | 269,712 |

lihood of conflict for the contiguous dyads is given directly by its estimated coefficient, while the influence for the other two groups is determined by adding the coefficient of the appropriate interactive variable to this term. The effect of interdependence among the major-power pairs, for example, is the sum of the coefficient of DEPEND$_L$ plus the coefficient of MAJPOWR * DEPEND$_L$. The use of interactive terms insures that the large number of nonrelevant dyads, nearly 250,000 of our 271,000 cases, for whom the probability of conflict is very low, does not distort our understanding of the causes of conflict for those dyads for which conflict is comparatively common—the contiguous and major-power pairs.

## Table 7.3. MID Onset and Involvement, All Dyads, 1950–92

| Variable | | ONSET | | INVOLVEMENT | |
|---|---|---|---|---|---|
| | | PEACEYRS Correction | GEE | PEACEYRS Correction | GEE |
| Lower Dependence$_{t-1}$ | ß | -40.5 | -122 | -34.0 | -182 |
| | SE$_{ß}$ | 22.1 | 53 | 21.8 | 66 |
| | p | .07 | .02 | .12 | .006 |
| Major Power*Lower Dependence$_{t-1}$ | | 2.84 | 27.2 | 23.5 | 1.91 |
| | | 69.81 | 120.2 | 101.9 | 194.5 |
| | | .97 | .82 | .82 | .99 |
| Not Relevant*Lower Dependence$_{t-1}$ | | 57.5 | 127 | 60.8 | 167 |
| | | 23.1 | 54 | 26.8 | 82 |
| | | .01 | .02 | .007 | .04 |
| Joint Democracy$_{t-1}$ | | -0.00151 | -0.000722 | -0.00228 | -0.00116 |
| | | 0.00076 | 0.000918 | 0.00074 | 0.00092 |
| | | .05 | .43 | .002 | .21 |
| Major Power*Joint Democracy$_{t-1}$ | | -0.00313 | -0.00382 | -0.00326 | -0.00390 |
| | | 0.00115 | 0.00142 | 0.00118 | 0.00146 |
| | | .007 | .007 | .006 | .008 |
| Not Relevant*Joint Democracy$_{t-1}$ | | -0.00348 | -0.00292 | -0.00515 | -0.00384 |
| | | 0.00140 | 0.00139 | 0.00140 | 0.00135 |
| | | .01 | .04 | <.001 | .004 |
| Contiguity | | 0.961 | 1.61 | 0.315 | 1.16 |
| | | 0.231 | 0.31 | 0.231 | 0.30 |
| | | <.001 | <.001 | .11 | <.001 |
| Log Distance | | -0.235 | -0.381 | -0.234 | -0.437 |
| | | 0.068 | 0.091 | 0.070 | 0.096 |
| | | <.001 | <.001 | <.001 | <.001 |
| Major Power*Log Distance | | -0.0906 | 0.0356 | -0.0663 | -0.0254 |
| | | 0.1431 | 0.1971 | 0.1355 | 0.207 |
| | | .53 | .86 | .63 | .90 |
| Not Relevant*Log Distance | | -0.951 | -0.841 | -0.697 | -0.594 |
| | | 0.142 | 0.156 | 0.209 | 0.236 |
| | | <.001 | <.001 | <.001 | .01 |
| Allied$_{t-1}$ | | -0.663 | -1.02 | -0.565 | -1.07 |
| | | 0.181 | 0.24 | 0.168 | 0.24 |
| | | <.001 | <.001 | <.001 | <.001 |

**Table 7.3. Continued**

| Variable | ONSET | | INVOLVEMENT | |
|---|---|---|---|---|
| | PEACEYRS Correction | GEE | PEACEYRS Correction | GEE |
| Major Power*Allied$_{t-1}$ | 0.638 | 0.652 | 0.757 | 0.755 |
| | 0.356 | 0.419 | 0.324 | 0.411 |
| | .07 | .12 | .02 | .07 |
| Not Relevant*Allied$_{t-1}$ | 0.057 | 0.301 | -0.234 | 0.00608 |
| | 0.320 | 0.356 | 0.338 | 0.40198 |
| | .32 | .40 | .49 | .99 |
| Log Capability Ratio$_{t-1}$ | -0.117 | -0.105 | -0.166 | -0.164 |
| | 0.055 | 0.073 | 0.055 | 0.076 |
| | .03 | .15 | .002 | .03 |
| Major Power* Capability Ratio$_{t-1}$ | -0.288 | -0.310 | -0.240 | -0.245 |
| | 0.089 | 0.122 | 0.079 | 0.116 |
| | <.001 | .01 | .002 | .04 |
| Not Relevant* Capability Ratio$_{t-1}$ | -0.185 | -0.139 | -0.363 | -0.313 |
| | 0.110 | 0.123 | 0.109 | 0.13 |
| | .09 | .26 | <.001 | .02 |
| Major Power | 1.85 | 1.71 | 1.62 | 1.64 |
| | 0.979 | 1.36 | 0.99 | 1.52 |
| | .06 | .21 | .10 | .28 |
| Not Politically Relevant | 4.96 | 4.19 | 3.29 | 2.55 |
| | 1.16 | 1.36 | 1.68 | 1.94 |
| | <.001 | <.001 | .05 | .19 |
| Constant | -0.0680 | -0.90 | 1.34 | 0.374 |
| | 0.5738 | 0.76 | 0.55 | 0.771 |
| | .50 | .24 | .02 | .63 |
| $X^2$ | 1857.2 | 1348.9 | 2273.4 | 995.4 |
| $X^2$ d.f. | 22 | 18 | 22 | 18 |
| P of $X^2$ | <.0001 | <.0001 | <.0001 | <.0001 |
| Pseudo-$R^2$ | .39 | – | .46 | – |
| N | 271,262 | 269,712 | 271,951 | 270,400 |

The results of estimating the expanded equation are given in table 7.3. In the first two columns, we report coefficients for models predicting the onset of militarized disputes. As before, we use both Beck et al.'s approach (column 1) and GEE (column 2) to correct for autocorrelation. In columns 3 and 4, we use the same specification and the same corrections to predict states' *involvement* in disputes. With this dependent variable, every year that a pair of states is involved in a dispute, not just the first, is coded as an instance of conflict. This is the specification we favor on theoretical grounds and have used in our previous research (Oneal et al., 1996; Oneal and Ray, 1997; Oneal and Russett, 1997).

The results reported in table 7.3 indicate that economically important trade does reduce conflict among contiguous pairs of states, whether conflict is measured as the onset of or involvement in a militarized dispute. DEPEND$_L$, which reveals the benefits of interdependence for these most conflictual dyads, is statistically significant for both dependent variables, at the .02 level for onsets and .006 for dispute involvement, when temporal dependence is corrected using GEE. It is significant for the onset of disputes with the peace-years splines (p < .07) and nearly so (p < .12) for dispute involvement. As in previous analyses, the association is stronger and the coefficient larger with GEE. The coefficients of MAJPOWR*DEPEND$_L$ are far from statistical significance. Trade for this second subset of conflict-prone dyads reduces conflict, and the effect is not statistically different from that for the contiguous pairs, as we previously reported (Oneal and Russett, 1997).

The influence of trade for other dyads, the nonrelevant pairs, is different. The net effect of interdependence on the likelihood of conflict for these dyads is positive in three of the four analyses. For example, for the onset of a dispute with Beck et al.'s correction (column 1 in table 7.3), the coefficient of DEPEND$_L$ is -40.5 and that for NOTREL*DEPEND$_L$ is 57.5. The sum of these terms, 17.0, is positive, indicating that interdependence increases the likelihood of a dispute. The net effect of trade is found, however, by multiplying the sum of these coefficients times the value of DEPEND$_L$, which for this group is very small. The mean value of DEPEND$_L$ for the nonrelevant cases is only .00023, compared to .0037 for the contiguous pairs; and the median is actually zero. Consequently, the effect of trade on the likelihood of conflict among this subset of cases, as we show below, is trivial.

There are significant differences in the effects of joint democracy, being allied, and the capability ratio for the three subsets of cases. Joint democracy has the least effect in restraining violence among the contiguous pairs. Its influence alone is not statistically significant when GEE is used, but is significant for both onsets (p < .05) and dispute involvement (p < .002) using the PEACEYRS correction. Furthermore, the interactive terms show that joint democracy does significantly reduce conflict among both the major-power pairs and the nonrelevant dyads. The peace-inducing benefit of an alliance is substantially reduced if one of the states is a major power, as shown by the significant positive sign of MAJPOWR*ALLIED in three of the four analyses presented in table 7.3 The capability ratio has less influence on conflict among the contiguous pairs than among dyads involving a major power. The major powers enjoy very favorable balances of power vis-à-vis the many small states with which they are paired. Finally, the coefficient of NOTREL*DISTANCE is large and significant in all the analyses, indicating that accounting for the influence of geographical distance is especially important for this subset of cases.[7]

## Substantive Effects

Attention is usually focussed on the statistical significance of estimated coefficients; but as McCloskey (1993) has argued, it is the *substantive* significance of our results that ultimately matters. Indeed it becomes increasingly important to consider the practical implications of our findings as the size of the sample increases.[8] We can make our results more concrete by estimating the effect of each of our theoretical variables on the likelihood that a militarized dispute will commence. First, we calculated a baseline probability for each of the three subsets of cases against which to make comparisons. We set the bilateral trade-to-GDP measure at the median for each subset because it is more representative. Each of the other continuous variables, including PEACEYRS1 - PEACEYRS4 when appropriate, was made equal to the mean value for the group, and we postulated that the pair of states was not allied. We then estimated the annual probability of the onset of a militarized dispute for this 'typical' dyad for each of three subsets of cases—contiguous, major-power, or nonrelevant dyads—using the estimated coefficients in columns 1 and 2, table 7.3.[9] Next, we adjusted the most theoretically interesting variables in turn by adding one standard deviation to DEPENDL or the logarithm of the capability ratio, or by making both members of the dyad fully democratic or allied.[10]

The annual probabilities of a dyad being involved in a dispute under these various conditions are given in table 7.4. The likelihood of a dispute under the baseline conditions is .063 for the contiguous dyads using Beck et al.'s method. This drops to .039 if the lower trade-to-GDP measure is increased by a standard deviation, a reduction in danger of 38 percent. The result produced with GEE is even more dramatic; the likelihood of a dispute goes from .106 to .025 with greater trade. The benefit of economic interdependence for this most conflict prone set of countries are greater than that of joint democracy or a one standard deviation increase in the capability ratio with either method of correcting for dependence in the time series. They are greater than the effects of being allied in the GEE analysis and nearly as large if Beck et al.'s correction is used.

For the dyads composed of at least one major power, the baseline probability is .0061 with Beck et al.'s method and .0084 with GEE, less than one-tenth the risk of conflict experienced by contiguous pairs of states. For this subset of cases, too, economically important trade has pacific benefits. The danger of a dispute drops by 16 percent in column one and by 35 percent when GEE is used. Joint democracy has much larger benefits for this subset of cases, lowering the incidence of conflict by 70 percent in both estimations. An increase in the capability ratio also increases substantially the prospects for peace. Being allied raises the prospects of conflict for this group of countries if GEE is used but has little effect with Beck et al.'s technique. Interdependence does increase the probability of a dispute for the noncontiguous, non-major-power dyads; but as shown in the last section of table 7.4, the substantive effect is very small. The baseline rate is only .00028 when calculated with Beck et al.'s method and

.00048 with GEE. The probability of conflict goes to .00029 and .00049 if the lower trade-to-GDP ratio is raised by one standard deviation, an increase of only 2 or 3 percent of an already small probability of conflict. The substantive effect of trade can be expressed in another way. If the annual probability of a dispute were increased from .00048 to .00049 for our 243,000 observations for the nonrelevant dyads, 1950-92, there would be a net increase of two disputes; but there would have been 810 fewer disputes among the contiguous pairs if their rate of conflict dropped from .106 to .025. Joint democracy and the creation of an alliance have important benefits for the nonrelevant dyads, at least when assessed relative to their baseline rate.

**Table 7.4. Annual Probabilities of MID Onsets, 1950–92**

|   |   | PEACEYRS Correction | GEE |
|---|---|:---:|:---:|
| **Contiguous Dyads** | | | |
| 1 | Baseline: Lower trade-to-GDP ratio at median for group; Joint democracy, log capability ratio at means for group; states not allied. | .063 | .106 |
| 2 | Lower trade-to-GDP ratio increased by 1 std. dev.; other variables at baseline values. | .039 | .025 |
| 3 | Both states made fully democratic; other variables at baseline values. | .043 | .089 |
| 4 | States made allied; other variables at baseline values. | .033 | .041 |
| 5 | Log capability ratio increased by 1 std. dev.; other variables at baseline values. | .054 | .093 |
| **Major-Power Dyads** | | | |
| 1 | Baseline: Lower trade-to-GDP ratio at median for group; joint democracy, log capability ratio at means for group; states not allied. | .0061 | .0084 |
| 2 | Lower trade-to-GDP ratio increased by 1 std. dev.; other variables at baseline values. | .0051 | .0055 |
| 3 | Both states made fully democratic; other variables at baseline values. | .0018 | .0025 |
| 4 | States made allied; other variables at baseline values. | .0060 | .0058 |
| 5 | Log capability ratio increased by 1 std. dev.; other variables at baseline values. | .0029 | .0040 |
| **Non-Relevant Dyads** | | | |
| 1 | Baseline: Lower trade-to-GDP ratio at median for group; joint democracy, log capability ratio at means for group; states not allied. | .00028 | .00048 |
| 2 | Lower trade-to-GDP ratio increased by 1 std. dev.; other variables at baseline values. | .00029 | .00049 |
| 3 | Both states made fully democratic; other variables at baseline values. | .00006 | .00016 |
| 4 | States made allied; other variables at baseline values. | .00015 | .00024 |
| 5 | Log capability ratio increased by 1 std. dev.; other variables at baseline values. | .00018 | .00035 |

*Note*: Based on the estimated coefficients in Columns 1 and 2 in Table 7.3.

## The Liberal Peace

We have reassessed the liberal peace using the specification recommended by Barbieri (1998a), which incorporates Beck, Katz, and Tucker's (1998) correction for temporal dependence. We found that interdependence significantly reduced the likelihood of conflict, 1950–92, among contiguous and major-power pairs—the so-called politically relevant dyads, as we had previously reported. Joint democracy has important pacific benefits in this test, too.

We then modified our analyses in four steps to clarify the influence of economically important trade on interstate relations. First, we used the General Estimating Equation and adjusted for autocorrelation as an alternative to Beck et al.'s recommended method. Then we changed the specification of the regression equation, using the lower and higher trade-to-GDP ratios and introducing better controls for geographical distance. Third, we included in our analyses all pairs of states for which missing data regarding trade could reasonably be assumed to indicate that no (or little) bilateral trade occurred. Finally, we considered the consequences of interdependence for three subsets of cases separately: contiguous states, pairs of states that include a major power, and all other dyads.

The results of these additional analyses provide abundant support for the liberal peace. Economic interdependence and joint democracy are generally associated with a reduction in interstate violence, whether measured as the onset of or involvement in a militarized dispute. The evidence is strongest when the largest number of cases is analyzed and when temporal dependence in the dyadic time series is taken into account using GEE. Estimating an expanded equation, in which the effects of the theoretical variables are computed for the contiguous states, major power pairs, and the nonrelevant dyads separately using interactive terms, provides the clearest indication of the promise that expanded economic relations have for international relations. Trade sharply reduces the onset of or involvement in militarized disputes among the contiguous and major-power pairs—the dyads, as Maoz and Russett (1993) correctly perceived, with meaningful levels of conflict to be explained. A one standard deviation increase in the trade-to-GDP ratio lowers the likelihood of conflict for a contiguous dyad by 38 to 76 percent below the baseline rate for this group. These results have important implications for policymaking, as Russett (2003) makes clear with regard to Sino-American relations. Trade has no substantive effect on the likelihood of conflict for the nonrelevant dyads. The slight 2–4 percent increase in their low annual probability of a dispute, less than five chances in 10,000, is probably spurious, as trade acts as an indicator of at least some level of interstate interaction.

Future research needs to clarify the functional form that best expresses the link between interdependence and peaceful interstate relations and to consider further the proper technique for estimating logistic regression analyses with pooled time-series data. More attention also needs to be paid to influences that may condition the effects of interdependence and democracy, as Mansfield and

Pollins (2001) recommend in their recent review of the literature.[11] Mousseau (2000) reports that at least a minimal level of economic development is necessary for democracy to have a substantial pacific benefit; Hegre in this volume finds that commercial ties are a greater force for peace between developed states; and Gelpi and Grieco (2003) argue that democratic institutions increase the conflict-reducing effect of trade. None of these studies presents a radical challenge to the liberal peace because all indicate that democracy and trade have important pacific benefits for the great majority of states. Further investigation of these conditional effects is certainly warranted (Mousseau, Hegre, and Oneal, 2003). However, especially because each of these studies was done without considering the interactive effects proposed by the other two. It is also important in future research to address the complex causal relations linking democracy, interdependence, alliances and other international organizations, and conflict; Russett and Oneal (2001) is only a preliminary effort. It seems clear for now, however, that economically important trade does have important pacific benefits.

# Notes

This is a slightly revised version of Oneal and Russett (1999c). We remain grateful for financial support from the Carnegie Corporation of New York, the Ford Foundation, and the National Science Foundation, and to Soo Yeon Kim for providing us with much of our data. Katherine Barbieri, Neal Beck, Bruno S. Frey, Gerald Schneider, and Richard Tucker provided helpful comments. Our data are available at http://www.yale.edu/unsy/democ.htm or http://bama.ua.edu/~joneal/jpr_data/

1. Green, Kim, and Yoon (2001) offered a more recent methodological critique, suggesting the use of a fixed effects model in testing the liberal peace. This technique is problematic, however, especially for the analysis of dichotomous dependent variables (Beck and Katz, 2001; King, 2001). Even with this method, however, there is strong support for the liberals' theses regarding democracy and interdependence (Oneal and Russett, 2001).

2. By 'change in the level of force' we mean movement along the standard 0-4 COW scale of hostility. These changes do not show up in the COW data because multiyear disputes are coded in all years at the highest level of hostility reached at any time during its duration. We thank Jacob Sullivan for research assistance on this matter.

3. The price level of GDP, which equals the PPP of GDP relative to the U.S. dollar divided by the exchange rate, was used to convert real GDPs in current prices into the exchange-rate based measure of national income (Summers et al., 1995).

4. Adding 10 to each of the DEMOC-AUTOC scores, as Barbieri (1998a) did, means that JNTDEM will equal zero if one state in a dyad has a score of -10, whatever the regime score of the other state. We found little difference in our results when 11 was added to avoid this result, however.

5. The analysis in column 3 of table 7.2 includes 271,262 dyads. Complete data for all variables other than trade are available only for an additional 33,669 dyads.

6. Initially we did include interactive terms involving the higher dependence ratio in the specification. All were statistically insignificant except for the one for the dyads that

are neither contiguous nor involve a major power. This can safely be ignored for the sake of simplicity because, as we show below, trade does not have a substantively important effect on the likelihood of conflict for this group. There was additional evidence in this analysis that asymmetric trade does not increase the onset of disputes among the contiguous dyads because the sign of the coefficient of $DEPEND_H$ was negative, though insignificant.

7. The sign of NOTREL is unexpectedly positive, but this coefficient must be interpreted in conjunction with those of the theoretical variables for this subset of cases. As shown in the next section, the nonrelevant dyads have a very low likelihood of conflict.

8. A common, but erroneous, belief holds that a large sample virtually guarantees a statistically significant finding. A large sample only increases the likelihood that small substantive effects will be detected.

9. A dyad can be both contiguous and a major-power pair. In estimating the probabilities reported in table IV, we have assumed that the contiguous dyad does not include a major power and the major-power dyad is not contiguous.

10. These adjustments are designed to provide comparable effects. A one standard deviation change in the trade-to-GDP or capability ratios is relatively large because of the skewness of both variables. Making both states' DEMOC-AUTOC score equal to +10 (and, thus, JNTDEM 400) and making the states allies is, therefore, reasonable.

11. See their edited volume (Mansfield and Pollins, 2003) for suggestions regarding other timely research strategies.

## CHAPTER 8

# Modeling Dynamics in the Study of Conflict:
# A Comment on Oneal and Russett

*Nathaniel Beck*

Oneal and Russett (hereinafter 'OR') offer some new analyses on the role of trade in reducing conflict. These new analyses are largely a response to the work of Katherine Barbieri, but there is also some discussion about the best way to model dynamics in the dyad-year analysis of international conflict (that is, with a binary dependent variable). While OR are comfortable with the event-history based methods that I espouse, they propose two alternatives that they prefer (and that yield a stronger pacific effect of trade). The alternatives are: (1) modeling dynamics via the Generalized Estimating Equation (GEE) of Liung and Zeger (1986) rather than the use of the temporal splines (PEACEYRS correction or event-history methods) and (2) analyzing all years of a conflict, rather than only the first year of each conflict (dropping subsequent years from the analysis). In this brief comment I consider each of these two alternatives separately, and argue that neither of OR's alternative analyses are appropriate for the dispute data. This is not to say that the GEE is never right for binary dependent variable longitudinal data, since the experience of over a decade is that it is a very useful method for some types of longitudinal data. Nor is this to say that scholars should always consider only the onset of an event, but that for the current enterprise either we should analyze onsets or, as we shall see, use a more complicated model which can adequately treat ongoing events. In the brief conclusion I return to the issue of when one might want to use alternative methods.

I work with the data and specification as given by OR. Given my purposes, it makes most sense to work with OR's preferred data and specification, that is, with missing IMF trade values set to zero. Thus I work with the analyses presented in their tables 7.2 (All Dyads) and 7.3 (ONSET). I do no analysis on dyads with missing trade data (their tables 7.1 and the left columns of table 7.2).

As a consequence I do not contribute to the debate between Barbieri and OR, and the results presented here are orthogonal to the main issue that divides Barbieri and OR, namely, the treatment of dyads with missing IMF trade data. But, however researchers choose to resolve the missing data issue, the issues raised here are also relevant to studying the impact of trade on conflict.

Since this comment focuses on my differences with OR, I should be clear on where we agree. First, I had no difficulty exactly replicating their results. Second, if one accepts the OR position on missing trade data, I agree with them that the results reported in the PEACEYRS correction columns in table 7.2 (All Dyads) and in table 7.3 (ONSET) provide reasonable estimates of the effect of trade (and other variables, though I focus here on trade) on conflict. These results, as interpreted by both OR and myself, indicate that trade has a significant pacific effect on the *onset* of a dispute, both when we consider all dyads (table 7.2) and when we consider only dyads made up of adjacent nonmajor powers (table 7.3).[1] Thus I also agree with the translation of these results into probabilities in their table 7.4, in the column marked PEACEYRS correction.

OR and I differ in that I find that their GEE analyses do not adequately correct for temporal dependence in the data. Their GEE findings on the pacific impact of trade are much stronger than those obtained with the event-history (PEACEYRS) method. Looking only at the onset of conflict, the trade coefficient in the GEE analysis is either twice (All Dyads) or three times (nonmajor power PRDs) that obtained with event-history methods; it is five times greater when analyzing all years of a dispute. Looking at probabilities (table 7.4), the GEE estimates yield a substantive effect of trade on the probability of conflict twice as large as that found using the event-history methods (for nonmajor power PRDs). It makes a great deal of difference whether we estimate the logits using GEE or the event-history methods. In the second section of my response I will show the logit estimates using the event-history PEACEYRS correction are the ones we should believe.

OR also argue that it is better to analyze data including all years of a dispute (INVOLVEMENT)—treating each year of a dispute the same as the first year of a dispute—rather than just analyzing the first year of a dispute (ONSET) while dropping all subsequent years of the dispute from the analysis.[2] OR cite Blainey (1988) in arguing that 'the beginning of wars, the prolonging of wars, the ending of wars and the prolonging or shortening of periods of peace all share the same causal framework. The same explanatory framework and the same factors are vital in understanding each stage in the sequel of war and peace'. Analyses of ONSET and INVOLVEMENT produce similar results using the event-history methods. However, GEE analysis indicates that the pacific impact of trade on INVOLVEMENT is only half that on ONSET. I show why the two analyses differ and also show that it is the analysis of ONSET that is of interest.

The issues raised in this reply go beyond the study of conflict and trade. As we as a discipline become more methodologically sophisticated, and as programs such as Stata make sophisticated analysis easier, we see more attention paid to 'details' such as temporal dependence in binary models. As we see in the current case, the particular method chosen to deal with these details can make a big difference. It is therefore important that we begin to think about which of these technical treatments is appropriate for any particular data set. In some cases this will be GEE; in other cases, it will be the event-history approach. Sometimes we will choose to analyze all years of an event; other times we will limit ourselves to analyzing the onset of an event. But we must look at methods as more than routines in a statistical package, and think about the models that underlay the various methods. For the OR analysis of conflict and trade, we shall see that the event-history analysis of the onset of disputes is the reasonable way to proceed. In the conclusion, I briefly discuss when the alternative methods might be preferred.

## GEE versus Event-History for Conflict Data

The event-history (PEACEYRS) method I prefer has its underpinnings spelled out in Beck, Katz, and Tucker (1998). But the basic idea behind it is extremely simple and intuitive: the key piece of information in dyad-year conflict data sets is the time between conflicts. While we often see event-history modelers examine the time between events, it is uncontroversial that we can model event-history data as a sequence of conditional binary dependent variable (logit or probit) models (Sueyoshi, 1995). I first apply this argument to the conflict data and then provide some analyses.

In my work I have chosen to model the event histories of peace as the discrete-time (logit) version of the most common model used by event-history analysts, that is, the Cox (1972) semi-parametric proportional hazards model. But while this model is flexible, it of course makes assumptions, in particular, proportionality of the hazards (Box-Steffensmeier and Zorn, 2001). Thus it cannot be claimed that the PEACEYRS approach is correct, but it can be claimed that it is derived from a very flexible and very commonly used event-history model. My preferred approach requires no new statistical work, and is very intuitive.

This is not to claim that the event-history approach is always preferred for binary longitudinal data. There are surely many data sets where the time between events (ones) is not the best way to conceive of the information in the data set. The prototypical biostatistical data set of Liang and Zeger, modeling children's illness as a function of mother's stress, is probably not appropriate for the event-history approach, since the number of consecutive periods between illnesses is probably not the ideal way to model these data. But the various theories of the cause of peace and conflict, when studied in a binary dyad-year context, seem to me to focus exactly on why some dyads remain at peace longer than do other dyads.

What of OR's claim that '[it] is no more surprising, then, that the statistical significance of interdependence [trade] declines in the presence of the PEACEYRS variables . . . than that a measure of inflation will be less significant in a regression that also includes a control for the money supply'[?] A more

correct analogy would be 'it is no more surprising that the significance of interdependence declines in the presence of the PEACEYRS variables than that controlling for extensive serial correlation of the errors causes many independent
variables to lose statistical significance in time-series analyses.' Omitting the
PEACEYRS variables is equivalent to assuming that data can be modeled ignoring the temporal dependence in the data. The *exact* analogue to adding the
PEACEYRS variables to the logits is the move from duration-independent (exponential) models to models that allow for duration dependence (including the
Cox proportional hazards model). It is uncontroversial that incorrect use of duration-independent event-history models leads to inefficient estimation and incorrect standard errors in the presence of duration dependence; this is true
whether we incorrectly use the continuous-time exponential model or the discrete-time ordinary logit. Including the PEACEYRS variables in the logit is like
correctly modeling the error term in a time-series analysis and is no more op-
tional with dependent binary time-series cross-section data than with simple
time-series data. Some models may be duration-independent, but it is up to the
researcher to test for that. I return to the tests for the OR model below.

Does the Liang and Zeger GEE solve OR's problem of modeling dependent
data without introducing the troublesome PEACEYRS variables?[3] The GEE was
designed to deal with panel data with a binary (or more complicated) dependent
variable. It is a very general fix-up, and sees the temporal dependence of observations as a nuisance which has its primary impact on the estimated standard
errors. It is almost certainly the case that using the GEE is better than ignoring
the issue of interdependent observations, but no one is claiming that ignoring
interdependence is a good thing.

The first problem with GEE is that it is a bit of a black box. Unlike my preferred event-history approach, it is a bit hard to tell exactly what GEE is doing
to the OR data. For example, OR never even tell us what the estimated correlation between the observations is; in these analyses they view the temporal aspects of the data simply as a nuisance impeding estimation, rather than a feature
of the data that is to be modeled. To put this more technically, GEE is a quasi-
maximum likelihood approach that takes the ordinary logit model for the data
but then 'fixes' the various equations used to estimate the model parameters.
Thus, in using GEE estimates for prediction purposes, one would simply use the
standard logit prediction formulae, ignoring any temporal dependence in the
data. GEE does not provide a model for temporal dependence; such dependence
simply enters the black box used in the maximization.[4]

But even if we feel we understand the GEE, are its assumptions relevant to
the OR data? The GEE assumption (which, I stress, does *not* enter the marginal
model relating disputes to the independent variables) is that the conflict dependent variable (conditional, of course, on the covariates) follows a first-order autoregressive (AR1) pattern, that is, the correlation of $y_{i,t}$ and $y_{i,t-1}$ is $\rho$. The correlation of adjacent observations is identical for all observations (with that
correlation being squared for observations two years apart, and so forth). This
means that if we observe a dyad in conflict last year, the correlation with this

year's conflict is the same as if the dyad were at peace last year; similarly, the correlation between a dyadic observation in year twenty and twenty-one of peace is the same as that between year one and year two of peace (and a year of dispute followed by a year of peace). This is very different from the event-history findings (Beck, Katz, and Tucker, 1998), which show that disputes are more likely to break out after a very short spell of peace than after a long spell of peace.

The simple AR1 pattern is particularly odd for the OR INVOLVEMENT measure. Here, as we shall see, the conditional probability of a dispute following a year of dispute is dramatically higher than the conditional probability of a dispute following a year of peace. But the GEE assumes that the correlation between adjacent temporal observations is the same, regardless of whether the prior observation was one of peace or war. AR1 models may be perfectly appropriate for economic time-series, where good years follow good and bad years follow bad, but such a model seems completely inadequate to capture the dynamics of the INVOLVEMENT data. While this problem, as we shall see, is most severe for the INVOLVEMENT analysis, it is also present, though in less severe form, for the ONSET analysis.

How does one tell which approach to use in practice? To see if the PEACEYRS approach is necessary, one simply adds the PEACEYRS (spline) variables to the specification and then tests the null hypothesis that those variables do not belong in the specification, using an ordinary $\chi^2$ test. Thus one does not need to resort to a purely theoretical argument concerning whether the event-history approach is necessary; the data indicate whether it is. If we do not reject the null hypothesis that the PEACEYRS variables do not belong in the specification, we can then do ordinary logit (or its GEE analogue). I now turn to an analysis of the OR results.

## Data Analysis

To focus attention on the difference between GEE and event-history approaches, I work with the exact specifications used by OR to generate their results in tables 7.2 (All Dyads) and 7.3 (ONSET).[5] For reasons of space, I show results only for the critical OR variable, the ratio of dyadic trade to GDP for the less trade dependent partner (denoted TRADE here).[6]

All the OR results use Huber robust corrected standard errors, which allow for dyadic observations to be correlated in some unspecified way. There is no disagreement that this is a useful approach for this type of data. However, to see what GEE and PEACEYRS are doing to the data, I first present the results of an ordinary logit analysis which ignores dynamics, and then show the effect of each of the 'fixes' with (column marked 'Robust') and without ('ML') the impact of using robust standard errors. Results are in table 8.1 corresponding to the OR analyses of ONSET, first for all dyads and then for PRDs only.

**Table 8.1. The Effect of Trade on Conflict**

| Correction | All Dyads ONSET β | ML | Robust[a] | PRDs Only ONSET β | ML | Robust[a] | INVOLVEMENT β | ML | Robust[a] |
|---|---|---|---|---|---|---|---|---|---|
| None | -118.9 | 18.6 | 45.9 | -108.8 | 17.6 | 52.2 | -168.0 | 20.2 | 73.4 |
| GEE | -115.7 | 21.2 | 42.9 | -105.4 | 20.9 | 48.3 | -169.4 | 20.9 | 73.6 |
| ρ (GEE) | .15 | | | .20 | | | .03 | | |
| PEACEYRS | -51.9 | 14.9 | 23.4 | -28.7 | 13.0 | 22.3 | -32.6 | 14.4 | 28.0 |
| Test of PEACEYRS[b] | 337.2 | | | 328.3 | | | 587.3 | | |

[a]Clustering by dyad
[b]$\chi_4^2$ statistic for $H_0$:*PEACEYRS* not needed in specification, robust variance estimates

The results are easy to summarize: GEE results are essentially identical to ordinary logit results, both in estimated coefficients and standard errors. The slight difference between the GEE results reported by OR and their earlier results (Oneal and Russett, 1997) based on ordinary logit (beyond some changes in the data and slight changes in the specification) arises because the current GEE results also report robust standard errors. Thus the move to Huber robust standard errors changes OR's estimated standard errors by between 100 percent and 300 percent. The GEE analyses change estimated coefficients by under 3 percent and standard errors by less than 15 percent.[7]

GEE by itself has almost no effect on either ordinary logit estimates or standard errors. Thus, to believe the GEE results, one would have to believe that there is trivial temporal dependence in the data. With the data displaying long sequences of peace, such a belief is hard to maintain. Note that GEE estimates the correlation of adjacent observations as between .15 and .20. Such minimal correlation obviously has only a trivial effect on coefficient estimates and standard errors.

The $\chi^2$ tests of whether the PEACEYRS variables belong in the specification indicate that we can clearly reject the null hypothesis that they do not belong; that is, the data show duration dependence. The reported $\chi^2$ statistics are quite large, indicating that the PEACEYRS variables are important predictors of disputes. Thus, analyses that omit the PEACEYRS variables, or otherwise fail to correct for duration dependence, will tend to be overly optimistic.

What about the notion that the PEACEYRS and TRADE variables are highly similar, and so inclusion of both makes it impossible to see the true effect of either? If we simply regress TRADE on the four components of the PEACEYRS spline, the $R^2$ for all dyads is .005 and for PRDs .015. In other words, TRADE is not very well predicted by the temporal spline. The large impact of controlling for duration dependence in the analysis cannot be because TRADE and the PEACEYRS spline are essentially the same variable; they are clearly not.

Since the GEE correction clearly adds nothing to the analysis of the onset of disputes, the OR GEE results are the same as their previously reported ordinary logit analyses with robust standard errors. Robust standard errors are clearly useful, but they do not attempt to model the dynamics of the onset of disputes. The event-history analyses do exactly this. There may be superior alternatives to the event-history methods, but there is no doubt in my mind that the correct results in table 8.1 are those using the PEACEYRS correction (with Huber robust standard errors). These show that trade has a statistically significant pacific impact on the *onset* of disputes for all dyads, but a nonstatistically significant impact for PRDs (with a slightly more positive, and statistically significant, finding for PRDs not involving major powers).

## Should We Analyze All Years of a Dispute?

The greatest difference between the GEE and event-history analyses is when analyzing INVOLVEMENT (for PRDs). The estimated effect of trade is about five times larger for the GEE analysis than for the event-history analysis; the p-value for trade in the GEE analysis is less than .01 while the event-history analysis indicates that the pacific impact of trade is far from statistically significant. It should also be noted that the event-history approach yields roughly the same estimated impact of trade on disputes, whether we analyze all the years of a dispute or only the onset of disputes. Why is the difference between the two methods so much greater for INVOLVEMENT than for ONSET?

To answer this question, we must first look a bit at the structure of the dispute data. Limiting ourselves to PRDs, the data set contains 28,155 dyad-years (observations); of these, 1,396 (5 percent) were years involving disputes. Of these, 896 were new disputes, leaving 500 dispute years as the second or subsequent year of an ongoing dispute. Thus, the probability of a new dispute occurring is just over 3 percent, but if it does occur, the probability of it continuing is over 35 percent.

The OR analysis of INVOLVEMENT does not use the information that the conditional probability of a year of dispute following a previous year of dispute is much higher than the conditional probability of a year of dispute following a year of peace. Their logit specification contains no variables that would allow the probability of a dispute to be vastly higher if it immediately follows a previous year with a dispute. Modelers of binary longitudinal data should never ignore this dynamic information.

But why is the event-history analysis not affected by the move to INVOLVEMENT? The answer is that the PEACEYRS variables allow for the fact that the probability of a dispute immediately following a dispute is much higher than immediately following a year of peace. If we look at the shape of the PEACEYR splines for ONSET and INVOLVEMENT, we see that the decline in the probability of a dispute over time is much steeper for the INVOLVEMENT analysis. This reflects the higher likelihood that a dispute will immediately follow a dispute when analyzing INVOLVEMENT. It is therefore more important to correct for duration dependence when we analyze all years of a dispute. While, as we shall see, it is preferable to analyze ONSET, the event-history method is adequate to guard against a serious mis-estimate if we study INVOLVEMENT, at least for this data set.

Looking at the right hand columns of table 8.1, we see that the GEE approach does nothing to correct for the difference in the conditional probability of dispute depending on whether it follows a dispute or a year of peace. The estimated correlation from the GEE analysis for INVOLVEMENT is therefore a tiny .03; this masks the high correlation between observations in sequences of peace and sequences of disputes. With such a minuscule serial correlation, the GEE results are almost identical to the ordinary logit results; as in the analysis of ONSET, the only difference between the OR results reported in their table 7.3 and their previously reported results have to do with the use of Huber robust standard errors.[8]

Another way to see the issue is to note that analysts of binary time-series-cross-section data frequently attempt to model the transition process—they model P(yi,t=1|yi,t-1=0) and then P(yi,t=1|yi,t-1=1) (Amemiya, 1985; Ware, Lipsitz, and Speizer, 1988). These analysts invariably allow the parameters of the process governing transitions from zero to be different from those governing the transitions from one (perhaps testing for the equality of those coefficients). Thus, they attempt to model both the process of transition from peace to dispute and the process that keeps dyads disputing given they are already disputing.[9] But, contra Blainey, the parameters (and even the independent variables) in these two processes are allowed to differ. While it would be nice to have a unified theory of the beginning and ending of disputes, would anyone maintain a priori that the two processes must be identical? But this is what OR maintain in their model of INVOLVEMENT.

Transition analysts extend the ordinary logit model used by OR to allow for an interaction between the model parameters and whether the previous year was one of peace or dispute. As shown in Beck et al. (2001), this is equivalent to estimating two separate logits, one for observations following a year of peace, the other for observations following a year of dispute. Note that the logit conditioning on a prior year of peace is essentially the same as the logit analysis for ONSET, assuming no duration dependence (that is, it does not contain the PEACEYRS variables).[10] The second logit is essentially the duration independent model for lengths of conflict.[11] Since the event-history approach is more general, I prefer it, but it is of interest to see how a standard transition model estimates the parameters of the OR logit.

## Data Analysis

The transition model is estimated by creating a dummy variable that equals 1 whenever a dyad experienced a dispute in the previous year. Since we are modeling INVOLVEMENT, there is no distinction made between second years of ongoing disputes and two disputes which occur in consecutive years. The transition model is estimated with ordinary logit but includes both the dummy variable marking the prior dispute status of the dyad and all interactions between the substantive variables and that dummy variable. The first observation for each dyad is dropped from the analysis. A comparison of the OR logit estimates for INVOLVEMENT for all PRDs and the transition model estimates is in table 8.2.[12]

**Table 8.2. Logit and Transition Models of Involvement: PRDs**

| | | | Transition | | | |
| | Logit | | LAGGED PEACE | | LAGGED DISPUTE | |
| Variable[a] | β | SE[b] | β | SE[b] | β | SE[b] |
|---|---|---|---|---|---|---|
| TRADE | -168.00 | 73.43 | -50.18 | 28.13 | -195.84 | 106.61 |
| DEMOCRACY | -.0027 | .0007 | -.0020 | .0006 | -.0013 | .0009 |
| CONTIGUITY | 1.31 | .26 | 1.71 | .25 | -.73 | .30 |
| DISTANCE | -.45 | .09 | -.34 | .08 | -.21 | .19 |
| MAJOR POWER | .91 | .27 | .41 | .24 | .42 | .29 |
| ALLIES | -.99 | .20 | -.57 | .18 | -.58 | .22 |
| CAPABILITY | -.30 | .06 | -.09 | .05 | -.25 | .08 |
| Constant | .51 | .69 | -2.00 | .59 | 3.09 | .78 |

[a]All variables as in OR, table 7.3.
[b]All standard errors are Huber robust, clustering on the dyad.

We note a number of differences between the transition from peace to disputes and the continuation of disputes: contiguity enhances the chance of a dispute occurring but actually shortens the length of a dispute once it occurs, whereas capability disparity has little effect on the outbreak of disputes but does seem to shorten those that do break out. Given the issues in this comment, however, I focus on the constant term and the coefficient on TRADE. The very different constant terms in the models for transitions from peace and from prior disputes shows what we have seen before: there is a much higher probability of a dispute in a year following a dispute than in a year following a year of peace. This is nothing more than a restatement of the conditional probabilities noted at the beginning of this section.

The large pacific impact of trade in the OR analysis of INVOLVEMENT is a combination of the large effect of trade in shortening the length of a dispute once it breaks out and a much smaller impact of trade in inhibiting disputes. It is probably not surprising that dyads that continue to maintain high trade do not engage in long disputes.

But our interest here is on whether trade inhibits disputes. The transition model yields more positive findings, and statistically significant ones, on the pacific impact of trade than does the event-history analysis. This is because the transition model only allows for the probability of a dispute to be different in the first year of a spell of peace, with no duration dependence in subsequent years.[13] But even if we take the transition model findings as accurate, they are much closer to the event-history findings than they are to the ordinary logit (and GEE) findings. The various event-history analyses I have presented yield a coefficient on TRADE which varies from about -30 to -50, with corresponding t-ratios of between about 1.3 and 2.2; contrast this to the estimated impact of TRADE on INVOLVEMENT using ordinary logit (or GEE) of -168 (with a t-ratio of 2.3). It is clearly the very high estimate obtained by the ordinary logit analysis of INVOLVEMENT that is out of line.

## Conclusion

I have no problem with any of the OR analyses using the event-history (*PEACEYRS*) method. These indicate that trade has a statistically significant pacific impact if we look at all dyads, and a similar-sized effect (either marginally statistically significant or insignificant) if we look only at PRDs or subsets of PRDs (whether all dispute years or only the onset of disputes). The substantive pacific impact of trade is as OR compute it using the event-history methods.

But the GEE results, which show a much stronger pacific impact of trade, are not correct. The GEE model of the interdependence of the data is not consistent with the temporal interdependence manifested in the conflict dyad-year data. In essence, the GEE results are identical to the ordinary logit results that ignore temporal dependence. If one accepts the argument made in Beck, Katz, and Tucker (1998) that the original findings of Oneal and Russett (1997)—that trade has pacific effects—are flawed, then the GEE results reported here by OR must be equally flawed. The problem with GEE (or other nonevent-history methods) is particularly severe for analyses that include all years of a conflict (INVOLVEMENT), since the temporal dependence in that dependent variable is much greater than in the ONSET variable. It is hard to imagine a situation where one would want to model the duration of disputes as being identical to the duration of years of peace, and so it is hard to imagine a situation where it would be appropriate to analyze a data set containing all years of ongoing conflicts.

This does not mean that GEE is never useful, nor that the event-history method preferred here is always right. There will clearly be cases where the GEE approach is preferred to the event-history method. Specifically, we would prefer GEE in data that mixes short spells of zeros and ones (cooperation and conflict) so that the event-history approach, that analyzes the lengths of these spells, becomes less interesting. The various biomedical panels where GEE has been used are all of this type. For such data, either GEE or the transition model would be appropriate. But the OR conflict data is not of this type. Thus their GEE analyses, either of the onset of conflict or all years of conflict, do not produce estimates that we should accept. If we accept the OR specification and decisions about how to treat missing trade data, then we can believe their event-history findings that trade has a pacific impact, although an impact more modest than those found by the alternative methods they prefer.

The event-history methods do not solve all, or even most, of the statistical problems in the dyad-year conflict data. There are myriad issues that remain, with the most important being either spatial dependence or the interrelationship of dyads that share a common partner. While work is being done in this area (Gleditsch and Ward, 2000), clearly much remains to be done on these issues. But any future methodological advances also must allow for the modeling of temporal dependence. One very nice feature of the discrete-time event-history approach is that it should combine easily with methods that treat other problems. It is, of course, high time to start analyzing those other problems.

# Notes

I wish to thank the always collegial John Oneal and Bruce Russett for providing their data, and, in particular, John Oneal for answering all my queries and meeting all my requests. Much of the thinking in this chapter reflects an ongoing dialogue with Simon Jackman and Chris Zorn who provided very helpful comments on GEE. The editors of this volume have also been of great help, each in their own way. A complete file of my statistical results is available on my web site at http://weber.ucsd.edu/~nbeck. The data used were kindly made available by John Oneal and may be obtained from http://www.yale.edu/unsy/democ/democ1.htm.

1. OR report P < .07 on the latter finding, but the correct one-tailed test would allow for rejection of the null that trade does decrease the probability of a dispute with P < .04. In some analyses, slight modifications change coefficients and standard errors enough so that some p-values move across the conventional .05 threshold. Clearly it cannot matter much whether P=.06 or .04, and so we should not worry much about whether results are marginally statistically significant or insignificant.

2. In the MID coding, it is possible for a new dispute, that is a dispute with a new id code, to immediately follow another dispute. Both OR and I would keep both these years of dispute in the analysis. Thus, of the 1,078 onsets of disputes in the full data set, 283 were new disputes that immediately followed a previous dispute, and are coded as ONSET=1. Where we differ is when disputes span more than one year. The analysis of ONSET simply drops all the latter years of the dispute from the analysis while INVOLVEMENT retains them, treating the latter years as if they were identical to years with a new dispute following immediately after a previous one.

3. See Zorn (2001) for a good discussion of GEE relevant to political science. It should be stressed that GEE allows for a variety of other interrelationships beyond the autoregressive processes used by OR; the discussion here is limited to the first-order autoregressive analyses used by OR. It should also be noted that there are a variety of extensions to GEE which may improve matters; these are discussed by Zorn.

4. In this it is a bit like the Huber robust standard errors that both OR and I use here. These also take the model for the probability of a conflict as the logit model, and then fix the standard errors. The Huber correction does not change the estimated model coefficients at all; the GEE correction does. But neither method changes the underlying logit model that P(Y=1)=logit($\beta$). Since I use the Huber robust errors, I obviously cannot claim that it is never right to use nonmodel-based methods. But they are never the best approach.

5. The analyses based on table III are limited to PRDs only, rather than following OR's approach of analyzing all dyads with a full interaction model that breaks them down into three subsets: nonmajor power contiguous dyads, major power dyads and non-relevant dyads. Since OR find no statistically significant difference between major power and contiguous dyads (the two subtypes of PRDs), and no effect of trade in non-PRDs,

there is little loss in simply analyzing all PRDs, which is more conventional. In any event, my results for PRDs are very similar to their results. But there are small differences in the analyses I present and those of OR because of my decision not to distinguish PRDs involving a major power from those involving contiguous nonmajor powers, and my analyzing only the PRD subset (with a dummy variable for whether the PRD contains a major power). I stress the differences are slight and in no way are part of the argument about the differences between us. The slight change in methods does, however, sometimes cause small (and uninteresting) movements across the P=.05 conventional value. Similarly, to keep the big issues clear, I do not consider a variety of alternative combinations of methods. In particular, if we combine GEE, robust errors, and event-history, we get results that are more favorable to the liberal peace argument, though they are much closer to the event-history results than the GEE results of OR. This is another argument for focusing on the general size of coefficients rather than on whether some particular coefficient happens to be significant at some arbitrary level.

6. When comparable, my results are identical to those provided by OR.

7. One can also view the differences between the ML and Huber standard errors as a test of specification. If the model estimated is correct, the Huber and ML standard errors should be similar (since the Huber 'sandwich' would then reduce to the ML variance-covariance estimator). Looking only at PRDs and ONSET, we see that ordinary logit is heavily misspecified, with the Huber standard errors being three times larger than their ML counterparts. The GEE model is also misspecified, with the Huber errors being two and a half times larger than their ML counterparts. While the event-history model is still misspecified, it does much better than either ordinary logit or GEE, with the Huber standard errors being only 50 percent larger than their ML counterparts. Thus neither ordinary logit nor GEE accounts for the dyadic dependence in the data; the event-history analysis does not fully account for this dependence, but does a much better job than the other two estimators. The data therefore indicate that neither the ordinary logit nor the GEE come close to modeling adequately the interdependence in the observations for any given dyad.

8. To see that the GEE estimate of the correlation of the observations is highly suspect, note that the standard test for whether the errors in a probit analysis of the INVOLVEMENT specification is based on generalized residuals (Beck, Epstein, Jackman, and O'Halloran, 2001; Poirier and Ruud, 1988). (Probit is used here because it has much simpler mathematical properties than does logit. As is usual, probit and logit are substantively similar.) The serial correlation of those generalized residuals is .58 (for the same specification as the ordinary logit in table 8.2), yielding a P value for the test of the null hypothesis of serially uncorrelated errors as close to zero as one could possibly imagine. While serial correlation of the errors is not the same as correlation of the dependent variable, the two are highly related by construction. This analysis indicates that the GEE estimate of $\rho$=.03 is highly implausible at best.

9. See Jackman (2000) for an application of the transition model to the dispute data.

10. The two approaches are not identical, in that the transition model drops the first year a dyad is observed, since we do not know whether the first year followed a year of dispute or a year of peace. The first year in the logit conditioning of prior peace is the second year of a spell of peace, while the logit conditioning on a prior year of dispute yields the probability of peace in the first year of a spell of peace. Thus the transition model allows for the probability of a dispute to vary depending on whether it is the first year of a spell of peace or any subsequent year, but does not allow the probability of a dispute to vary otherwise; the event-history approach allows for a much more flexible

modeling of the effect of time, and is thus more general than the transition model. Also note that the transition model can be generalized by allowing for different independent variables to enter the two different transition equations, though I do not pursue that here.

11. I do not study duration dependence in lengths of spells of conflict because we have too few of these spells and they are generally too short to allow for meaningful analysis. In other datasets we might meaningfully model lengths of sequences of zeros and ones; these two will initially be analyzed separately, though one could then test for equality of coefficients between the two analyses.

12. For convenience, the table displays the transition coefficients separately for years following peace (LAGGED PEACE), and years following disputes (LAGGED DISPUTE). As noted, it is irrelevant whether these results are obtained from two separate logits or one logit with interactive terms. The former facilitates interpretation while the latter allows for easier hypothesis tests. The two methods yield *identical* results and the results in table 8.2 are identical to those we would observe from the full interaction model. In symbols, if LAGDISP is the lagged dispute dummy, the interactive model estimates a logit of disputes on the independent variables, x, LAGDISP and their product. In table 8.2, the coefficients in the 'Lagged Peace' column are the coefficients on the relevant x (and the constant term), and the coefficients in the 'Lagged Dispute' column are the sum of the coefficients on the relevant x and its interaction with LAGDISP. The constant term in the latter column is just the sum of the constant term in the 'Lagged Peace' column and the coefficient on LAGDISP. It is, of course, easiest to get standard errors on the sum of two coefficients by estimating two separate logits depending on whether LAGDISP is zero or one. The full algebra may be found in the various cited references.

13. If we append the PEACEYRS variables to the transition model, the coefficient on *TRADE* drops to -20 with a robust standard error of 17, which are even weaker than those estimated by the straight event-history methods.

# CHAPTER 9

# Modeling Conflict While Studying Dynamics: A Response to Nathaniel Beck

*John R. Oneal and Bruce Russett*

Our exchange with Neal Beck and his colleagues (Oneal and Russett, 1997; Beck, Katz, and Tucker, 1998; Oneal and Russett, 1999c), which culminates in this volume, has been unusually productive. There has been progress in assessing the influence of economic interdependence on interstate relations and in addressing methodological problems associated with the analysis of binary dependent variables. Because we are international relations scholars, not statisticians, we are primarily interested in the substantive implications of our dialogue. Consequently, we first present in this response new tests of liberal theory using data that have only recently become available. These confirm the pacific benefits of economic interdependence and democracy, whether Beck's method, the General Estimating Equation (GEE), or an alternative correction for temporal dependence is used. *Our basic finding that trade reduces conflict is thus no longer at issue between us and Beck.* In the process of testing liberal theory, we have tried to become informed consumers of others' statistical expertise, so we conclude by sharing some thoughts about addressing dependence in logistic analyses of pooled time series.

## Confirming the Liberal Peace

In this section, we report several new tests of the pacific benefits of economic interdependence for the period 1886–1992. The opportunity for these analyses is presented by Kristian Gleditsch's (2002a) recent compilation of data regarding states' bilateral trade and their gross domestic products (GDPs), 1950–92. Gleditsch has supplemented the IMF's (1997) *Direction of Trade* statistics and

179

the GDP data in the Penn World Tables (Summers et al., 1995) with information from additional sources. There are two particularly important advantages to using Gleditsch's data. First, it includes observations from within the Soviet bloc during the Cold War—cases absent from the IMF data. Second, by consulting additional sources, Gleditsch has been able to find values for most of the other missing data and, where values are still unknown, there is greater reason to believe that no trade existed. Thus, the debate regarding missing values of trade in the *Direction of Trade* is, for practical purposes, eliminated.[1]

For the pre–World War II period, we use the economic data we have collected, which have been discussed in detail elsewhere (Oneal and Russett, 1999b; Russett and Oneal, 2001). The primary sources of our early trade data are *The Statesman's Yearbook* (e.g., Epstein, 1913) and the League of Nations (various years), which were carefully compared to Katherine Barbieri's (1998b) bilateral trade data. Maddison (1995) provides estimates of per capita GDPs for a large number of countries, which permit us to estimate GDPs for many other countries as well. With the publication of Gleditsch's economic data for the post–World War II period and our assembly of the data for the pre–World War I and interwar periods, we believe that the state-of-the-art dataset on interstate commercial relations, 1885–1992, is at hand.

In addition to Gleditsch's new data regarding trade-related interdependence, we also use Zeev Maoz's (1999) revised data on militarized interstate disputes (MIDs). Maoz has shown that past efforts to produce dyadic variables from the Correlates of War (COW) project's state-level MIDs file (Jones, Bremer, and Singer, 1996) are problematic to a degree. For example, individual states on one side of a multilateral contest may never have threatened, displayed, or used force against particular states on the opposing side. Maoz has corrected this problem and others to produce more accurate data for dyadic analyses. Following Beck's suggestion in chapter 8, we analyze the onset of militarized disputes, rather than dispute involvement; but we return to this issue when discussing our results.

There is little need to discuss our other variables. Their definitions and the sources of our information have been explained in our earlier contribution to this volume. We adopt the specification, based on the weak-link assumption, from several recent publications (e.g., Oneal and Russett, 1999b, Russett and Oneal, 2001). We postulate that the likelihood of the onset of a militarized dispute is a function of the lower democracy score and the lower bilateral trade-to-GDP ratio ($DEPEND_L$) in a dyad; the logged ratio of the two states' military capabilities; indicators of whether the pair is allied, whether they are contiguous, and whether either is a major power; and the logarithm of the distance separating them. Our model has evolved from that of Bremer (1992) and Maoz and Russett (1993). Bennett and Stam (2000); Hegre (2000); Mousseau (2000); Gartzke, Li, and Boehmer (2001); Zeng and King (2001); Heagerty, Ward, and Gleditsch (2002) among others have used similar specifications.

In table 9.1 we present the results of several estimations for the politically relevant dyads, 1886–1992, using different corrections for dependence in the time series. We focus on this subset of cases for two reasons. First, Beck concurs that interdependence significantly reduces conflict when all dyads are analyzed; but it is marginally insignificant when he limits his analysis to the politically relevant dyads, pairs that are either contiguous or include a major power. This set of cases, therefore, warrants further analysis. Beck acknowledges, however, that interdependence is significantly associated with peace for the subset of contiguous dyads. Second, the politically relevant dyads are the states that suffer an appreciable risk of interstate conflict.[2] Indeed, as we show in chapter 7 and Beck confirms, the benefit of trade is greatest for those states most prone to conflict—the contiguous pairs. We follow Beck's example by confining our discussion to the lower trade-to-GDP ratio (DEPEND$_L$); but in all the tests, the lower democracy score is very significant and substantively important. We report in table 9.1 the reduction in the probability of the onset of a dispute from a one standard-deviation increase in interdependence, as a means of making its practical importance apparent. As before, this evaluation is made by reference to a 'typical' dyad. For comparison, we present in the last column the reduction in risk associated with the two states becoming allied.

**Table 9.1. The Effect of Trade/GDP (DEPEND$_L$) on the Onset of a Militarized Interstate Dispute, 1886–1992**

Politically relevant dyads

| Estimator | β | SE$_β$ | p* | Reduction in risk (DEPEND$_L$) (%) | Reduction in risk (Allies) (%) |
|---|---|---|---|---|---|
| Logistic regression | -48.9 | 14.4 | .001 | -38 | -45 |
| PEACEYRS | -27.7 | 8.9 | .001 | -24 | -20 |
| GEE | -43.7 | 13.2 | .001 | -34 | -44 |
| WSEV | -48.9 | 15.8 | .001 | -38 | -45 |
| Range | | | | 24–38 | 20–45 |

*One-tailed tests.
n=43,492–43,567

The first row gives the results of a logistic regression analysis. In this and all our other tests we report robust standard errors. These allow for unspecified correlation within the dyadic time series. The estimated coefficient of the trade variable is significant at the .001 level (one-tailed test). The reduction in the probability of conflict from increasing the economic importance of trade is 38 percent, which is a little less than that associated with making the members of the dyad allies (45 percent). With Beck, Katz, and Tucker's (1998) correction for duration dependence (PEACEYRS), the coefficient of DEPEND$_L$ is again significant at the .001 level, as seen in the second row.[3] The reduction in the probability of conflict is 24 percent, which is greater than the 20 percent drop if the states become allies.

In light of the attention their work has received, it is important to note that the lower trade-to-GDP ratio is significant (p < .004) even if our analysis is limited to 1950–85, as in Oneal and Russett (1997) and Beck, Katz, and Tucker

(1998); and its coefficient is large ($\beta$ = 40.3, $SE_\beta$ = 15.3). Including the approximately 5,500 additional cases contained in Gleditsch (2002a), drawn primarily from within the Soviet bloc, improves the results; but refinements to the specification (especially controlling for the distance separating states) and improvements in the quality of the data (particularly in the measure of conflict) are also important. In short, economic interdependence reduced interstate conflict during the Cold War, in both the West and the East and elsewhere. Evidence from the pre–World War II years lends additional support to liberal theory.

In the third row, we report the results of an analysis using GEE with a correction for a first-order autoregressive process. As in chapter 7, the effect is nearly equal to the results of a logistic regression with robust standard errors. There is a 34 percent reduction in risk (p < .001) with GEE; making the pair of states allies reduces the probability of the onset of a dispute by 44 percent.[4]

This much is clear from the results presented thus far: The pacific benefit of economic interdependence is statistically significant and substantively important in all analyses, whether dependence in the time series is corrected using Beck's preferred method or an alternative.

In his reply, Beck draws attention to the similarity of the results using logistic regression and GEE, concluding that this is an indictment of GEE. In our analyses, too, the reduction in risk in the GEE analysis (-34 percent) is closer to that derived from logistic regression (-38 percent) than to the results using his suggested correction for temporal dependence (-24 percent). His reasoning is this: Even with robust standard errors, logistic regression does not explicitly control for temporal dependence; the results of using GEE are similar to those of logistic analysis; therefore, GEE must not adequately account for temporal dependence. But is it obvious that the coefficient of DEPEND$_L$ produced by logistic analysis is too large?

Zorn (2001) shows that GEE offers the potential for unbiased estimates of the coefficients and, with robust standard errors, yields estimates of their variances that are consistent even if the correlation matrix is misspecified. If we were working with a continuous dependent variable and were concerned about temporal dependence, the standard practice would be to adjust the data for autocorrelation using information contained in the residuals from a first-stage estimation. This is possible because the estimated coefficients in the first stage are unbiased and consistent even if autocorrelation is present. Though the estimation is inefficient, the primary concern when data are autocorrelated is the consistency or reliability of an effect, as indicated by the size of the standard error relative to the estimated coefficient, not the magnitude of the coefficient itself.

Heagerty, Ward, and Gleditsch (2002) recently proposed a correction for spatial correlations across the pooled time series that also addresses the problem of temporal dependence. It does so in a manner consistent with the view that it is the standard error, not the coefficient, which is in doubt. Heagerty et al. note that the experiences of dyads at a single point in time are not independent, in part due to the contagion of interstate conflict. Failing to take this into account confounds standard estimators of variance. As a remedy, they propose the Window Subsampling Empirical Variance (WSEV) estimator, where estimations of variance drawn from different subsamples of the data through time are averaged; this produces consistent estimates of the variances of the regression coefficients. The essence of the method is straightforward. Instead of using dyads to define the clusters for producing robust standard errors, the WSEV estimator uses slices of time. When these slices include more than one year, adjustment is also being made for autocorrelation. Thus, the WSEV estimator addresses both spatial and temporal dimensions of dependence among the dyad-year observations.[5]

We broke our analysis of disputes, 1886–1992, into five periods of historical significance: 1886–1903, 1904–14, 1920–39, 1951–73, and 1974–92.[6] The four breakpoints in time correspond to the formation of the Entente Cordiale between France and Great Britain in 1904, the outbreak of World War I, the interwar years, the Cold War period, and the era of détente between the United States and the USSR. Thus, we are assuming that the geographical pattern of disputes was similar within each of these periods. By estimating robust standard errors using these multiyear clusters, we are allowing for temporal as well as spatial dependence in the data.

The results of reestimating the regression model using Heagerty et al.'s estimator are presented in the fourth row of table 9.1. The estimated coefficient is the same as in row 1. Whether we cluster our observations by dyad, as is normally done in generating robust standard errors, or by historical period, the coefficient (-48.9) is the same. Both methods begin with the premise that this estimate is unbiased. Thus, the effect of interdependence on the probability of a militarized dispute is also the same: a reduction in risk of 38 percent. With the WSEV estimator, the estimated coefficient is again significant at the .001 level.[7]

As noted in chapter 7, we have two principal concerns about Beck, Katz, and Tucker's (1998) method. First, it does not give primacy to the theoretically derived model. Rather, it introduces the PEACEYRS splines into the specification of the regression equation as coequals of the theoretical terms. As Beck stresses in his reply, his correction explicitly models the temporal dynamics; but no theoretical justification for this modeling is presented. Second, to the extent that the theoretical variables are correlated with the years of peace, these terms apportion to themselves some of the variance in the dependent variable that would have been explained by the theoretical terms if the splines had been omitted. In his reply, Beck notes that $DEPEND_L$ is not well predicted by the PEACEYRS splines. He concludes that the impact of controlling for duration dependence cannot be because the two variables are essentially the same. But, of course, the introduction of the splines into the model does account for the reduction in the magnitude of the coefficient and the statistical significance of the trade-to-GDP ratio; nothing else has changed.[8] As Beck and Tucker (1996) acknowledged at an early stage, their solution for duration dependence requires that the 'effects of time and the covariates are separable' (p. 11), a cautionary note not included in their 1998 article with Katz. Separating the effects of time and the covariates is often difficult in the social sciences.[9]

Based on table 9.1, there can be little doubt that economically important commerce is associated with more peaceful interstate relations. In the four estimations reported there, the level of statistical significance is never less than .001. More importantly, the estimated reduction in the likelihood of a militarized dispute ranges from 24 percent to 38 percent. This can be compared to the benefit of the two states becoming allied (33–45 percent). The effect of an alliance is less robust temporally (Russett and Oneal, 2001: 195), however, and may be positively dangerous when a major power is involved (Oneal and Russett, 1997).

## Fatal Disputes and the Benefits of Interdependence

Despite the strong results reported thus far, these analyses understate the case for the liberal peace. Focusing attention on particularly serious disputes—those involving fatalities among the combatants—makes the pacific benefit of interdependence even more apparent. Table 9.2 presents the results of using the same estimators in analyses of the onset of fatal disputes, conflicts that resulted in the death of at least one combatant. Many disputes are in actuality of limited severity and pose little real danger to peace. For example, on several occasions Peru seized American fishing boats that entered the territorial waters it claimed. This is coded by the COW project as an actual use of force (four on a 5-point scale), though there was little risk of armed conflict between the two countries.

**Table 9.2. The Effect of Trade/GDP (DEPEND$_L$) on the Onset of a Fatal Militarized Interstate Dispute, 1886–1992**

Politically relevant dyads

| Estimator | β | SE$_β$ | p* | Reduction in risk (DEPEND$_L$) (%) | Reduction in risk (Allies) (%) |
|---|---|---|---|---|---|
| Logistic regression | -123 | 39 | .001 | -71 | -56 |
| PEACEYRS | -86 | 25 | .001 | -58 | -34 |
| GEE | -115 | 37 | .001 | -68 | -56 |
| WSEV | -123 | 48 | .005 | -71 | -56 |
| Range | | | | 58–71 | 34–56 |

*One-tailed tests.
n=43,359–43,433

Limiting the analysis to fatal disputes not only focuses attention on particularly serious cases, it also reduces the bias in the reporting of conflict at the low end of the spectrum. The use of even minimal force in Europe, for example, rifle fire across an international boundary, is unlikely to go unreported in the Western media from which the COW data are primarily gleaned; such incidents in many parts of Africa are apt routinely to go unnoticed. An examination of fatal disputes should reduce the regional disparity in the media's attentiveness because disputes with fatalities are more newsworthy. As in our analyses of the onset of all MIDs, we coded our fatal disputes variable 1 in the first year that a dyad was involved in a dispute with at least one military death; it equals zero otherwise.

The results reported in table 9.2 show the dramatic effect that economically important trade has on the likelihood that a dyad will experience a fatal dispute. Using Beck's PEACEYRS correction, interdependent states are 58 percent less likely than the typical pair of states to be involved in a conflict with military fatalities. This is only a little less than the 68 percent reduction in risk if GEE is used or the improvement of 71 percent with WSEV. In each of the four analyses, a high level of commerce reduces the likelihood of a dispute more than making the pair of states allies; and the coefficient of the trade-to-GDP ratio is significant at least at the .005 level in all cases.

In the past, we have argued that analyzing all years of a dispute is a way to weight serious conflicts more heavily. As Beck et al. (1998) noted, and Beck confirms in his reply in this volume, interdependent states have conflicts of shorter duration than states not linked by economically important trade. This finding, widely ignored, is important because long conflicts are most apt to involve the loss of life. Analyzing the onset of fatal disputes is a better way of focusing attention on serious disputes for the reasons Beck has emphasized; but the results reported in table 9.2 show clearly that our earlier publications—including those based on dispute involvement, rather than onset—have not exaggerated the pacific benefit of interdependence. Indeed, all the reductions in risk reported in table 9.2, including that using the PEACEYRS correction, are greater than any we have previously reported.[10]

## Advantages and Disadvantages of PEACEYRS

We began this piece by declaring our *bona fides*: we are students of international relations, not methodologists. Still, our experience as consumers of the statistical expertise of others may have given us some insight into the advantages and disadvantages of various means for correcting for dependence in the time series. We have stated our reservations about Beck's PEACEYRS correction, but we are really methodological pluralists. Good theory must pass a variety of statistical tests employing different estimators, specifications of the regression model, definitions of variables, and samples of cases. The more tests passed, the greater our confidence in the hypothesis being tested. Beck has proposed a valuable method for analyzing binary data. It is intuitively appealing and easy to implement computationally. The support for the importance of interdependence that has been generated using the PEACEYRS correction in both our contributions to this volume and elsewhere is important evidence for the liberal peace.[11] We have shown here that this evidence is even stronger if the best, most complete data on trade and disputes are used, especially if attention is focused on conflicts involving fatalities among the combatants.

Beck's correction for temporal dependence should be used with care, however. As he notes in his reply, 'the information in the dyad year conflict data sets is exactly the time between conflicts' (p. 3). He then proposes to test theoretical explanations of this information while controlling for the time elapsed since the last dispute. Obviously what is being explained is closely related to the correction he has proposed. The estimated influences of the theoretical terms will be reduced if the time since the last conflict is correlated with their current values. If a dyad has a history of economically important trade, for example, each subsequent year of peace counts for less and less in support of the liberal thesis. Controlling for duration dependence discounts the experience of peaceful, interdependent states through time, even though the theory predicts that high levels of trade, investment, and so forth lead to protracted periods of peace.

Certainly, the time elapsed since the last conflict is a good predictor of the prospects for continued peace; but nothing is explained by noting that the hazard of conflict changes over time, as Beck et al. (1998) acknowledge. Why does a history of peaceful relations reduce the present likelihood of conflict? Or, alternatively stated, why does a dispute make another more likely in the near term? We do not know of anyone who has offered an explanation; and as Bennett (1999) cautions, our choice of methods should be dictated by theory. Neither 'bureaucratic inertia' nor 'a loss of control by decision makers over events' is a satisfying response when all our theories begin with the assumption that national leaders are rational actors. If sunk costs account for the phenomenon, what is their nature and how can they be measured directly?

Beck often calls his technique a correction for temporal dependence, but it is clearly not an adjustment for autoregression. The PEACEYRS splines are introduced directly into the model; no use is made of information about correlations in the errors of prediction over time.[12] Beck's approach is better thought of as a correction for duration dependence. It is an effort to address the problem of endogeneity, not to resolve autocorrelation. This is its real contribution. It provides a means to test our theories while controlling in a simple fashion for the influence of past conflict on current events. But it is possible that the explanatory variables in the model have long-term effects, too: the current likelihood of conflict may be a function of a dyad's history of economic ties as well as its history of militarized disputes. Controlling for the years of peace alone does not allow for this possibility. Nor does Beck's correction provide a rich account of the influence of past conflict. The effect of a recent dispute on current relations is apt to be different depending on whether it was an isolated incident or part of an enduring rivalry. Consequently, controlling for the years of peace provides a first approximation in addressing the problem of endogeneity and uncovering causal relations; but it does not allow for the possibility that the explanatory variables, too, will have long-term effects. Vector-autoregression and distributed-lags models are superior in both regards, at least when, as in the current case, there is an abundance of observations (Oneal, 2003; Oneal, Russett, and Berbaum, 2003).

# Conclusion

The analyses we report here confirm that economically important trade has statistically significant and substantively important pacific benefits. Democracy, too, is a potent force for peace in the analyses we conducted. Using the most complete information to measure interdependence (Gleditsch, 2002a; Russett and Oneal, 2001) and the best data on militarized disputes (Maoz, 1999) provides even stronger evidence for the liberal peace than we have reported before. Economically important trade is closely associated with peace whatever method is used to take into account temporal dependence in the time series. More importantly, trade's effect on the risk of interstate conflict is substantial, especially for the most serious disputes—those involving fatalities. A high level of interdependence reduces the likelihood of a fatal dispute by 58 percent if we control for the years of peace; the estimate is 68 percent with the General Estimating Equation (AR1). These results show clearly that we have not oversold the pacific virtues of interdependence in previous publications. The importance of interdependence is also evident in comparison to the restraining effect of an alliance. Moreover, commercial ties are a more reliable force for peace than is a military pact, especially for small states (Oneal and Russett, 1997; Russett and Oneal, 2001: 195).

National leaders sometimes make decisions that affect the lives of millions of people. Political scientists should provide them with the best scientific evidence possible; but we can also remind them that, in choosing wisely, they should minimize the joint danger of accepting a false hypothesis and of rejecting a true one. In making this determination, it is important that policymakers consider the costs of these type I and type II errors. Often decisions involve unhappy trade-offs, but there is abundant evidence that economic openness and interdependence increase prosperity because they lead to specialization according to comparative advantage and economies of scale. Current social-scientific research confirms the promise of liberalism: greater prosperity *and* more years of peace.

# Notes

We gratefully acknowledge the helpful comments of Margit Bussmann, Dan Reiter, Jaroslav Tir, Mike Ward, and Chris Zorn on earlier drafts of this chapter. Of course, they are not responsible for the way we have used their advice. Neal Beck has patiently tried to improve our methodological skills. Others should be so fortunate as to have such a gadfly. The log-files of our regression analyses are posted at http://bama.ua.edu/~joneal /sage_book

1. Gleditsch (2002a) uses trade and GDP data expressed in international prices, as Summers et al. (1995) and we have done (Oneal and Russett, 1997, 1999b; Russett and Oneal, 2001). His data can be found on ftp://isere.colorado.edu/pub/ksg/trade.zip.

2. As reported in chapter 7, the mean probability of a dispute for a pair of states that are neither contiguous nor include a major power is about .0004. We could reduce even this very low probability by identifying regional powers, as Maoz (1996) and Gates and

McLaughlin (1996) have done; but their analyses indicate that the results are not sensitive to this refinement.

3. Using linear instead of cubic splines yields very similar results to those reported in the tables.

4. The estimated coefficients in the different analyses can only be roughly compared because a logistic curve is being fitted. The effect of a change in interdependence is not solely a function of its coefficient; it is also affected by the magnitude of the other coefficients and the constant.

5. We are grateful to Mike Ward for drawing our attention to this point.

6. We use independent variables measured in year t to explain disputes in year t+1, so democracy, interdependence, and so forth in 1885 explain conflict in 1886. There are insufficient trade data for the years of World War I and World War II and for the immediate post–World War II period (1946–49).

7. We obtained similar results using WSEV and 10-year slices of time to define the subsamples. Utilizing actual historical periods seems preferable to analyses with equal time periods of arbitrary length. WSEV can also be used in combination with Beck's correction, as Heagerty et al. note. Then the coefficient of the trade-to-GDP ratio (27.7) is significant at the .02 level. This is consistent with the results they report using data from Russett and Oneal (2001).

8. Achen (2000) notes that the same thing often occurs in the analysis of continuous variables when a lagged dependent variable is included on the right-hand side of the regression equation—at times even causing a reversal in the signs of coefficients. Consequently, he has urged caution in employing lagged dependent variables. It is probably best to report results using several estimators when analyzing either continuous or discrete data.

9. It is possible to modify Beck's method to insure that the effects of the theoretical variables and time are distinguished. If we regress the years of peace on the theoretically specified variables (the lower trade-to-GDP ratio, the lower democracy score, the capability ratio, etc.), we can create residuals for all observations that are independent of the explanatory model. These residuals can be used to create four splines. Using the PEACEYRS residuals to correct for duration dependence yields a substantive effect very similar to what is reported in row 2, table 9.1; but the estimated coefficient in this regression is more than seven times its standard error.

10. The reduction in the likelihood of a dispute for the politically relevant dyads was estimated at 29 percent in Oneal, Oneal, Maoz, and Russett (1996), 40 percent in Oneal and Russett (1997), 33 percent (Oneal and Russett 1999b), and 43 percent in Russett and Oneal (2001).

11. See Oneal and Russett (1999a, b); Bennett and Stam (2000); Hegre (2000); Mousseau (2000); Gartzke, Li, and Boehmer (2001); Boehmer, Gartzke, and Nordstrom (2000); King and Zeng (2001); Mousseau, Hegre, and Oneal (2003); and Heagerty, Ward, and Gleditsch (2002).

12. In his reply, Beck sometimes discusses autocorrelation, which is a symptom of the errors of prediction, and sometimes the correlation between $y_{i,t}$ and $y_{i,t-1}$. He also says that it is hard to believe GEE's low estimates of $\rho$ when there are long sequences of peace. In our analyses of all onsets, the correlation ($\rho$) between adjacent residuals is .24, which is not excessive; the correlation between adjacent values of ONSET is .35.

# CHAPTER 10

# The Trade and Conflict Debate: Exploring the Frontier

*Rafael Reuveny*

The relationship between bilateral trade and political conflict and cooperation is controversial. According to one group of studies, trade generates cooperation and amity. A second group of studies argues that trade causes conflict and hostility. According to a third position, trade rises with cooperation and falls with conflict.[1] A fourth position yet argues that bilateral trade and political conflict and cooperation flows do not affect each other.[2]

Most contemporary studies of trade and conflict employ statistical methods.[3] However, their results differ, supporting each of the above positions. Of course, the results of statistical studies may differ due to differences in samples, data, and measures. However, at a more fundamental level, the results also may differ due to differences in theoretical model specification, and particularly if models omit different parts of the 'true' trade-conflict relationship.

I generally believe that before one considers empirical issues, one needs to consider theory. To that end, I first identify several important theoretical issues that so far have largely been ignored in the literature. Second, I present a new micro-founded theoretical approach to the study of the trade-conflict relationship that incorporate these issues. Finally, I evaluate the empirical implications of this new theoretical approach.

In this chapter I do not conduct new empirical analysis; rather, I synthesize a number of my previous single and coauthored studies.[4] Based on this synthesis, I conclude that existing studies may well miss important theoretical parts of the trade-conflict puzzle, namely, the simultaneous nature of the trade-conflict relationship, the variation of the relationship across goods and dyads, the dynamic nature of conflict, and the multicountry nature of trade and conflict. The empirical results shown here illustrate the importance of these issues.

The theoretical issues at the center of this chapter have not been ignored completely in the trade-conflict literature. However, they have been far from the forefront of contemporary research, and they have not been studied together in a single model.

## The Missing Parts of the Puzzle

I identify seven theoretical elements that have been generally absent from most statistical models of trade and conflict. Several prominent scholars have started to consider the importance of these missing parts of the puzzle, but their comments have not received much attention in the literature so far.

One group of studies defines conflict as the dependent variable and trade as one of a number of independent variables.[5] A second group of studies defines trade as the dependent variable and conflict as one of a number of independent variables.[6] Implicitly or explicitly, these two groups assume a different direction of causality (trade causes conflict, or conflict causes trade). Statistically, a finding that trade affects conflict may reflect the fact that conflict affects trade, and vice versa. It also may imply that the two forces affect each other. In fact, Reuveny and Kang (1996a, 1998) find a reciprocal Granger causality between trade and conflict. Studies that ignore this reciprocity face the risk of simultaneity bias.[7]

A second issue pertains to the actors whose behavior is to be modeled. Studies that explain the determinants of conflict assume (implicitly or explicitly) that a state unitary actor decides on the level of conflict. Studies that explain the determinants of trade assume that a unitary state actor decides the level of trade. In the real world, these two conceptualizations of the state translate to different actors: Governments choose the level of conflict and exporters and importers determine the level of trade (Sayrs, 1989; Pollins 1989a,b; Ward, 1995). However, trade-conflict studies typically assume that nations are unitary actors.

A third issue involves conflict dynamics. Many studies have demonstrated that the choice of conflict follows a dynamic interaction, or action-reaction process. Inertia and reciprocity are central concepts in this literature.[8] Reciprocity is the tendency of nations to retaliate with the same type of action that was directed at them. Inertia is the tendency of current actions to depend on their own past values. Despite the empirical support the action-reaction model has received in the conflict literature, action-reaction conflict dynamics is typically not included in trade-conflict statistical models.[9]

Moving to a fourth issue, certain traded goods naturally can be more important to countries than other goods. For example, some goods have no domestic substitutes, while other goods could play a central role in the domestic economy. Hence, the sensitivity of trade to conflict might vary across goods. The extent to which trade affects conflict also may change across traded goods because the gains from trade vary.[10] Moreover, as traders lobby governments, their efforts may affect political relations. These efforts typically vary across sectors. However, the overwhelming majority of studies employ total trade data, implicitly or explicitly assuming that the relationship between trade and conflict does not vary across goods. Ignoring the composition of trade may distort inferences on the modeled trade-conflict relationship by mixing the qualities of different goods.[11]

Fifth, one could expect that the trade-conflict relationship will vary across dyads. Action-reaction dynamic conflict models find that reciprocity and inertia vary across dyads. So does the importance of bilateral trade to nations. The relationship between trade and conflict generally is observed to be more intense among rivals than among allies. Other differences across dyads also are possible, depending on forces such as political regime, trade composition, and economic freedom. Despite this, trade-conflict studies typically pool the data of many dyads, assuming there is a universal relationship. If the relationship does change across dyads, the change simply cannot be detected by the pooling method. Hence, pooling may distort our understanding of the trade-conflict nexus as if we would combine the tail and the leg of an elephant into a 'tail-leg' organ.[12]

Sixth, as noted by McMillan (1997), most trade-conflict studies use the dyad as their unit of analysis. A considerable smaller group of studies perform a monadic analysis. The reasons for either choice are not well developed. Another possibility, which is not explicitly considered by McMillan, is that the trade-conflict flows of one dyad affect the trade-conflict flows of another. If dyads are indeed affected by other dyads, pure dyadic or monadic trade-conflict models are missing variables, which could distort empirical inference.

Finally, many contemporary trade-conflict studies generally measure conflict based on the Militarized Interstate Disputes data. The MID data suppress the cooperation side of the conflict-cooperation continuum into one phenomenon, i.e. no conflict. Moreover, while the MID data distinguish among different dispute types (e.g., war, show of force, verbal warning), trade-conflict studies typically treat all the MIDs as if they are the same political events, coding a variable to one when a MID of any type is reported, and zero otherwise.[13] As noted by Polachek and Robst (1998) and James et al. (2000), this practice is problematic. It implies that the relationship between trade and conflict (or other forces and conflict for that matter) does not depend on the intensity of conflict or cooperation, which is a brave assumption. Alternatively, one could conceptualize conflict and cooperation as a variable that can take on varying intensities. This approach is taken in the next section.

## The Basic Dyadic Model

It is possible to study the relationship between trade and conflict at the monadic, the dyadic, or the multicountry (or systemic) level of analysis. In some of my trade-conflict studies, I employ a dyadic model, which is described in this section.[14] In this model, I assume that the trade-conflict flows of one dyad are not affected by the flows in another dyad, returning to this complicated issue later.

Trade-conflict models in the literature typically have a macro flavor, without specifying the details of how conflict and trade interact. My model offers a more micro-founded approach. Several authors have developed micro-founded static models of trade and conflict, explaining either conflict or trade, but not both.[15] My approach differs from these studies in that it attends to the issues of simultaneity, variation across dyads, variation across goods, dynamic conflict interaction, conflict intensity, and the separate behavior of traders and governments.

I conceptualize conflict and cooperation as a continuum of actions. In each country of a trading dyad, the modeled actors are an exporter, an importer, and a government, all of which are rational goal-maximizers. I assume that the two governments in the model do not trade, and the four traders (two importers and two exporters) do not determine the level of conflict. At any given level of bilateral trade, governments determine the level of conflict to send toward a trade-partner country. At any given level of bilateral conflict, exporters choose the level of export, and importers choose the level of import.[16] The bilateral trade flow is determined in economic equilibrium, where the level of import (demand) must equal the level of export (supply), for each bilateral trade flow. The model has two parts, focusing on trade and conflict, respectively.

## Trade

The trade part of the model describes the behavior of importers in country k and exporters in country j, in dyad j-k. For each good and at each price, one equation specifies the quantity imported by k from j, and a second equation specifies the quantity exported by j to k. I assume that importers prefer to import from a friendly country and exporters prefer to export to a friendly country, which is motivated as follows. First, traders may wish to punish hostile countries by trading less with them. As conflict rises, traders also may reduce trade, fearing that governments may restrict trade with rivals. Finally, a rise in conflict may imply greater cost, which reduces trade.[17] One also could think of mechanisms that increase trade as conflict rises. I maintain the standard approach, returning to these mechanisms later.

The mathematical formulation of the trade part of the model modifies the works of Armington (1969), Geraci and Prewo (1982), and Bergstrand (1985).[18] As in these studies, I use the term *good* to denote a traded commodity, and the term *product* to denote a location-specific good. For instance, oil is a good, and Mexican and Saudi oils consumed in Japan are two products. It is assumed that importers distinguish between products based on their country of origin, and exporters distinguish between products based on their destination country.

There are n goods in the model, each imported from N origins and exported to N destinations. $Q_{ijk}$ is the quantity of good i produced in nation j and consumed in nation k (a product), and $P_{ijk}$ is its free on-board price in the producer's currency. $F_{ijk} \geq 1$ denotes transport costs, $E_{jk}$ is the value of the currency of k in terms of the currency of j, and $t_{ijk}$ is the tariff k imposes on a product $Q_{ijk}$. Hence, the price paid by consumers in k—$P^*_{ijk}$—is given by $P_{ijk} * F_{ijk} (1+t_{ijk})/E_{jk}$.

The status of j-k relations as viewed by importers is modeled as $b_{ijk} = \exp(\gamma_{ik} C^{jk})$, where $\gamma_{ik} > 0$ determines the importance of good i to k, $C^{jk}$ is the status of the relations between j and k, $C^{jk} = f(C_{jk}, C_{kj})$, $C_{jk}$ is the level of conflict/cooperation sent from j toward k, and $C_{kj}$ is the level sent from k toward j. The status of bilateral relations as viewed by exporters is modeled with $a_{ijk} = \exp(-\delta_{ij}CC^{jk})$, where $\delta_{ij}>0$ determines the importance of good i to j.[19]

As usual, importers in k are assumed to maximize utility by choosing the quantities of products to import from each j ($Q_{ijk}^D$), and exporters are assumed to maximize profit by choosing the quantity of products to export to each k ($Q_{ijk}^S$), both taking prices as given.[20] The utility maximization by importers gives the demand in k for good i imported from j.

$$Q_{ijk}^{D} = \frac{b_{ijk}^{\sigma_{ik}} P_{ijk}^{*-\sigma_{ik}} M_{ik}}{\sum_{j=1}^{N}(b_{ijk}^{\sigma_{ik}} P_{ijk}^{*1-\sigma_{ik}})} \tag{10.1}$$

The profit maximization by exporters gives j's export of good i to k.

$$Q_{ijk}^{S} = \frac{P_{ijk}^{\tau_{ij}} X_{ij}}{a_{ijk}^{\tau_{ij}+1}\sum_{k=1}^{N} a_{ijk}^{-\tau_{ij}} P_{ijk}^{\tau_{ij}+1}} \tag{10.2}$$

In equation 10.1, $0<\sigma_{ik}<\infty$ is the elasticity of substitution among products in k, and $M_{ik}$ is the total expenditure on imports of good i in country k. In equation 10.2, $0<\tau_{ij}<\infty$ is the elasticity of substitution among products in j, and $X_{ij}$ is the total expenditure on producing exports of good i in country j. Equation 10.1 implies that as j-k relations deteriorate, less good i is demanded by consumers in k from producers in j, and equation 10.2 implies that less good i is supplied by producers in j to consumers in k.[21]

The equilibrium price and quantity of the bilateral trade flow from j to k are determined by the condition demand (in equation 10.1) equals supply (in equation 10.2), for each good. Figure 10.1 presents this condition graphically for good i. At $E_1$, export supply is given by $Q^{S1}_{ijk}$ and import demand is given by $Q^{D1}_{ijk}$. As conflict rises, $Q^{S1}_{ijk}$ falls to $Q^{S2}_{ijk}$ and $Q^{D1}_{ijk}$ falls to $Q^{D2}_{ijk}$. The system then moves to $E_2$ and trade quantity falls. This effect will be stronger when demand and supply are more price elastic. The shift down of import demand reduces price, while the shift up of export supply increases it, ceteris paribus. Hence, the monetary value of bilateral trade (price times quantity) may rise, fall, or remain unchanged when conflict rises. The effect of conflict on trade price and value may change across dyads and goods, since the price elasticities of demand and supply change across dyads and goods. In other words, figure 10.1 implies that the theoretical effect of conflict on bilateral trade value and price is unclear.[22]

**Figure 10.1. Disaggregated Bilateral Trade and Conflict**

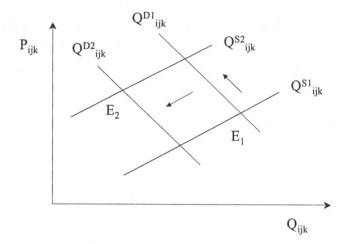

*Note:* The arrows indicate the movements of the supply and demand curves, respectively, when the level of conflict rises.

Pollins (1989b), Gowa (1994), Morrow (1998), and others assume that the value of bilateral trade falls with conflict and rises with cooperation. Polachek (1980, 1992, 1997) assumes that conflict raises the bilateral import price and lowers the export price, and Pollins (1989a) assumes that trade prices do not change with conflict. However, my model shows that the trade price and trade values may rise or fall with conflict (or cooperation). The ambiguous effect of conflict on trade prices in the model has important implications for the effect of trade on conflict and cooperation, an issue to which I turn next.

## Conflict

The conflict part of the model extends the important work of Polachek (1980, 1992, 1997). He assumes that leaders' utility rises with national consumption and with the conflict they send toward another nation. Leaders are assumed to be rational unitary actors that maximize utility by choosing the level of conflict.[23] Polachek also assumes that as conflict rises, export price falls and import price rises, or the terms of trade decline. The mathematical tension between the utility gained from conflict and the utility lost from the declining terms of trade due to conflict drives the optimal solution. Polachek's model implies that the level of conflict the leaders of nation $j$ send toward nation $k$ falls with the trade between $j$ and $k$. Formally, the government of $j$ maximizes utility by choosing $C_{jk}$, taking $j$'s trade with $k$ as given. The solution of this optimization problem shows that $C_{jk}$ depends on the quantities and prices of the traded goods that flow between countries $j$ and $k$ (i.e., $Q_{ijk}$, $Q_{ikj}$, $P_{ijk}$, $P_{ikj}$).

Polachek's model does not specify the details of the process that determines the effect of trade on conflict. Such details generally are not considered in the statistical literature. One might address these details by assuming that a leader's stay in power depends on the support of a coalition of diverse trading interests. The conflict decision involves the inputs received from this coalition. As trade rises, some groups in the coalition gain and some groups lose. The distribution of gains and losses depends also on the economic sectors to which groups belong, because comparative advantages and the levels of political power vary by sectors. Groups that have more to gain from trade than other groups are more likely to oppose conflict. If leaders get much support from politically powerful groups that stand to lose when trade falls with a certain trade partner, they are likely to be less hostile toward that particular partner.[24]

This story implies that trade may cause conflict or cooperation, or simply leave conflict unaffected. In contrast, the effect of trade on conflict in Polachek's model is negative. One way to integrate the two competing scenarios is to embed Polachek's conflict model within a simultaneous trade-conflict framework.

Polachek assumes that hostility lowers bilateral export prices and raises import prices. However, we have seen that trade prices may rise or fall with hostility, and the effect of hostility on prices may change across goods and dyads. Hence, the effect of conflict on the terms of trade of various sectors is not uniform. Some groups will observe a deterioration of terms of trade, others will observe an improvement. Consequently, they may see conflict with a trade partner differently. The overall effect of trade on conflict cannot be determined a priori since it depends on the political strength of groups in affecting leaders' decisions.

Next, I incorporate action-reaction dynamics into the model. I assume that leaders first consider the effect of trade, as described above, and then consider reciprocity and inertia.[25] Equation 10.3 is a standard action-reaction model, where t is time, $C_{jkt}$ is conflict sent from j to k, $C_{jkt-1}$ is $C_{jk}$ at time t-1, $C_{kjt}$ is conflict sent from k to j, $a_0$ is an intercept, $a_1$ determines reciprocity, $a_2$ determines inertia, and $e_{jkt}$ represents surprise moves by j toward k.

$$C_{jk_t} = a_0 + a_1 C_{kj_t} + a_2 C_{jk_{t-1}} + e_{jk_t} \qquad (10.3)$$

Equation 10.3 implies that if $a_1 > 0$, j extends hostility in return for k's hostility (or amity in return for amity). If $a_2 > 0$, j's past action induces the same type of action. As usual, I assume that reciprocity is positive. Equation 10.3 can be derived mathematically based on the partial adjustment model, showing that $a_2 = 1 - \gamma$, where $-\infty < \gamma < \infty$ is a deep parameter. It also can be shown that when $0 < \gamma < 2$, equation 10.3 implies that j's actions agree with its conflict goal. Assuming that governments are rational actors (i.e., goals correspond to actions), I expect $0 < \gamma < 2$.

Equation 10.4 adds the effect of trade into equation 10.3, so that the overall conflict from j to k is given by:

$$C_{jk_t} = a_0 + a_1 C_{kj_t} + a_2 C_{jk_{t-1}} + \sum_{i=1}^{n} [ \beta_{iP} P_{ijk_t} + \beta_{iQ} Q_{ijk_t} + \delta_{iP} P_{ikj_t} + \delta_{iQ} Q_{ikj_t} ] + e_{jk_t} \quad (10.4)$$

where, $\beta_{iP}$, $\beta_{iQ}$, $\delta_{iP}$ and $\delta_{iQ}$ are good-specific coefficients.[26]

## Full Model

The full model is based on equations 10.1, 10.2, and 10.4. For each good, there are two import-demand and export-supply equations: one for flow from j to k, and the other for the flow from k to j. As usual, demand equals supply for each flow.[27] Two other equations constrain the sum of the trade values of all goods to be equal to the total trade values in each direction. Equation 10.4 also is written for each flow. Hence, for n goods, the model includes 4n+4 equations per dyad.

We can summarize the implications of the full model with the following four hypotheses:

$H_1$ trade and conflict will affect each other (simultaneity)
$H_2$ the trade quantities will decline with conflict
$H_3$ the relationship between trade and conflict will change across dyads
$H_4$ the relationship between trade and conflict will change across goods.

## Empirical Analysis from the Basic Model

The empirical analysis requires data on bilateral trade prices and quantities, which are not easy to obtain for many countries. Italianer (1986) developed a unique data set of yearly bilateral trade prices, quantities, and values, for a few industrialized countries, from 1963 to 1980, disaggregated along the five categories of agriculture and fishery, energy, ores and minerals, manufactured goods, and miscellaneous consumer goods. The European Union generates similar trade data from 1979 to the present.[28] Using these trade data, I have conducted two empirical analyses. One analysis employs total trade (or n=1). A second employs disaggregated trade data for five goods (or n=5). The analysis from total trade data includes all the dyads formed among the United States, (West) Germany, Japan, and the (former) USSR. The analysis from disaggregated trade data does not include the USSR due to data limitations.[29]

The level of conflict is measured based on the Conflict and Peace Data Bank (COPDAB) and the World Event Interaction Survey (WEIS).[30] In using events data, some studies employ one variable for conflict and one for cooperation (Sayrs, 1989; Ward and Rajmaira, 1992). Other studies aggregate the levels of conflict (with a negative sign) and cooperation (with a positive sign), generating net conflict (Richardson, 1960; Polachek, 1980, 1992, 1997; Pollins, 1989a, b; Goldstein and Freeman, 1990). As basically seen in all empirical measures, net conflict has pluses and minuses. On the minus side, the use of net conflict does not allow us to investigate whether processes involving conflict and cooperation differ. On the plus side, net conflict indicates the overall level of political relations, which is important for trade and conflict (Polachek, 1980, 1992, 1997; Pollins, 1989a, b), and it keeps the empirical analysis tractable. Given the complexity of my model, in the studies reported here I employ net conflict.[31]

According to the model, the trade-conflict nexus can vary across dyads. Estimating the model by pooling the data of many dyads does not allow us to evaluate this property of the model. Accordingly, I estimate the model separately for each dyad.

Turning to a summary of the empirical results from total trade, net conflict exhibits positive reciprocity, and the inertia coefficient $\gamma$ is always in the 0–2 range, both as expected. The effects of total trade and conflict on each other are generally significant, supporting $H_1$. The signs of the effects of conflict on trade quantity partially support $H_2$. The effect of trade on conflict is mixed and at times not significant, supporting $H_3$. The proportion of nonsignificant effects of trade on conflict is larger than the proportion of nonsignificant effects of conflict on trade, indicating a weaker effect of trade on conflict than of conflict on trade. This result could be related to the sample I have used, because in the period studied, relations between the United States, Japan, and Germany were basically friendly.

I also find that at times trade rises with conflict, which disagrees with $H_2$ and contemporary theory, indicating the presence of forces pushing to raise trade when conflict rises.[32] These forces have been typically ignored in the literature. However, one can certainly think about mechanisms explaining why trade may rise with conflict. For example, conflict may force countries to agree to policies imposed by other countries (including more trade), groups that gain from trade may trade more with a hostile nation, and groups that lose from trade may reduce trade with a friendly nation. Leaders also may use trade to appease a hostile partner or to stimulate trade with a rival as part of a larger plan (e.g., creating trade dependence, future gains).

The results illustrate that the relationship between trade and conflict varies across dyads. If dyads are grouped according to East–West blocs, a rise in conflict raises West–West import, weakly reduces West–West export, and has a mixed effect on East–West trade. These results agree with casual historical observation. Although they traditionally have been allies, Western countries have disputed at times. When conflict rose, particularly following trade disputes, they opened their markets for import. As for the mixed effect of conflict on East–West trade, at times the West used trade with the USSR to mitigate West–USSR conflict. At other times, it reduced trade to punish the USSR.

The potential sensitivity of import and export to conflict is studied from the import and export price elasticities, a question which also has not been examined so far. Japanese–German trade is the least sensitive to conflict; USSR's trade with Japan is the most sensitive to conflict, followed by USA–USSR and USSR–Germany trade. These results may well reflect attempts of countries belonging to the opposing East–West blocs not to become overly dependent on each other.

Trade generally generates cooperation sent from the USSR to the West. This effect is greatest for USA–USSR trade, followed by that of USSR–Germany and USSR–Japan trade. Trade also generates conflict sent from the West to the USSR–

with the greatest effect on actions from the USA to the USSR. The effect of trade on West–West relations is weak and negative. These results may be explained as follows. The importance of East–West trade (resulting in trade gains) for the USSR was generally higher than for the West. The conflict-inducing effect of trade on USA–USSR relations may reflect USA fears that the USSR gained more in relative terms. Overall, the analysis of total trade implies that the relationship between trade and conflict has been more intense for East–West dyads than for West–West dyads. This pattern may seem obvious. However, the fact that the results are intuitive lends support to the model.

The empirical model from disaggregated trade is more complex. Given the available data, this complexity presents problems of estimation, due to the large number of independent variables. I therefore investigate each good separately, which is a practice used in many trade studies and in the few trade-conflict studies that have employed disaggregated trade data.[33]

The analysis of disaggregated trade data has employed dyads formed among the United States, Germany, and Japan. Due to the relatively low conflict intensity among these countries, one could expect that in these dyads conflict will not affect trade. However, as suggested by Polachek and Robst (1998), lower level conflict also could affect trade. Indeed, the results show that trade generally declines with conflict. Two other findings are that the effect of conflict on disaggregated trade is more significant than the effect of trade on conflict, and in some of the cases disaggregated trade rises with conflict, both of which replicate the spirit of results from total trade.

Ranking the sensitivity of goods to conflict according to price elasticities, we find that energy is the most sensitive, followed by agriculture and fishery, manufactured goods, miscellaneous consumer goods, and ores and minerals (the least sensitive). Trade in energy is most sensitive to conflict, which might be expected. Changing the origin and destination of manufactured goods is harder, as they tend to have more country-specific qualities, which is reflected in their low sensitivity to conflict relative to energy. Trade in ores and minerals also is generally hard to diversify, due to its relatively small number of sources.

Across goods, a rise in the quantity of trade in agriculture and fishery—and less so in energy—generates cooperation. For ores and minerals, manufactured goods, and miscellaneous consumer goods, the effect of trade quantity on conflict is mixed. A rise in trade prices of agriculture and fishery, energy, and (to a lesser extent) ores-minerals causes conflict, whereas the effect for manufactured goods and miscellaneous consumer goods is mixed. The mixed nature of these results supports hypothesis $H_4$, illustrating that using total trade in empirical analysis could introduce aggregation bias.

## Multicountry Analysis

So far, I have assumed that the trade-conflict flows in one dyad are not affected by the flows in another dyad. Relaxing this assumption, one could ask several questions. For example, does conflict from A to B depend on trade from A to C? Does trade from A to C depend on conflict from B to C? In principle, we should be able to modify the basic dyadic model to include trade-conflict flows among more countries. However, the theoretical foundations for a general-equilibrium, optimization-based trade-conflict model have not been developed yet. Still, the importance of multicountry trade-conflict relationships can be explored empirically. This issue is explored by Kang and Reuveny (2001).

In a multicountry model of trade and conflict, there are many possible interactions between trade-conflict flows. For example, the trade flows of one dyad may affect the trade flows of another dyad without involving any political considerations (e.g., through the economic forces of trade creation or diversion). The conflict flows of one dyad may affect the conflict flows of another dyad without involving any trade considerations (e.g., through action-reaction processes, as in Goldstein and Freeman, 1990). However, the trade (conflict) flows of one dyad also may affect the conflict (trade) flows of other dyads.

Consider conflicting countries A and C. Country A might regard the trade of C with B as a security threat if trade benefits C, and therefore might express hostility toward both B and C. Or, consider allied countries A and C. If B is not an enemy of A, then A might regard trade between C and B as beneficial to its own security, because when C trades with B, C gains. Since C is an ally of A, A also benefits. And yet, when trade between A and B rises, C may increase conflict with A and B, as it sees this trade as a threat to its economic position in B's markets.

Moving to the effect of conflict on trade, when relations improve between allies, trade may rise among them because they would like to support each other. A case involving rivals is more complicated. For example, A may restrict exports to B, suspecting that B may ship them to C, thus strengthening C. Or, suppose that A and B are allies facing conflict with C. When A–C conflict rises, A and B may trade more as they gain economically from trade, and may restrict trade with C, suspecting that C's relative gain is greater. A and B also may use their trade with C as a tool to mitigate conflict. However, since the gains from trade with C for A and B and the strength of their conflict with C may differ, the effect of A–C conflict on A–C trade and B–C trade may differ.

Kang and Reuveny (2001) study these relationships with a vector-autoregression model (VAR). In a VAR model, each of the conflict and trade flows between N countries is regressed on the lagged values of all the flows in the system. The effect of the lags of the trade flow from A to B on current trade from B to A is denoted as trade reciprocity.[34] Trade flows also may exhibit inertia due to slow changing economic factors. In the conflict equations, the VAR setup links to the action-reaction approach, which I have utilized in the basic dyadic model. The random components in the VAR represent factors such as unexpected changes in consumer tastes (in the trade equations) or unexpected changes of political positions (in the conflict equations).

The empirical analysis employs the USA, the (former) USSR, and (West) Germany. This triangle is used to illustrate the empirical power of the approach.[35]

Quarterly trade flows are measured by the ratios of the monetary values of exports and their bilateral trade prices. Trade values are obtained from the IMF and bilateral trade prices are obtained from Italianer (1986) and the European Union. The measure of conflict and cooperation is constructed from COPDAB and WEIS data and is conceptualized as net conflict. The sample period runs from the first quarter of 1963 to the fourth quarter of 1991.

The results show that the trade-conflict flows of one dyad are affected by those of other dyads. As trade rises in one dyad, trade also increases in other dyads. Other effects depend on particular dyads. For example, an increase in trade between the USSR and Germany brings more conflict between members of all the dyads in the system. But an increase in trade between the USA and Germany brings more cooperation between the USSR and Germany. As before, the claim that an increase in cooperation raises trade is only partially supported.[36] While Kang and Reuveny (2001) have investigated only one case, it could well be that the relationships between trade-conflict in other dyads also are subject to multicountry effects.

## Conclusion

This chapter has synthesized research on the variation of trade-conflict across goods and dyads, the simultaneity of trade and conflict, the dynamics of conflict in a trade-conflict setup, and the systemic nature of trade-conflict relationships. The importance of these issues has been noted previously in the literature, however they have rarely been analyzed. The basic dyadic model presented makes the following predictions: bilateral trade-conflict should affect each other; trade quantity should decline with conflict; conflict should exhibit reciprocity and inertia; conflict may rise or fall with trade; the relationship between trade-conflict should vary across goods and dyads; and the value of trade may rise or fall with conflict. Another contention is that the trade-conflict flows of one dyad will be affected by the flows in other dyads. The empirical results generally support these predictions. [37]

When it comes to policymaking, this essay suggests a need for caution. The optimistic liberal assertion that free trade will reduce conflicts among nations is based on the celebrated Ricardian model, showing that free trade generates more economic benefits than costs. Liberals take this result one step further, arguing that rational agents therefore will conclude that it is better to trade than to fight.

I do not dispute the argument that free trade generates more economic benefits than costs. However, international actors have political goals in addition to economic goals. In deciding whether to embrace free trade, policymakers need to consider all the costs and benefits from trade, not only the economic costs and benefits. In some situations free trade may not be a powerful pacifying tool, as is argued by liberals, and in some cases it may even promote conflict.[38]

Several potentially important issues might be evaluated in future research: First, the empirical research synthesized here is based on a relatively small sample of countries. Currently, the bilateral trade data required by the model are available for only a few countries, and only since 1963. As more data become available, the scope of the empirical analysis could be broadened. Second, I have found that in a number of cases more conflict results in more trade, which—while logically plausible—warrants further investigation. Third, future research could consider more goods. Similarly, future models could distinguish between different conflict types (e.g., verbal conflict, non-fatal militarized conflict, fatal militarized conflict), as well as distinguish between conflict and cooperation. Fourth, this essay demonstrates that there are reasons to believe that dyads are affected by other dyads. Future research could attempt to transform the basic dyadic model presented here into a multicountry model of trade and conflict.

Finally, existing models do not take into account the future costs and benefits of one's current choices in a dynamic optimization setup. The model presented here includes explicit conflict dynamics, but does not employ dynamic optimization. Developing a dynamic optimization-based trade-conflict model is a worthy research extension. One could approach this complex mathematical problem by using the model of Reuveny and Maxwell (1998), which focuses on the dynamics of free trade and arms races. To the extent that arms races and conflicts are associated, the model of Reuveny and Maxwell could serve as a platform for the development of a dynamic model of the relationship between trade and conflict.

In the end, I believe that the relationship between bilateral trade and political conflict and cooperation is more complex than the one envisioned by contemporary theories. Regardless of the nature of future research, I propose that trade and conflict need to be investigated using a dynamic simultaneous model that includes traders and governments as separate actors, distinguishes across goods, and employs a multicountry approach. Studies that ignore these features risk missing important forces in the relationship between bilateral trade and conflict and cooperation.

# Notes

I would like to thank Rhonda Butts for editorial assistance.

1. This position constitutes a reversal of the direction of the causality between trade and conflict, relative to the first two positions.

2. For detailed reviews of these studies see, for example, Reuveny (1999a, 2000), Barbieri and Schneider (1999), McMillan (1997), and Sayrs (1990).

3. To simplify the presentation, I will use the terms 'bilateral trade' and 'trade' interchangeably, and the terms 'political conflict/cooperation' and 'conflict' interchangeably.

4. This chapter synthesizes my work in Reuveny (1999a, b, 2000, 2001a, b), Reuveny and Kang (1996a, b, 1998, 2003), Kang and Reuveny (2001), and Reuveny and Maxwell (1998).

5. For example, see Polachek (1980, 1992, 1997), Gasiorowski (1986), Sayrs (1989), Barbieri (1996a), Schneider and Schulze (2002b), Gartzke and Li (2001), and Russett and Oneal (2001).

6. For example, see Pollins (1989a, b), Bergeijk (1994), Gowa (1994), Morrow et al. (1998, 1999) and Barbieri and Levy (1999).

7. While the issue of trade and conflict simultaneity is typically ignored, several studies briefly note its importance (Pollins, 1989a, b; Sayrs, 1990; Polachek, 1992; Barbieri, 1996a).

8. This literature can be traced back to Richardson (1960) and Boulding (1962). Ward (1981: 230) summarizes this approach by positing a golden rule that guides nations: 'Do unto others what they have recently done unto you.' For a review, see for example, Goldstein and Freeman (1990).

9. Sayrs (1989) includes action-reaction dynamics in a model of the effect of trade on conflict, but only for one side in a dyad.

10. For example, countries that trade in goods for which they have no readily available substitutes are more likely to be affected by trade changes.

11. See Arad et al. (1983), Domke (1988) and Pollins (1989a, b). Morrow et al. (1998) warn that to be 'correct', trade-and-conflict theories must find support from disaggregated trade, and Polachek (1992) and Polachek and McDonald (1992) warn that total trade data may bias results. Sayrs (1990) and McMillan (1997) note there is little knowledge on how trade and conflict vary across goods.

12. Gasiorowski (1986) and Polachek (1997) find that the effect of trade on conflict varies across dyads. Polachek (1980), Gasiorowski and Polachek (1982), Pollins (1989b) and Sayrs (1989, 1990) suspect that trade and conflict vary across dyads, and Sayrs (1990), Pollins (reported in Sayrs, 1990) and Polachek (1997) explicitly call for statistical models from single dyads. The general limitations of the use of pooling method in political studies are discussed in Achen (1986) and Ward (1987).

13. As noted by Russett and Oneal (2001), part of the reason for that practice has to do with the paucity of MID events.

14. For technical details, see Reuveny (2001a,b) and Reuveny and Kang (2003).

15. Schneider and Schulze (2002b) explain the level of conflict by adding a military sector to a two-sector, factor specific trade model, where the military sector gains from both hostility and trade. Gartzke and Li (2001) explain the discrete choice of conflict versus no conflict based on a game theoretic framework with three actors: state A, state B, and the market. Pollins (1989a) models import demand as a function of conflict. Polachek (1980, 1992, 1997) explains the level of conflict using a model to which I will return later.

16. The assumption that trade is performed by importers and exporters and not by governments is commonly used in economics. The assumption that conflict decisions are made by governments—as opposed to importers (consumers) and exporters (producers)—should not require any justification.

17. For an elaboration on these mechanisms, see Pollins (1989a, b), Gowa (1994), and Morrow et al. (1998).

18. For examples using this approach, see Deardorff and Stern (1986), Italianer (1986), Pollins (1989a, b), Bergstrand (1989), and Marquez (1992).

19. The symbol f denotes a positive monotonic function, and $-\infty < C^{jk}$, $C_{jk}$, $C_{kj} < \infty$. Negative $C^{jk}$, $C_{jk}$ and $C_{kj}$ denote hostility and positive values denote friendliness. Also, $b_{ijk}$ approaches zero for high conflict and infinity for high cooperation, and $a_{ijk}$ approaches infinity for high conflict and zero for high cooperation.

20. These are standard assumptions in economics. Utility is assumed to take the form of constant elasticity of substitution (CES) function, and production technology is assumed to take the form of a constant elasticity of transformation (CET) function, both of which are widely used in economics.

21. Similar equations are written for $Q_{ikj}^{D}$ and $Q_{ikj}^{S}$. As is usual in economics, $Q_{ijk}^{D}$ falls with price, tariffs, and domestic currency devaluation and rises with total import expendi-

tures on good i in country k, and $Q_{ijk}^S$ rises with price and j's total expenditures on producing the exports of good i.

22. For a given upshift of supply, the less price elastic demand is, the harder it is for importers to substitute this import. The rise in price will be greater and the decline in quantity will be smaller. Similarly, for a given downshift of demand, the less price elastic supply is, the harder it is for exporters to substitute this export. The fall in price will be greater and the decline in quantity will be smaller.

23. Polachek does not study why leaders' utility rises with conflict. However, logically, one could argue that rational leaders choosing to engage in conflict find this option beneficial.

24. Schneider and Schulze (2003, this volume) also address these issues.

25. This assumption simplifies the modeling of a complicated problem, for which an all-encompassing, optimization-based mathematical model has not yet been developed.

26. To simplify, the price-quantity part of Equation (4) assumes a linear form, as in Polachek (1980, 1992). A similar equation to (4) is written for $C_{kjt}$.

27. In equations (1) and (2), $C^{jk}$ and $C^{kj}$ are replaced by a linear combination of $C_{jk}$ and $C_{kj}$, respectively, and the denominators are measured by the multilateral import and export prices.

28. The price data include transportation cost.

29. Tariffs are approximated by the ratio of custom revenues to imports, as in many trade studies. Exchange rates are taken from the IMF's *International Financial Statistics* and the UN's *Trade Statistics*. For details, see Reuveny (2001a, b).

30. The two data sources are combined, as is done in Reuveny and Kang (1996b). On COPDAB, see Azar (1984), and on WEIS, see World Event Interaction Survey (1993).

31. Pollins (1989a), Goldstein and Freeman (1990), and Reuveny and Kang (1996b) report that the spirit of results from the separate measures of conflict and cooperation and net conflict differs little.

32. This empirical finding does not invalidate the model's structure because it implies only a different assumption on the signs of $\gamma_{ik}$ ($\gamma_{ij}$) and $\delta_{ik}$ ($\delta_{ij}$) in $a_{ijk}$ and $b_{ijk}$ from Equations (1) and (2). Levy (1998), Barbieri and Levy (1999), and Morrow et al. (1998, 1999) report findings in the same spirit.

33. For a similar approach, see the trade and conflict studies of Gasiorowski and Polachek (1982) and Polachek and McDonald (1992), and the pure bilateral trade studies of Arad Hirsch, and Tovias (1983) and Bergstrand (1989).

34. Trade reciprocity may be more intense among rivals, but peaceful countries are also attentive to it (Baldwin, 1984).

35. The USA–USSR–Germany triangle has received considerable attention in the literature because, during the Cold War, Germany was both the largest Western trade partner of the USSR and an important member in the alliance with the USA facing the USSR. For examples of studies focusing on this triangle, see Kang and Reuveny (2001).

36. To illustrate, a rise in Germany–USSR cooperation does not raise trade in any of the dyads in the system.

37. On the models prediction about the value of trade, see Reuveny and Kang (2003).

38. Illustrating this complexity, Reuveny (1999a, b) shows that the Israel–Palestine bilateral trade and economic relations are important contributors to the current Israel–Palestine cycle of violence. In this particular case, the liberal paradigm does not seem to hold.

# CHAPTER 11

# Development and the Liberal Peace: What Does It Take to Be a Trading State?

*Håvard Hegre*

States that trade extensively with each other seldom fight wars with each other. This classic, liberal thesis is based on a twofold idea: First, trade between two states increases the economic costs of war between them. Second, a side-effect of trade is improved communication between the inhabitants of the trading states. This reduces the chances of misunderstanding and helps to build institutions for the peaceful resolution of conflict.

In recent years, the peace-through-interdependence hypothesis has generated enormous interest among international relations scholars. A host of theoretical and empirical investigations have refined and strengthened the argument. However, even when explicitly using economic incentives to explain state behavior, very few studies have taken into account the more structural economic factors. An exception is Richard Rosecrance's *The Rise of the Trading State* (1986). Rosecrance is concerned with explaining why states choose trading-state strategies rather than military-political ones. Peaceful trading strategies enjoy greater efficacy today than before, he holds, and one of the reasons is industrial-technological development.

In this article, I connect Rosecrance's arguments to the empirical literature on trade and conflict, and go on to argue that the relationship between trade and conflict is contingent on the level of development. Within the empirical framework set out by Bremer (1992) and Maoz and Russett (1993), I will investigate the importance of socioeconomic development for the relationship between trade and conflict, drawing mainly on Rosecrance's arguments. While concentrating on the importance of socioeconomic development for the trade-promotes-peace hypothesis, I will also touch upon its importance for the democratic peace.

Empirically, the models used by Oneal and Russett (1997, 1999c) and Barbieri (1996a) will be my point of departure. However, I propose two major improvements compared to their models. First, I construct a new measure of interdependence based on the residuals from a gravity model of trade. In contrast to measures currently in use, the gravity model measure is independent of the relative size of the two countries in the dyad. In addition, its distribution is symmetric rather than highly skewed, which makes for ease of interpretation. Second, I employ the Cox regression model put forward in Raknerud and Hegre (1997). As shown there (and by Beck, Katz, and Tucker, 1998), proper modeling of temporal dependence is essential if any valid conclusions are to be drawn concerning the relationship between interdependence and conflict. The statistical model used here allows precise modeling of such dependence.

In the next section, I look more closely into the idea that trade leads to peace, and elaborate on Rosecrance's argument that socioeconomic development affects the relationship between trade and conflict. In section 3, the statistical model and measurement issues are accounted for. The results from the Cox regression analysis are presented in section 4. In the final section, I conclude that there is a negative relationship between trade and conflict, but that this is, to a certain extent, restricted to dyads consisting of two developed dyads.

One may see the peace-through-interdependence hypothesis as part of a more general 'liberal peace', where the democratic peace is another important factor. Since it is the citizens of the state who have to do the fighting and bear the economic burden of war, they will be likely to restrict their country's participation in war participation if they have the opportunity to influence its policies (cf. Kant, 1795/1991: 100). Even if the economy and the population of the country as a whole will suffer from war and from the loss of trade, narrower groups may be much less affected. A democratic regime helps to prevent such groups from forcing through policies that are detrimental to the majority of the population.

Consequently, the analyses reported here control for regime type. The results suggest that the democratic peace, too, requires a minimum level of development to be efficient.

## Development, Trade, and Conflict

Classic liberals have argued that an increase in free trade will diminish the frequency of war. This is supposed to happen both through processes within the individual state that moved toward free trade and laissez-faire economies, and through changes in the relations between the trading states. Thus, the argument involves both the dyadic and the nation level.

Eméric Crucé (1590–1648) was among the first to note a dyadic argument for trade to promote peace—namely, that trade between two states creates common interests (cf. Oneal and Russett, 1997: 268). In the words of Montesquieu (1748/1991, Book XX, ch. II), 'the natural effect of commerce is to bring about peace. Two nations which trade together, render themselves reciprocally dependent: if the one has an interest in buying the other has an interest in selling; and all unions are based upon mutual needs' (quoted in Hirschman, 1945/1980: 10). The underlying assumption is that war disrupts the trade bonds between the two states. Mutual dependence, then, acts as a form of economic deterrence: If it is sufficiently high, the expected costs of a war-induced cut in trade exceed the expected gain from a war.

At the nation (or monadic) level, Crucé argued that trade increased the prosperity and political power of the peaceful, productive members of society (Oneal and Russett, 1997: 268). Kant, Paine, Bentham, James Mill, and John Stuart Mill all argued for free trade, liberty for individuals *and* for republican or democratic government. These ideas were linked in the liberal opposition to mercantilism: Accumulating gold was seen by mercantilists as equivalent to increasing state power, since wars were financed largely through the state's gold reserves and through loans. All economic and individual interests were necessarily subordinated to the pursuit of state power. The liberal opposition to the traditional political systems then automatically meant an opposition to its economic doctrine: 'Mercantilism was seen to arise from the nature of aristocratic states, and therefore the political priority of liberals was to topple the interventionist, power-seeking state structures that were the legacy of the eighteenth century' (Buzan, 1984: 600).

Richard Rosecrance's (1986) argument is monadic as well: States are forced to make a choice between expanding territory or increasing trade as a basis for increasing wealth, power, and welfare. In a military-political strategy, increasing territory through conquest is seen as the primary means to increase wealth: 'The state with the greatest land mass would have the largest population, the greatest stock of natural resources, and presumably as well the largest wealth' (1986: 6–7). The alternative strategy for increasing wealth is to encourage international trade. However, as argued by the liberal theorists, these two strategies are antithetical. To a large extent, states have to choose one of the two.

The dyadic and monadic levels are interrelated. If two states change their general strategies (toward all states) from military-political to trading-state strategies, the relationship between them changes from military competition to a trading relationship. The likelihood of war between them will decrease, independently of the cost-benefit calculations over the loss of the bilateral trade versus the gains from war. If only one state changes its orientation, the risk of conflict should also, at least on average, decrease to some degree.

A series of large-N empirical studies at the dyadic level have found a positive relationship between trade and peace (Bennett and Stam, 2000: Kim, 1998, 1999; Oneal et al., 1996, 1997; 1999b,c; Polachek, 1980, 1999; Russett and Oneal, 2001; Russett, Oneal, and Davis, 1998). Still, there are dissenting voices: Barbieri (1996a) concludes that extensive trade bonds *increase* the likelihood of conflict rather than decreasing it, while Beck and colleagues (Beck, Katz, and Tucker, 1998; Beck and Tucker, 1997) find no relationship between trade and conflict when controlling for temporal dependence.

However, the liberal peace hypothesis may depend in part on the structure of the economies of the states in question. Norman Angell in the *The Great Illusion* (1910/1938), frequently considered the modern ancestor of interdependence theory, stresses how things have changed in the modern world. When nations fear their neighbors, this is 'based on the universal assumption that a nation, in order to find outlets for expanding population and increasing industry, is necessarily pushed to territorial expansion and the exercise of political force against others'. Angell 'attempts to show that . . . [this assumption] belongs to a stage of development out of which we have passed' (1938: 115). Modernization and industrialization have fundamentally changed the extent to which war is profitable.

Rosecrance (1986) argues that the incentives for states to choose between the trading world and the military-political one change with economic development.[1] The two worlds have always coexisted, but historical developments have made the trading world increasingly more attractive to states. Rosecrance points out that development alters four variables that are crucial to the calculations of the leader of a state: it increases the potential gains from trade, the economic costs of war, and the political costs of war, as well as decreasing the utility of occupying territories relative to the pursuit of trade policies.

First, development directly affects the possibility for and the gains from trade:

> Industrial and population growth strengthen interdependence and make it harder to achieve national objectives autonomously. When technology was rudimentary and population sparse, states had little contact with one another and did not generally get in each other's way. With the commercial and industrial revolutions, however, they were brought into closer proximity. As the Industrial Revolution demanded energy resources— great quantities of food, coal, iron, water power, and petroleum—the number of states that could be fully independent declined. (Rosecrance, 1986: 25)

Likewise, development furnishes states with access to better transport and communications technology and infrastructure—within and between states— which in turn increases both the volume and the utility of trade by reducing the transaction costs.[2]

The choice between the trading world and the military-political world is also related to how easy or difficult it is to conquer territory, and to govern such territory once it has been taken. Rosecrance (1986: 32–38, 155–162) holds that the costs of war have increased enormously with the industrialization of warfare. The price of producing one tank or one fighter has become far higher, yet such items do not last correspondingly longer in the battlefield (in confrontation with an opponent with the same technological level). In addition, the accelerating pace of technological change renders weapons and units obsolete more and more quickly. Moreover, modern weapons are more destructive, and sophisticated factories and elaborate infrastructure take more time to reconstruct if damaged. In addition, Rosecrance argues, the political costs of warfare are higher in industrialized societies.

Rosecrance also points out (159) that development affects the costs of holding the occupied territory by force and the likelihood of making this profitable. Illegitimate governments will face stiffer opposition from the population and have a hard time levying taxes from them. He argues that these problems will increase—the higher the level of education is—in the occupied territory.[3] Arguably, military force may secure the access to raw materials in the occupied territory as easily in a developed area as in an underdeveloped area even when faced with a hostile population. This is counterbalanced, however, by the reduction in transport costs brought about by development and technological improvements, making trade a relatively more attractive means of obtaining access to raw materials. Moreover, complex economies rely on the access to a broad range of raw materials. The occupation of a single country cannot ensure access to more than a few different goods, which decreases the utility of conquest for developed states compared to simpler economies (cf. Brooks, 1999).

On the other hand, Liberman (1993) argues that industrialized countries are more valuable prizes for an expansionist country. He also counters Rosecrance's contention that the political costs of occupation are higher in developed countries by pointing to the relative ease with which Nazi Germany could make the manufacturing sectors in the countries it had occupied—each of them fairly developed even by modern standards—contribute to its own war economy.

Likewise, advanced weapons may cause less collateral damage. This is most evident when a technologically superior power fights a lesser state (e.g., the United States vs. Iraq), but may also apply to a war between two developed states. Economic development further means that states, through improved organization and a larger tax base, have more resources to spend on the military. This tends to reduce the relative costs of war.

Rosecrance's argument may be summarized by seeing how development affects the utility calculations of states. Since the costs of seizing and holding a territory increase with increased development, and the relative utility of occupying the territory decreases, the chance that the expected utility of occupation exceeds the expected costs will decrease with increased development. Likewise, since the utility of trade increases with increased development, then increased development also makes it more likely that the expected costs of breaking the trade bonds will exceed the gains to be expected from occupation.

We should, then, expect *the probability of interstate war and militarized disputes to decrease with increasing development*. Moreover, development strengthens the effect of interdependence—there is an interaction effect between the two variables. A certain level of development may even be a *prerequisite* for the liberal peace to work. Below, I will test empirically whether these expectations hold for the post–World War II period.

## Research Design

The present study, like all the studies cited above, simply assume that trade causes peace, and not vice versa. How can this be justified? Realists stress the dominance of security issues over economic issues. Anticipating the costs of broken trade ties in wartime, a state will have an incentive to limit its trade with other states if it perceives the probability of war with them in the near future to be high. A rupture of international trade may also create losses beyond the loss of the gains from trade. The economy will have to readjust; it will lose productivity; and social problems may emerge from the ensuing unemployment. All in all, the country may be worse off than if the trade ties never had existed (see also Buzan, 1984: 620–621; Hirschman, 1945/1980: 26–29). In the realist view, the trade-promotes-peace finding depends entirely on a faulty assumption concerning the direction of causation. Assuming the reverse flow of causation, comparable studies have found that the level of trade between states depends on alliance bonds between them (Morrow, Siverson, and Tabares, 1998) or on war history (Gowa and Mansfield, 1993).

The question of direction of causation has been subjected to empirical tests. Polachek (1980) and Gasiorowski and Polachek (1982) conclude that past values for the trade variable are much better at predicting present values of cooperation and conflict than past values for the conflict variable are for predicting present values of trade. Kim (1998, 1999) and Oneal and Russett (2001b) reach a similar conclusion. Reuveny and Kang (1996a, 1998), on the other hand, find that the relationship between trade and conflict/cooperation is largely reciprocal.

The question of the direction of causation is not settled. What is fairly well established, however, is that trade and conflict are inversely related. For my purposes—seeing how socioeconomic development affects the relationship between trade and conflict—the direction of causation between trade and conflict is less important than the fact that there is a relationship between the two variables, and that this is likely to change with changing levels of development.

## Temporal and Spatial Domain

This study covers the period 1950–92. The analysis is limited to an extension of Maoz and Russett's (1992) relevant dyads. I have included all dyads whose members are either two major powers, allied, or contiguous, or have intercapital distance less than 3,000 km.[4]

## The Cox Regression Model

As in Raknerud and Hegre (1997), I employ a variant of the Cox regression model to minimize the problems of dependence between observational units, inconsistent censoring, and the untenable assumption of stationarity. Readers are referred to that article for details. The advantage of the Cox regression model is that it allows observations on dyads to be recorded on the finest possible time-scale to keep track of the succession of events. This allows inclusion of an exact variable for the duration of peace in the dyad. The main idea of Cox regression is the assumption that the hazard of war $\lambda_d(t)$ for dyad $d$ can be factorized into a parametric function of (time-dependent) variables and a nonparametric function of time itself (the baseline hazard):

$$\lambda_d(t) = \alpha(t)\exp(\sum_{j=1}^{p} \beta_j X_j^d(t)) \qquad (11.1)$$

In (11.1), $\alpha(t)$ is the baseline hazard: an arbitrary function reflecting unob-served variables at the system level. $X_j^d(t)$ is a (possibly time-dependent) ex-planatory variable for dyad $d$; $\beta$ is the corresponding regression coefficient; and $p$ is the number of explanatory variables. All legitimate explanatory variables are known prior to $t$—they must be a part of the history up until immediately before $t$. Given that there is an outbreak of dyad war at time $t_w$, the probability that this war outbreak will happen in dyad $d$ is:

$$\text{Pr(war in dyad } d| \text{ a war breaks out at } t_w) = \frac{\exp(\sum_{j=1}^{p} \beta_j X_j^d(t_w))}{\sum_{i \in R_{t_w}} \exp(\sum_{j=1}^{p} \beta_j X_j^i(t_w))} \qquad (11.2)$$

where $R_{t_w}$ is the *risk set* at $t_w$: the set of dyads that are at peace immediately be-fore $t_w$. The parameters $\beta$ can be interpreted in terms of a *relative* probability of war.[5]

## Measuring Development

The analysis was run using two different indicators of economic development: Gross domestic product per capita and energy consumption per capita. Both indicators were log-transformed, reflecting the view that the marginal effect of development on conflict behavior is diminishing. To create a dyadic measure I used the value for the poorer of the two countries in the dyad. This follows Oneal and Russett (1997: 275–276), who argue that the likelihood of conflict is primarily a function of the degree of political constraint experienced by the least constrained state in the dyad. They consequently use the trade dependence value for that state for which the dyadic trade poses the lowest economy dependence, on the basis of the 'weak-link assumption' (Dixon, 1994: 23).

Data on GDP per capita were taken from the RGDPCH variable from the Penn World Table (Mark 5.6) (see Summers and Heston, 1991). This variable measures real GDP per capita in constant dollars, calculated with the Chain in-dex. Data on energy consumption were taken from the Correlates of War Project dataset on national capabilities, found on the EUGene home page.[6] Several missing cases were filled in by means of linear interpolation.

## Measuring Interdependence

### Least Dependent and Salience

Barbieri (1996a) argues for the use of dyadic trade flow (imports + exports) between two states relative to total trade as a measure of one state's dependence on another. She combines the two-partner dependence figures into a measure of the size of a trading relationship defined as $Salience_{ij} = \sqrt{TradeShare_i * TradeShare_j}$

Oneal and Russett (1997) suggest using the dyadic trade flow relative to gross domestic product as a measure of one state's dependence on another. They use the value for the less dependent (the one with the lowest trade-to-GDP ratio) state as their dyadic measure. As for the development variable above, their choice is based on the weak-link assumption (Dixon, 1994). These two measures are highly correlated, and yield comparable results when my trade dataset is used (see Hegre, 1998 for a comparison).

Both measures vary with the size of the country's economy. A given amount of trade will be less significant for a country with a large GDP than it will for a smaller country. This means that the level of dependence is also dependent on the size of economy (see Hegre, 2001). Moreover, when creating a dyadic measure, we need to note that the size of the smaller state's economy will set a ceiling on the larger country's dependence. When Oneal and Russett's weak-link formula is used, the larger country's dependence will, in most cases, be coded as the level of interdependence. The same thing will tend to happen with Barbieri's measure, although to a lesser degree. This is potentially problematic, since the interdependence measure will function as a proxy for country size. To see this problem, consider the USA: in the entire period studied here, it was by far the largest economy in the world. In all the dyads it forms part of (with USA–Japan, USA–Canada, and USA–Germany being the exceptions), the value for 'least dependent' is extremely low. The USA has made use of its military power in a large number of militarized disputes. Is this because it is economically independent, or because it is a military superpower? Disputes with the USA form a large portion of the MID dataset. To what extent does this affect the study of the trade-conflict relationship?

Another problem with the two measures is that their distributions are extremely skewed to the right (cf. the summary statistics in appendix 11.2). This creates difficulties in interpreting the results from a generalized linear model analysis. To minimize this problem, I have log-transformed the Salience measure. Zeros have been handled by adding 0.02 to all values before calculating the logarithm.

## Level of Interdependence as Deviation from Expected Trade

The contamination of relative size in the interdependence variable is partly solved by entering a control for relative size in the model. Still, it would be useful to have a measure of interdependence which is independent of the sizes of the states in the dyad, absolutely, as well as relative to each other. Following the lead given by Russett (1967: 123–125), we may obtain this by assessing how much trade we might expect in the dyad, and then measuring the deviation of the observed trade level from this predicted level.

Once we have such a measure, the question of symmetry may be treated through a measure of relative capabilities or relative size. This is more appropriate, since it is extremely difficult to disentangle the contribution of military and political power preponderance from economic preponderance. With such a measure of interdependence, a measure of relative size, and the interaction term of these two variables, we may get more precise answers.

## The Gravity Model

I will use an economic model of international trade as my point of departure in order to formulate a realistic zero model of trade in a dyad: How much trade is to be expected in the dyad if political factors are not accounted for? The gravity model is an old model of human interaction, employed extensively in geography and regional science.[7] One of the first to use this model to study trade flows was Linneman (1966), who has modeled trade in a dyad *ij* as:

$$trade_{ij} = \frac{GNP_i * GNP_j}{dist_{ij}}$$

Dist$_{ij}$ is usually measured as the geographical distance between the capitals of the states. The model reflects that, ceteris paribus, states trade more with states that have large GNPs than they do with smaller economies. Likewise, states trade more with neighboring states than with distant ones. To this model I will add contiguity, since large countries may share a long border with extensive trade opportunities although their capitals are located far from each other.

The multiplicative gravity model is rendered linear when taking the logarithms of all terms. The model may thus be formulated as:

$$\ln(trade_{ij}) = \alpha + \beta_1 \ln(GNP_i) + \beta_2 \ln(GNP_j) + \beta_3 \ln(dist_{ij}) + \beta_4 contiguity_{ij} + \varepsilon$$

I estimate this by means of separate OLS regressions for each year, as the dependent variable is at the interval level and probably assumes a normal distribution. The data on bilateral trade, distance, and GNP are described below. Since the gravity model was estimated separately for each year, trade and GDP figures in current dollars were used. A summary of the analyses is reported in appendix

11.1. The residuals from these estimations were used as my measure of interdependence.

## Trade Data

Like Oneal and Russett (1997) I use the International Monetary Fund's *Direction of Trade* (1997) data. This source was supplemented with Faber and Nierop's *World Export Data, 1948–83* (1989, subsequently called WED), which has more complete information for non-IMF members.[8] The IMF dataset contains information on exports from state 1 to state 2 as well as imports to state 2 from 1. The WED data report exports only. There are considerable discrepancies between the three figures. To minimize errors, I calculated the average between the three figures where all were available and reported as larger than 0.[9] If one of three figures were missing or reported to be 0, I calculated the average of the remaining two. If two were missing, or 0, the third was used. Finally, if both sources reported 0 or missing data, I followed Oneal and Russett's example in treating it as an instance of negligible trade. The smallest unit in the IMF dataset is $0.1 million. Any exports or imports less than $0.05 million would be rounded down to 0. Thus, I recoded all cases reported as having zero trade to $0.02 million for the gravity-model estimation to allow log-transformation.

The information on trade level was lagged with one year, to minimize problems in assessing the direction of causality. Thus, for dispute outbreaks in 1950, the interdependence measures were calculated on the basis of the 1949 trade figures.

## Gravity Model Measure of Interdependence

The residuals from the OLS estimation of the gravity-model of trade were used as my measure of interdependence. This measure may be interpreted as the natural logarithm of the trade observed in the dyad, divided by the trade predicted from the gravity model. This measure is only weakly correlated with the other interdependence measures: $r = 0.26$ with Barbieri's Salience, $r = 0.22$ with Oneal and Russett's Least dependent measure, and $r = 0.63$ with the natural logarithm of Salience. Salience and Least dependent are correlated by $r = 0.65$ in my compilation of the data.

## Trade-to-GDP Ratio and Salience

To ensure comparability with previous studies, I also compiled Oneal and Russett's trade-to-GDP ratio and Barbieri's Salience measure on the basis of this trade dataset. These variables were scaled to range from 0 to 100, and are to be interpreted as the value of the dyadic trade as a percentage of GDP.

# The Dependent Variable: Fatal Dispute

The dependent variable is a subset of the Militarized Interstate Disputes compiled by the Correlates of War Project (Jones, Bremer, and Singer, 1996). Only disputes where at least one of the two states in the dyad experienced at least one fatality resulting from the dispute were included. Although limiting the number of disputes will in itself reduce the power of the analysis, I expect only a slight reduction in significance for the regime and interdependence variables.[10] Disputes with battle deaths are more clear-cut examples of militarized disputes than those not involving fatalities. Moreover, there is reason to suspect that militarized disputes between rich democracies are overreported in the MID dataset. Hereafter, I will refer to outbreaks with battle deaths as fatal disputes.

# Control Variables

Are there any variables that might confound the relationship between interdependence and militarized conflict? The set of control variables chosen here builds on Raknerud and Hegre (1997).

## Contiguity

Contiguity is defined as sharing a land border or having less than 25 miles of sea between the two states. Contiguity through colonies is not counted as contiguity here. A contiguous dyad is defined as a high-relevance dyad.

## Major Powers

By definition, major powers have the means to interact with a large proportion of the states in the system—as well as an interest in so doing. They are therefore expected to participate more in militarized disputes than other states. For the same reason, Oneal and Russett include dyads containing major powers in their set of relevant dyads. I have coded each dyad as consisting of zero, one, or two major powers. The information on power status is taken from the Correlates of War Project (Small and Singer, 1982).

Dyads consisting of two major powers are defined as high-relevance dyads and included in the dataset. Dyads consisting of only one major power, on the other hand, are not included—a different choice from that of Maoz and Russett (1992). The justification for this is that the number of dyads containing one major power is dependent on the number of states in the system. It is, then, following the discussion on the relevance of dyads in Raknerud and Hegre (1997), necessary to treat them together with the low-relevance dyads. The category One major power distinguishes these dyads from the other low-relevance dyads.

## Allies

Dyads related through alliances have a lower probability of war, ceteris paribus (Bremer, 1992). I used an update[11] to 1992 of the COW alliance dataset (Singer and Small, 1966a; Small and Singer, 1969) to code this variable, and added some alliances from Oren (1990). The nonaggression pact category was excluded since this usually applies to potential enemies rather than between potential allies in war (see Raknerud and Hegre, 1997: 394 for an empirical validation of this choice).

## Brevity of Peace and War History

The probability of peace between two states in a future period is duration-dependent (Beck and Katz, 1997; Beck, Katz, and Tucker, 1998; Raknerud and Hegre, 1997): The longer the peace has lasted, the greater its chances of continuing. Time is needed to heal wounds and reestablish normal relations after an interstate conflict; moreover, the creation of new states is often followed by tensions in the first period due to uncertainties in definitions of borders, and so forth. The Brevity of peace variable is a function of the number of days since the current peace began—the time since the last fatal dispute in the dyad ended, or, if they have not had any wars, since the youngest state in the dyad achieved independence. Recall that all disputing dyads are excluded from the dataset. The number of days in peace was transformed into a decaying function using the formula:

$$Exp\left( -\frac{Days\ in\ peace}{\alpha} \right),$$

where $\alpha$ was set to 3,162 to model the assumption that the hazard of a fatal dispute is halved every six years. The variable varies from 1 for observations of dyads just after the peace began to 0 for dyads that have had peace for a large number of years.

The variable was coded from the Correlates of War datasets on militarized disputes (Jones, Bremer, and Singer, 1996) and on system membership (taken from the Peace Science Society website). When coding the variable, I made use of information from 1816 and onward, unlike Beck, Katz, and Tucker (1998), who only coded peace-years from 1950 onward. This is not a trivial difference, as information on the alliance alignment of World War II is ignored in their analysis, as is the entry of new states in the two decades before 1950 (India and Pakistan, among others).

If the peace was preceded by a fatal dispute between the states, we may expect the risk of new dispute to be higher than if the peace started with one of the countries gaining system membership. I have included a variable called past dispute to distinguish the two types from each other.

## Regime Type

As noted above, liberal economic and political theory have been interconnected ever since the eighteenth century. The trade-promotes-peace hypothesis is closely related to another liberal tenet—that democracies do not fight each other (cf. Oneal and Russett, 1998; Russett, 1998). It is necessary to control for the regime-type combination in the dyad.

The regime-type variable denotes whether the dyad consists of two democracies, two nondemocracies, or one democracy and one nondemocracy (here called politically mixed dyads), or whether one or both countries have missing regime data or are coded as being in transition. Regime data were taken from Polity IIId (Gurr, Jaggers, and Moore, 1989; Jaggers and Gurr, 1995; McLaughlin et al., 1998). A democracy is defined as a country that receives a score of 6 or higher on the institutionalized democracy index in Polity.

Oneal and Russett used the lower score of the two countries in the dyad as the corresponding control variable. I chose the categorical variable described above instead, for several reasons: First, in the politically mixed dyads we find higher proneness for war than in the nondemocratic dyads (Beck and Jackman, 1998; Gleditsch and Hegre, 1997; Raknerud and Hegre, 1997). Oneal and Russett's measure does not account for this. The bimodal distribution of the democracy variable allows this simplification without much loss of data. Finally, the category Missing regime data allows the inclusion of dyads where information on regime type is missing, cases that are omitted by Oneal and Russett.

## Size Asymmetry

Two measures of asymmetry were tested. The GDP ratio variable is based on the two countries' population and GDP. The variable is calculated by the following formula:

$$SizeRatio = \ln\left(\sqrt{\frac{GDP_{country\_1}}{GDP_{country\_2}} * \frac{Population_{country\_1}}{Population_{country\_2}}}\right)$$

The objective of the formula is to average the two ratios. This averaged ratio is then log-transformed to avoid outliers. Data on GDP and population were taken from the Penn World Tables (Mark 5.6) (see Summers and Heston, 1991).

I also made use of the traditional measure of asymmetry, the capability ratio or the ratio of the states' score on the COW military capabilities index (Singer, Bremer, and Stuckey, 1972). This index gives equal weight to the states' total population, urban population, energy consumption, iron and steel production, military expenditures, and size of the armed forces. The source for this variable is the same as for energy consumption per capita.

*GDP for the Gravity Model*

Data on GDP were taken from Penn World Table (Mark 5.6) (see Summers and Heston, 1991). For the gravity model, the current dollar value of GDP was used (the Penn CGDP variable). GDP was calculated by multiplying the GDP per capita variable by the population variable.

*Distance for the Gravity Model*

Dyadic distance is defined as the beeline distance between the capitals of the two states. I used the data computed for Gleditsch (1995).

# Results

## Development, Interdependence, and Fatal Disputes

Results from the Cox regression estimation using the gravity-model measure of interdependence are reported in table 11.1. The column labeled Model Ia supports the conclusion of Oneal and Russett (1997).[12] The parameter estimate (found in the top row of each cell) for the interdependence variable is –0.13: Thus, dyads with high levels of trade relative to the prediction from the gravity model have a much lower risk of fatal disputes than dyads with a low trade level relative to the prediction. The estimated standard errors and *p*-values appear in the second and third rows in each cell. In contrast to Beck, Katz, and Tucker (1998) and Oneal and Russett (1999c), the parameter estimate for interdependence is highly significant even when controlling for temporal dependence.

In column Ib, the development variable was added to the model. The estimates for interdependence and for development (GDP per capita) emerge as both negative and strongly significant. The probability of militarized conflict decreases with increasing trade *and* with increased development. The development variable clearly improves the model's goodness-of-fit, increasing log likelihood by 4.9.

However, I expected the effect of interdependence to be strengthened by increased development. In column Ic, the interaction term between interdependence and development was added to the model. This improves the fit considerably: Log likelihood is increased by 4.4 points, which is significantly different from 0 (*p*=0.003). Development thus seems to be a crucial factor for the liberal peace.

The estimate has a negative sign, as hypothesized: the pacifying effect of trade increases with increased development. With the interaction term present, the estimate for interdependence is positive, implying that, in some circumstances, greater interdependence may *increase* the probability of fatal disputes.

**Table 11.1. Risk of Fatal Dispute, Gravity Model, GDP/cap Measure of Development, 1950–92**

| Variable | Category | Model Ia | Model Ib | Model Ic |
|---|---|---|---|---|
| Interdependence: Residual from gravity model of trade | | -0.13<br>0.038<br><0.0005 | -0.13<br>0.039<br>0.001 | 0.87<br>0.29<br>0.002 |
| Development: GDP per capita | | | -0.48<br>0.18<br>0.009 | -0.70<br>0.16<br><0.0005 |
| Interdependence* development Interaction | | | | -0.14<br>0.040<br><0.0005 |
| Regime type | Two democracies | -0.11<br>0.39<br>0.77 | 0.28<br>0.40<br>0.48 | 0.34<br>0.39<br>0.39 |
| | Two autocracies | 0.14<br>0.24<br>0.55 | 0.019<br>0.26<br>0.94 | -0.045<br>0.25<br>0.86 |
| | Missing regime Data | -0.68<br>0.77<br>0.38 | -0.91<br>0.78<br>0.25 | -0.76<br>0.76<br>0.32 |
| Relevance | Contiguity | 3.07<br>0.35<br><0.0005 | 3.03<br>0.35<br><0.0005 | 3.02<br>0.34<br><0.0005 |
| | Alliance | 0.013<br>0.25<br>0.96 | 0.06<br>0.25<br>0.80 | 0.007<br>0.25<br>0.98 |
| | One major power | -0.19<br>0.36<br>0.60 | -0.14<br>0.37<br>0.70 | 0.001<br>0.36<br>0.998 |
| | Two major powers | 0.40<br>0.52<br>0.44 | 0.52<br>0.53<br>0.33 | 0.47<br>0.53<br>0.37 |
| Size asymmetry: ln(Ratio of GDP and population) | | 0.15<br>0.08<br>0.068 | 0.18<br>0.09<br>0.041 | 0.15<br>0.09<br>0.088 |
| Peace history | Brevity of peace: exp(–days in Peace/3,162) | 3.13<br>0.33<br><0.0005 | 2.75<br>0.39<br><0.0005 | 2.60<br>0.36<br><0.0005 |
| | Past dispute | 1.69<br>0.27<br><0.0005 | 1.82<br>0.27<br><0.0005 | 1.87<br>0.27<br><0.0005 |
| Log likelihood | | -456.49 | -451.58 | -447.19 |
| No. of disputes (failures) | | 103 | 103 | 103 |
| No. of observations | | 266,094 | 266,094 | 266,094 |

*Note:* The figures in each cell are: Parameter estimate, Robust standard error, *p*-value (two-sided test).

To ease the interpretation of results, the parameter estimates in column Ic are shown in figure 11.1 for actual ranges for the two variables. The vertical axis denotes the estimated risk of fatal disputes relative to a baseline dyad.The baseline dyad is here defined as a dyad with mean value for development and trade equal to the gravity model prediction (a residual equal to 0). In the upper right-hand corner of the floor of the figure we find dyads consisting of two states that are rich (9.8 corresponds to U.S. GDP per capita in 1990; $18,000 per capita) and that have negligible trade bonds. This dyad is estimated to be 30 percent more war prone than the baseline. The interdependence measure is the natural logarithm of the ratio between observed and expected trade. Multiplying trade by $e = 2.7$ is equivalent to increasing the interdependence measure by one unit. For the rich dyad, this reduces the risk of war by 40 percent.

**Figure 11.1. Relative Risk of Fatal Dispute as a Function of Interdependence and GDP per Capita, 1950–92**

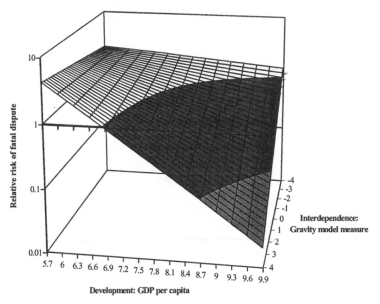

In the lower left-hand corner we find a highly interdependent dyad where the poorer state is very poor (5.7 corresponds to $300 per capita, e.g., a dyad involving, say, Chad or Ethiopia in the mid-1980s). Interdependence for such a dyad is estimated to have the opposite effect: Increasing the interdependence by one unit[13] *raises* the risk of dispute by 7 percent. Greater interdependence is estimated to increase the risk of fatal dispute for dyads where the poorer state has a GDP per capita lower than $500. Mali and Malawi were close to this figure in the early 1990s, and as much as 10 percent of the observations in the period 1950–92 were below this threshold. Figure 11.1 demonstrates clearly that interdependence works best for developed economies, as the theoretical discussion implied. The development variable reduces the risk of dispute for the entire plotted range of values.

The figure is based on the results in column Ic in table 11.1. The development variable is estimated to be of substantial importance. For a dyad with 0 on the interdependence variable (i.e., with a trade level equal to what the gravity model predicts), an increase in development by the factor $e = 2.7$ reduces the risk of dispute to one half. The 10th percentile dyad in terms of GDP per capita is estimated to be 5.7 times more dispute-prone than the 90th percentile dyad. The 10th percentile is 6.2 or approximately $500—roughly equal to the level of Mali or Malawi in the 1990s. The 90th percentile is approximately 8.7 or $6,000, corresponding to the level of Denmark or Sweden in the 1950s, or to Greece or South Korea in the late 1980s (see appendix 2).

In table 11.2, the analysis is reproduced using the ln(Salience) measure of interdependence and energy consumption per capita as indicator of development. The results are very similar to those of table 11.1. Both trade and development reduce the probability of fatal militarized disputes. Since this analysis includes 50 percent more observations, the significance levels are generally lower. Interestingly, the $p$-value for ln(Salience) drops dramatically when we include the interaction term between interdependence and development (compare Models IIa and IIb with Model IIc).

Figure 11.2 plots the estimates in model IIc in the same way as Model Ic was plotted in figure 11.1. We see how the interaction between interdependence and development is even more marked in Model IIc. For a dyad with 2.0 as the lowest ln(energy consumption per capita)—for example, two Western European countries in the 1990s an increase in trade by the factor $e = 2.7$ reduces the likelihood of fatal dispute by 60 percent. For a dyad with lowest ln(energy consumption per capita) = –4.0—the level of Chad or Ethiopia in the 1980s—this increase in the trade level is estimated to increase the risk of fatal dispute by 34 percent. The estimated effect of interdependence is peace-promoting only above –2.47, or the level of Bangladesh in 1992. More than one-fourth of the observations in the sample are under that threshold—29 countries had lower values than this in 1992.

For an average interdependent dyad (with ln(Salience) = 5.5), the estimated effect of development is stronger in Model IIc than in Model Ic. In other words, increasing energy consumption per capita by the factor $e = 2.7$ decreases the risk of fatal dispute by more than 80 percent.

The characteristic feature of Cox regression is the nonparametric baseline hazard. Combined with my choice of calendar time as the time variable in the survival analysis, this implies that all comparisons are done cross-sectionally, not over time. The advantage of this is that the results are immune to spurious effects from factors that vary systematically over time (cf. Raknerud and Hegre,

**Table 11.2. Risk of Fatal Dispute, ln(Salience) Measure of Interdependence, Energy/CAP Measure of Development, 1950–92**

| Variable | Category | Model IIa | Model IIb | Model IIc |
|---|---|---|---|---|
| Interdependence: ln(Salience) | | -0.13 | -0.11 | -0.47 |
| | | 0.075 | 0.077 | 0.12 |
| | | 0.076 | 0.15 | <0.0005 |
| Development: Energy consumption per capita | | | -0.23 | -0.64 |
| | | | 0.063 | 0.11 |
| | | | <0.0005 | <0.0005 |
| Interdependence* development interaction | | | | -0.19 |
| | | | | 0.042 |
| | | | | <0.0005 |
| Regime type | Two democracies | -0.43 | -0.19 | -0.10 |
| | | 0.37 | 0.37 | 0.37 |
| | | 0.25 | 0.60 | 0.77 |
| | Two autocracies | -0.22 | -0.35 | -0.32 |
| | | 0.18 | 0.18 | 0.19 |
| | | 0.23 | 0.055 | 0.083 |
| | Missing regime data | -0.66 | -0.91 | -0.72 |
| | | 0.53 | 0.53 | 0.52 |
| | | 0.21 | 0.086 | 0.17 |
| Relevance | Contiguity | 2.50 | 2.42 | 2.46 |
| | | 0.26 | 0.26 | 0.26 |
| | | <0.0005 | <0.0005 | <0.0005 |
| | Alliance | -0.15 | -0.23 | -0.018 |
| | | 0.19 | 0.20 | 0.21 |
| | | 0.43 | 0.24 | 0.93 |
| | One major power | -0.027 | 0.06 | 0.30 |
| | | 0.26 | 0.26 | 0.28 |
| | | 0.92 | 0.81 | 0.28 |
| | Two major powers | 1.05 | 1.24 | 1.56 |
| | | 0.39 | 0.40 | 0.41 |
| | | 0.008 | 0.002 | <0.0005 |
| Size asymmetry: ln(Capability ratio) | | 0.079 | 0.078 | 0.076 |
| | | 0.040 | 0.041 | 0.041 |
| | | 0.05 | 0.056 | 0.065 |
| Peace history | Brevity of peace: exp(–days in peace/3,162) | 2.94 | 2.61 | 2.49 |
| | | 0.28 | 0.30 | 0.30 |
| | | <0.0005 | <0.0005 | <0.0005 |
| | Past dispute | 1.89 | 2.04 | 1.97 |
| | | 0.21 | 0.22 | 0.21 |
| | | <0.0005 | <0.0005 | <0.0005 |
| Log likelihood | | -757.85 | -750.82 | -742.02 |
| No. of disputes (failures) | | 149 | 149 | 149 |
| No. of observations | | 343,148 | 343,148 | 343,148 |

*Note:* The figures in each cell are: Parameter estimate, Robust standard error, *p*-value (two-sided test).

1997). If current-dollar GDP/cap had been used as the measure of development, this would have yielded exactly the same parameter estimates as with constant-dollar figures. The difference between the two measures would be reflected only in the baseline hazard. The advantage of this for the present analysis is that we know that the effects of all variables are purely cross-sectional. Any trends in variables over time are disregarded. It is *relative* wealth and *relative* interdependence that makes the difference in the models estimated in tables 11.1 and 11.2. However, if we want to know whether the possible increase in average wealth and average interdependence has changed the world, the parameter estimates of the Cox regression model give no answer. To validate this, I estimated the data using exponential regression. This is equivalent to setting $\alpha(t) = 1$ in equation 1. The parameter estimates emerging from that analysis were virtually unchanged from the results in table 11.1—indicating that the effect of development is not only cross-sectional but also temporal. The results give reason to expect the interstate system to become more peaceful as its member-states become more developed.

**Figure 11.2. Relative Risk of Fatal Dispute as a Function of ln(Salience) and Energy Consumption per Capita, 1950–92**

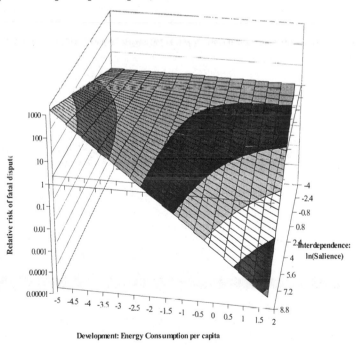

*Note:* The figure is based on the results in column IIc in table 11.2.

## Control Variable Puzzles

Among the control variables, only contiguity, brevity of peace, and past dispute are significant in all the reported models. They are, however, both strong and highly significant. The contiguous dyads have a hazard of dispute 10–20 times higher than the baseline[14]. The brevity of peace variable is as important for the hazard of dispute in a dyad as is contiguity. The parameter estimate indicates that the risk of dispute is approximately 10–20 times higher in the first year after a dispute than after some 40 years in peace. There is considerable support for the idea of temporal dependence in the data, further strengthened by the past dispute variable. Not surprisingly, the analysis shows that whether the members of a dyad have been enemies in a dispute earlier is important for the risk of a new dispute: The estimated hazard is 5–7 times higher for such dyads. This comes in addition to the increase in risk modeled by the brevity of peace variable. Half a year after a fatal dispute, Model Ic estimates the risk of fatal disputes to be 75 times higher than for a dyad that has never had a dispute and has coexisted peacefully for many years.[15] The significance of these variables is substantial.

In table 11.1, the GDP/population size ratio was used as indicator of size asymmetry since this variable led to the least reduction in the number of cases with data. In table 11.2, I used the capability ratio, for the same reason.[16] The variables for size asymmetry are close to statistical significance in both tables, but in the opposite direction of what has been found in comparable studies (e.g., Barbieri, 1996a; Oneal and Russett, 1997). The estimate for two major powers is positive but significant only in table 11.2.

The regime variables never reach statistical significance, despite the many studies that have found support for the democratic peace (e.g., Bremer, 1992; Doyle, 1986; Maoz and Russett, 1993; Raknerud and Hegre, 1997). Likewise, the alliance and major power variables are insignificant.

The discrepancy between these results and previous studies is in part due to the brevity of peace and past dispute variables. When the models are estimated without them, alliance and asymmetry emerge with negative and significant estimates. It may be debated how the two variables should be interpreted. The principle of conditioning on all events that precede the event we analyze to avoid temporal dependence is a strong argument for including these variables. However, with brevity of peace as the exception, the variables in the model are dyad attributes that change slowly. When estimating the models without the development and the two history variables, we see that a contiguous, politically mixed dyad of two major powers is among the most likely to wage a first dispute. Using the peace history variable to predict later disputes may mean partly subsuming these explanations under this variable.

A closer look at the data can shed more light on the puzzle. For 55 percent of the dispute outbreaks in the dataset we find that the two countries are previous enemies in disputes, as compared to 2.7 percent for the nondispute observations. Contrary to what might be expected, the double-democratic dyads in the dataset have had past disputes more frequently than any other regime combinations: 5.6 percent in contrast to 1.8 percent for the double autocratic dyads and 2.9 percent for the politically mixed ones. One reason is that double-democratic dyads on average have existed for a longer time; another reason may be the regime changes in Germany, Italy, and Japan after World War II. In 10 of the 12 double democratic disputes (83 percent) there had been a past war. This is high, but not that far from the baseline of 55 percent.

**Table 11.3. Effect on the Risk of Fatal Dispute, Model Including Interaction between Regime Type and Development, 1950–92**

| Variable | Category | Parameter estimate | Robust standard error | p-value (two-sided test) |
|---|---|---|---|---|
| Interdependence: Gravity model measure | | 0.78 | 0.30 | 0.010 |
| Development | | -1.07 | 0.21 | <0.0005 |
| Interdependence* development interaction | | -0.13 | 0.043 | 0.002 |
| Regime type | Two democracies | 0.36 | 2.16 | 0.87 |
| | Two autocracies | -4.99 | 1.86 | 0.007 |
| | Missing regime data | 1.59 | 8.15 | 0.85 |
| Interaction: Regime type* development | Development*Two democracies | 0.027 | 0.30 | 0.93 |
| | Development*Two autocracies | 0.72 | 0.27 | 0.008 |
| | Development*Missing regime data | -0.42 | 1.31 | 0.75 |
| Relevance | Contiguity | 2.96 | 0.35 | <0.0005 |
| | Alliance | 0.030 | 0.26 | 0.91 |
| | One major power | 0.064 | 0.37 | 0.86 |
| | Two major powers | 0.58 | 0.54 | 0.28 |
| Asymmetry: ln(Geometric average of GDP) | | 0.14 | 0.09 | 0.12 |
| Peace history | Brevity of peace: exp(–Days in peace/3,162) | 2.50 | 0.37 | <0.0005 |
| | Past dispute | 1.84 | 0.28 | <0.0005 |
| Log likelihood | | -443.95 | | |
| No. of disputes (failures) | | 103 | | |
| No. of observations | | 266,094 | | |

A trivariate analysis of the relationship between regime type, past war, and dispute outbreak shows that regime type does make less of a difference for dyads with a past war than for dyads with a peaceful history: For the former group, the probabilities for politically mixed dyads and double-autocratic dyads are 2.5

and 5 times higher than for double-democratic dyads, respectively. The corresponding figures for the latter group are 5 and 6.5. This change is sufficient for the parameter estimates to drop considerably in terms of statistical significance.

Still, the estimate for two democracies is significant only when we remove the development variable in addition to the peace-history variables.[17] Might it be that the democratic peace also requires a certain level of economic development? This is suggested by Mousseau (1998, 2000), who finds the democratic peace to be restricted to the developed world. Mousseau explains this with norms generated by intensive market economies, but it may also be due to the fact that poor, illiterate citizens are less capable of constraining their political leaders than rich, well-educated ones. To test this, I added the interaction term between development and regime type to Model Ic. The results are presented in table 11.3.

**Figure 11.3. Relative Risk as a Function of Development for Different Regime Categories, Gravity Model Measure 1950–92**

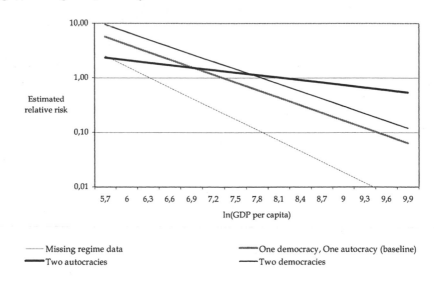

The results in table 11.3 give some support for the hypothesis of interaction between development and the democratic peace. Dyads consisting of two autocracies are estimated to be significantly different from the baseline. Figure 11.3 is presented to ease the interpretation of these estimates. Here, the estimated risks relative to the baseline are plotted as functions of development for the four categories of regime type combinations. The slope of the line representing two autocracies is clearly different from the others: For this category, increased development does less to reduce the risk of disputes. One interpretation of this result is that there is a monadic democratic peace for developed dyads: Dyads with at least one democracy are significantly less dispute-prone than are dyads with no democracies.[18] For dyads that contain at least one underdeveloped country, the opposite is the case: Dyads with no democracies are significantly less prone to fatal disputes than are dyads with at least one democracy (recall that the development variable records the value for the less developed country of the dyad). It is not possible to tell from this model which of the two aspects is stronger—the developed democratic peace, or the underdeveloped autocratic peace.

Estimating the model in table 11.2 with corresponding interaction terms yielded comparable results, although the differences were less significant.

## Conclusion

This chapter has investigated to what extent the positive association between trade and peace is contingent on the trading partners' levels of socioeconomic development. Does the level of development have any influence on how the importance of the trade between countries is inversely related to conflict between them? And, by extension, does the democratic peace require a certain amount of development, too?

These questions were investigated empirically at the dyadic level using Cox regression for a wide range of dyads for the period 1950–92. As a first step toward answering these questions, I introduced an alternative measure of interdependence that is not dependent on the difference in size between the states in the dyad. When this measure was used, the analysis supported the hypothesis that trade is inversely related to militarized conflict. To a somewhat lesser degree, the same conclusion may be drawn from an analysis using the natural logarithm of a measure of interdependence based on the share of the total trade formed by the bilateral trade (i.e., ln(Salience), cf. Barbieri, 1996a).

I then included indicators for socioeconomic development and interaction terms between development and interdependence in the analysis. This demonstrated that development indeed is important for the peace-through-interdependence hypothesis, as indicated by Rosecrance. For dyads containing one state that is less developed than Bangladesh, for instance, interdependence seems to have no peace-conducive effect at all. Interdependence may even have the opposite effect. Development on its own seems to be a considerably stronger factor for keeping peace although development in one case was estimated to increase the hazard of fatal militarized disputes for extremely noninterdependent dyads.

The inclusion of the development variable obliterated the effect of regime type on the probability of fatal dispute. At first glance, the democratic peace seemed to be explained by the level of development. However, the inclusion of an interaction term between dyadic regime type and development demonstrated that development in the dyad decreased the risk of fatal dispute markedly more for dyads containing at least one democracy than for purely autocratic dyads.

To some extent, these results are at odds with earlier research. Maoz and Russett (1992: 257) concluded that 'the notion that democracies do not fight one another *because* they are rich is flatly rejected'. Oneal et al. (1996: 18) reported that '[d]yadic wealth is not included in the analyses we will report, however, because it never proved significant when [the interdependence measure] was in the equation'. However, a reanalysis of their model using their data (i.e., the data for Oneal and Russett, 1997) without the interaction term between development and interdependence, showed that GDP per capita was *positively* related to conflict. When adding the interaction term to the model, however, the results were very similar to those reported here. The discrepancies between the findings are most likely due to this interaction term.

Two important caveats to the conclusion reached here should be noted: First, the analysis presented here covers the years 1950–92. The major part of this period was characterized by the Cold War. Farber and Gowa (1995) warn against concluding that there is a democratic peace, since it may only be found in the post-1945 period—which coincides with the Cold War. This objection of course applies as much to the results in this analysis as to the studies of the democratic peace.

Second, the development measure uses the value for the least developed state, based on the weak-link assumption. All dyads consisting of one developed and one underdeveloped state are counted as underdeveloped. Any disputes in such dyads are counted as being in less developed dyads. If such disputes are overrepresented in the world, this will be disguised by this analysis. Moreover, the structural factors described by Galtung (1971) may serve to perpetuate developmental inequalities in the world. In that case, it is not tenable to assume that development is exogenous to the model. The question of asymmetry of development is intrinsically connected to asymmetry of trade, as trade between a developed and an underdeveloped state is almost invariably asymmetric in the rich state's favor. Barbieri (1996a) has argued that asymmetric trade bonds do not hinder militarized conflicts—rather the opposite. In Hegre (2001) I also find that trade is likely to reduce conflict the most in dyads where the two countries are roughly of the same economic size. The significant interaction between development and interdependence which I find may also be consistent with this.

**Appendix 11.1. Results of Gravity Model Regressions**

| Year | Intercept | ln(GDP country 1) | ln(GDP country 2) | ln(Distance) | Contiguous |
|------|-----------|-------------------|-------------------|--------------|------------|
| 1949 | 5.760 | 0.264 | 0.125 | -0.972 | 0.689 |
| 1950 | 5.398 | 0.251 | 0.128 | -0.912 | 0.682 |
| 1951 | 5.359 | 0.272 | 0.140 | -0.918 | 0.614 |
| 1952 | 5.075 | 0.281 | 0.168 | -0.907 | 0.319 |
| 1953 | 4.965 | 0.287 | 0.177 | -0.920 | 0.133 |
| 1954 | 5.559 | 0.250 | 0.160 | -0.936 | 0.160 |
| 1955 | 5.792 | 0.251 | 0.149 | -0.929 | 0.489 |
| 1956 | 6.431 | 0.240 | 0.124 | -0.972 | 0.497 |
| 1957 | 6.944 | 0.225 | 0.130 | -1.019 | 0.442 |
| 1958 | 7.178 | 0.222 | 0.113 | -1.028 | 0.286 |
| 1959 | 7.360 | 0.232 | 0.120 | -1.061 | 0.388 |
| 1960 | 2.146 | 0.460 | 0.388 | -1.094 | 0.384 |
| 1961 | 2.108 | 0.458 | 0.390 | -1.099 | 0.484 |
| 1962 | 2.326 | 0.452 | 0.396 | -1.133 | 0.299 |
| 1963 | 2.427 | 0.455 | 0.396 | -1.138 | 0.275 |
| 1964 | 2.502 | 0.456 | 0.377 | -1.125 | 0.319 |
| 1965 | 1.879 | 0.467 | 0.375 | -1.050 | 0.479 |
| 1966 | 1.459 | 0.481 | 0.392 | -1.036 | 0.340 |
| 1967 | 1.603 | 0.478 | 0.399 | -1.064 | 0.417 |
| 1968 | 1.619 | 0.494 | 0.399 | -1.099 | 0.513 |
| 1969 | 1.622 | 0.495 | 0.408 | -1.102 | 0.418 |
| 1970 | -3.562 | 0.809 | 0.644 | -1.096 | 0.513 |
| 1971 | -1.972 | 0.736 | 0.515 | -1.069 | 0.523 |
| 1972 | -1.160 | 0.754 | 0.508 | -1.195 | 0.567 |
| 1973 | 0.149 | 0.672 | 0.514 | -1.245 | 0.347 |
| 1974 | 0.423 | 0.637 | 0.524 | -1.234 | 0.375 |
| 1975 | -0.425 | 0.666 | 0.600 | -1.273 | 0.355 |
| 1976 | -0.709 | 0.669 | 0.572 | -1.220 | 0.344 |
| 1977 | -2.540 | 0.783 | 0.644 | -1.215 | 0.311 |
| 1978 | -1.956 | 0.742 | 0.615 | -1.211 | 0.299 |
| 1979 | -0.921 | 0.687 | 0.622 | -1.274 | 0.143 |
| 1980 | -2.633 | 0.767 | 0.732 | -1.303 | 0.313 |
| 1981 | -2.484 | 0.722 | 0.682 | -1.227 | 0.513 |
| 1982 | -2.387 | 0.722 | 0.669 | -1.245 | 0.507 |
| 1983 | -2.731 | 0.718 | 0.706 | -1.262 | 0.423 |
| 1984 | -4.317 | 0.762 | 0.842 | -1.304 | 0.407 |
| 1985 | -6.898 | 0.967 | 0.895 | -1.319 | 0.354 |
| 1986 | -3.818 | 0.749 | 0.841 | -1.352 | 0.266 |
| 1987 | -0.177 | 0.647 | 0.572 | -1.319 | 0.461 |
| 1988 | 1.250 | 0.557 | 0.499 | -1.273 | 0.611 |
| 1989 | 3.313 | 0.462 | 0.395 | -1.261 | 0.829 |
| 1990 | 6.926 | 0.307 | 0.219 | -1.242 | 0.815 |
| 1991 | 7.354 | 0.204 | 0.184 | -1.123 | 0.912 |
| 1992 | 8.520 | 0.198 | 0.161 | -1.186 | 0.948 |

**Appendix 11.2. Descriptive Statistics**

| Variable | Mean | St. dev. | Percentiles | | |
|---|---|---|---|---|---|
| | | | 10% | Median | 90% |
| Gravity-model measure | −0.054 | 1.88 | -2.43 | 0.085 | 2.14 |
| Ln(Salience) | 5.45 | 5.41 | -3.91 | 7.70 | 10.33 |
| Least dependent | 0.16 | 0.57 | 0 | 0.02 | 0.38 |
| Lowest GDP per capita | 7.33 | 0.93 | 6.19 | 7.23 | 8.67 |
| Lowest energy consumption/capita | −1.38 | 1.78 | −3.73 | −1.33 | 1.13 |
| Size asymmetry: GDP and population | 1.58 | 1.28 | 0.21 | 1.27 | 3.41 |
| Size asymmetry: Military capabilities | 0.15 | 2.33 | −2.70 | 0.089 | 3.09 |
| Time in peace | 0.24 | 0.27 | 0.0012 | 0.13 | 0.68 |

# Notes

This article is a slightly revised version of Hegre (2000). The research represented here has been supported by the Ryoichi Sasakawa Young Leaders Fellowship Fund, The Research Council of Norway, and by the U.S. National Science Foundation. I am grateful to Katherine Barbieri, Scott Gates, Kristian Skrede Gleditsch, Nils Petter Gleditsch, Leif Helland, Jon Hovi, Soo Yeon Kim, Michael Mousseau, John Oneal, Bruce Russett, Gerald Schneider, Indra de Soysa, Richard Tucker, and Michael D. Ward as well as to *JPR*'s reviewers for comments on earlier versions of this work. The dataset and Stata do files used in this analysis are available at www.prio.no/cwp/datasets.asp (see under Hegre, 2000 in the chronological list). The findings and conclusions expressed in the chapter are entirely those of the author, and do not represent the views of the author's current employer, the World Bank.

1. Rosecrance's argument is to some extent systemic, since the spread of technology and industrialization is quicker than the initial development of it. However, sizeable differences persist in the level of development. Rosecrance's argument, then, applies at the nation-state and dyadic level as well.

2. This argument may also be found in the 'new growth theory' in economics. If there are economies of scale in the production of a good and a large market for it, firms will specialize (see Ethier, 1995: 52–58). However, to run manufacturing plants sufficiently large to benefit from economies of scale, firms need capital, skilled labor, and a developed infrastructure. Thus, developed countries are in a better position to enjoy the gains from trade due to economies of scale (cf. Krugman, 1981). Accordingly, it may be hypothesized that the more developed countries will trade more, relative to their GDP, than less developed ones.

3. We might add to Rosecrance's argument that the more developed a country is, the easier it is for the inhabitants to take their assets with them when fleeing the country. If this is so, it is not certain that increased wealth in a society makes it a richer prize.

4. The inclusion of nonrelevant dyads with inter-capital distance up to 3,000 km means a significantly larger spatial domain than the relevant dyads. Still, only a quarter of all dyads were included. The reasons for the limitation are purely technical. A dataset with 500,000 cases is much more manageable than one with 2,000,000.

5. See Raknerud and Hegre (1997) for a discussion of the interpretation of the parameter estimates.

6. http://wizard.ucr.edu/cps/eugene/eugene.html.

7. The gravity model was originally developed in geography. It has also been used to study other forms of international interaction (Gleditsch, 1968). Earlier uses of the grav-

ity model to study the trade and conflict issue are found in Gowa and Mansfield (1993) and Pollins (1989b).

8. Most earlier studies of the liberal peace (e.g., Oneal and Russett, 1997, 1999c; Barbieri, 1996a) exclude the non-IMF members from their samples—most notably, these studies omitted all countries in the Warszaw Pact.

9. The figures for imports were weighted down by the factor 0.96, the average exports/imports ratio in the DOT dataset. This discrepancy is due to the reporting of imports as c.i.f. and exports as f.o.b.

10. In a trial run with Oneal and Russett's (1997) dataset, I replaced their dependent variable with mine. This in fact resulted in a higher level of significance for their interdependence variable, in spite of the loss of cases.

11. This dataset was obtained from the COW project in 1995 through personal communication with J. David Singer.

12. In Hegre (1999) I report the results for the same model using Oneal and Russett's (nontransformed) measure of interdependence. The size and sign of the parameter estimate obtained there was close to what they found, but the standard error of the estimate was too large to dismiss a hypothesis of no relationship between interdependence and conflict.

13. Which is equivalent with reducing trade to $1/e = 0.37$, or reducing with 73 percent.

14. The estimated relative hazards of '10–20 times higher than the baseline' is arrived at by computing the exponential of the parameter estimate; $\exp(2.42) = 11.2$ and $\exp(3.07) = 21.5$.

15. This estimated relative hazard is computed by the formula $\exp(2.60 + 1.87 * \exp(-188/3,162)) = 75$, where 188 is the number of days that equals a half year and 3,162 the value for $\alpha$.

16. I also tried using the capability ration in table 11.1 and vice versa. This did not alter the results except for a loss of significance due to the loss of cases.

17. Moreover, in Raknerud and Hegre (1997) we found support for the democratic peace when controlling for exactly the same history variables (but that study was of war and included a longer time-frame and more outbreaks to analyze).

18. The line for two democracies is above that of one democracy, one autocracy, but this difference is not significant.

# CHAPTER 12

# Institutions, Interdependence, and International Conflict

*Edward D. Mansfield and Jon C. Pevehouse*

Over the past few decades, there has been a surge of interest in the relationship between international trade and political conflict. Among both policymakers and scholars, the view that heightened trade inhibits conflict is gaining currency. Nonetheless, this view has also attracted various critics. Some of them argue that increasing commerce is a source of political discord, while others maintain that economic exchange has no systematic influence on hostilities.

These debates have given rise to a burgeoning empirical literature, the bulk of which addresses the effects of trade flows on conflict. Such research, however, has largely ignored the institutional context in which trade is conducted. In a number of recent studies, we have argued that this omission obscures the relationship between commerce and conflict (Mansfield and Pevehouse, 2000; Mansfield, Pevehouse, and Bearce, 1999–2000). Members of preferential trading arrangements (PTAs)—a set of institutions that includes free trade areas, common markets, and customs unions—are less likely to become involved in militarized disputes than other states. Moreover, the effects of trade flows on hostilities depend centrally on whether commercial partners are PTA members. Heightened trade does much more to dampen antagonism between parties to the same PTA than between other states.

Our earlier tests of this argument followed many prior studies in analyzing 'politically relevant' pairs of states—that is, those that either are geographically contiguous or include a major power—during the period from 1950 to 1985. Here, we analyze a far broader sample of country-pairs, an expanded temporal domain, as well as multiple datasets on the flow of trade. Our findings continue to indicate that trade flows have a more pronounced influence on the prospects of belligerence between PTA members than between other states and that

233

among parties to the same preferential grouping, the likelihood of a military dispute declines precipitously as commerce increases.

## The Relationship between Trade and Conflict

As the editors discuss in the introduction to this book, debates over the relationship between trade and conflict generally revolve around three core arguments. The first is that open economic exchange reduces the prospect of interstate hostilities. Central to this claim, which is a pillar of liberal theories of international relations (Doyle, 1997; Keohane, 1990; Rosecrance, 1986; Stein, 1993), is the view that open trade fosters dependence among countries by promoting specialization in the production of goods and services. Extensive dependence, in turn, raises the cost of conflict between trade partners, thereby deterring its onset, since hostilities usually disrupt international economic relations.

The second argument, which stands in contrast to liberal theories, is advanced by neomercantilists and others who stress that interdependence can be a source of friction between states. Some of these observers point out that rising trade increases the range of economic issues over which political disputes can occur (Waltz, 1970: 205, 222). Others emphasize that the distribution of the efficiency gains stemming from foreign commerce can influence the relative political-military power of trading states (Hirschman, [1945] 1980). Past research has shown that these power changes often contribute to military conflict (Gilpin, 1981; Levy, 1989a). Still other critics of the liberal position contend that states prefer to minimize their economic dependence and that military expansion is one way to meet this objective. As such, rising trade can create incentives for states to engage in military actions designed to decrease their economic vulnerability (Gilpin, 1981; Liberman, 1996).

The third argument is that trade has no strong bearing on conflict. Among the most outspoken adherents of this position are realists, who attribute the outbreak of hostilities to the anarchic nature of the international system and power relations between states rather than international economic factors (e.g., Buzan, 1984; Gilpin, 1987; Mearsheimer, 1990). The vast bulk of the literature bearing on these competing claims is composed of quantitative analyses that address whether bilateral trade flows have affected military disputes during the past fifty years.[1] The results of most of these analyses accord with the liberal argument. In a seminal study, for example, Polachek (1980) examined 30 pairs of countries from 1958 to 1967 and concluded that higher levels of trade dampen conflict. More recently, Oneal and Russett (1997, 1999c, this volume; Russett and Oneal, 2001; Russett, Oneal, and Davis, 1998) conducted a series of studies covering a much longer span of time than Polachek's analysis. They also found a strong, inverse relationship between commerce and militarized disputes.

Nonetheless, evidence supporting the liberal position has not gone unchallenged. Barbieri (1996a,b), for instance, found that heightened trade promotes hostilities. Another strand of literature has criticized the statistical procedures used to derive much of the empirical support for the liberal argument. This body of work has concluded that when more appropriate estimation techniques are used, there is no systematic relationship between trade and military disputes (Beck and Katz, 1997; Beck, Katz, and Tucker, 1998; Beck and Tucker, 1996).[2]

## Preferential Trading Arrangements and Conflict

Existing research on the links between commerce and conflict has focused almost exclusively on the effects of trade flows. Very little attention has been devoted to the influence of international institutions designed to shape trade. In a number of recent studies, however, we have argued that analyses ignoring the effects of PTAs risk arriving at misleading conclusions about the relationship between commerce and conflict (Mansfield and Pevehouse, 2000; Mansfield, Pevehouse, and Bearce, 1999–2000). PTAs inhibit political-military disputes between contracting parties, and the pacifying effects of these arrangements grow more pronounced as trade flows rise between member-states. In the same vein, the high levels of trade that liberals view as contributing to peace are much more likely to inhibit hostilities between parties to the same PTA than between other states. Preferential groupings minimize conflict by both holding out the promise of economic gains and providing institutional mechanisms to deal with the negative political-military externalities stemming from economic interaction.

A primary reason why PTAs help to dampen conflict is that hostilities threaten the economic benefits that states expect to realize from membership. These expected benefits include increased trade, heightened investment, and protection from shocks to the global trading system. Preferential arrangements generally reduce trade barriers among members and make it difficult for members to subsequently raise these barriers. Consequently, acceding to a PTA helps a country to insure against the damage that would be caused if other members of the arrangement become increasingly protectionist, an especially important concern if the PTA includes this state's major trading partners (Fernández and Portes, 1998; Mansfield, 1998; Whalley, 1998; Yarbrough and Yarbrough, 1992). Moreover, as trade barriers decline within a preferential grouping, member-states have good reason to anticipate the expansion of trade and the deepening of economic integration.

In addition, PTAs can create the expectation of increased investment for members. Firms locating investments in a country that belongs to a PTA gain preferential access to each participant's market. Further, since PTAs reduce the ability of governments to behave opportunistically, firms investing in a contracting party limit the prospect that these investments will be undermined by state actions (Fernández and Portes, 1998; Yarbrough and Yarbrough, 1992). Indeed, even a group of states marked by few economic complementarities—and therefore with few efficiency gains to be derived by lowering trade barriers—may believe that forming a PTA will prompt a surge in foreign investment.[3]

Finally, states entering PTAs have reason to anticipate gaining protection from adverse shocks to the global trading system and increased bargaining power in international negotiations. If, for example, the trading system becomes weakened, then commercial relations among key partners could be undermined, generating considerable economic harm. Joining a PTA that includes some of these partners helps limit such damage by guaranteeing preferential access to their markets (Mansfield, 1998; Whalley, 1998). In fact, the growing fear of many states about being isolated from key international markets has contributed heavily to the recent rush of states to enter PTAs (de Melo and Panagariya, 1993: 5–6; Yarbrough and Yarbrough, 1992: 105–106). Further, countries acceding to a preferential arrangement often expect to bolster their position in international economic negotiations, since the grouping has more leverage with respect to third parties than any individual member. As in the case of Southern Cone countries that achieved more favorable terms in certain negotiations with the European Union after forming MERCOSUR (Thurston, 1995), the gains derived from joining forces with several partners rather than negotiating alone are often particularly striking when bargaining with a very powerful state or another PTA.

Hence, there are a wide variety of benefits that states entering a PTA have reason to anticipate. Interstate conflict can scuttle these expected gains by undermining commitments to sustain commercial liberalization, inhibiting investment on the part of firms that are reluctant to operate in unstable regions, and damaging the bargaining power of members in negotiations with third parties. The adverse economic consequences of hostilities within PTAs are generally well understood by the members of such arrangements. For instance, it is widely recognized that the participants in MERCOSUR looked forward to reaping substantial economic gains from this arrangement (Guedes de Costa, 1998; Peña, 1993). Since its members also realized that MERCOSUR's economic goals would be threatened by political antagonism, they implemented a series of measures intended to facilitate cooperation in the region (Smith, 1993). Such measures have contributed to the diminution of tensions between Brazil and Argentina. More generally, Hirst (1998: 113) points out that 'regional security cooperation has become a spill-around effect of the expansion of economic ties among Southern Cone countries'.

While PTAs diminish the prospects for conflict by raising members' expectations of economic gain, the benefits of membership are likely to appear especially large when countries trade extensively. Preferential groupings help to deepen integration and avert the future erosion of economic relations, thereby holding out the promise that trade between key partners will continue to flourish, if not expand. Since hostilities threaten to scuttle existing trade relations as well as future economic gains, states that trade heavily and participate in the same PTA have a particularly strong incentive to avoid conflict. Under these conditions, members' economic expectations are likely to be met, rendering them hesitant to take actions that place the gains from commercial integration at risk. While political disputes may not immediately affect either trade flows or

PTAs (Mansfield, Milner, and Rosendorf, 2002; Morrow, Siverson, and Taberes, 1998), conflicts can drag on and escalate, gradually damaging the institution and economic relations among member-states. The upshot is that PTA members marked by extensive commercial ties have good reason to avoid the use of force.[4]

Preferential arrangements help dampen conflicts which may arise *because of* extensive commercial interactions as well. Close economic relations increase the costs of military conflict, but also can stimulate disputes—for example, over the distribution of gains and losses from economic exchange—that may create political-military tensions if they are not contained (Stein, 1993). PTAs help to contain such tensions by creating a forum for bargaining and negotiation among members that facilitates the resolution of disagreements before open hostilities break out (Nye, 1971: 109). Regardless of how much trade members conduct, many PTAs have developed vehicles—such as dispute-settlement mechanisms—to mediate both economic and political conflicts. For example, ASEAN is widely credited for managing discord in Southeast Asia (Amer, 1999; Huxley, 1996), and MERCOSUR has performed a similar function throughout the Southern Cone (Manzetti, 1993–94; Smith, 1993).

Equally, by fostering reciprocity among members, PTAs address concerns about the distribution of the gains and losses from foreign commerce that often impede international economic cooperation (Grieco, 1990; Mastanduno, 1991). These arrangements help to ensure that economic concessions made by one participant are repaid rather than exploited by its counterparts (Fernández and Portes, 1998: 213). Preferential groupings also improve the flow of information about the gains and losses accruing to members, thereby reducing their uncertainty about the distribution of benefits stemming from economic activity. More generally, PTAs aid in the establishment of focal points that forestall breakdowns in cooperation by shaping states' expectations about what constitutes acceptable behavior and by facilitating the identification of deviations from such behavior (Garrett and Weingast, 1993).

## The Research Design

In sum, we argue that PTAs tend to inhibit political-military conflict between members, that preferential groupings are increasingly likely to dampen conflict as trade flows rise, and that high levels of trade are more likely to reduce tensions between PTA members than between other states. We are hardly alone in positing that PTAs influence the likelihood of interstate belligerence (Keynes, 1919: 249; Machlup, 1977: 143; Nye, 1971); yet until recently, virtually no empirical research had been conducted on this topic.

In an effort to fill this important gap in the literature, we previously extended a well-known study by Oneal and Russett (1997) that addressed the determinants of militarized disputes (MIDs) from 1950 to 1985 within politically relevant dyads—pairs of states that either are geographically contiguous or include a major power. Oneal and Russett set out to analyze the effects on MIDs of democracy and economic interdependence, holding constant interstate power relations, political-military alliances, and economic growth, each of which has been linked to the onset of conflict in prior research. To their model, we added a variable indicating whether each pair of countries participated in the same PTA (Mansfield, Pevehouse, and Bearce, 1999–2000). We found strong evidence that PTA membership reduces the likelihood of military disputes. In a subsequent study, we addressed whether PTAs influence the relationship between trade flows and disputes (Mansfield and Pevehouse, 2000). Consistent with the argument advanced above, our findings indicated that, for states that do not belong to the same PTA, the flow of trade has little affect on MIDs. For PTA members, however, heightened trade inhibits hostilities. In addition, parties to the same PTA are less prone to engage in military disputes than others states, an influence that grows larger as the flow of trade expands.

Here, we broaden our tests of these arguments by analyzing a wider range of country-pairs and a longer period of time than in previous research. Building on another study by Oneal and Russett (1999c), we examine the onset of MIDs within all pairs of states in the interstate system from 1950 to 1992. Working with this broader and longer sample should help to assess the robustness of our earlier findings concerning the influence of both PTAs and trade flows on hostilities. We also compare our results across two datasets on trade flows, since recent research by Oneal and Russett (1999c) and Barbieri (1996a, 1998) suggests that differences between these data strongly influence the observed relationship between commerce and conflict.

## The Statistical Model

We begin by estimating the following model:

$$\text{ONSET}_{ij} = \beta_0 + \beta_1\text{JNTDEM}_{ij} + \beta_2\text{DISTANCE}_{ij} + \beta_3\text{MAJPOW}_{ij} + \beta_4\text{ALLIES}_{ij} + \beta_5\text{CAPRATIO}_{ij} + \beta_6\text{TRADE}_{ij} + \beta_7\text{GDP}_L + \beta_8\text{GDP}_H + \beta_9\text{PTA}_{ij} + \beta_{10}(\text{TRADE}_{ij} \times \text{PTA}_{ij}) + \beta_{11}(\text{GDP}_L \times \text{PTA}_{ij}) + \beta_{12}(\text{GDP}_H \times \text{PTA}_{ij}) + \beta_{13}\text{HEGEMONY} + \beta_{14}\text{GATT}_{ij} + \beta_{15}\text{TAU-B}_{ij} + e_{ij}$$

where $\text{ONSET}_{ij}$ is the probability of the onset of a militarized interstate dispute between two states, $i$ and $j$, in a given year, $t$.[5] The observed value of this variable is dichotomous—it equals 1 if a dispute breaks out between these countries in $t$ and 0 otherwise.

The first five independent variables are taken directly from Oneal and Russett's (1999c) study. In light of the voluminous literature on the democratic peace, it is important to control for the influence of regime type. Jaggers and Gurr (1995) have developed a widely used index of regime type that ranges from 0 (least democratic) to 20 (most democratic).[6] $\text{JNTDEM}_{ij}$ is computed by multiplying the value of this index for state $i$ by the value for state $j$ in year $t$-1. The bulk of the literature on the democratic peace concludes that democratic country-pairs are more peaceful than other dyads, suggesting that an inverse relationship should exist between JNTDEM$_{ij}$ and the probability of a militarized dispute (e.g., Doyle, 1997; Russett and Oneal, 2001).

Next, DISTANCE$_{ij}$ is the natural logarithm of the capital-to-capital distance between countries $i$ and $j$.[7] States which are geographically proximate to one another have much greater opportunity to enter into a dispute and more issues to fight over than distant states (Siverson and Starr, 1991). Equally, states in close proximity tend to conduct more trade and have a greater likelihood of entering the same PTA than other countries (Deardorff, 1998; Mansfield, Milner, and Rosendorff, 2002). As such, we need to ensure that any observed relationship between disputes and either trade or PTAs is not due to the effects of distance.

In addition, it is widely understood that political-military relations between states influence their proneness to hostilities (e.g., Gilpin, 1981; Levy, 1989a). We therefore address the effects of three crucial political-military factors. First, MAJPOW$_{ij}$ equals 1 if state $i$ or state $j$ is a major power in year $t$-1, as defined by the Correlates of War (COW) project, and 0 otherwise.[8] Second, we include ALLIES$_{ij}$ to account for the influence of political-military alliances on conflict. This variable is coded 1 if states $i$ and $j$ are allied in year $t$-1 and 0 otherwise. Third, to control for the dyadic balance of power, we introduce CAPRATIO$_{ij}$. This variable is the natural logarithm of the ratio of the stronger state's military capabilities to the weaker state's capabilities in year $t$-1. To calculate annual values of CAPRATIO$_{ij}$, we rely on the COW national military capabilities index, which is based on each state's total population, urban population, energy consumption, iron and steel production, military manpower, and military expenditures (Mansfield, 1994; Singer, Bremer, and Stuckey, 1972; Singer and Small, 1993).

The remaining independent variables are drawn from our earlier work on preferential trading arrangements and military conflict (Mansfield and Pevehouse, 2000). As previously noted, one of Oneal and Russett's (1999c) chief purposes was to address the influence of interdependence on military disputes. To measure interdependence, they computed the sum of the exports and imports between $i$ and $j$ and then divided this sum by each state's gross domestic product (GDP). Oneal and Russett labeled the higher of the two resulting values DEPEND$_H$ and the lower one DEPEND$_L$. In contrast, we disaggregate these variables into their constituent parts. It is widely acknowledged that more powerful states are disproportionately prone to become involved in military confrontations and that economically large states tend to be political powerful. Hence, any observed relationship between MIDs and either DEPEND$_H$ or DEPEND$_L$ may reflect the influence of GDP rather than trade. For this reason, we analyze separately state $i$'s GDP, state $j$'s GDP, and the volume of commerce between them.

TRADE$_{ij}$ is the total amount of state $i$'s exports to and imports from state $j$ in year $t$-1 (expressed in constant U.S. dollars). It is derived by multiplying DE-

$PEND_H$ by the GDP of both state $i$ and state $j$, creating two values of bilateral trade for each dyad in each year. When the resulting figures differ, we use the higher one. We also include $GDP_H$ and $GDP_L$, which are the gross domestic products in year $t$-1 (expressed in constant U.S. dollars) of the state with the higher and the lower national income, respectively.[9]

To capture the influence of membership in a preferential trading arrangement, we introduce $PTA_{ij}$, a dichotomous variable that equals 1 if states $i$ and $j$ are parties to the same PTA in year $t$-1 and 0 otherwise.[10] Because we contend that the impact of trade flows on military hostilities is influenced by PTA membership, we include $TRADE_{ij} \times PTA_{ij}$. We also include $GDP_H \times PTA_{ij}$ and $GDP_L \times PTA_{ij}$ to assess whether there is an interactive effect between economic size and membership in a preferential economic grouping.

Various studies have found that whether the international system is marked by a hegemon influences the prospects for military conflict between great powers; equally, there is some evidence that this factor affects the likelihood of disputes involving smaller states (Gilpin, 1981; Mansfield, 1994). Since hegemony also has been linked to both the openness of international trade and the probability of states entering a PTA (Gilpin, 1987; Mansfield, 1998; Mansfield, Milner, and Rosendorff, 2002), it is especially important for us to address the impact of this factor. We do so by including HEGEMONY, which is a yearly measure (in $t$-1) of the percentage of total global GDP generated by the largest state in the system (which is the United States for the entire period covered in this analysis).

Although our argument is that PTAs inhibit conflict, they may not be the only international commercial institutions that have such an effect. The General Agreement on Trade and Tariffs (GATT) established the infrastructure for the global trading system during the period examined here and, like PTAs, may have created a setting that reduced the likelihood of military conflict between members. Moreover, since many PTAs were formed under the GATT's authority, we need to make sure that any observed relationship between PTAs and conflict is not simply an outgrowth of GATT membership. To this end, we include $GATT_{ij}$, which equals 1 if states $i$ and $j$ are GATT members in year $t$-1 and 0 otherwise.

We also include a measure of the similarity of states' preferences that has been widely used in models like ours (Gartzke, 1998, 2000; Mansfield and Pevehouse, 2000: 796–797; Russett and Oneal, 2001: 228–237). Developed by Gartzke (1998), this measure is based on voting records in the United Nations General Assembly. Despite the obvious limitations associated with using the votes of UN members to measure their underlying foreign policy preferences, analyzing these preferences is important. States with similar preferences are unlikely to become embroiled in military conflicts and are quite likely to have close economic ties. To ensure that any observed effect of PTAs or trade flows does not stem from the influence of states' preferences, we include Gartzke's measure of the similarity of state $i$'s and state $j$'s UN voting profiles in year $t$-1, labeled $TAU\text{-}B_{ij}$. Finally, $e_{it}$ is a stochastic error term.

## Table 12.1. Effects of Trade Flows and PTAs on MIDs, 1950–92

| Variable | ONSET | No EC[a] | No Imputed Data[b] | Barbieri[c] |
|---|---|---|---|---|
| Intercept | 4.768*** | 4.833*** | 3.745** | 4.652*** |
| | (3.93) | (3.94) | (2.98) | (3.64) |
| JNTDEM$_{ij}$ | -0.002** | -0.002** | -0.002*** | -0.002** |
| | (-3.12) | (-2.98) | (-3.42) | (-2.78) |
| MAJPOW$_{ij}$ | 1.074*** | 1.131*** | 0.731** | 0.579* |
| | (4.61) | (4.91) | (3.09) | (2.49) |
| ALLIES$_{ij}$ | -0.187 | -0.178 | 0.030 | 0.020 |
| | (-0.87) | (-0.85) | (0.12) | (0.09) |
| DISTANCE$_{ij}$ | -1.116*** | -1.127*** | -0.832*** | -0.827*** |
| | (-10.15) | (-10.15) | (-6.80) | (-6.68) |
| CAPRATIO$_{ij}$ | -0.229*** | -0.222*** | -0.216*** | -0.193*** |
| | (-4.07) | (-3.93) | (-3.37) | (-3.29) |
| TRADE$_{ij}$ | $-1.02 \times 10^{-8}$ | $-1.12 \times 10^{-8}$ | $-5.87 \times 10^{-9}$ | $-6.32 \times 10^{-6}$ |
| | (-1.57) | (-1.69) | (-0.99) | (-0.99) |
| GDP$_L$ | $7.35 \times 10^{-10}$* | $7.60 \times 10^{-10}$* | $7.15 \times 10^{-10}$* | $4.87 \times 10^{-10}$ |
| | (2.07) | (2.12) | (2.34) | (1.86) |
| GDP$_H$ | $7.18 \times 10^{-10}$*** | $6.95 \times 10^{-10}$*** | $6.30 \times 10^{-10}$*** | $5.90 \times 10^{-10}$*** |
| | (8.41) | (7.97) | (6.90) | (6.21) |
| PTA$_{ij}$ | 0.322 | 0.287 | 0.246 | 0.226 |
| | (1.38) | (1.23) | (1.09) | (0.99) |
| TRADE$_{ij}$ × PTA$_{ij}$ | $-3.17 \times 10^{-8}$* | $-3.44 \times 10^{-8}$*** | $-2.82 \times 10^{-8}$* | $-1.97 \times 10^{-5}$* |
| | (-2.19) | (-2.74) | (-2.44) | (-2.10) |
| GDP$_L$ × PTA$_{ij}$ | $6.53 \times 10^{-12}$ | $5.28 \times 10^{-9}$** | $-2.07 \times 10^{-10}$ | $3.07 \times 10^{-11}$ |
| | (0.05) | (2.71) | (-0.17) | (0.03) |
| GDP$_H$ × PTA$_{ij}$ | $5.18 \times 10^{-10}$ | $3.05 \times 10^{-10}$ | $5.24 \times 10^{-10}$ | $4.91 \times 10^{-10}$ |
| | (1.60) | (0.77) | (1.68) | (1.49) |
| HEGEMONY | 6.882 | 6.610 | 2.065 | -3.730 |
| | (1.41) | (1.35) | (0.40) | (-0.72) |
| GATT$_{ij}$ | -0.171 | -0.174 | -0.210 | -0.222 |
| | (-0.76) | (-0.79) | (-0.99) | (-1.08) |
| TAU-B$_{ij}$ | -0.768*** | -0.735*** | -0.568** | -0.672*** |
| | (-4.27) | (-4.12) | (-2.85) | (-3.23) |
| $\chi^2$ | 1,155.54*** | 1,162.49*** | 976.64*** | 1,044.33*** |
| Log likelihood | -3,392.52 | -3,379.91 | -2,578.34 | -2,449.84 |
| N | 203,687 | 202,671 | 104,861 | 93,345 |

*Note:* These parameters are estimated using logistic regression, after including a natural cubic spline function with three knots. Figures in parentheses are asymptotic $z$-statistics computed using clustered Huber standard errors.

[a] Estimation excludes dyads where both states are members of the EC.
[b] Estimation excludes imputed data from Oneal and Russett's (1999c) dataset.
[c] Barbieri's (1996a) data on trade flows are used to code TRADE$_{ij}$.
*** $p \leq .001$; ** $p \leq .01$; * $p \leq .05$. Two-tailed tests are conducted for all estimates.

Since the dependent variable being analyzed is dichotomous, logistic regression is used to estimate the model. To account for any temporal dependence in the data, we follow the tack suggested by Beck in this volume and elsewhere (Beck and Katz, 1997; Beck, Katz, and Tucker, 1998; Beck and Tucker, 1996), namely, introducing a natural cubic spline function with three knots of the number of years that have elapsed since a MID last began between states $i$ and $j$.[11] We also rely on clustered Huber standard errors to take account of any heteroskedasticity as well as the grouped nature of the data.

## The Findings

Initial estimates of the model are presented in the first column of table 12.1 (labeled ONSET). In our model, the coefficient of $TRADE_{ij}$ measures the influence of trade flows on disputes for states that do not belong to the same PTA.[12] Clearly, this influence is weak: the estimate of $TRADE_{ij}$ is negative, but it is not statistically significant. Hence, outside of a preferential trading arrangement, the flow of commerce has little influence on the prospect of military hostilities. In marked contrast, however, heightened trade does serve to dampen conflict between PTA members, as indicated by the negative and statistically significant estimate of $TRADE_{ij} \times PTA_{ij}$. It also should be noted that we attach little importance to the estimate of $PTA_{ij}$, since by itself, this estimate reflects the influence of a preferential arrangement on conflict when members engage in no trade and have no national income (i.e., when $TRADE_{ij} = GDP_L = GDP_H = 0$). Obviously, that is not a substantively meaningful situation. Further, this estimate is not statistically significant.

These findings accord with our argument and correspond with our previous results (Mansfield and Pevehouse, 2000). So, too, do the estimated effects of national income. As in our earlier study, the estimates of $GDP_L$ and $GDP_H$ are both positive and statistically significant, indicating that economically large states outside PTAs are more prone to conflict than their smaller counterparts. However, neither the estimate of $GDP_H \times PTA_{ij}$ nor that of $GDP_L \times PTA_{ij}$ is statistically significant, suggesting that economic size has little influence on the probability of disputes between PTA members.

The negative and statistically significant estimates of $JNTDEM_{ij}$, $DISTANCE_{ij}$, $CAPRATIO_{ij}$, and $TAU\text{-}B_{ij}$ also conform with prior findings.[13] More democratic dyads experience a lower probability of disputes than less democratic country-pairs. Equally, as the distance between states increases and the disparity in their capabilities widens, the likelihood of conflict between them declines. Greater similarity in UN voting patterns (which, recall, is a proxy for the similarity of underlying foreign policy preferences) also reduces the prospect of interstate hostilities. Interestingly, though, neither the estimate of $ALLIES_{ij}$ nor that of $GATT_{ij}$ is statistically significant. The latter result is especially noteworthy since it suggests that the conflict-inhibiting effects of PTAs do not stem from a more general tendency for international commercial institutions to dampen hostilities among the contracting parties.

To more fully analyze the links between commerce and conflict, it is useful to assess the magnitude of the estimated effects of both trade and PTAs on military disputes. To do so, we generate the predicted probability of a dispute's outbreak for PTA members and for non-PTA members while varying the amount of commerce being conducted. To compute these probabilities, all continuous variables except $TRADE_{ij}$ (and $TRADE_{ij} \times PTA_{ij}$) are set to their medians; and $ALLIES_{ij}$, $GATT_{ij}$, and $MAJPOW_{ij}$ are set to 0, which is the modal value of each of these variables. Within our dataset, the annual value of bilateral trade ranges from \$0 to upwards of \$100,000,000. We begin by setting $TRADE_{ij}$ to \$25,000,000 and then calculate the predicated probability of a dispute for PTA members and for non-PTA members, respectively. Next, we do likewise after increasing the value of $TRADE_{ij}$ to \$50,000,000.

This increase in commerce yields about a 65 percent reduction in the predicted probability of hostilities for states that belong to the same PTA, but only about a 25 percent decrease for other states. Further, for a pair of states conducting \$25,000,000 of yearly trade, PTA membership cuts the predicted probability of conflict by roughly 35 percent. For a country-pair conducting \$50,000,000 of trade, however, the reduction in the likelihood of conflict stemming from PTA membership rises to about 70 percent. Clearly, then, PTA membership tends to inhibit conflict and this effect grows quite large as the flow of trade increases. Moreover, the effects of trade flows on belligerence are much larger for participants in a preferential grouping than other states.

Interestingly, though, such groupings do little to inhibit conflict at the very lowest levels of trade. In fact, for states that conduct no trade, PTA membership actually gives rise to a slight increase in the predicted probability of a military dispute. This finding is not entirely surprising. As Nye (1971: 187) observed, whether regional economic arrangements foster peace depends on their capacity to promote integration among member-states. Hence, arrangements that do not increase economic activity among participants are unlikely to encourage the resolution of political discord. Moreover, if expectations regarding the gains from regional integration are unmet—which is quite likely to be the case if little or no trade is conducted within a PTA—it is not hard to understand why political tensions might flare up between member-states.

As trade rises, however, the pacifying influence of preferential arrangements becomes quite evident. Given even a relatively modest amount of trade, PTA membership yields a dramatic reduction in the prospect of hostilities. Having generated some initial estimates of our model and analyzed the magnitude of the effects of trade and PTAs on conflict, it is important to assess the robustness of our findings. To begin, we consider the implications of including the European Community (EC) in our sample of PTAs. We then analyze whether the measurement and coding of both bilateral trade and the onset of disputes bear on the results.

## The Influence of the EC

Among the PTAs included in our sample, there has been a remarkable amount of commercial interaction and lack of armed conflict within the EC. Indeed, many observers maintain that a key source of the peace in Western Europe since World War II has been the extensive economic ties among members of the EC and the European Union (e.g., Nye, 1971: 115; Wallace, 1994). We therefore need to ensure that the strong, inverse relationship between trade flows and military disputes within PTAs is not simply an outgrowth of the EC. To this end, we delete all observations where both $i$ and $j$ are parties to the EC in year $t$-1 and then generate another set of estimates. As shown in the second column of table 12.1, the signs, sizes, and significance levels of these estimates are very similar to those when observations composed of EC members are included in the sample. The only noteworthy difference is that the new estimates of $TRADE_{ij}$ × $PTA_{ij}$ and $GDP_L$ × $PTA_{ij}$ are statistically significant at the .01 level. Hence, there is no indication that our results are being driven by the EC.

## Measuring Trade

Like most existing studies of the relationship between bilateral commerce and conflict, Oneal and Russett (1999c) draw their trade data from the International Monetary Fund's (IMF's) *Direction of Trade Statistics*. The IMF, however, does not distinguish between situations in which two states conduct no trade (or a trivially small amount of trade) in a given year and situations in which trade data are missing (either because the two states do not engage in trade or no reliable information is available on the trade they do conduct). Oneal and Russett (1999c: 425) elect to treat missing data on foreign commerce as though the states in question conduct no economic exchange. To ensure that this decision does not unduly influence our results, we reestimate the model after omitting observations where Oneal and Russett code missing trade data as a trade flow equal to 0. Doing so reduces the sample by nearly half.

The parameter estimates based on this smaller sample—which are reported in the third column of table 12.1—are much the same as our initial estimates. The coefficients of both $TRADE_{ij}$ and $TRADE_{ij}$ × $PTA_{ij}$ are negative, and the latter coefficient is statistically significant whereas the former is not. Equally, the remaining estimates are quite similar to those in the first column of table 12.1, which are derived using the entire sample of dyads in Oneal and Russett's dataset.[14]

In contrast to Oneal and Russett, Barbieri (1996a, 1998) has attempted to distinguish between cases where the IMF trade data are missing and cases where so little trade is conducted that the IMF does not report any commercial activity. Consequently, her figures on bilateral commerce differ from those of Oneal and Russett, although their trade data are highly correlated ($r = .94$). To further assess the robustness of our results, we reestimate our model using Barbieri's trade data. As shown in the last column of table 12.1, the effects of trade flows and PTAs—as well as the other variables in our model—continue to correspond very closely to our earlier findings when her data are analyzed.

## The Dependent Variable

Thus far, we have treated military disputes as a homogeneous class of events, a tack taken in almost all studies of commerce and conflict. However, as we have argued elsewhere (Mansfield and Pevehouse, 2000), it is also useful to determine whether the effects of PTAs and trade flows depend on whether low-intensity or more violent interstate disputes are analyzed. To address this issue, we redefine $ONSET_{ij}$ as a trichotomous variable that equals 2 if a violent dispute broke out between states $i$ and $j$ in year $t$, 1 if a nonviolent dispute began between them, and 0 otherwise. The COW Project codes MIDs on a five-point scale, where higher values correspond to more violent episodes (Jones, Bremer, and Singer, 1996). Following past research, we define violent disputes as those MIDs coded as a 4 or 5 on this scale and nonviolent MIDs are those coded 1, 2, or 3 (Bueno de Mesquita and Siverson, 1997; Gowa, 1999). To estimate this model, we utilize a multinomial logit specification.[15]

The results presented in table 12.2 indicate that both estimates of $TRADE_{ij}$ are negative, but only the one associated with violent MIDs is statistically significant. Thus, outside of PTAs, higher levels of trade have little influence on whether states threaten to use force, but a stronger influence on whether states actually use force. Between PTA members, in contrast, greater trade flows dampen the outbreak of both violent and nonviolent MIDs, since both estimates of $TRADE_{ij} \times PTA_{ij}$ are negative and significant. Moreover, as in our earlier analysis, the absolute value of each estimate of $TRADE_{ij} \times PTA_{ij}$ is much larger than the corresponding estimate of $TRADE_{ij}$, providing further evidence that commercial flows have a more pronounced influence on hostilities between PTA members than on those between other states. Most of the remaining variables have a uniform influence on nonviolent and violent disputes, although $GDP_H \times PTA_{ij}$, $GDP_L \times PTA_{ij}$, HEGEMONY, and $JNTDEM_{ij}$ deviate from this pattern. The latter result is especially interesting. While democracy strongly inhibits the outbreak of violent hostilities, it is only weakly related to nonviolent disputes. This accords with the findings of Gowa (1999: 61) that democracies engage in low-intensity MIDs about as frequently as nondemocracies.

Rather than relying on a multinomial logit specification, some observers argue that a censored probit model should be used to analyze the determinants of disputes. The latter model accounts for any selection effects arising if the same factors that contribute to the onset of a MID also contribute to its escalation to war (Reed, 2000). Although we will not review the results in full, it should be noted that censored probit estimates of our model produce no evidence of a selection effect. More specifically, the estimate of the selection parameter ($\rho$) is not statistically significant, regardless of whether the EC is included or excluded from the set of PTAs and whether the complete sample of dyads is analyzed or the imputed trade data are excluded.[16]

**Table 12.2. Multinomial Logit Estimates of the Effects of Trade Flows and PTAs on MIDs, 1950–92**

| Variable | Nonviolent MIDs | Violent MIDs |
|---|---|---|
| Intercept | 7.690*** | 3.743** |
| | (4.33) | (2.88) |
| JNTDEM$_{ij}$ | -0.002 | -0.002*** |
| | (-1.69) | (-3.31) |
| MAJPOW$_{ij}$ | 2.014*** | 0.774*** |
| | (6.95) | (3.31) |
| ALLIES$_{ij}$ | -0.246 | -0.062 |
| | (-0.88) | (-0.29) |
| DISTANCE$_{ij}$ | -1.193*** | -1.082*** |
| | (-10.14) | (-11.17) |
| CAPRATIO$_{ij}$ | -0.238** | -0.188** |
| | (-3.15) | (-2.95) |
| TRADE$_{ij}$ | $-7.53 \times 10^{-8}$ | $-1.54 \times 10^{-8}$** |
| | (-1.37) | (-2.72) |
| GDP$_L$ | $1.23 \times 10^{-9}$*** | $1.08 \times 10^{-9}$** |
| | (2.94) | (2.73) |
| GDP$_H$ | $5.72 \times 10^{-10}$*** | $6.98 \times 10^{-10}$*** |
| | (4.93) | (6.20) |
| PTA$_{ij}$ | 0.557 | 0.206 |
| | (1.73) | (0.99) |
| TRADE$_{ij}$ × PTA$_{ij}$ | $-7.48 \times 10^{-7}$** | $-3.48 \times 10^{-8}$** |
| | (-3.15) | (-3.07) |
| GDP$_L$ × PTA$_{ij}$ | $9.78 \times 10^{-9}$*** | $-3.96 \times 10^{-10}$ |
| | (3.82) | (-0.24) |
| GDP$_H$ × PTA$_{ij}$ | $-9.82 \times 10^{-10}$ | $6.55 \times 10^{-10}$* |
| | (-1.11) | (2.25) |
| HEGEMONY | -20.407* | 8.641 |
| | (-2.24) | (1.54) |
| GATT$_{ij}$ | -0.285 | -0.139 |
| | (-1.00) | (-0.69) |
| TAU-B$_{ij}$ | -0.838** | -0.740*** |
| | (-2.85) | (-3.79) |
| $\chi^2$ | 2,171.11*** | |
| Log likelihood | -4,225.64 | |
| N | 203,964 | |

*Note:* These parameters are estimated using a multinomial logit model, after including one natural cubic spline function with three knots for nonviolent MIDs and a second such function for violent MIDs. Figures in parentheses are asymptotic $z$-statistics computed using clustered Huber standard errors.

\*\*\* $p \leq .001$; \*\* $p \leq .01$; \* $p \leq .05$. Two-tailed tests are conducted for all estimates.

In sum, there is limited evidence that heightened trade between non-PTA members inhibits conflict when we disaggregate nonviolent and violent disputes. Nonetheless, our results continue to yield strong support for the argument that membership in preferential trading arrangements dampens antagonism and that this effect grows stronger and larger as trade flows rise. Although these institutions are obviously not a panacea for conflicts, they provide real benefits in lessening tensions between nation-states, even when controlling for a host of other political, economic, and military factors that could influence the propensity for hostilities.[17]

## Conclusion

Recently, a burgeoning literature has emerged on the relationship between foreign trade and political conflict. The vast majority of such studies focus on the impact of bilateral trade flows on belligerence, but give very short shrift to how international commercial institutions condition this relationship. By doing so, researchers risk presenting a distorted view of these links. Both theory and empirical investigation indicate that preferential trading arrangements dampen military disputes and strongly influence the effects of trade flows on hostilities.

PTAs inhibit discord through a variety of means, most centrally by generating the expectation of future economic gains on the part of members. Since disputes threaten to scuttle these gains, participants in the same PTA have reason to avoid involvement in military conflicts. In addition, many preferential groupings create a forum for bargaining and negotiation that reduces tensions among participants, helps to resolve conflicts that do occur, and promotes the establishment of focal points that shape states' expectations and facilitate the identification of deviations from accepted norms. Moreover, the tendency for preferential arrangements to inhibit disputes becomes more pronounced as trade flows rise. For PTA members that trade extensively, the future stream of gains from membership is likely to seem particularly large, thereby creating a potent deterrent to the use of force.

Our past findings and those reported here accord with these arguments. Preferential groupings tend to dampen conflict between members. Further, trade flows have a relatively weak influence on the outbreak of hostilities between states that do not belong to the same PTA, but exert a strong and sizeable effect on the likelihood of military disputes between PTA members. These results are at odds with the view that trade has little systematic impact on conflict. They also contradict the unqualified claim that increased trade reduces the prospect of belligerence. Instead, there is considerable evidence that whether foreign commerce promotes peace hinges on the institutional setting in which it is conducted.[18] As such, the relationship between economic exchange and the outbreak of hostilities seems to be much more nuanced than most existing studies suggest.

While our analysis helps to clarify the links between commerce and conflict, it also points to some avenues for further research. One key issue is whether there are significant variations across PTAs in the extent to which these institutions dampen interstate disputes. Moreover, it is obviously crucial to determine the source of any such variations; for example, whether they stem from differences in the degree of economic integration across PTAs, the institutional characteristics of these arrangements, or the range of economic policies that preferential groupings coordinate. Further, our analysis centered on the Cold War era, since that period is the focus of most extant empirical work on trade and conflict and since comprehensive data on PTAs are not available for earlier periods. Clearly, though, our argument is not specific to the years since World War II and it would be useful to analyze whether the effects of preferential groupings on political-military relations are stable over time.

Additional research on these and other related topics is likely to have important implications for both the study and practice of international relations. In recent years, there has been a sharp rise in preferential trading arrangements throughout the globe. Virtually all parties to the World Trade Organization belong to at least one such arrangement and this trend shows no sign of abating (WTO, 1995). The economic implications of these developments have been widely studied and fiercely debated. Analyses of their impact on political-military relations, however, have been sparse. Our findings indicate that, especially if contemporary PTAs are characterized by extensive commercial ties among members, the recent proliferation of these arrangements is likely to augur well for promoting cooperation and inhibiting political disputes.

# Notes

For helpful comments on earlier versions of this chapter, we are grateful to the editors of this book, Helen Milner, and seminar participants at the University of Wisconsin and the 2001 annual meeting of the American Political Science Association.

1. For overviews of this literature, see Mansfield and Pollins (2001); McMillan (1997); Schneider, Barbieri, and Gleditsch (this volume); and Stein (1993). For a discussion of recent theoretical, empirical, and methodological advances in research on the relationship between economic interdependence and political conflict, see Mansfield and Pollins (2003).

2. Subsequent applications of these techniques have yielded results that more closely conform to the liberal view (Beck, this volume; Bennett and Stam, 2000; Russett and Oneal, 2001).

3. For example, such was the case for members of the Association of Southeast Asian Nations (ASEAN). See Saxonhouse (1993: 410–411).

4. It is obvious that if member-states calculate that the economic gains from participating in a PTA could be easily replaced or if they heavily discount these gains, then PTAs may do little to dampen conflict, regardless of how much trade takes place among members. Further, regardless of the anticipated gains from participating in a PTA, a member may determine that attacking a partner would yield even greater gains. But as long as key trade partners expect the benefits from PTA membership to outweigh the

costs of participation and the potential benefits associated with military disputes, the prospect of antagonism is likely to be small. See Mansfield, Pevehouse, and Bearce (1999–2000).

5. Data on MIDs are taken from Jones, Bremer, and Singer (1996).

6. More precisely, this index is *REGIME TYPE = DEMOCRACY – AUTOCRACY*, where *DEMOCRACY* is an 11-point measure of a state's democratic characteristics and *AUTOCRACY* is an 11-point measure of its autocratic characteristics. Note that the original derivation of this index yielded scores ranging from -10 to 10 (Jaggers and Gurr, 1995). To generate values of *JNTDEM$_{ij}$*, Oneal and Russett add 10 to every state's annual score.

7. Or major ports for the United States, USSR/Russia, and Canada.

8. For the entirety of this analysis, the major powers are China, France, Great Britain, USSR/Russia, and the United States. See Singer and Small (1994).

9. Data on GDP are taken from Summers and Heston (1988, 1991). Where they do not furnish data for an observation in Oneal and Russett's study, we rely on data from Maddison (1995) and the *World Bank Development Indicators* (various years).

10. These data are taken from de Melo and Panagariya (1993), Hartland-Thunberg (1980), Mansfield and Bronson (1997), Pomfret (1997), and WTO (1995). They are the same data used in Mansfield and Pevehouse (2000).

11. Oneal and Russett (1999c) also use this technique. We use Richard Tucker's STATA ado-file to create the spline and the SPBASE command for the creation of the knots. We do not report the estimates of the spline, although it should be noted that the base and each knot are statistically significant in each estimation.

12. On the interpretation of models that include interaction terms, see Friedrich (1982).

13. See Gartzke (2000), Mansfield and Pevehouse (2000), Oneal and Russett (1997, 1999c), and Russett, Oneal, and Davis (1998).

14. The results are also quite similar to those in table 12.1 when we exclude all observations in which *TRADE$_{ij}$* is coded as 0 (that is, observations where Oneal and Russett code missing trade data as a trade flow equal to 0 and those where the IMF codes a trade flow as 0).

15. We compute two spline functions for this model: one for the time since a pair of states were involved in a violent MID and a second for the time since a pair of states were involved in a nonviolent MID. Each function is included in the multinomial logit estimation.

16. Since the distribution of our dependent variable is highly skewed (due to the rarity with which MIDs break out), we also assessed the robustness of the estimation by using King and Zeng's (2001) rare-events logit procedure. The results are much the same as those discussed earlier: the estimate of *TRADE$_{ij}$* is negative and not statistically significant, while the estimate of *TRADE$_{ij}$ × PTA$_{ij}$* is negative and statistically significant (at the .05 level). Thus, our analysis is not affected by any rare-events bias.

17. As in our previous work, we are sensitive to potential problems of reverse causality that could arise if MIDs influence PTA membership. To address this issue, we estimate a model predicting membership in a PTA that includes the following independent variables: MIDs, regime type, trade flows, GDP, alliances, distance, the distribution of capabilities, major-power status, hegemony, GATT membership, UN voting similarity, a spline function (with three knots) of the time since the dyad last participated in a common PTA, and the percentage of states in the global system that participate in a PTA. (On the latter variable, see Mansfield (1998).) The results yield no evidence that MIDs have a

statistically significant influence on PTAs, a finding that accords with our prior research (Mansfield and Pevehouse, 2000: 798; Mansfield, Milner, and Rosendorf, 2002).

18. On this point, see Keohane (1990) and Stein (1993).

# CHAPTER 13

# Globalization and Internal Conflict

*Håvard Hegre, Ranveig Gissinger, and Nils Petter Gleditsch*

Trade, foreign investment, and other forms of economic interdependence have grown throughout the post–World War II period, along with a stronger global political consciousness and increased regional cooperation. After the end of the Cold War, not only have these phenomena accelerated, but the lack of any opposing world system has also given them a near-universal character. In a cultural sense, too, the world is becoming a single arena. English is spreading rapidly as a global means of communication for science, commerce, and the transmission of news. New information technology has drastically reduced the costs of the worldwide dissemination of knowledge and opinion. 'Globalization' is employed as an umbrella term for these economic, political, and cultural processes. We use it here as a value-neutral term, in contrast to words like dependency or integration, which for many people carry negative or positive connotations. We use the term globalization mainly in the sense of an increasingly open economy.

During the period of emerging globalization, economic growth has generally continued in the industrial and post-industrial countries, while a number of newly industrialized countries have taken off. At the political level, the 'Third Wave' has brought democratic government to a greater part of the world than in any previous period. Many serious environmental problems in highly developed countries are being tackled with strategies combining national action and international collaboration.

On the other hand the former Soviet Union, parts of Africa, and war-torn nations elsewhere are in decline economically, and the most successful economies in Asia have shown clear signs of economic strain. Domestic economic inequality is increasing in most parts of the world. Politically, many new democracies have a poor human rights record, and their political systems appear to be weakly rooted in civil society. Environmental decline continues in many, perhaps most, developing countries. Even in the highly developed world new environmental problems such as global warming emerge as serious threats to human welfare.

Various authors have linked all of these phenomena, positive as well as negative, to effects of globalization. Indeed, globalization is emerging as a key formula embodying most of the modern world's ills—or its promises. In this chapter, we concentrate on the implications of globalization for *internal armed conflict*. This is a topic that has been studied less intensively than the social and economic consequences, even less than the implications of globalization for interstate conflict.[1] But the disagreements regarding the consequences of globalization for internal armed conflict are as sharp as in any other such debates. Economic development will be an important intervening variable in the analysis, but we are also concerned with political development, notably democratization.

The debate on globalization has moved far beyond the academic arena—to government and to civil society. As the violent demonstrations in Seattle, Prague, Quebec, Gothenburg, and Genova indicate, antiglobalization forces are galvanized into action on the streets. Movements such as Attac that are devoted to challenging liberalization of the global economy are spreading. Coalitions against globalization are formed by some unlikely partners: They include supporters of populist American politicians, who want to terminate U.S. involvement in multilateral treaties and see an end to the United Nations system, organized labor interested in protecting domestic markets and jobs, developing world supporters with anti-imperialist leanings, anarchists, and environmentalists.

While the term globalization is relatively new, the issue of whether or not global structures and agents benefit poor countries, or indeed exploit them, has been at the core of social research on the problems of development for decades. Issues of development and underdevelopment were discussed within the framework of modernization theory and structural theory,[2] discussions mirrored in the current debate. While neoliberal and modernization theorists view closer international economic contact as a strong factor in the modernization of poorer countries, the loose coalition of antiglobalists, whom we will call structuralists, emphasize the harmful effects of economic integration. Structuralists argue that foreign direct investment and trade are forms of capitalist exploitation of developing societies, and that they promote poverty and societal disarray and conflict within the developing world. In contrast, neoliberal models blame internal processes of poor governance and unsuccessful development policies and downplay international processes as the cause of underdevelopment.

In this chapter we will make an attempt to test some of these arguments. In order to do so, we have to simplify them, hopefully not to a point where they can no longer be recognized by their proponents.

# The Liberal Model

We first summarize the liberal model in figure 13.1: An open economy leads to a higher level of economic development. In turn, this leads to peace, both directly and through the promotion of democracy. In developing this model, we were inspired by the overall perspective of liberal conflict theorists such as Weede (1995) and Russett and Oneal (2001), drawing on Manchester liberalism and on what Russett and Oneal in particular have identified as a Kantian mode of thinking in international affairs. While these scholars have developed their argument mostly in relation to building a secure foundation for international peace, there is also a solid basis for a liberal argument about domestic peace. Since internal conflict is the overwhelmingly dominant form of conflict today (Wallensteen and Sollenberg, 2001), the political importance of this is obvious.

**Figure 13.1. A Liberal Model**

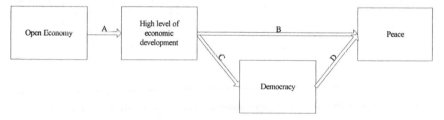

Economists (e.g., Dollar, 1992; Dollar and Kraay, 2001a; Levine and Renelt, 1992; Sala-I-Martin, 1997), sociologists (Firebaugh and Beck, 1994), and political scientists (de Soysa and Oneal, 1999) are among the many who have found that countries with more open economies tend to have higher growth rates. This raises the hope that they should eventually reach a higher level of welfare (arrow A), whether measured as per capita income or by other measures such as the Human Development Index or the reduction in the number of poor people (Dollar and Kraay, 2001a, b). During the period of globalization, formerly closed economies, such as China and Vietnam, have experienced considerable economic growth and reduction in poverty after moving to modernize their economies through foreign trade and greater use of the market mechanism.

The link from development directly to domestic peace (arrow B) is one of the most robust findings in the World Bank studies and other work on civil war. Collier and Hoeffler's (2001) 'predation theory' assumes that there will always be someone who has sufficient grievances to be willing to start a rebellion against the government. Whatever the motivation, the rebellion can be carried out only if it is financially viable. (In a more cynical variant of the theory, greed is the sole motivation). As welfare grows, the opportunity costs of participating in violent insurrection are higher. This increases the recruitment costs for the rebel group and thereby reduces the financial viability of the rebellion. Civil war is particularly likely in countries that have a relatively high dependence on primary commodities exports, since control over such primary commodities provides an attractive source of income for the rebel organization, again increasing the financial viability of rebellion. Development may reduce the value of this control relative to other sources of income, which also reduces the financial viability of rebellion. Moreover, Collier and Hoeffler (2001) and Fearon and Laitin (2001) note that the governments of rich countries are likely to be sufficiently strong to deter most rebellions.

The link from development to democracy (arrow C) is a classic in modernization theory dating back to Lipset's famous article over forty years ago, which proclaimed that 'the more well-to-do a nation, the greater the chances it will sustain democracy' (Lipset, 1959: 75). Higher income and better education for the lower strata would lead to a more compromise-oriented view of politics. Rich countries also have greater surpluses to distribute; this permits modernization through education, occupational mobility, free flow of information, and organizational experience. Taken together, these factors encourage adaptability and compromise, tolerance, and moderation. Increased access to material and thus political resources, together with greater institutional diversity, were seen to act as preconditions for stable democracy. These views have found support in several empirical studies (Burkhart and Lewis-Beck, 1994; Londregan and Poole, 1996; Przeworski et al., 2000). Przeworski et al. (2000: 88) point out that the relationship between democracy and development may come about in two ways: either because democracies 'may be more likely to emerge as countries develop economically, or, having been established for whatever reasons, democracies may be more likely to survive in developed countries.'

The link from democracy to civil peace (arrow D) is slightly more complex. In democratic countries the decision-making system tends to enjoy greater acceptance among the general population, so dissatisfaction is not frequently expressed in the form of serious challenges to the regime. Dissatisfaction can be channeled through the political system, with a low probability of outright rebellion. However, rebellion is also unlikely under a harshly authoritarian regime, which can effectively repress the opposition or even deter it from ever arising. Thus, it is in intermediate regimes, in semidemocracies, that we are particularly likely to find higher levels of internal conflict (Hegre et al., 2001).

Tying together these various links then, we expect globalization to have a general peace-building effect on the internal affairs in nations which participate in it.

## The Structuralist Model

The structuralist school of thought argues that an open economy is more likely to lead to increased conflict. We have summarized this argument in the simple model in figure 13.2. According to structuralist theory, the penetration of trade and foreign capital into peripheral economies leads to the exploitation of local human and natural resources, and to a transfer of profit back to the imperial centers. This process results in impoverishment, inequality, and injustice. The production of raw materials in poor countries serves to prevent competence-building, and the economy remains export-oriented. Ties are created between the local power elite and foreign interests; this in turn increases income inequality in the poor countries. The production of raw materials will keep inequality high and the level of welfare low.

**Figure 13.2. A Structuralist Model**

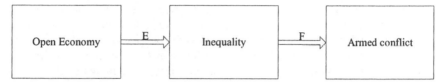

In the 1960s dependency theory focused mostly on exploitation through trade. Later versions of dependency theory paid more attention to foreign direct investment (FDI). Galtung (1971), for instance, depicts economic relationships between core and peripheral countries as characterized by an alliance between the elites within the two countries, which in particular is carried out at the expense of the periphery within the periphery country. To a lesser extent the relationship is at the expense of the periphery in the core country, too. In sum, increasing the intensity of this relationship of structural imperialism should increase inequality in both countries, but the most in the poor country. In a classical and influential study, Bornschier and Chase-Dunn (1985) looked at the consequences of the policies of multinational corporations in the periphery. Based on a study of 72 countries for the period 1950–77, they concluded that foreign capital increased inequality in poor countries. The price of a globally marketed product is approximately the same anywhere. In the North, most people may be able to afford a given product, whereas in the periphery only the elite can afford it. According to Bornschier and Chase-Dunn, if there is little inequality in the poor country, no one will be able to afford the product in question. Thus, as far as the multinational firm is concerned, a certain degree of inequality is desirable.

Dependency theory claimed that FDI in less-developed countries reduces economic growth while inequality increases. Foreign investment was thought less likely to contribute to public revenue, less likely to encourage indigenous entrepreneurship, less likely to promote links to other industries in the domestic economy, and more likely to use inappropriate capital-intensive technology (Firebaugh, 1992: 106). Similar arguments are frequently repeated in the current political debate about globalization (e.g., in Martin and Schumann, 1998).

More in the economic mainstream, Kuznets (1955) argued that inequality is relatively low in agricultural societies because most people are engaged in small farming and have fairly similar incomes. With industrialization and urbanization, inequality will initially increase, since wages in the industrializing sector are generally higher (in addition, inequality is supposed to be higher in the modernizing sector, too). As the labor force shifts from the agricultural sector to production in the modern sector where wages are higher, inequality will initially increase as long as the modern sector labor force is a minority, but will decrease as the transition is completed. (In addition, as workers become integrated into the new industrial culture, they will organize to struggle for higher wages and better legal protection, and gradually the inequality within the modern sector will be reduced). This process is often referred to as sector dualism (Nielsen and Alderson, 1995), and the inverted-U shaped relationship is referred to as the Kuznets U-curve. To the extent that trade and foreign investment mainly benefit the modern sector, and accelerate its expansion, we expect the effect of globalization to have different effects on inequality at different levels of development.

Structuralist writers are critical of this line of reasoning, however. In their view, worldwide capitalism is premised on inequality being maintained at a high level.

In economic theory, the factor-price equalization theorem also implies different effects for rich and poor countries, although in the opposite direction: With trade, developing countries specialize in goods that are intensive in unskilled labor, and hence push up wages for unskilled labor (cf. Aghion and Williamson, 1998). Developed countries specialize in goods that are intensive in skilled labor and in capital, and thereby depress wages for unskilled labor. This leads to a hypothesized increased inequality in developed countries and reduced inequality in developing countries—which is the opposite effect as that predicted by the structuralist model and the Kuznets curve.

Today reference is frequently made to increasing income inequality not just in the poor countries but also in the rich countries. Some scholars have sought an explanation in terms of technological change; others have cited high immigration. Increasingly, however, globalization is being singled out as the culprit (Wood, 1994). Imported cheap textiles and electronic goods compete successfully with Western products (Bhagwati and Kosters, 1994), producing an increasing number of unemployed. A new group of 'working poor' is emerging because of weakening of the labor movement and because of companies' efforts to compete with low-cost countries. Multinational companies threaten their Western workers that if costs are not kept down, factories may be moved to countries with lower wages. To take but one example, between 1990 and 1994 the Swiss–Swedish firm Asea Brown Boveri (ABB) closed down 40,000 jobs in North America and in Europe and created over 20,000 jobs in Eastern Europe— mostly in Poland. Average hourly wages in a Western country were almost 12 times higher than in Poland (Thurow, 1996: 168). To avert massive job losses, workers in Western countries have had to moderate their demands for higher wages. The real median income of families has barely increased since the early 1970s, and although the poverty rate has declined slightly, numerous children are still growing up in poverty. Employment has been growing strongly in the USA since the early 1980s, but it is less impressive if we take into account the population growth and the low salaries in many jobs. So goes the antiglobalist story, leading to the rhetorical question whether the United States is becoming a Third World country, since millions of people live under conditions similar to those found in poor countries (Luttwak, 1993; 118, 125).

This development is consistent with the prediction from the factor price equalization theorem, and have been confirmed empirically for developed countries (see Nielsen and Alderson, 1995: 678). But has it been accompanied by the predicted decrease in inequality in developing countries? Not according to Korzeniewicz and Moran (1997), who find world income inequality to have increased since 1965, and in particular since 1980. The signs of the estimates for independent variables associated with low level of development in Nielsen and Alderson (1995) also indicate that inequality has been increasing in the developing world.

Inequality, in turn, is seen as giving rise to conflict. Theories of relative deprivation argue that while absolute poverty may lead to apathy and inactivity, comparisons with those in the same society who do better may inspire radical action and even violence. Many revolutions have been based on egalitarian ideas like 'all men are created equal' or 'liberty, equality, fraternity'. And numerous empirical studies by Boswell and Dixon (1990), Muller and Seligson (1987), and others have found a positive relationship between inequality and conflict. In a survey Lichbach (1989) suggested that these findings might be spurious because they failed to include control variables like the level of economic development and political regime type. Scholars had focused on relative deprivation at the cost of ignoring more important explanatory factors. A puzzle in this connection is how economic inequality, which changes only slowly, can cause armed conflict to erupt at a particular time (Muller, 1988). Using the data on income inequality generated by Deininger and Squire (1996), several researchers (e.g., Collier and Hoeffler, 2001) have failed to find a significant relationship between inequality and political violence. In fact, inequality, is among the grievance factors largely dismissed by Collier and Hoeffler.

Within the structuralist mode of thinking, then, the main link is from globalization via inequality to internal conflict. We could have added increased political instability and the erosion of democracy to the model. The main reason why we have not done so is that it is the liberal model, rather than the structural model that clearly specifies a link between the political system and violence. We will nevertheless discuss some such links when we come to our empirical work.

## The Advance of Globalization

If we are to be able to test these notions empirically, we need to know at what point in history globalization is supposed to have entered and set the stage for greater inequality and violence—or for prosperity and peace. Globalization is obviously not a new phenomenon. Europe and China were connected hundreds or years ago by the 'silk route' and traders transferred such culturally pervasive items as noodles and gunpowder from China to Europe. By the end of the nineteenth century foreign trade exceeded 30 percent of GDP in several European countries and statistics in both liberal and structural writings indicate a declining trend in trade dependency since that time. If indeed the increasing absolute volume of trade was more than matched by increasing domestic production, we would have to ask whether the phenomenon of globalization itself was a fiction of the imagination. This would also call into question a basic premise for why it should have all the beneficial or negative effects posited by the liberals and the structuralists respectively.

However, Alesina et al. (2000) indicate that the apparent stagnation of globalization as measured by trade over GDP is based on an expanding set of nations. This provides a poor basis for comparison if the new nations included in the aggregate figures have lower trade dependency. When limiting for comparison over time to nine European countries with long data series, they find that the average trade/GDP ratio was roughly stable from the previous turn of the century until about 1930. Then it dropped and stayed down during the depression and war years. After World War II it rose rapidly to the pre-1930 level where it stayed until it started rising again in the early 1970s. Similarly, when comparing a larger sample of 61 countries from 1950, which shows that trade openness has picked up remarkably from the end of the 1970s and continues to rise. This is precisely the period identified by many as the age of globalization. During this period we have seen a massive relative decline in transportation costs. Statistics for foreign direct investment show an immense increase in this same period. Even greater expansion is reported for electronic communication, where the limitations imposed by geographical distance are largely eliminated. It *does* make sense, then, to speak of an era of globalization from the 1970s. We will test the consequences of globalization for the period 1970–97, and we would expect the rapid globalization in the later two-thirds of this period to have some consequences for conflict.[3] We therefore now move to an examination of these links, based on the broad models outlined earlier.

## Comparing the Models Empirically

### Globalization and Growth

We first investigate arrow A in figure 13.1, the liberal model: Does economic openness lead to a high level of economic development? Table 13.1 presents the results from an time-series cross-sections OLS regression analysis with growth as the dependent variable. Growth is measured as a country's average annual GDP per capita growth in four-year periods.[4] The first four-year period starts in 1970 and ends in 1973. The last period starts in 1994 and ends in 1997. We include a fairly standard set of control variables: the natural logarithm of the initial level of GNP per capita measured in constant 1995 USD dollars, gross domestic investment (GDI) as a percentage of GDP, financial depth (M2), secondary school enrollment (percent of relevant age group), agriculture value added as percentage of total value added, population growth in percent, and government consumption as percentage of GDP.[5] All these variables were taken from World Bank (1999) indicators. We calculated the mean of all years with data within the period for these variables. Since growth is likely to affect investment, financial depth, and our globalization variables, we lagged these three variables by one period to minimize endogeneity bias.[6] We also included indicator variables for eight regions and each of the time periods to minimize omitted variable bias (the parameter estimates are not shown here).[7] In addition, we included a variable denoting whether a civil war started in the country during the period.

In column A, we operationalize economic openness as trade (imports + exports) as a percentage of GDP. To decrease the effect of a few very high values, we took the natural logarithm of the variable.[8] In column B, we use the natural logarithm of foreign direct investment (FDI, net inflows in reporting country as a percentage of GDP) as our measure of openness.[9] In column C, we use Sachs and Warner's (1995) indicator as a measure of openness. In this measure, countries are coded as open if it maintained reasonably low tariffs and quotas, and did not have an excessively high black market exchange rate premium, was not socialist, and avoided extreme state control of its export sector. The dataset spans the period 1950–92. The data for GDP growth, FDI, and trade were also taken from World Bank (1999) indicators. All these variables were coded for the first year in the period. The data for civil wars were taken from the Correlates of War project and supplemented with wars for the 1993–97 period from Collier and Hoeffler (2001). The GNP per capita, trade, and primary commodities variables were all centered to minimize collinearity problems in the interaction models.

The estimates for lagged trade and FDI are both positive, but not statistically significant. The results do not support arrow A in figure 13.1 as clearly as other studies have. Estimating these models with nonlagged globalization variables, however, shows a positive and significant relationship. The implication of this is that the results reported here do not give a basis for concluding that high levels of trade or foreign direct investment relative to domestic production *cause* higher rates of growth, but that growth most often is associated with increased importance of trade and foreign investment. The Sachs and Warner indicator, on the other hand, is positive and significant.[10] Countries that are open, according to their definition, grow on average by more than two percentage points more than nonopen countries.[11] Note the 'convergence effect' in the results: The estimate for ln(GNP per capita) is negative, implying that poorer countries grow faster than richer. This contributes to reduced global inequality, as developing countries catch up with the developed ones. This appears to contradict the results of Korzeniewicz and Moran (1997). Note, however, that the impact of GNP per capita to some extent is offset by other control variables that are correlated with GNP per capita (e.g., investment, population growth, and civil war). In sum, the convergence effect may be fairly small.

**Table 13.1. Globalization and Economic Growth, 1970–97, OLS**

| Independent variable | 1A Trade, OLS | 1A* Trade, 2SLS | 1B FDI, OLS | 1C Sachs and Warner openness, OLS (1970–93) | 1D Trade, GNP per head interaction, OLS | 1E Trade, primary commodities exports inter-action, OLS |
|---|---|---|---|---|---|---|
| Trade/GDP (centered, lagged) | 0.20 (0.60) | 0.19 (0.63) | | | 0.02 (0.06) | 0.06 (0.14) |
| FDI/GDP (lagged) | | | 0.13 (1.00) | | | |
| Sachs/Warner openness | | | | 2.33 (4.45) | | |
| ln(GNP per capita) (centered, lagged) | −0.92 (−2.70) | −0.82 (−3.24) | −0.69 (−2.05) | −0.62 (−1.42) | −0.88 (−2.78) | −1.40 (−3.14) |
| Trade/GDP*ln(GNP per capita) (lagged) | | | | | 0.33 (2.17) | |
| Ln(Primary commodities exports/Total Trade/GDP) (lagged) | | | | | | −0.30 (−0.75) |
| Primary commodities* Trade/GDP (centered, lagged) | | | | | | −0.40 (−2.38) |
| GDI/GDP (lagged) | 0.046 (1.54) | 0.063 (2.29) | 0.041 (1.36) | 0.034 (0.92) | 0.054 (1.76) | −0.074 (−0.18) |
| M2/GDP (lagged) | 0.0095 (0.78) | 0.0076 (0.78) | 0.017 (1.54) | −0.016 (−1.53) | 0.010 (0.90) | −0.015 (−1.20) |
| New civil war in period | −2.86 (−4.33) | −2.75 (−4.18) | −2.76 (−3.94) | −2.64 (−3.79) | −2.89 (−4.27) | −2.57 (−3.25) |
| Secondary schooling | −0.0095 (−0.80) | −0.0099 (−0.99) | −0.0028 (−0.24) | −0.012 (−1.00) | −0.0098 (−0.84) | −0.0095 (−0.68) |
| Agriculture as share of value added | −0.081 (−3.59) | −0.069 (−3.32) | −0.078 (−3.44) | −0.060 (−2.68) | −0.086 (−3.86) | −0.13 (−4.04) |
| Population growth (%) | −0.73 (−2.50) | −0.74 (−3.68) | −0.35 (−1.41) | −0.69 (−2.72) | −0.75 (−2.52) | −1.24 (−3.63) |
| Govt. consumption as share of GDP | −0.12 (−2.74) | −0.11 (−3.81) | −0.14 (−3.66) | −0.097 (−2.48) | −0.11 (−2.53) | −0.15 (−3.10) |
| Constant | 7.56 | 6.46 | 6.96 | 5.81 | 7.16 | 11.82 |
| N | 511 | 506 | 474 | 402 | 511 | 352 |
| $R^2$ | 0.30 | 0.35 | 0.31 | 0.36 | 0.31 | 0.40 |

*Note:* Regression coefficients (with *t*-values in parentheses). The dependent variable is growth in GDP per capita. All models estimated with robust standard errors (Huber/White/sandwich estimator of variance).

According to some versions of the structuralist model, trade may be beneficial for rich countries but not for poor ones; neither is it good for primary goods exporters. To test this, we estimated a model with an interaction term between trade/GDP and initial GNP per capita (Model 1D). The interaction term is positive and significant: Trade seems to be less beneficial for poor countries than for rich countries. However, some caveats should be noted: First, the magnitude of the interaction term relative to the GNP per capita term implies that even the least developed countries are estimated to grow faster than developed countries, whether they have a high trade-to-GDP ratio or not. Second, the corresponding interaction term for the Sachs and Warner openness indicator (not reported here) is negative, but negligible in magnitude and not significant. According to that measure, economic openness is equally beneficial for all countries. Finally, the problem with correlation between trade/GDP and size mentioned above (fn. 9) is even more relevant here. Consistent with this, excluding India and China from the analysis significantly reduces the magnitude of the estimate for the interaction term.

The results for the primary commodities exports variable and its interaction with trade/GDP (Model 1E) yield estimates pointing in the same direction: Countries for which primary commodities form a large share of the total exports seems not to benefit from globalization measured as trade/GDP, as implied by the structural model. However, this interaction term is identical to a variable denoting the extent to which the economy is dependent on primary commodities exports. Primary commodities-dependent economies have been shown to grow more slowly than more diversified economies (cf. Sachs and Warner, 1997; Sachs, 1999), but this is ordinarily explained by internal mechanisms, not by the dependence on the rich world to which structuralists would attribute the finding: In particular, the 'Dutch disease' explanation suggests that resource-abundant economies tend to allocate less labor and capital to manufacturing. This is harmful if manufacturing is characterized by learning-by-doing or by economies of scale.

The estimates for the control variables are roughly consistent with earlier studies. Moreover, as others have also found (cf. Collier, 1999; Murdoch and Sandler, 2002), the onset of civil wars is extremely detrimental to economic development. In the first four-year period of the war, average annual growth is reduced to somewhere in the range of 2.5 to three percentage points.

## Globalization and Inequality

Table 13.2 presents results of tests of arrow E in figure 13.2: Is economic openness associated with higher inequality? The dependent variable is the average Gini coefficient for income inequality for the same periods as in table 13.1. The Gini coefficient ranges from under 20 (low inequality) to over 60 (high inequality) in the sample. The inequality data were taken from Deininger and Squire (1996). To maximize the number of observations, missing data points were filled in by means of an imputation model. Since inequality changes only slowly in most countries, there is extensive autocorrelation in the series.[12] To account for that we estimated the model using OLS with panel-corrected standard errors (Beck and Katz, 1995), assuming country-specific AR(1) processes.[13] The result from this estimation is reported in table 13.2, column A.

We include a set of control variables in the model, based on Ahluwalia (1976) and Nielsen and Alderson (1995), that to some extent explain the Kuznets curve: Earlier studies find a high level of education (represented by secondary school enrollment) to reduce inequality, a high population growth to be associated with high inequality, sector dualism (operationalized as the difference between the share of the labor force in agriculture and the share of agriculture in GDP, cf. Nielsen and Alderson 1995) to be positively related to inequality, and urban share of population and Marxist-Leninist economic system to be negatively related to inequality. We have also included democracy, assuming that democratic regimes are likely to carry out more redistribution, and GNP per capita and the square of GNP per capita in the model. We investigate the same indicators of globalization as in table 13.1.

**Table 13.2. Globalization and Inequality, 1970–97, OLS with Panel-Corrected Standard Errors**

| Variable | 2A<br>Trade/GDP;<br>No Interaction<br>term | 2B<br>Trade/GDP;<br>Interaction<br>terms | 2C<br>FDI/GDP;<br>Interaction<br>terms | 2D<br>Sachs/<br>Warner<br>openness | 2E<br>Trade/GDP;<br>Prim. comm. dep.<br>interaction terms* |
|---|---|---|---|---|---|
| Constant | 43.9 | 44.1 | 44.6 | 46.9 | 42.6 |
| Ln(Trade/GDP) | 0.61<br>(1.42) | 0.51<br>(1.11) | | | 0.98<br>(1.88) |
| Ln(Trade/GDP)*<br>ln(GNP per capita) | | −0.99<br>(−3.10) | | | −1.27<br>(−2.97) |
| FDI/GDP | | | 0.41<br>(0.67) | | |
| FDI/GDP*ln(GNP<br>per capita) | | | −0.042<br>(−0.48) | | |
| Sachs/Warner<br>openness | | | | −2.61<br>(−4.96) | |
| S-W Openness *<br>ln(GNP per capita) | | | | −0.66<br>(−1.33) | |
| Share of exports<br>primary goods | | | | | 0.043<br>(3.11) |
| Primary goods *<br>ln(Trade/GDP) | | | | | −0.036<br>(−1.80) |

**Table 13.2. Continued**

| Variable | 2A<br>Trade/GDP;<br>No Interaction<br>term | 2B<br>Trade/GDP;<br>Interaction<br>terms | 2C<br>FDI/GDP;<br>Interaction<br>terms | 2D<br>Sachs/<br>Warner<br>openness | 2E<br>Trade/GDP;<br>Prim. comm. dep.<br>interaction terms[*] |
|---|---|---|---|---|---|
| Ln(GNP per capita) | −0.61<br>(−1.69) | −0.89<br>(−2.45) | −0.87<br>(−1.86) | 0.56<br>(1.17) | 0.21<br>(0.47) |
| $(ln(GNP per capita))^2$ | −0.88<br>(−12.61) | −0.63<br>( 6.59) | −0.87<br>(−7.06) | −0.74<br>(−3.92) | −0.85<br>(−4.89) |
| Democracy | 0.11<br>(3.36) | 0.37<br>(2.28) | 0.32<br>(1.78) | 0.25<br>(1.09) | 0.29<br>(1.17) |
| Democracy*ln (GNP per capita) | | −0.038<br>(−1.79) | −0.029<br>(−1.21) | −0.028<br>(−0.95) | −0.031<br>(−0.95) |
| Secondary school enrollment (%) | −0.13<br>(−9.26) | −0.13<br>(−8.31) | −0.12<br>(−5.50) | −0.13<br>(−6.24) | −0.11<br>(−6.59) |
| Population growth (%) | 0.42<br>(3.01) | 0.29<br>(1.26) | 0.28<br>(0.60) | −0.14<br>(−0.41) | 0.36<br>(1.02) |
| Sector dualism (%) | 0.024<br>(1.11) | 0.012<br>(0.51) | 0.019<br>(0.78) | 0.025<br>(1.24) | 0.047<br>(1.89) |
| Urban population (% of total pop.) | 0.077<br>(4.14) | 0.083<br>(3.93) | 0.073<br>(3.38) | 0.065<br>(2.80) | 0.076<br>(3.54) |
| Marxist-leninist | −6.57<br>(−9.60) | 6.23<br>(−8.41) | −7.74<br>(−6.33) | −5.49<br>(−2.01) | −6.06<br>(−4.44) |
| N | 597 | 597 | 565 | 474 | 367 |
| No. of countries | 117 | 117 | 116 | 97 | 81 |
| $R^2$ | 0.964 | 0.961 | 0.961 | 0.975 | |

*Note:* Regression coefficients (with *t*-values in parentheses). Models A–D were estimated using OLS with panel-corrected standard errors (Beck and Katz, 1995), assuming panel-specific auto-correlation coefficients. Model E was estimated using FGLS (Greene, 1997: 511–513).

The results for the control variables are generally in line with earlier studies (Ahluwalia, 1976: Nielsen and Alderson, 1995): Education reduces inequality, and population growth and sector dualism increases it. In contrast to Ahluwalia, we find the share of urban population to increase inequality. This estimate is highly and negatively correlated with the estimate for GNP per capita, however, so the inconsistency may be due to collinearity. We find, as do Nielsen and Alderson (1995), that democracy is associated with high inequality.

The results in model 2A weakly support the argument reflected in arrow E in figure 13.2: A high level of trade relative to GDP is associated with high income inequality, although the relationship is not statistically significant.[14] However, as in the analysis of economic growth, there are reasons to believe that the relationship between economic openness and inequality is contingent on development.

The discussion of the structuralist model above implies that globalization should affect poor and rich countries differently.[15] To account for that, we added the interaction term between ln(Trade/GDP) and ln(GNP per capita) to the model. We also created an interaction term between democracy and ln(GNP per capita). The results are presented in table 13.2, column B.

The estimates indicate that high levels of trade and democracy are associated with high income inequality in poor countries only. The predicted Gini coefficients are plotted as functions of GNP per capita for three levels of trade in figure 13.3. For the countries with the lowest incomes per capita, those with trade/GNP at the 90th percentile are estimated to have a Gini coefficient more than two points above those with a trade level at the mean, and the least open economies more than two points under the average trader. For the countries with high income per capita, this relationship is completely reversed. This interaction effect reinforces the support for arrow E in figure 13.2: Trade is particularly likely to increase income inequality in low-income countries. This may not necessarily mean that only the elites in the periphery reap the benefits of trade, however, as suggested by Galtung (1971). Trade is likely to primarily affect the modern sector, and to accelerate the labor shift toward the modern sector. According to the sector dualism argument, this will lead to an increased Gini coefficient as long as the majority of the labor force still is in the low-wage traditional sector. Hence, a much more substantial part of the population than the 'elite' may benefit even when inequality increases.

In column C in table 13.2, we present the results from the corresponding model for ln(FDI/capita).[16] We do not find any significant relationship between the flow of foreign direct investment and inequality.[17] Column D shows that the Sachs and Warner indicator of economic openness is negatively related to inequality. This association is strongest for countries with a high level of GNP per capita, but open countries are estimated to have less inequality for all levels of development.

As discussed in relation to table 13.1, exposure to global trade may be particularly harmful for countries that are heavily dependent on primary commodities. To explore this, we added (as in table 13.1) the share of primary commodities in total merchandise exports, and this variable's interaction term with ln(Trade/GDP). The results are reported in column 2E. High dependence on primary commodities is associated with a high level of income inequality: the estimate 0.043 indicates that a country with mean GNP per capita where primary commodities make up 60 percent of the exports have a Gini coefficient 2.1 percentage points higher than one with only 10 percent primary commodities exports.[18] The negative interaction term for the interaction term indicates that this relationship between primary commodities dependence and inequality attenuates the relationship between trade and inequality. The estimate for the interaction term is not statistically significant, however.

**Figure 13.3. Estimated Effect of Trade on Income Inequality, by GNP per Capita, 1970–97**

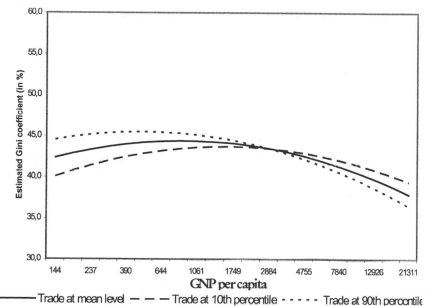

## Globalization and Civil War

Table 13.3 reports results from a calendar-time Cox regression analysis estimating how the globalization variables influence the risks of outbreak of civil war. The model is based on Hegre et al. (2001). The interpretation of the estimates of the model is very similar to the interpretation of logistic regression estimates.[19] The data for civil war were taken from the Correlates of War project, and again supplemented with a few additional wars from Collier and Hoeffler (2001).

This analysis allows us to test arrows B, D, and F in figures 13.1 and 13.2. The analysis controls for the level of democracy, GNP per capita, proximity of regime change, proximity of civil war, interstate war, ethnic heterogeneity, and the logarithm of the size of the country's population. Population is a crucial control variable in this analysis, since it has a high negative correlation with trade/GDP (cf. fn. 6). Without this control, trade/GDP may be acting as a proxy for population size. The number of battle deaths from political violence are more likely to exceed 1,000 per year in a more populous country . Thus, civil war is more frequent the larger the country (Collier and Hoeffler, 2001).

We use the Polity 98d democracy index and its square term as our measure of level of democracy. Proximity of regime change is measured as exp(–days since regime change/527), which assumes that the impact of a regime change on

**Table 13.3. Globalization and Civil War, 1960–92, Cox Regression**

|  | 3A | 3B | 3C | 3D |
|---|---|---|---|---|
| Ln(Trade/GDP) (lagged by one year) | 0.10 (0.31) | 0.13 (0.31) |  |  |
| FDI/GDP (lagged by one year) |  |  | –0.045 (–0.68) |  |
| Inequality |  |  |  | 0.0067 (0.32) |
| GDP per capita (lagged by one year) | –0.49 (–2.51) | –0.43 (–3.00) | –0.41 (–2.37) | –0.40 (–3.14) |
| GDP per capita squared (lagged by one year) | –0.18 (–1.82) | –0.18 (–2.24) | –0.20 (–1.73) | –0.13 (–1.75) |
| Proximity of civil war (eight year half-life) | 1.06 (2.04) | 1.29 (3.26) | 1.46 (3.49) | 1.54 (4.29) |
| Interstate war | 0.75 (1.09) | 0.94 (2.29) | 1.32 (3.18) | 0.67 (1.73) |
| Ln(Population) | 0.31 (2.15) | 0.30 (2.27) | 0.26 (2.26) | 0.19 (2.32) |
| Proximity of regime change (half year half-life) | 1.80 (3.67) | 1.79 (4.30) | 2.14 (5.00) | 1.73 (3.97) |
| Democracy | –0.028 (–1.18) |  |  |  |
| Democracy squared | 0.0015 (0.23) |  |  |  |
| Ethnic heterogeneity | 0.65 (1.22) |  |  |  |
| log likelihood |  |  |  |  |
| No. of civil wars | 42 | 53 | 36 | 56 |
| No. of countries | 144 | 172 | 164 | 158 |

*Note:* Regression coefficients (with *t*-values in parentheses).

the probability of civil war is initially high and then reduced at a constant rate with a half-life of six months.[20] The proximity of civil war variable is constructed along the same lines, but with a half-life of eight years. The interstate war variable records whether a civil war was ongoing at the time of observation. Ethnic heterogeneity is measured as $(1-s^2)$ where $s$ is the share of the population in the country that belongs to the largest ethnic group.

We use the same source for GDP per capita as for tables 13.1 and 13.2, but supplement it with figures from Penn World Tables Mark 5.6 (Summers and Heston, 1991), and log-transform this variable, too. The trade/GDP, FDI/GDP, and GDP per capita variables were sampled the year before the observation year to minimize problems of endogeneity. Both the trade/GDP and GDP per capita variables were log transformed. As in Hibbs (1973) and Hegre et al. (2001), we included the square of ln(GDP per capita). The inequality variable was measured the same year as the observation.

The results of this estimation are shown in table 13.3. In column 3A, we find no impact of trade/GDP on the hazard of civil war, controlling for all the variables mentioned above.[21] Note that, in contrast to Hegre et al. (2001), there is no discernible relationship between the level of democracy and the hazard of civil war (arrow D in figure 13.1). This is mainly due to the inclusion of the GDP per capita variable, which is correlated with democracy ($r = 0.51$). This creates problematic collinearity in the model, which again hurts the precision of the estimates for both variables. Given the debate around whether development causes democracy or vice versa, one may discuss which of the two variables should be taken out. However, since we are focusing on economic factors in this chapter, we reestimated the model without the level of democracy variables.[22] We also removed the ethnic heterogeneity variable, which is never significant at the 0.05 level with this dataset. The results are presented as model B in table 13.3. The estimates are very close to those in model A, but the standard errors are invariably smaller because of the higher number of cases available for analysis and because of the removal of the collinearity problems. In model C, we find no relationship between the flow of foreign direct investment and the hazard of civil war.

Models A–C show that there is no direct effect of trade openness or the flow of foreign investment on the risk of civil war. The structuralist model (cf. figure 13.2), however, implies that an open economy should increase the risk of civil war through increased income inequality (arrows E and F). We found some relationship between trade exposure and inequality for poor countries in table 13.2, but can we find any trace of the other part of this relationship? In model 3D we add the Gini coefficient to the model. Like Collier and Hoeffler (2001), we find no systematic relationship between inequality and civil war—the estimate is virtually zero.[23]

The liberal model (figure 13.1) does not predict a direct relationship between economic openness and the hazard of civil war. Globalization works through the effect of trade on growth. In table 13.1, we found some evidence for economic openness to increase growth as suggested by arrow A. Arrow B implies that there is a direct, negative relationship between GDP per capita and the hazard of civil war. The estimates for the variable and its square term are negative. Figure 13.4 plots the estimated relationship between GDP per capita and the hazard of civil war, based on the estimates in model 3B. The figure shows that the hazard of civil war is roughly unchanged when increasing GDP per capita up to approximately USD 1,500 (the level of Guatemala or Ukraine in 1997), and then decreasing at an increasing rate for each multiplicative increase in GDP per capita.

All of the control variables retained in models 3B–3D are significant: Population size is positively associated with the risk of civil war. The existence of an interstate war in the country is also positively correlated with civil wars, although this result is quite sensitive to sample variations. The proximity of civil war variable captures the fact that civil wars are likely to be followed by another civil war (in addition to being a proxy for unmeasured characteristics that increase the likelihood of civil war, cf. Collier and Hoeffler, 2001). The proximity of regime change, on the other hand, partly reflects the fact that a change in the institutional setup often lead to violent protest, and partly the fact that regime change often is an integral part of the process leading up to a civil war. This suggests that it would be useful to analyze how globalization affects the likelihood of regime change. This is done in table 13.4.

**Figure 13.4. The Estimated Relationship between GDP per Capita and Civil War**

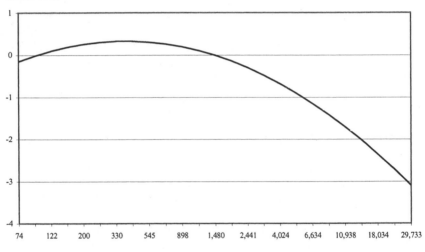

*Note:* The figure plots the natural logarithm of the estimated risk of civil war relative to the baseline, which has GDP per capita at the mean.

## Globalization and the Duration of Political Institutions

The analysis reported in this section builds on Gates et al. (2001). The dependent variable in table 13.4 is the duration of a polity, that is, the time between two regime changes in a country. A regime change is defined as a substantial change in the system for recruitment of the executive, the degree to which the executive is constrained by a balancing institution, and the share of the population participating in elections. The conceptualization and data were drawn from Gurr (1974) and Vanhanen (2000).[24] Here, we use log-logistic regression, with the duration of the polity as the time variable as is common in survival analyses. The hazard of failure increases initially, peaks after 3–4 years, and then falls. The parameter estimates are reported in time-ratio form, implying that they are estimates of the change to the median survival time effected by one unit's increase on the independent variable (cf. Collett, 1994: 205). Figures in parentheses are estimated t-scores, testing the hypothesis that ln(time ratio) $<>$ 0. T-scores are negative when the estimated time ratio is less than one. The economic variables are measured as in table 13.3, and sampled once for every five years such that they refer to a time between (and including) the year of the observed regime change or up to five years before the change.

**Table 13.4. Globalization and Duration of Political Systems, 1960–97, Log-logistic Regression**

|  | 4A | 4B | 4C | 4D | 4E |
|---|---|---|---|---|---|
|  | All Regime types, trade | All Regime types, FDI | Autocracies | Inconsistent regimes | Democracies |
| Ln(Trade/GDP) | 1.13 (1.26) |  | 0.84 (−1.06) | 1.27 (1.87) | 2.27 (3.24) |
| FDI/GDP |  | 1.05 (1.37) |  |  |  |
| Ln(GDP per capita) | 1.18 (2.79) | 1.15 (1.87) | 1.24 (3.40) | 1.01 (0.14) | 1.59 (4.11) |
| Autocracy | 2.51 (6.95) | 2.05 (4.53) |  |  |  |
| Democracy | 5.45 (9.98) | 5.01 (8.14) |  |  |  |
| Avg. dist. from political pos. of neighbors | 0.54 (−2.25) | 0.64 (−1.32) | 0.32 (−2.61) | 0.75 (−0.75) | 6.73 (2.18) |
| Proximity of independence | 2.04 (3.56) | 2.47 (3.13) | 4.79 (4.16) | 1.42 (1.29) | 0.55 (−1.25) |
| Gamma (95% c. i.) | 0.73 (0.68, 0.79) | 0.71 (0.65, 0.77) | 0.69 (0.61, 0.78) | 0.70 (0.63, 0.78) | 0.72 (0.58, 0.89) |
| 2ll change (d.f.) | 140.91 (6) | 86.68 (6) | 31.19 (4) | 8.75 (4) |  |
| No. of failures | 504 | 335 | 188 | 252 | 64 |
| No. of polities | 630 | 455 | 218 | 286 | 126 |

*Note:* Regression coefficients (with *t*-values in parentheses).

Columns 4A and 4B investigate how trade/GDP and FDI/GDP affect the hazard rate of all type of polities. Both estimates are positive, but not statistically significant. Increasing trade by a factor of $e=2.7$ is estimated to increase the survival time by 13 percent. Increasing FDI by the same factor only increases regime survival by 5 percent.

The estimate for GDP per capita is positive, clearly significant, and non-trivial in magnitude. Increasing GDP per capita by $e=2.7$ (approximately the difference between Bolivia and Panama, or between Mongolia and the Philippines) increases the expected survival time with 18 percent in model 4A.

The distance between a state's political setup and that of its neighbors affects stability. On average, polities surrounded by countries with diametrically different political systems live only half as long as those neighboring their political kins. Surprisingly, the first polities following a country's independence are more stable than those coming later: A political system put together at the country's independence day may expect to last twice as long as one commencing 60–70 years later, ceteribus paribus.

We distinguish between three regime types: autocracies, democracies, and in-between (inconsistent) regimes as defined in Gates et al. (2001). We control for the average distance between the political system in the country and those of the neighboring country. This variable ranges from 0 to 1. A fully consistent democracy bordering only consistent autocracies would be coded with a 1.[25] We also control for the proximity of independence. This variable takes the value 1 on the first day of independence and decreases at a constant rate with a half-life of 16 years.[26] We also tried controlling for population size to make sure Trade/GDP does not act as a proxy for country size, but this variable was never close to statistical significance. We report the estimated time ratios, or how many times longer the median survival time is estimated to be if the independent variable is increased with one unit.

The estimates for autocracy and democracy show that both autocracies and democracies are much more stable than the reference category 'Inconsistent regimes'. The inconsistent regimes have an estimated median survival time of 2.6 years.[27] Controlling for the other variables, autocracies are estimated to survive 2.5 times longer, and democracies 5.5 times longer.

The liberal model, however, does not imply that development enhances the stability of nondemocratic political systems (cf. Przeworski et al., 2000). On the other hand, it is often argued that nondemocratic regimes have a harder time surviving when faced with economic openness. To assess the hypothesis more precisely, we estimated the model in column 4A separately for each of the three regime types.

Column 4C reports the analysis for autocracies. The median survival time for this subset is 6.5 years. Here, economic openness is associated with a shorter expected polity duration, although the estimate is not significant. Autocratic states with a high GNP per capita, on the other hand, are more stable than autocracies with a low GNP per capita.[28] This relationship is stronger than the average relationship between development and stability.

Interestingly, the control variables also have very different impacts on policy duration in the three subsets. The political distance to the neighborhood significantly reduces expected survival time: autocracies surrounded by democracies are more likely to experience regime changes than autocracies in more homogenous surroundings (cf. Gleditsch, 2002b for a more elaborate study of this). Finally, the median survival time increases more rapidly with time since independence in the autocratic subset than for all regimes.

Column 4D presents the model estimated for in-between regimes. Although this is the subset with the highest number of polities and failures, none of the variables reach the 5 percent level of significance. This probably reflects the highly heterogenous nature of this class of polities. Economic openness is estimated to increase regime stability, and is the variable that is closest to the 5 percent significance level. Increasing trade by a factor of 2.7 increases estimated survival time by 1.27. The other three variables in the model does not seem to alter the stability of these inconsistent, frequently short-lived polities.

Column 4E shows how the variables in the model affect the stability of democracies. This is the most stable subgroup, with median survival time of 9.6 years in the 1960–97 period. Despite the low number of cases (126 polities with 64 failures), the estimates are very clearly defined: Economic openness clearly increases the likely duration of the polity. The 2.7 factor increase in trade increases estimated duration by as much as 127 percent. Increasing the level of GDP per capita has the strongest impact on duration in democracies. Democracies in sub-Saharan Africa may expect to live only 1/8 as long as those of Western Europe.[29] Hence, the analysis not only supports arrow C in the liberal model (figure 13.1), which predicted that a high level of development should lead to or stabilize democracy. There seems also to be a direct effect of an open economy on the stability of democracies, which is not found for the other regime types.

Strangely, the prospects for democratic survival are not reduced by being surrounded by autocracies and inconsistent regimes. On the contrary, it seems that democratic institutions thrive particularly well in such conditions.

For democracies, the estimate for proximity of independence is less than one, but not statistically significant—democracy is not more stable in new states. Breaking the analysis up into the three subsets suggests an explanation of why polities in new states seems to be most stable: Autocracies are clearly more stable when states are young, and since they account for a large fraction of the polities they contribute the most to the estimate in model 4A. When states have existed for some time, autocratic political systems seems to be less viable. Although the estimate for proximity of independence in democracies is not statistically significant, it is consistent with the trajectory postulated by modernization theory. As noted in connection with the civil war model (table 13.3), there is endogeneity in this model, too. Just as foreign investors and prospective trading partners may anticipate civil war, they may anticipate regime change. An unknown portion of the positive estimate for trade and FDI is due to this anticipation. However, the endogeneity argument cannot explain the considerable differences in the estimates for trade/GDP between the three regime types. This may indicate that globalization really increases democratic stability. Moreover, if the anticipation biases the estimates in the destabilizing direction, this implies that the true estimate for autocracies, purged of endogeneity, should be even lower: Globalization may be associated with the democratization of autocracies.

## Conclusion

In this chapter, we have outlined and compared two models of how globalization is likely to affect the risk of civil war. Overall, we find considerably more support for the liberal model than for the structuralist, antiglobalist model. Trade does appear to have a capacity for increasing internal peace—not directly, but via trade's beneficial effects on growth and increased political stability.

Overall, we find economic openness to be associated with higher growth. This is particularly clear when using the Sachs and Warner measure of economic openness. Measured as trade/GDP, it is unclear whether globalization causes growth or vice versa, but there is evidently a positive relationship between the two variables. Our results give no support to the idea that globalization reduces growth, not even for poor countries. We found some evidence that trade increases income inequality. However, in contrast to the robust link established between income inequality and violent crime (Fajnzylber, Lederman, and Loayza, 2002), we do not find any relationship between inequality and civil war. In sum, the beneficial effect of trade and foreign investment outweighs whatever violence may be generated by increased inequality. We find that economic openness is associated with greater stability of political systems. This effect is particularly strong for democracies, but also positive for inconsistent regimes and autocracies. Finally, in our analysis of the factors increasing the likelihood of civil war, we find no direct impact of economic openness. However, countries with a high income per capita and a stable political system have considerably lower risk of civil war than those without. Hence, since we find economic openness to increase average income and political stability, we do find an indirect conflict-reducing effect of globalization.

However, we note three caveats to this conclusion: First, our empirical investigation makes use of data at a fairly high level of violence and it remains to be seen whether more evidence can be found for the structuralist thesis using data on lower-level violence. Second, while the effects of globalization may be largely successful overall, the question still remains whether some parts of the world are being marginalized in the process of globalization and suffer from some of the ills described by the structuralists. Our tentative judgment would be that great parts of Africa and some other areas marred by poverty, poor governance, and conflict are victims of too little globalization rather than too much. While it does not seem very plausible to us that successful globalization in some regions should be contingent on marginalization in others, this remains to be investigated rigorously. Third, our indicators of globalization fail to capture certain aspects of international trade that are clearly related to civil war: In countries such as Angola, Sierra Leone, and Liberia the exports of diamonds, timber, and drugs have financed rebel groups and militarily adventurous state leaders. Likewise, these groups have acquired weapons through the international market for arms. More liberal and efficient international trade has increased the incentives for wars in many places. Still, our results indicate that this is balanced by the beneficial effects of globalization. This particular type of trade must be handled by targeted sanctions and regulations, not by reducing economic openness in general.

## Notes

The theoretical part of this chapter borrows heavily from Gissinger and Gleditsch (1999). The empirical analysis is new. An earlier version was presented to the World Bank Conference on the Economics and Politics of Civil War: Launching the Case-Study Project, Soria Moria conference center, Oslo, 11–12 June 2001. We are grateful for comments from the participants of that meeting, and from Indra de Soysa, Gunnar Eskeland, Erik Gartzke, John Randa, and Erich Weede. We also acknowledge the assistance of Naima Mouhleb, Håvard Strand, and Lars Wilhelmsen. The findings and conclusions expressed in the chapter are entirely those of the authors and do not necessarily represent the views of the World Bank.

1. In particular, there is an extensive debate about trade and conflict, as shown by Schneider and Barbieri (1999) and most of the chapters in this volume.

2. We might have used 'dependency theory' for this line of thought. However, we avoid this term, since it is associated with a particular historical period. The current objections to the neoliberal model are similar in many ways to those of the 1970s, but the term dependency theory seems to be dead.

3. For a more detailed discussion of these trends, see de Soysa and Gleditsch (2001).

4. All the independent variables in table 13.1 change slowly. Hence, using the four-year period as our time unit rather than the year does not involve much loss of information. At the same time, analysing four year periods lessens the problems with autocorrelation.

5. We also tried controlling for democracy, using data from Polity III (Jaggers and Gurr, 1995). This variable is never significant. Since missing observations for the variable removes a number of cases from the analysis, and introduces collinearity, we present the results without it.

6. We also ran two-stage least square regressions where these three variables were instrumented. This analysis yielded very similar results, so the use of lagged variables seems sufficient to avoid endogeneity bias. When estimating the model with a non-lagged trade/GDP variable, the trade variable obtains a positive and significant estimate. Furthermore, we ran a feasible generalized least square (FGLS) regression (Greene, 1997: 511–513) to ascertain that autocorrelation in the series does not produce another type of bias. The estimates for the variables of interest were quite similar in this estimation, too, and there was not evidence of any problematic autocorrelation. The results from these estimations are available at http://www.prio.no/cwp/datasets.asp.

7. The region indicators were included to partly account for other factors that influence countries' growth rates. The eight regions are West Europe and North America, East Europe, South Asia, East Asia, Central Asia, Middle East, and North Africa, Africa South of Sahara, and Latin America. The period indicators account for worldwide fluctuations in growth rates. The estimates for each of the region and period indicator variables are available at http://www.prio.no/cwp/datasets.asp.

8. The trade/GDP, FDI/GDP, and GNP per capita variables were centered by subtracting the mean of each variable from all observations to minimize collinearity when creating interaction term. The implication of this is that the constant term is to be interpreted as the growth rate when these variables are at their mean for models 1A and 1B. In model 1D, the interpretation of the parameter estimate and the estimated t-value for each

of the two main terms in the interaction construction is their effect/significance when the other variable is at the mean (cf. Friedrich, 1982).

9. Negative values were replaced with 0.1%.

10. One possible reason for the inconsistency between the Sachs and Warner indicator results and the trade/GDP and FDI/GDP variables, is that the denominator in the latter variables imply that they are negatively correlated with the size of the economies. Large countries trade less relative to GDP because they have larger internal markets. Hence, the trade-to-GDP ratio might act as a proxy for size rather than for economic openness. The two largest developing countries, India and China, have recently opened up their economies and increased their growth rate (Dollar and Kraay, 2002), but their relatively low trade-to-GDP ratios pull down the estimate for this variable.

11. We also estimated the model including a lagged Sachs and Warner openness indicator to minimize endogeneity. The parameter estimate for the lagged variable is smaller (1.03) but statistically significant.

12. Estimating an FGLS model with a common autocorrelation coefficient indicated a coefficient of 0.55. We also estimated various other models, all yielding similar substantive conclusions. These results are reported in the log files available at http://www.prio.no/cwp/datasets.asp.

13. We also estimated the model using a Feasible Generalized Least Squares model (Greene, 1997: 511–513), which yielded very similar results. Model 2D could be estimated using only FGLS because of a high number of gaps in the country series.

14. An increase in inequality does not necessarily imply that anyone gets poorer in an absolute sense. Dollar and Kraay (2001a, b) estimate that the increase in average income resulting from the economic openness is so large that the net average effect is that trade lifts people out of poverty, even though trade may be associated with inequality. We do not investigate the net effect of trade on poverty reduction here.

15. Alderson and Nielsen (1999: 621) also find that foreign investment increases inequality in noncore (i.e., developing) countries only.

16. For a number of observations, FDI were zero or negative. These were replaced with FDI/GDP = 0.1% before log-transforming.

17. This is in contrast to Alderson and Nielsen (1999), who find a significant positive relationship between foreign capital stock and inequality, and also a positive estimate for the flow of foreign investment.

18. The primary commodities variable is highly correlated with ln(GNP per capita) and washes out the effect of the GNP/capita main term.

19. The Cox regression model estimates log relative risk of civil war (relative to a baseline), whereas the logistic regression model yields estimates of log odds of civil war. For rare events as civil wars, however, these measures are roughly similar. See Hegre et al. (2001) for a justification of the model. The use of the Cox regression model deviates from standard use of survival models as Cox regression, as we use calendar time as the time variable. The dataset samples all countries not already in civil war once for each time there is an outbreak of civil war. This allows estimating the relative risks of civil war breaking out in a country with certain characteristics, given that a civil war has broken out somewhere.

20. The denominator 527 in the expression determines the half-life of six months. Hegre et al. (2001) finds this half-life to maximize the likelihood of the model.

21. This is inconsistent with the results of the State Failure Project (Esty et al., 1998; see also King and Zeng, 2001), who find trade/GDP to be one of the most robust predictors of civil war. This discrepancy is mostly due to Esty et al.'s failure to control for

population. To a lesser extent, the discrepancy may also be caused by their broader definition of the dependent variable, which also includes abrupt regime changes (cf. the results in table 13.4).

22. The results reported in table 13.4 below show that democracies are the most stable political systems, and hence are least likely to have regime changes that we find to be strongly associated with civil war. Moreover, the inconsistent regimes, those that are neither consistent democracies nor autocracies, are the least stable. Hence, it is possible to trace an indirect relationship between regime type and the hazard of civil war.

23. Since there is an inverted U-curve relationship between both development and inequality and development and civil war (cf. figure 13.4), we would expect to find a stronger relationship between inequality and civil war if we omit the GNP per capita variables. Estimating the model without these variables does increase the magnitude of the estimate for inequality, but it is still not significant ($t=1.34$). Hence, there is little support for the idea that the GNP per capita variable masks the effect of the inequality variable.

24. Full definitions and sources are found in Gates et al. (2001).

25. This measure is also explained in Gates et al. (2001).

26. We tried out different half-life values, ranging from 0.5 to 16 years. Setting the half-life to 16 years gave the best fit to the data.

27. The 95% confidence interval for this estimate is (2.0, 3.0). This estimate is considerably lower than the one reported in Hegre et al. (2001). This is due to a more inclusive definition of regime change, and the fact that political changes occured more often in the late twentieth century than in the 1800–1960 period.

28. This result contradicts the results of Przeworski et al. (2000: 124), who find that autocracies tend to change into democracies slightly more often when the level of income is increased. This difference in results may be due to a different set of control variables, but is more likely to be due to the fact that Przeworski et al. do not distinguish between autocracies and inconsistent regimes.

29. Although this analysis takes duration dependence into account, the difference between the African and Western European democracies' chances of survival is not as dramatic as it may sound. Since the definition of regime change is quite wide in this analysis, a 'failure' may equally well lead an slightly inconsistent democracy toward a more stable democratic setup as to a total breakdown in the democratic system. Such changes, however, are less likely in the old democracies in Western Europe, because they have reached a point where increasing suffrage and parliamentary control cannot be further increased. These effects are more fully discussed in Gates et al. (2001).

# CHAPTER 14

# The Trade-Disruption Hypothesis and the Liberal Economic Theory of Peace

## *Katherine Barbieri and Jack S. Levy*

The systematic analysis of the relationship between economic interdependence and international conflict emerged in the mid-1990s as a thriving research program, one that involved both proponents and critics of the long-standing liberal belief that interdependence promotes peace. While most of the literature has focused on the impact of trade on conflict, our finding that war did not systematically and significantly reduce trade between seven minor power dyads over the last century (Barbieri and Levy, 1999) helped to trigger a secondary debate on the impact of war on trade. Anderton and Carter (2001a) extended the analysis of the impact of war on trade to major power as well as minor power dyads, and their findings raised questions about the generality of our findings. A debate ensued (Barbieri and Levy, 2001; Anderton and Carter, 2001b). This debate has enormous implications for the trade-promotes-peace hypothesis and liberal international theory more generally. The assumption that war reduces trade is one of the central causal mechanisms underlying the liberal proposition that trade promotes peace.[1]

In this chapter we present our original study of the impact of war on trade (Barbieri and Levy, 1999), summarize the Anderton and Carter (2001a) study, and note some of the ways in which it differs from our own analysis. Anderton and Carter (2001a) are more interested in extending our analysis to major power dyads and determining the extent to which our empirical findings are generalizable than in questioning the validity of our findings in our particular sample of cases. We have challenged the strength of their findings elsewhere (Barbieri and Levy, 2001), and rather than reproducing that entire critique here we simply summarize some of the major points of contention.

## The Theoretical and Empirical Debate

In recent years there has been a surge of interest in the relationship between trade and militarized international conflict, as scholars have begun to reformulate long-standing arguments and to test these theoretical propositions systematically against the empirical evidence. The primary focus has been on the question of whether trade promotes peace, and scholars have generally framed the debate in terms of the 'paradigm wars' between liberalism and realism.

Liberals advance a number of interrelated theoretical arguments in support of the proposition that trade promotes peace. The most compelling of these is that trade generates economic benefits for both parties, and that the anticipation that conflict will disrupt trade and lead to a loss or reduction of the gains from trade deters political leaders from conflict against key trading partners (Polachek, 1980, 1992; Oneal and Russett, 1997; Doyle, 1997).[2] Realists and others argue either that trade has a negligible impact on conflict (Buzan, 1984; Levy, 1989a: 260–262, 2003; Ripsman and Blanchard, 1996/97), or that trade—and particularly asymmetric trade—actually increases conflict between trading partners (Barbieri, 1995, 1996a, 2002).[3] Scholars on both sides of this debate have recently begun to generate empirical evidence to bolster their theoretical arguments.[4]

Although contemporary liberal and realist theories disagree about the effects of trade on conflict, they appear to agree on the effects of conflict on trade. Both imply that trade and other forms of economic interchange between states will cease or be drastically reduced once states are engaged in serious conflicts with each other. The liberal hypothesis that trade deters conflict is based on the premise that conflict will substantially reduce trade or adversely affect the terms of trade. Realist theories imply that trade, particularly in strategic goods, will terminate between adversaries because of relative gains concerns (Waltz, 1979; Grieco, 1990; Huntington, 1993). Fearing that its adversary will reap relative gains from the continuation of trade and exploit those gains to increase its relative military power and potential, at least one state will perceive an incentive to cease trade.[5] If relative gains concerns exist during peacetime, we expect them to be even greater during wartime. Similarly, once states prove themselves to be adversaries in war, there should be a heightened sensitivity to concerns about security externalities and thus a reduction or elimination of trade between wartime enemies.

Contrary to both liberal and realist theories of interdependence and war, however, there are numerous historical cases of trading with the enemy during wartime, including trade in strategic goods that directly affect the ability of a state to prosecute the war. This is quite evident from numerous historical accounts (Giltner, 1997; Levy and Barbieri, 2001).[6] For example, the Baltic trade was so essential to the economy of the Netherlands in their Eighty Years' War with Spain (1565–1648) that the Dutch served as carriers of naval stores for the Spanish. In this way the Dutch earned the monies to pay the forces that protected Dutch frontiers against Spanish attack, while Spain secured the stores that helped maintain its fleets engaged in the protection of Spanish commerce against Dutch attacks (Howard, 1976: 44). Or consider the Seven Years' War of the mid-eighteenth century, in which British insurance companies continued to insure French naval and commercial ships and to pay enormous sums to replace ships that were actively being searched and destroyed by British warships (Pares, 1963). Trading with the enemy was also widespread during the War of 1812 and the Crimean War (Levy, 1998), and this phenomenon has not ceased in this century.[7]

Trading with the enemy—whether directly or indirectly through neutral states—is an interesting phenomenon in itself and one that has important implications for contemporary theories about the relationship between economic interdependence and peace. The liberal hypothesis that trade deters conflict rests on the assumption that conflict reduces trade and, hence, the welfare gains from trade, so that systematic evidence that states trade with the enemy during wartime would undercut this central causal mechanism of the liberal proposition. Such evidence would also undercut the strong implication of realist theory that relative gains concerns will lead one or both adversaries to terminate trade in order to deny the other the ability to convert relative gains into usable military power.

Thus both liberal and realist theories generate the strong hypothesis that the outbreak of war substantially reduces levels of trade, at least while the war is underway. Whether trade will remain depressed after the termination of war, or whether it will quickly return to prewar levels, is less well specified. Liberal theories imply that the loss of the gains from trade refers not only to the losses suffered during the war itself but also to the adverse impact of war on the future trading relationship, at least for a while.[8] It is conceivable, though less likely, that in some circumstances political leaders are concerned only with the loss of trade during the war and expect a rapid recovery after the war. Clearly, the deterrent effects of the anticipated loss of trade will be lower if leaders expect that trade will resume immediately after the termination of war. Thus we conclude that liberal theories predict both a reduction of trade during war and only a delayed and gradual recovery of trade after war under most conditions, but that the intrawar effect is on average stronger than the postwar effect.

Similarly, realists do not clearly specify what happens to trade after a war is over. Under some conditions war resolves outstanding disputes and creates conditions for profitable trade soon after the termination of war.[9] Under other conditions mutual threat perceptions remain high after the end of war because of fears that the adversary may use gains from trade to enhance its military power and potential for leverage in future conflicts, perhaps motivated by the loser's incentives to recover its losses.[10] Our reading indicates that the second set of conditions is more common, with the prediction of a slow recovery of trade after war being weaker than the prediction of the reduction of trade during war.

Many of the same arguments about the impact of war on trade should apply to militarized conflict short of war, largely because of fears of escalation to war. Because of uncertainties about escalation, however, the causal effects should be somewhat weaker, whether motivated by liberal concerns of the loss of welfare gains from trade or by realist concerns for relative gains. We would hypothesize that the impact of war on trade should be greater than the impact of militarized disputes on trade.[11] Consequently, trading with the enemy in wartime is more of an anomaly for contemporary liberal or realist theories of interdependence and war than is trading with the adversary during a period of militarized disputes or rivalry, and for this reason our empirical study focuses on the impact of war rather than of more generalized forms of conflict.

Our argument, then, is that the impact of conflict (and particularly war) on trade has enormous implications for the impact of trade on conflict in contemporary liberal and realist models of the relationship between economic interdependence and conflict. We are careful to distinguish, however, between liberal and realist paradigms of international politics and contemporary scholars' *applications* of those paradigms to the question of the relationship between economic interdependence and conflict. Our argument is not that liberal and realist paradigms are incapable of explaining the trading with-the-enemy phenomenon, but rather that liberal and realist theories of interdependence and conflict, as they are now formulated in the literature, do not adequately deal with this phenomenon.

As we argue later, liberal theory can help explain this phenomenon by incorporating the political power and interests of key societal groups, and realism can do so by incorporating third parties into its conceptualization of relative gains. Applications of these paradigms to the interdependence and conflict debates, however, are framed much more narrowly. Both liberals and realists focus primarily on the dyadic level, ignore the role of domestic actors and third parties, and are consequently unable to account for the important phenomenon of trading with the enemy.[12] Moreover, because the impact of conflict on trade is central to theories of the impact of trade on conflict, current liberal and realist theories fail to provide a satisfactory explanation of the consequences of economic interdependence for international conflict. By demonstrating that war—the most serious manifestation of conflict—does not systematically reduce levels of trade between states, we hope to emphasize the need to construct a more complete and more accurate theory of the relationship between economic interdependence and militarized interstate conflict.

## Empirical Literature on Conflict and Trade

In spite of its theoretical importance, scholars have devoted remarkably little systematic attention to either the phenomenon of trading with the enemy or to the broader question of the impact of war on trade. Historians have examined particular instances of this phenomenon (Giltner, 1997), and recent theoretical work on the security externalities of trade (Gowa, 1994; Morrow, 1997; Werner, 1997) have important implications for this question,[13] but there are few systematic empirical studies of the frequency and importance of trade with the enemy or the conditions under which this is most likely to occur.[14]

Similarly, there has been relatively little systematic research on the broader question of the impact of war on trade.[15] One of the few studies to focus on war per se is Mansfield (1994), whose systemic-level study shows that less trade is conducted during periods in which major powers are involved in wars against each other or against other states.[16] Others focus on the impact of cooperative and conflictual relationships defined more broadly. Pollins (1989a, b) constructs a model of bilateral trade flows and finds that for the 1960–75 period cooperative political relations between states increases trade between them. As noted, Gowa (1994) finds that trade is higher among allies than among adversaries, which she interprets in terms of the security externalities of trade.

Most scholars who have empirically examined the impact of conflict on trade and the impact of trade on conflict concede that the true nature of the relationship between these two variables is probably reciprocal and that current models fail to capture the relative importance of these causal paths. Polachek (1980: 63), for example, notes in one of his early studies that it is impossible to determine 'whether trade diminishes conflict, or whether in fact the reverse is true, and it is really conflict that reduces trade'.

Concerns that unidirectional models of the conflict–trade relationship are misspecified have led scholars to apply Granger causality analysis (Freeman, 1983) in an attempt to disentangle the effects of conflict on trade and the effect of trade on conflict. Gasiorowski and Polachek (1982) examine the USA–Warsaw Pact relationship from 1967 to 1978, use the COPDAB data to measure conflict and cooperation, and conclude that Granger causality for short lag periods runs overwhelmingly from trade to conflict and not from conflict to trade. If true, this is a puzzling finding because it simultaneously supports the liberal prediction that trade depresses conflict while undercutting the central causal mechanism of the liberal hypothesis—the anticipation that conflict reduces trade and consequently the welfare gains from trade will deter states from conflictual behavior.

Reuveny and Kang (1996a) criticize the use of pooled time-series analysis in Gasiorowski and Polachek (1982) and other studies, on the grounds that this technique might mask dyad-specific effects. Instead, they examine the trade–conflict relationship for sixteen individual dyads from 1960 to the early 1990s, combining the COPDAB and WEIS events data sets. Reuveny and Kang (1996a) find that although the causal relationship between conflict/cooperation and trade is dyad-dependent, it is largely reciprocal. In a subsequent study Reuveny and Kang (1998) disaggregate trade by commodity group, and they find that Granger causality from conflict to trade is more pronounced in 'strategic goods' than in other goods, though they acknowledge the ambiguity of the strategic goods concept.

They also find that patterns of causality are generally not affected by the presence of a political rivalry, though in the U.S.–USSR and U.S.–China dyads bilateral trade in some goods increases as political relations improve.

Recent dyadic-level work on the impact of conflict on trade has moved the debate forward and has contributed to larger debates regarding the relationship between economic interdependence and conflict. The fact that these studies have been limited to three decades of the Cold War period, and thus to a relatively unique set of international and domestic conditions, significantly reduces our confidence that the results of these studies can be generalized to other international systems—either those of the past or those that will emerge in the future. Our more general theoretical concerns lead us to focus on a more extended temporal domain and to construct a research design consistent with that objective.

Our aims are both descriptive and explanatory. We want to describe the phenomenon of trade between adversaries and to explain why states continue to trade with their enemies both during and immediately after wars. We focus on wars rather than a broader category of conflictual events because it is for war that the hypothesized causal mechanisms should be the strongest and the trading with the enemy phenomenon the most anomalous for contemporary liberal and realist theories of interdependence and war.

## Research Design

We have argued that contemporary liberal and realist theories of economic interdependence and conflict strongly imply that conflict between trading partners will significantly reduce the level of trade between them, particularly after the outbreak of war. There is some expectation that in the period after war trade will remain depressed and only slowly recover from prewar levels, and that in the period leading up to war trade will begin to decline. Declines in trade both before and after war, however, should be weaker than declines during war.

We investigate the extent to which war disrupts trading relationships using interrupted time series analyses (Lewis-Beck, 1979; Lewis-Beck and Alford, 1980).[17] This technique permits us to examine the level and trend in trade conducted before and following the outbreak of war. If war has a significant effect on trading relationships, we would expect to witness a decline in trade between adversaries that engage in war. Interrupted time-series analysis also permits us to examine both the long- and short-term impact of war. In addition, it permits us to assess whether or not the anticipation of war leads to a reduction in trade.

Testing hypotheses about the impact of war on trade poses a number of formidable methodological problems. One relates to the fact that many states do not provide complete reports of their trading activities during periods surrounding wars. There is a failure to report trade with allies as well as trade with adversaries, and consequently we cannot assume that the absence of trade reports implies the absence of trade. This is particularly true during World War I and World War II, where trade reports are incomplete but where there is ample evidence from secondary historical accounts that some trade continued between belligerents in these wars (Higham, 1983; Aarons and Loftus, 1994). In addition, states may have political and economic motivations for misreporting trade flow values, during both wartime and peacetime. We expect that the problem of misreporting would be greater during wartime, since states may wish to conceal trade ties with adversaries. If legal restrictions to trade are imposed, illegal activities will also be excluded from official statistics. Thus, the value of trade may be underrepresented in official reports. Thus, data limitations posed by inaccurate and incomplete information are difficult to overcome, and it is often hard to determine whether war seriously disrupts trade flows or simply the reporting of those flows.

In part, we address the problem of inaccurate reporting by one state by relying on the information provided by both states in a dyad. To do this, we rely on the import records for each side of the dyad. If one state is misrepresenting their trade values, our reliance on both states' reports provides a more balanced picture of the relationship.[18] Our measure of dyadic trade, therefore, is defined as the sum of Imports$_{ij}$ plus Imports$_{ji}$, where Imports$_{ij}$ is the flow from State j to State i and Imports$_{ji}$ is the flow from i to j, reported in USD millions. Trade data were derived from an extended and revised version of a trade database constructed by Barbieri (1995).[19] Data from the Correlates of War Project are used to identify the date of a state's participation in a given war (Small and Singer, 1982).[20]

The lack of available trade data, both for periods during war and for earlier historical eras, restricts the number of dyads that we can analyze. Since time series analysis requires that we have a continuous series of dyadic trade reports, both our spatial and temporal domains were restricted.[21] We began our investigation by examining the trade patterns for all dyads that experience a war at some time during the period 1870–1992, which corresponds to the availability of our trade data. We selected for our analysis those cases for which we had data available for at least ten years before and ten years after the outbreak of war.[22] The temporal domains for our time series range from 17 years to 122 years.

In most cases, the dyad analyzed has a much longer history of engaging in trade than our analysis portrays. When there were interruptions in the time series for data reports, we isolated the analysis to the years immediately before and after the war. In addition, we focus our attention on the impact of one war, even when dyads experience more than one war in their history. Dyads experiencing multiple wars in a short period of time proved difficult to analyze, since it was not easy to distinguish the effect of each war. For example, in the case of China and Japan, five wars occurred in the 1870–1992 period and several were so temporally proximate that it was impossible to distinguish the postwar trade recovery and the prewar trade trend.

From our selection process, we are left with only seven dyads: Argentina–UK, UK–China, Cyprus–Turkey, Greece–Turkey, Uganda–Tanzania, UK–Egypt, and USA–China. We recognize that our limited number of cases restricts our ability to generalize beyond our findings to other cases. The extent of the bias is hard to estimate, however, because it is unclear whether there is any systematic relationship between the availability of trade data surrounding a given war and the way in which the war affected the trading relationship.

One thing that is clear is that each of the wars in our sample is relatively short in duration, with all but one (Uganda–Tanzania) lasting less than a year. Although this is troubling in the sense that we might expect that longer wars have a greater impact on the reduction of bilateral trade between belligerents, we should note that short interstate wars are the norm rather than the exception in international politics.[23] Moreover, by restricting our analysis to short wars we effectively control for the effect of a change in GNP on bilateral trade because long wars are much more likely than short wars to have a significant effect on national economies. This enables us to isolate the direct impact of war on trade, which is the primary testable implication of liberal and realist theories of interdependence and war, as distinct from the impact of GNP on trade.[24]

We should also note that because of incomplete data our sample includes no cases of great power (major–major) war. We know from historical accounts of World War II and other cases (as mentioned earlier) that trading with the enemy occurs during great power wars (Levy and Barbieri 2001), but our analysis in this study will not formally permit us to generalize about the impact of great power war on bilateral trade, which is unfortunate.

Although our research design will not allow us to make inferences about how frequently or to what extent trade between wartime enemies occurs in the universe of all wars, it will allow us to demonstrate that this phenomenon occurs frequently enough to constitute a potential problem for contemporary liberal and realist theories of trade and conflict.

Let us return to the question of the proper measurement of trade in commercial liberal theory before we move on to the next section. Whereas we measure trade in terms of its value (see also Barbieri, 1995, 2003b), Anderton and Carter (2001a) argue that liberals emphasize trade volume rather than trade value in assessing the importance of trade. They attempt to measure trade volume by using the reporting state's consumer price index (CPI) to adjust trade values. Liberal political or trade theory, however, does not necessarily suggest that trade volume is more important than the value of trade ties. Presumably, a state that attaches greater value to small quantities of a good might be less willing to cut ties, compared to a country that conducts large quantities of trade in low value goods. In fact, one might expect that higher values, rather than higher quantities of trade, will have greater implications for the cost of forfeiting trade, during peace and wartime.

Anderton and Carter (2001a) make a valid point in questioning our use of unweighted price figures, and their analysis raises concerns for both of our studies. A better measure for both studies would permit us to incorporate both the quantity and price of goods traded. Yet, we argued that trade volume most likely declines during war, but the value of that trade increases, since prices on the limited goods traded would be higher than in peacetime. If anything, Anderton and Carter's comments about volume versus value simply highlights the need to incorporate information about quantity, price, alternative suppliers, and the actual commodities traded. Unfortunately, Anderton and Carter's solution of employing the CPI index of the reporting country to adjust trade values for inflationary trends does not solve the problem. It is not clear that the reporting state's CPI is applicable to its trade partner or that the bundle of goods used to calculate the CPI corresponds to the price changes for goods traded externally. Finally, we rely on information from each state in a dyad, rather than relying on only one state, as Anderton and Carter do, since this enables us to reduce the bias that results when one state tends to over or underreport the value of trade. In the end, Anderton and Carter's measure, like ours, ends up capturing trade value or at least a rough approximation of the value of trade conducted during wartime.[25]

## Statistical Techniques

For each dyad, we estimate the following equation (Lewis-Beck, 1979: 1132; Lewis-Beck and Alford, 1980: 747):[26]

$$\text{Trade}_t = \beta_0 + \beta_1 \text{Trend}_t + \beta_2 \text{War level}_t + \beta_3 \text{War rate}_t + \varepsilon_t,$$

where $\text{Trade}_t$ = the annual observation of dyadic trade flows in millions of USD, $\text{Trend}_t$ is a counter for each year of the series; war $\text{level}_t$ = a dichotomous variable that equals 0 for each observation before the outbreak of war and 1 for each year after the outbreak of war; and War $\text{rate}_t$ = a counter of years scored 0 before the outbreak of war and 1, 2, 3...once the war occurs. The parameters $\beta_0$ and $\beta_1$ allow us to estimate the level and slope of dyadic trade before the war, respectively; $\beta_2$ estimates the change in the level of trade after the war; and $\beta_3$ estimates the change in the slope after the war. In addition, we include an AR (1) adjustment parameter to address the problem of autocorrelation.[27]

Figure 14.1 illustrates the manner in which we can utilize interrupted time series techniques to assess the impact of war on trade.[28] Imagine two states whose trade increases each year, yielding the positive sloping line AB. If war has a substantial disruptive impact on trade, we would see a decline in the value of trade from B to B' accompanying the outbreak of war. The harm to the trading relationship may be temporary or permanent. If the reduction in trade were permanent, postwar trade would conform to a nonpositive slope, such as the negative slope illustrated by B'D. If the impact of war were temporary, we would see a recovery in trade, illustrated by the positive slope of B'C. If war were to have no impact, we would see a continuous trend in the trade relationship, regardless of the outbreak of war. We could also see an increase in trade at point B. Similarly, the risk of war may affect prewar trading levels, in which case we might witness a negative slope in trade prior to the outbreak of war.

## Empirical Analysis

It is useful to combine a statistical analysis based on interrupted time-series techniques with a visual examination of scatter plots of the dyadic trade flows for each of the seven dyads in the sample. Figure 14.2 illustrates the trade series

**Figure 14.1. Hypothetical Impact of War on Trade Flows**

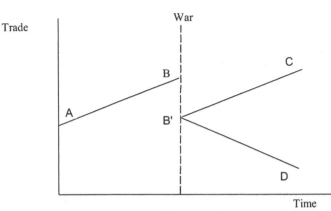

for each of our seven cases. The point at which a war interrupts the trade time-series is demarcated with a broken line. Findings that we obtain with the interrupted time-series analyses should be visible in an inspection of the scatter plots.

Table 14.1 reports the results of each dyadic analysis, with each column representing a different dyad. We are interested in assessing whether war has a significant effect on trade relations and whether that effect is temporary or permanent. The scatter plots in figure 14.2 are useful for discerning the patterns in trade relations, but our statistical analysis allows us to determine the magnitude and significance of the effect. We first consider whether or not war leads to a decline in the level of trade between states composing the dyads investigated. This information is revealed in the coefficient for the war level variable. A negative coefficient for this variable means that the outbreak of war leads to a decline in the level of trade between states. Looking at the results for all seven dyads, we see that in five instances (Argentina–UK, UK–China, UK–Egypt, Cyprus–Turkey, and Greece–Turkey) the coefficient has a negative sign. But this apparent decline in trade after the onset of war is only statistically significant for one dyad; the outbreak of the Falklands War led to a dramatic reduction in the level of trade between the United Kingdom and Argentina. These patterns are corroborated with our scatter plot in figure 14.2.

We also see that dyadic trade sometimes increases after the onset of war, as in our statistical analyses of the Uganda–Tanzania and USA–China dyads. None of these positive coefficients for the war level variable are statistically significant, however, and the pattern is not easily discerned in the scatter plots.

There are several reasons why we might witness an increase in trade associated with war. First, the trade level reflects the value of goods traded, rather than the quantity of commodities traded. If war leads to restrictions on trade and consequently to shortages and to higher prices for the goods that are traded, the result would be an increase in the value of goods traded, even if the volume of

**Table 14.1. The Impact of War on Dyadic Trade**

| Variables | Argentina –UK 1870–1992 Falkland (1982) | UK–China 1870–1913 Boxer R. (1900) | UK– Egypt 1948–92 Sinai (1956) | Cyprus– Turkey 1960–92 Turco- Cypriot (1974) | Greece– Turkey 1886–1911 Greco- Turkish (1897) | Uganda– Tanzania 1968–85 Ugandan- Tanzanian (1978) | USA– China 1870– 1913 Boxer R. (1900) |
|---|---|---|---|---|---|---|---|
| Constant | 49.607 | 103.449*** | 137.963 | -0.665 | 4.801*** | 11.129** | 5.860 |
|  | (67.717) | (4.462) | (153.760) | (20.135) | (0.668) | (2.979) | (3.361) |
| Trend$_t$ | 3.577*** | -2.091*** | -20.528** | 0.322 | -0.012 | -1.179* | 0.908*** |
|  | (0.990) | (0.242) | (9.053) | (2.280) | (0.093) | (0.456) | (0.186) |
| War level$_t$ | -462.398*** | -2.254 | -50.178 | -11.343 | -0.520 | 1.204 | 7.896 |
|  | (90.619) | (6.782) | (150.310) | (21.807) | (0.717) | (3.511) | (5.604) |
| War rate$_t$ | 30.299* | 5.252*** | 43.641** | 2.409 | -0.026 | 2.330** | 0.149 |
|  | (15.561) | (0.736) | (13.459) | (2.619) | (0.118) | (0.712) | (0.584) |
| AR(1) | 0.755*** | 0.225** | 0.763*** | 0.000 | 0.256 | -0.002 | 0.011 |
|  | (0.062) | (0.079) | (0.101) | (0.001) | (0.199) | (0.004) | (0.013) |
| $R^2$ | 0.78 | 0.81 | 0.83 | 0.21 | 0.28 | 0.50 | 0.79 |
| Adj. $R^2$ | 0.77 | 0.79 | 0.81 | 0.09 | 0.15 | 0.34 | 0.76 |

*Note:* Standard errors appear in parentheses. * $p \leq .05$, ** $p \leq .01$, *** $p \leq .001$

trade conducted were to decline. In addition, one of the motivations for war may be to create the conditions for an increase in trade.

A major objective for China's adversaries in the Boxer Rebellion was the opening up of China's trade. Therefore, it is not surprising that the war level variable for the USA and China is positive, with respect to the Boxer Rebellion. Although the UK–China dyad reveals a negative coefficient for the war level variable, trade does increase between these states after the Boxer Rebellion. China appears to open up to trade as a result of the war, but more slowly in the case of the United Kingdom than the United States.

In general, our findings for the war level variable demonstrate that trade suffers an immediate decline with the outbreak of war, but that the decline is rarely statistically significant. In fact, the decline is probably even less significant than our results reveal, since official reports exclude illegal trade carried on during wartime and thus underrepresent the trade being conducted. If the official reports reveal no dramatic decline in trade, we expect more accurate estimates of wartime trade with the enemy would reveal even less of a decline in trade. If anything, it might seem surprising that the official reports do not lead us to detect a more significant decline in trade levels for most cases. Admittedly, we are analyzing short wars, but all of these instances are cases that result in at least 1,000 battle-related deaths. That in itself seems serious enough to warrant an interruption in business as usual.

We next turn to the question of whether the outbreak of war has a permanent effect on a trading relationship. Liberal and realist theories of interdependence and war are less clear on this point, but we have argued that both theories imply that after a war between trading partners dyadic trade should usually (but not always) remain depressed and be slow to recover to prewar levels. A visual inspection of our scatter plots in figure 14.2 reveals that in most instances we see

## Figure 14.2. Dyadic Trade

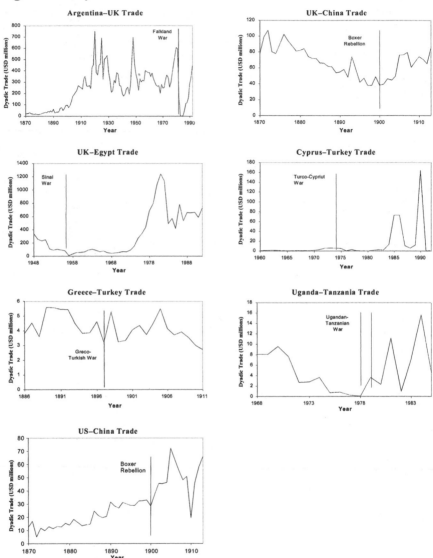

a rise in trade following the war. We can determine whether this trend is significant through the information provided in the war rate variable.

Table 14.1 reveals that in six of our dyadic analysis, the war rate variable is positive, meaning that the slope in the change of trade is positive for the postwar period (Argentina–UK, UK–China, UK–Egypt, Cyprus–Turkey, Uganda–Tanzania, and USA–China). In four of these six cases, the coefficient is statistically significant. This suggests that war's effect on trade is generally temporary.

In the majority of cases where war led to a decline in the level of dyadic trade (i.e., in four of the five cases with a negative war level variable), the war rate variable is positive. We find only one case (Greece–Turkey) with a negative war rate coefficient.

In the case of Greece and Turkey, we find negative coefficients for both the war rate and war level variables. One possible explanation for the failure of this trading relationship to recover from the war is that the postwar relationship is actually a prelude to other wars, the anticipation of which may keep trade low. The low levels of trade (averaging between 3 and 5.5 million dollars) and the negative trend in trade observed in the later years of the series may reflect a diminution in trade in the period leading up to the outbreak of the First Balkan War in 1912, the Second Balkan War in 1913, and the Greco–Turkish War in 1919. Unfortunately, we could not analyze the period surrounding the later wars, due to a lack of data for those periods.

The Greece–Turkey case raises the question of whether the anticipation of war leads to a deterioration in trade. The trend variable evaluates the prewar trading trend. A negative coefficient for this variable reveals that trade declines in each year prior to the war, while a positive coefficient for the trend variable reveals a positive slope in trade prior to the war. Table 14.1 reveals that our seven cases are nearly equally divided, where three dyads have a positive coefficient for the trend variable and four have a negative coefficient. Two of the three positive coefficients and two of the four negative coefficients are statistically significant. Trade, therefore, appears to be nearly equally likely to increase or to decrease in the period leading up to a war. In fact, we could imagine a set of equally plausible explanations for why the prewar period would experience either a positive or a negative trend. Hostilities may be so intense that they lead to restrictions or the breaking of trade ties even before the war occurs. Similarly, firms may be risk-averse and refrain from forging new deals with partners in a climate of uncertainty. On the other hand, businesses anticipating a war may rush to place orders or complete shipments for fear of a coming disruption to trade. For example, in some cases, legal restrictions to trade with the enemy still permit some allowances for firms to honor existing contracts. There would, therefore, be an incentive to increase trade prior to the war or at least to refrain from breaking trade ties.

To summarize, our empirical analysis demonstrates that there is some variation in the impact of war on trade across the dyads in our sample. In a majority of cases the outbreak of war appears to result in a decline in the level of dyadic trade, but for all but one dyad that decline is not statistically significant. In fact, we suspect that the real decline is even weaker than that suggested by our analysis based on official statistics, given the amount of illegal trade that may be conducted during wartime and excluded from official reports. Moreover, even when war leads to a decline in trade, that decline is almost always temporary; in general, trade increases in the postwar period. As to the period leading up to war, there is no systematic evidence that the anticipation of war usually results in a reduction in trade.

As mentioned, data limitations prevent us from providing a more comprehensive picture of the impact of war on trade. Governments often do not provide reports on wartime trade with the adversary. The fact that wartime trade data are also missing for other states suggests that the absence of trade reports does not necessarily imply the absence of trade. Even where data are complete, however, the fact that we are limited to annual data limits the number of observations, and this in turn makes it difficult to achieve levels of statistical significance with our interrupted time-series methods. This is compounded by the fact that nearly all of the wars in our sample are relatively short. As a result, in many cases we are left with a very small number of data points to measure the immediate impact of war on trade.

Our empirical tests of predictions of liberal and realist theories are also plagued by ambiguities in the theories, particularly for the period after the termination of war. Although both theoretical perspectives imply that trade will not quickly return to prewar levels after the termination of war, this is not a logical necessity, and there are some conditions under which we might expect a rapid recovery of trade. States may choose war as a means of opening up markets to trade, or they may want to rebuild the economies of their defeated adversaries in order to strengthen them and bring them into the balance of power against new enemies. Here we look at the aggregate effects of these contrary tendencies, but it would be useful in the future to hypothesize about the conditions under which trade increases immediately after war and to test these hypotheses against the evidence.

Our data are more reliable for periods after the termination of war, but the theoretical predictions are somewhat weaker. To the extent that political leaders' fears that war impedes trade is based both on the loss of trade during war and the slow recovery of trade after war, and to the extent that the experience of war generates hostility and continued sensitivity to relative gains, both liberal and realist theories predict that trade between wartime adversaries will not immediately return to prewar levels, but instead return slowly at best. If this is the prediction, it is clearly falsified by our analysis. In each of our cases trade increases quite rapidly within a few years after the end of war.

## Extending the Empirical Domain

Anderton and Carter (2001a) make an important contribution by extending the analysis of the war-trade relationship to 27 additional cases. Their analysis includes 14 major power dyads and 13 dyads that contain at least one minor power, and it includes both short and long wars. While we have questioned Anderton and Carter's (2001a) case selection, methodology, and other aspects of their research design, and argued that they have overstated the strength of their evidence (Barbieri and Levy, 2001), we believe that Anderton and Carter have demonstrated that in many cases war significantly reduces trade between adversaries. The fact that their analysis is based on a larger number of cases and greater diversity in the kinds of wars being analyzed, as compared to our own analysis, further enhances the credibility of their findings.[29] At the same time, our own findings of a number of other cases in which war does not have a significant negative impact on trade still stand, and Anderton and Carter do not challenge the internal validity of our findings for our particular cases. Because the total number of cases used to test the trade disruption hypothesis is still relatively small, we believe that the debate over the impact of war on trade is still up for grabs, and that this debate can be resolved only through further empirical research involving a larger number of cases.

Anderton and Carter (2001a) find that there is a statistically significant decline in the level of trade in 7 of the 14 major-power war dyads, with trade continuing to decline over the course of the war in a statistically significant manner in 8 of 14 cases (interestingly, 2 of the dyads exhibit a statistically significant increase in trade from the beginning to the end of the war).[30] Thus, for major powers, trade is significantly reduced in roughly half of the wars analyzed, with slightly more than a 50 percent chance that trade will continue to decline over the life of the war. In 12 of the 14 major power wars, there is a statistically significant increase in trade following the end of the war.

Anderton and Carter concede that the findings for their analysis of the impact of war on trade for 13 nonmajor power dyads are weaker than for the major power dyads. Their key indicator of the impact of war on trade levels is negative and statistically significant in 3 of 7 cases for major–minor short wars and 1 of 4 cases of major–minor long wars. This leaves 4 of 11 cases of mixed dyads for which war has a significant negative effect on trade. The 2 cases of minor–minor power dyads (1 long and 1 short war) each show a statistically significant impact of war on trade. Thus, for nonmajor power dyads, 6 of 13 cases show a significant impact of war on trade, basically the same percentage as for major power dyads. For the long wars, 3 of the 4 cases of mixed dyads continue to witness a significant decline in trade over the course of the war, while for the minor power long war, the dyad witnesses a significant increase in trade over the course of the war. Finally, in all of the cases of mixed dyad long wars, we see a significant increase in trade following the termination of war.

## Areas for Future Research

Some of the differences between Anderton and Carter's (2001a) findings and our own suggest potentially useful lines of inquiry for future research on the question of the impact of war on trade. The length of a war may be one factor influencing whether or not states witness a severe disruption in trade. The war-trade relationship might also vary for major power and nonmajor power dyads. Further research on both of these issues is required, because the major power dyads examined by Anderton and Carter all represent long wars. It is difficult to assess the relative importance and separate effects of the length of the war versus the types of participants in the war. We may find that it is the intensity of the conflict, be it a short or long war, major or minor power participants, that explains trade disruption. Clearly, more research is needed to uncover the variations that exist in the war-trade relationship across dyads. We should note in this context that while we believe that war's impact on trade varies across dyads and that more attention must be paid to the factors that might account for dyadic variations, Anderton and Carter (2001a) seem to argue that, based on their evidence, the trade-disruption hypothesis is invariant across different types of dyads and types of wars.

These different conclusions derive in part from different views as to what constitutes appropriate evidence for the trade-disruption hypothesis. One point of contention is that Anderton and Carter (2001a) believe that the recovery of trade after a war provides evidence in support of the trade-disruption hypothesis. While we understand the logic of their argument, we do not believe liberal theory is sufficiently specific about the postwar implications for trading relationships to suggest that a recovery to trade constitutes support of the trade-disruption hypothesis. For example, the anticipated trade-related costs that liberals expect to deter war may not only refer to the loss of trade during the war itself but may also include the adverse consequences that war could have on the long-term health of the trading relationship. A leader would be more deterred from engaging in conflict with a trading partner if she/he anticipated serious harm to the trading relationship in the long term, rather than just temporary reductions in trade during the war followed by a quick resumption of trade.

Preliminary evidence that dyadic trade sometimes declines with the outbreak of war, sometimes does not decline, and occasionally even increases, suggests that future research on this question should shift away from the aggregate impact of war on trade, and attempt instead to identify the conditions under which war leads to a decline in trade and the conditions under which it fails to do so. While the question of the net effects of war on trade is clearly an important question worth pursuing, there are other equally important questions that also need to be investigated. For example, it is important to examine what type of trade continues, in what type of goods, between what type of adversaries, in what type of wars, and with what impact on states' war efforts and domestic economies. These questions are particularly important if we want to understand how the anticipated disruption in trade and the trading relationship after the outbreak of war affects political leaders' decisions regarding the resort to war.

Future research must do a better job specifying the possible sources for variations in the trade-conflict relationship across dyads. Recently, Green, Kim, and Yoon (2001) have highlighted the problems inherent in pooled cross-sectional analyses often employed in international relations research. They argue that we must account for the heterogeneous nature of dyads contained in large samples. While their particular solutions have been subject to debate (Oneal and Russett, 2001a; Beck and Katz, 2001; King, 2001), Green, Kim, and Yoon (2001) raise the important point about the need to account for the variations that exist across cases in space and time, which is highly relevant to trade-conflict research. Reuveny (this volume) raises similar concerns in arguing that we need to look closely at dyad and commodity specific differences that exist in the trade-conflict relationship. He offers several examples of how we can move toward that goal through quantitative analysis. However, future research should also include qualitative analysis of specific cases. This will enable us to gain a richer understanding of the processes by which conflict affects trade and trade affects conflict.

Each of these research questions involves the objective impact of war on trade. An equally important set of questions concerns the expectations of political (and business) leaders regarding the impact of war on trade. This question of expectations is particularly important if our interest in the impact of war on trade is motivated by an interest in the more general liberal hypothesis that trade promotes peace, because it is the expectations of political leaders regarding the impact of war on trade that is relevant to their calculations of the costs and benefits of going to war and their decisions regarding war and peace.

Leaders' calculations regarding the likely economic costs of war are only one factor influencing their decisions, of course, and the relative weight of those economic factors must be compared to those of strategic, diplomatic, and domestic political considerations. Even if we were to accept Anderton and Carter's (2001a) findings that war has a statistically significant impact on trade half the time, it is not at all clear that this would be enough to induce leaders to decide against war, given the possible benefits of war anticipated by political leaders. This can be determined only by a more systematic empirical analysis of the extent to which trade considerations affect political decisions on questions of war and peace.[31]

This perspective leads to an important set of questions that require much more attention from researchers. What is the likely impact of war and trade as perceived by political and business leaders, and what is the impact of those expectations on their decisions? Do firms want to continue trade in search of profits or to cut back trade in an anticipation of increased transport and insurance costs? Are governments willing to permit trade to continue, either because of pressures from key economic groups or because of more general fears that the continuation of trade with the enemy is necessary for economic stability? Or are they driven by strategic concerns or patriotic pressures to prohibit trade? We should note that decisions to stop or reduce trade are not one-time decisions, and state policies on trading with the enemy may fluctuate as a function of the course of the war, its domestic economic impact, and demands from various domestic groups and organized political opposition.[32]

## Theoretical Implications and Conclusion

Our interrupted time-series analysis of patterns of war and trade for seven dyads demonstrates that the outbreak of war often fails to significantly reduce trade between adversaries, and that when trade does decline during war it often quickly returns to prewar levels after the end of war. Although the patterns do vary, although our limited sample precludes us from formally generalizing to other cases, and although Anderton and Carter's (2001a) study raises further questions about the generalizability of our findings, our analysis raises possible doubts about the validity of the hypothesis that trade between adversaries will cease or be significantly reduced after the outbreak of war.

This trade-disruption hypothesis clearly follows from both liberal and realist theories of economic interdependence and war, which suggest, respectively, that the fear of the loss of welfare gains from trade deters political leaders from conflictual behavior that runs a high risk of war, or that relative gains concerns lead to the cessation or significant reduction in trade between adversaries after the outbreak of war. Because these hypotheses play a pivotal role in liberal and realist theories of trade and war, and because our findings draw some support from detailed historical studies of the phenomenon of trade between adversaries during wartime, it seems clear that investigation of the question of the impact of war on trade should be a high priority for future research.

As we noted earlier, our argument here is not with liberal and realist paradigms themselves, but rather with specific applications of those paradigms to the question of the relationship between economic interdependence and conflict. Contemporary liberal and realist scholars have framed the debate over trade and conflict in excessively narrow terms—they both focus primarily on the dyadic level and ignore the role of domestic actors and third parties. This represents a substantial departure from the liberal and realist paradigms that have shaped much of the debate in the international relations field.

There are a number of possible explanations for the trading-with-the-enemy phenomenon, and nearly all of these are in fact quite compatible with broader conceptualizations of liberal or realist theory.[33] Political leaders may fear that a cutoff of trade would result in a loss of trade to a third party or the alienation of neutrals. Alternatively, they may anticipate that the continuation of trade during wartime may create the opportunity to make relative gains at the expense of third parties or to gain influence over the adversary by making him economically dependent. Each of these explanations is compatible with a realist framework.[34]

Political leaders may also be concerned about the domestic economic consequences and political costs of a cessation of trade. Key social groups may expect private gains from a continuation of trade with the enemy and may have the political power to block the government from imposing restrictions on such trade, as the government may be dependent on the economic support of leading commercial and financial interests for the financing of the war effort. Each of these explanations is compatible with a liberal (or Marxist) conceptual framework.

While debate continues about the aggregate effects of war on trade and of trade on war, it is clear that each of these relationships is conditional rather than universal, that scholars need to devote more attention to identifying the conditions under which each of these relationships holds, and that a complete specification of these conditions will involve some variables associated with liberal theories of interdependence and conflict and some variables associated with realist theories. Thus a fully satisfactory theory of trade and conflict will have to build on insights from both liberal and realist perspectives.[35] Such a theory will have to incorporate a range of key factors that enter political leaders' cost-benefit calculations regarding decisions for war and decisions to maintain or suspend trade in the event of war. These include leaders' fears of the impact of war on the welfare gains from trade; expectations of the impact of a cessation of trade on the domestic economy, on the ability to sustain the war effort, and on the support of key economic interest groups for the government and for the war effort; and expectations regarding the effects of the maintenance or cessation of trade on the relative position of potential economic and military rivals.

## Notes

This is a revised version of Barbieri and Levy (1999), in which we incorporate some material from Barbieri and Levy (2001). We would like to thank Martin Edwards, Andrew Enterline, John Geer, Peter Liberman, Helmut Norpoth, Brad Palmquist, Daniel Verdier, and especially Mark Crescenzi for their assistance and for their valuable comments; Michael Ault, Joseph Gochal, and Oliver Selwyn for their research assistance; and Stuart Bremer for providing war data and for helpful advice. The data used in this study are available at http://www.vanderbilt.edu/psci/barbieri/.

1. While Anderton and Carter (2001b) note the discrepancy between our primary focus on the empirical validity of the hypothesized linkage between trade and peace and their primary focus on the linkage between war and trade, they frame their initial study (Anderton and Carter, 2001a) in terms of the trade-promotes-peace hypothesis.

2. The underlying assumption is that trade is more efficient than conquest for expanding markets and investment opportunities (Rosecrance, 1986), at least in the last century.

3. The less dependent party may be tempted to use economic coercion to exploit the adversary's vulnerabilities and influence its behavior relating to security as well as economic issues (Baldwin, 1985), which can lead to counterthreats, conflict spirals, and war. In addition, resource scarcities can lead to economic competition and rivalry (Choucri and North, 1975) and under some conditions economic rivalries escalate to strategic rivalries and war (Levy and Ali, 1998).

4. For reviews of the theoretical arguments and empirical findings, see McMillan (1997), Barbieri and Schneider (1999), Mansfield and Pollins (2001), and Schneider, Barbieri, and Gleditsch (this volume).

5. Although some realists argue that strategic goods are especially important in relative gains concerns, Gowa (1994), who has been particularly influential in the contemporary literature, focuses on aggregate levels of trade. Gowa (1994) argues that states choose to trade with allies in order to avoid granting the gains from trade to adversaries, which may result in security externalities. It is not the adversary's increased income from trade that is of greatest concern, but the ability of the adversary to enjoy the gains arising from specialization (in international trade theory, gains from trade include both increased income and specialization). By permitting its adversary the opportunity to increase its productive efficiency and redirect resources away from alternative productive ventures, the adversary is better able to increase production of military resources and hence pose a potential challenge.

6. We use the term 'trading with the enemy' to refer broadly to trade, finance, and other forms of economic cooperation between adversaries. This is standard usage in the literature and also in many state statutes on 'trading with the enemy'.

7. Six days after Pearl Harbor a U.S. presidential edict created legislation for the granting of licensing arrangements for trading with the enemy, and there are countless examples of American firms doing business in strategic goods with Nazi Germany during World War II. Standard Oil of New Jersey, for example, sold oil to Germany through Switzerland while Allied forces suffered shortages, and Ford Motor Company sold trucks to Nazi forces in occupied France (Higham, 1983; Aarons and Luftus, 1994).

8. We might hypothesize that the impact of war on postwar trade will be a function of the duration of war and other measures of the seriousness of war. Alternatively, the key variable might be the type of war rather than its duration. Rasler and Thompson (1989) suggest that the economic impact of global wars (on GNP, public expenditures, and public debt) is greater than that of other interstate wars involving the great powers. See also Vasquez (1993: 52–53).

9. Victorious states sometimes have strong economic or strategic incentives to rebuild the economies of the losers after the war, which may increase trade, as illustrated by the experience of the United States and both Japan and Germany after World War II.

10. This is exacerbated by risk acceptance in the domain of losses, as prospect theory suggests (Levy, 1997).

11. Liberal and realist theories imply that trade between adversaries should be depressed during periods leading up to war, but not as much as during war itself.

12 Scholars have analyzed the effects of relative gains concerns in multipolar systems, but they have not applied these analyses to the phenomenon of wartime trade. See Snidal (1991a), Powell (1991), Gowa (1994), Lieberman (1996), Werner (1997).

13. For an economic model of the simultaneous presence of arming, conflict, and trade, but one that is based on a rather different set of assumptions, see Skaperdas (1996).

14. Liberman (1996) looks at trade between adversaries during periods of hostility prior to war (Britain and Germany, 1890–1914; United States and Japan, 1930–41), but we have argued that trade between adversaries during periods of rivalry or militarized conflict short of war is less anomalous than trade between enemies during war. Even Liberman (1996: 173) argues that 'relative gains block cooperation among states only at the brink of war,' which implies that trading with the enemy during wartime should not occur.

15. This reflects a more general lack of attention by international relations scholars to the economic consequences of war, though there have been some important recent exceptions (Organski and Kugler, 1980; Goldstein, 1988; Rasler and Thompson, 1989; and Modelski and Thompson, 1996).

16. This systemic-level finding does not necessarily imply that major power war reduces trade between states at the dyadic level, though this is a plausible hypothesis that needs to be tested.

17. In an earlier version of this chapter, we used ARIMA analysis to explore the impact of war on trade (Barbieri and Levy, 1997). The findings presented here are consistent with those derived from the ARIMA analysis.

18. The trade statistics reported by the importing nation are used to calculate dyadic trade unless these data are missing, in which case we rely upon the exporting nation's trade report.

19. A large portion of the data for the post–World War II statistics were derived from the International Monetary Fund's *Direction of Trade Statistics*, made available by the Inter-university Consortium for Political and Social Research.

20. We used a slightly extended version of the dataset reported in Small and Singer (1982).

21. We choose not to interpolate data points, since we are interested in discovering variations in trade flows and did not wish to assume a continuous trend in the series. Since it is difficult to distinguish missing trade reports from zero trade, we make no assumptions about the value of missing reports.

22. We have one exception to this rule. For the UK Egypt dyad, we had only eight years of data prior to the Sinai War. The cases that were excluded were far less complete, in terms of continuous series.

23. Of the wars since 1816 contained in the COW Interstate War dataset, approximately 67 percent lasted less than one year.

24. We thank Jacek Kugler for suggesting this point.

25. For other issues related to measurement, see Barbieri (2003a, b).

26. We used EViews Version 3.0 for all analyses performed here.

27. We investigated whether Autoregressive (AR) and Moving Average (MA) processes were present in the series by inspecting correlegrams. In preliminary tests, we identified an AR (1) process in many dyadic trade series. The models were estimated initially with a lagged dependent variable, which served to account for the process and allow us to overcome problems of autocorrelation. However, we follow the recommendation of reviewers that we include the AR (1) parameter and exclude the lagged dependent variable. Our results do not change significantly when using these alternative approaches. For details about EViews' estimation techniques, see the help file document, 'How EViews Estimates AR Models.'

28. Figure 14.1 is an adaptation of Figure 3 in Lewis-Beck (1979: 1130).

29. Of Anderton and Carter's (2001a) 27 dyads, five are from World War I, six are from World War II, and two are from the Korean War. The possibility that a state adopts similar policies toward its different wartime adversaries, or that allies adopt similar policies in order to maintain alliance cohesion, raises questions about the number of truly independent cases in their sample (Barbieri and Levy, 2001: 622).

30. Anderton and Carter (2001b) make the important point that if the anticipation of war leads to a substantial drop in trade between adversaries, as it sometimes does, we might fail to see a significant decline in trade with the outbreak of war because trade is already near zero and there is little room for further decline. Additional research is needed to uncover the impact that the anticipation of war might have on trade patterns.

31. The expectations and calculations of business leaders are also relevant. Their expectations about the impact of war on trade, and particularly on their own profits, will influence their own decisions as to whether to pressure the government to allow trade to continue and whether to attempt to circumvent any restrictions that the government might impose.

32. During the War of 1812, for example, the United States alternated between an economic embargo against British goods and much more open trading policies (Levy and Barbieri, 2001).

33. We analyze alternative explanations for the trading-with-the-enemy phenomenon more fully in Levy and Barbieri (2001).

34. This argument about the need to conceptualize relative gains in systemic rather than dyadic terms draws support from theoretical work on relative gains (Snidal, 1991a;

Powell, 1991), which suggests that relative gains concerns diminish as the number of actors in the system increases. For more specific theoretical discussions of the role of relative gains in trading relationships see Morrow (1997) and Werner (1997).

35. For a recent study that attempts to incorporate both liberal and realist hypotheses into a single theory of economic interdependence and conflict, see Papayoanou (1999).

# CHAPTER 15

# Does War Disrupt Trade?

*Charles H. Anderton and John R. Carter*

According to liberal theory, trade promotes peace because the disruption of trade by war makes war more costly. Barbieri and Levy (1999), however, have challenged the premise that war disrupts trade. Based on a careful analysis of seven war dyads, they concluded that 'in most cases war does not have a significant impact on trading relationships'. To explore the generality of their results, we extended the line of research by studying war's impact on trade in 27 dyads (Anderton and Carter 2001a). Contrary to Barbieri and Levy, we found that the weight of the evidence favored the conclusion that war disrupts trade. Barbieri and Levy (2001) responded that our evidence was insufficient to warrant this conclusion, eliciting our contrary assessment in Anderton and Carter (2001b).

In this volume we are pleased to join the exchange again with Barbieri and Levy. We ask simply and exclusively, 'Does war disrupt trade?' We highlight our research design and then summarize the empirical results. To anticipate, we conclude that the answer is affirmative for long wars but less clear for short wars. Our presentation is intentionally streamlined, with further details and discussion available in the earlier sources (Anderton and Carter, 2001a, b).

## Research Design

### Sample Selection and Data

We began with the list of interstate wars from the Correlates of War (COW) project. Among the various dyads (and dyadic possibilities from multination wars), we required that annual export and import data be available ten years before the war, during the war, and ten years after the war. We also required that a price index be available for deflating the trade data for each year of the analysis. If data were missing for one or more observations, we excluded the dyad from our analysis. Though not part of COW, we also included the UK/USA Revolutionary War dyad because trade and price data were available. These procedures led to the development of 27 dyadic data sets. Nineteen of these cases involved long wars spanning more than one calendar year. The other eight cases involved short wars beginning and ending within a single calendar year.

Most of our data came from *Abstract of British Historical Statistics* and *International Historical Statistics* (Mitchell, 1962, 1998a, b, c). Other sources included *Statistical Abstract of the United States* and *Historical Statistics of the United States* (Bureau of the Census, various years). These sources reported annual import and export values denominated in the currency of one of the trade partners. Imports plus exports yielded trade value for each dyad. To capture changes in real trade volume, we adjusted trade value for inflation. Ideally, a price index of traded goods would be used, but such an index was unavailable for many dyads. As a next best solution, we used the consumer price index of the nation whose currency denominated the trade value series.[1]

We constructed dyadic data series for ten years before the outbreak of war, through the war, to ten years after the termination of war. This limitation of sample length constrained the data requirements and allowed us to include some dyads that otherwise would have been excluded due to missing data. It also placed each dyad on an equal temporal footing while restricting the potential for trade trends to be altered by nonwar events.[2]

## Interrupted Time-Series Model

We used the multiple interrupted times-series design of Lewis-Beck and Alford (1980) to investigate formally the impact of war on trade. For each dyad we estimated the following equation:

$$\text{Ln(Real trade}_t) = \beta_0 + \beta_1 \text{Trend}_t + \beta_2 \text{War level}_t + \beta_3 \text{War trend}_t + \beta_4 \text{Peace level}_t + \beta_5 \text{Peace trend}_t + \varepsilon_t$$

Real trade is the annual observation of inflation-adjusted dyadic trade volume.[3] Trend is a counter for each year of the series. War level is a dichotomous variable that equals 0 for each year before the outbreak of war and 1 for the remaining years of the series. War trend is a counter scored 0 before war outbreak and then 1, 2, 3 . . . from the outbreak of war to the end of the series. Peace level is a dichotomous variable that equals 0 for each year before and during war and 1 for each year after the war. Peace trend is a counter scored 0 up through the last year of war and then 1, 2, 3 . . . to the end of the series. For wars occurring within a single calendar year, war trend and peace level drop out of the model, and peace trend is scored 0 for each year before the outbreak of war and then 1,2,3 . . . to the end of the series. This yields the equation used originally by Barbieri and Levy (1999) to study the impact of short wars on trade.

The parameters $\beta_0$ and $\beta_1$ in our model measure the level and rate of growth of real dyadic trade before the war. The parameters $\beta_2$ and $\beta_4$ capture whether war and war termination, respectively, cause a change in the level of real trade. $\beta_3$ and $\beta_5$ measure any change in the rate of growth of real trade during and after the war.

Figure 15.1 shows a prototype of the interrupted time-series model. Assume that real trade between two nations grows at 10 percent per year as shown along curve ABC in figure 15.1. If the onset of war disrupts trade, we would see a downdraft in the trade trend, say, from B to D ($\beta_2 < 0$). Furthermore, the growth in real trade may diminish during the war relative to the prewar rate. In figure 15.1, real trade grows at 3 percent during the war, rather than at the 10 percent rate prior to war ($\beta_3 < 0$). If the cessation of war leads to an immediate resumption of trade between the former combatants, there would be an updraft in the trade trend, for example, from E to F ($\beta_4 > 0$). Figure 15.1 shows real trade growing at 7 percent after the war ($\beta_5 > 0$).

# Empirical Analysis

## Long-War Dyads

We preview our statistical analysis by presenting in figure 15.2 a visual display of real trade flows for each of our 19 long-war dyads. The beginning and ending war years are demarcated with vertical lines. Casual inspection suggests clear support for the premise that war depresses trade. In 15 cases, trade is driven to near zero during the war before rebounding with peace. In one case (France/Germany 1870–71), trade falls with the onset of war, though not to zero, and then rebounds with peace. In the USA/China case, the decline is more gradual, and trade remains near zero after the war's end. Only in the cases of UK/China and USA/Mexico is support for the trade disruption premise not apparent.

Turning to the formal analysis, table 15.1 presents regression results for the 19 long-war dyads, which have been classified according to whether the nations are major or minor powers as defined by COW. Where appropriate, we report maximum likelihood estimates that allow for first-order autocorrelation (AR1); otherwise, we report ordinary least squares estimates (OLS). As previously indicated, the dependent variable is the natural logarithm of real trade flow. Consequently, the coefficients on the war and peace level variables measure vertical shifts in the trend line, while those on the corresponding trend variables measure changes in trade growth rates.

**Figure 15.1. Hypothetical Impact of War on Trade**

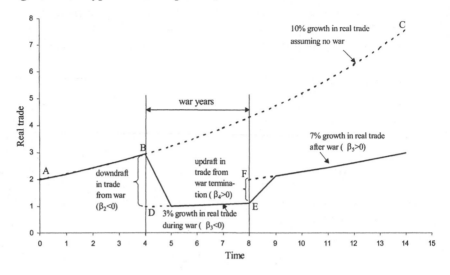

We are interested in whether war is associated with a significant downdraft in trade and/or a decline in the growth rate of trade. Hence, we focus on whether the coefficients $\beta_2$ on war level and $\beta_3$ on war trend are negative. Note that the trade disruption premise does not require that both $\beta_2$ and $\beta_3$ be negative. Even if $\beta_2$ is zero, trade disruption is evident if $\beta_3$ is negative.[4]

**Figure 15.2. Long-War Dyadic Trade Relationships**

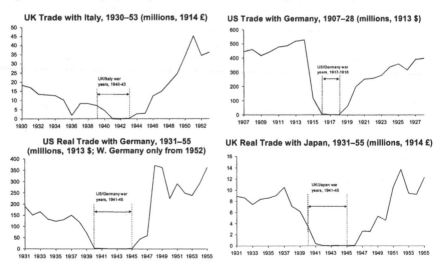

# Figure 15.2. Continued

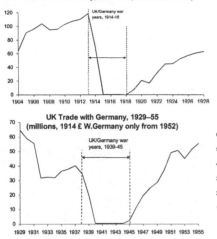

UK Trade with Germany, 1904–28 (millions, 1914 £)

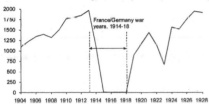

UK Trade with Germany, 1929–55
(millions, 1914 £ W.Germany only from 1952)

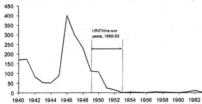

France Trade with Germany, 1904–28 (millions, 1914 francs)

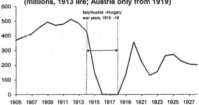

US Trade with China, 1940–63 (millions, 1938 $)

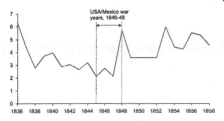

USA Trade with Mexico, 1836–58 (millions, 1913 $)

Italy Trade with Germany, 1905–28 (millions, 1913 lire)

Italy Trade with Austria/Hungary, 1905–28
(millions, 1913 lire; Austria only from 1919)

France Trade with Germany, 1860–81 (millions, 1914 francs)

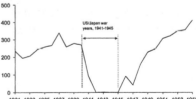

US Trade with Japan, 1931–55 (millions, 1913 $)

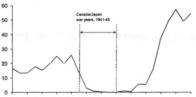

Canada Trade with Japan, 1931–55 (millions, 1913 CA $)

# Figure 15.2. Continued

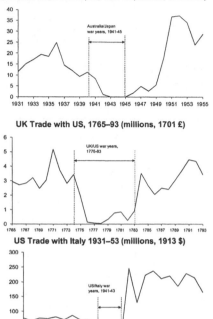

Australia Trade with Japan, 1931–55 (millions, 1938 AU £)

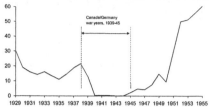

Canada Trade with Germany, 1929–55 (millions, 1913 CA $)

UK Trade with US, 1765–93 (millions, 1701 £)

UK Trade with China, 1940–63 (millions, 1929 £)

US Trade with Italy 1931–53 (millions, 1913 $)

*Note:* Trade is real merchandise trade (imports and exports) in all these graphs.

## Table 15.1. Impact of Long Wars ~~on Dynamic Trade~~

| Dyads (war years in parentheses) | Con-stant ($\beta_0$) | Trend ($\beta_1$) | War level ($\beta_2$) | War trend ($\beta_3$) | Peace level ($\beta_4$) | Peace trend ($\beta_5$) | Rho | $R^2$ |
|---|---|---|---|---|---|---|---|---|
| *Major/major long wars* | | | | | | | | |
| France/Germany, 1860–81 (1870–71) | 5.96* (0.03) | 0.05* (0.00) | -1.53* (0.10) | 0.46* (0.06) | 0.75* (0.05) | -0.50* (0.06) | | 0.99 |
| France/Germany, 1904–28 (1914–18) | 7.03* (0.42) | 0.06 (0.08) | -1.21 (0.86) | -1.35* (0.24) | 6.80* (0.74) | 1.37* (0.24) | | 0.92 |
| UK/Germany, 1904–28 (1914–18) | 4.33* (0.32) | 0.07 (0.06) | -0.71 (0.71) | -2.13* (0.19) | 8.59* (0.60) | 2.27* (0.19) | -0.33 (0.21) | 0.96 |
| Italy/Austria-Hungary, 1905–28 (1915–18) | 5.93* (0.34) | 0.05 (0.06) | -1.63* (0.88) | -1.73* (0.29) | 7.43* (0.68) | 1.67* (0.29) | -0.39* (0.21) | 0.91 |
| Italy/Germany, 1905–28 (1915–18) | 6.49* (0.21) | 0.06 (0.04) | -0.92 (0.56) | -1.35* (0.19) | 4.45* (0.44) | 1.48* (0.19) | -0.53* (0.19) | 0.92 |

## Table 15.1. Continued

| Dyads (war years in parentheses) | Con-stant ($\beta_0$) | Trend ($\beta_1$) | War level ($\beta_2$) | War trend ($\beta_3$) | Peace level ($\beta_4$) | Peace trend ($\beta_5$) | Rho | $R^2$ |
|---|---|---|---|---|---|---|---|---|
| USA/Germany, 1907–28 (1917–18) | 6.88* (0.89) | -0.38* (0.15) | -1.56 (1.20) | -0.70 (0.82) | 4.98* (0.83) | 1.22 (0.82) | 0.67* (0.17) | 0.91 |
| UK/Germany, 1929–55 (1939–45) | 3.98* (0.53) | -0.06 (0.10) | -2.95* (0.93) | -0.17 (0.20) | 3.78* (0.87) | 0.38* (0.20) | | 0.84 |
| UK/Italy, 1930–53 (1940–43) | 2.86* (0.65) | -0.13 (0.12) | -1.25 (1.49) | -1.05* (0.51) | 5.44* (1.19) | 1.49* (0.51) | | 0.83 |
| UK/Japan, 1931–55 (1941–45) | 2.29* (0.57) | -0.06 (0.11) | -2.66* (1.17) | -1.07* (0.33) | 5.48* (1.01) | 1.57* (0.33) | | 0.91 |
| USA/Germany, 1931–55 (1941–45) | 5.67* (0.49) | -0.25* (0.09) | -3.71* (1.01) | 0.24 (0.28) | 4.78* (0.87) | 0.17 (0.28) | | 0.90 |
| USA/Italy, 1931–53 (1941–43) | 4.29* (0.16) | 0.00 (0.03) | -9.67* (0.56) | 2.17* (0.24) | 4.22* (0.36) | -2.18* (0.24) | -0.69* (0.16) | 0.97 |
| USA/Japan, 1931–55 (1941–45) | 5.25* (0.34) | 0.08 (0.06) | -3.12* (0.75) | -0.93* (0.20) | 5.76* (0.64) | 1.04* (0.20) | -0.48* (0.19) | 0.91 |
| UK/China, 1940–63 (1950–53) | 1.46* (0.69) | 0.00 (0.12) | 0.74 (0.88) | -0.00 (0.37) | 0.06 (0.75) | 0.07 (0.37) | 0.58* (0.19) | 0.62 |
| USA/China, 1940–63 (1950–53) | 4.59* (0.59) | 0.07 (0.11) | 1.40 (1.37) | -1.71* (0.47) | 0.25 (1.09) | 1.72* (0.47) | | 0.85 |
| *Major/minor long wars* | | | | | | | | |
| UK/USA, 1765–93 (1775–83) | 1.14* (0.55) | -0.02 (0.10) | -2.22* (0.78) | 0.07 (0.16) | 1.60* (0.77) | 0.00 (0.16) | 0.29 (0.19) | 0.74 |
| Germany/Canada, 1929–55 (1939–45) | 2.95* (0.74) | -0.03 (0.14) | -1.75 (1.30) | -0.54* (0.28) | 4.10* (1.22) | 0.90* (0.28) | | 0.76 |
| Japan/Australia, 1931–55 (1941–45) | 2.85* (0.47) | -0.04 (0.09) | 0.62 (0.96) | -1.78* (0.27) | 6.61* (0.82) | 2.15* (0.27) | | 0.92 |
| Japan/Canada, 1931–55 (1941–45) | 2.71* (0.35) | 0.04 (0.07) | -0.30 (0.72) | -1.59* (0.20) | 4.66* (0.62) | 2.08* (0.20) | | 0.95 |
| *Minor/minor long wars* | | | | | | | | |
| USA/Mexico, 1836–58 (1846–48) | 1.51* (0.08) | -0.07* (0.02) | -0.57* (0.28) | 0.46* (0.12) | -0.28 (0.19) | -0.35* (0.12) | -0.49* (0.22) | 0.70 |

*Note:* Standard errors are shown in parentheses. An asterisk indicates a two-tailed p-value less than 10 percent. The alternative hypotheses on $\beta_2$ and $\beta_3$ are one-sided. Regressions are estimated using Time Series Processor (TSP) Version 4.4. AR1 results are reported if the absolute value of the t-statistic on rho exceeds 1.3; otherwise OLS results are reported.

Summarizing our results for the sample of 19 long wars, we find that 16 (84 percent) of the $\beta_2$ coefficients on war level are negative, and 9 (47 percent) are statistically significant at the 0.05 level (one-sided). Fourteen (74 percent) of the $\beta_3$ coefficients on war trend are negative, while 11 (58 percent) are significant. Taking the coefficients together, in 17 of 19 cases (89 percent) at least one of the coefficients, $\beta_2$

or $\beta_3$, is negative and significant. Hence, in the vast majority of long-war dyads, we find statistically significant trade disruption at some point in the war cycle.

**Figure 15.3. Short-War Dyadic Trade Relationships**

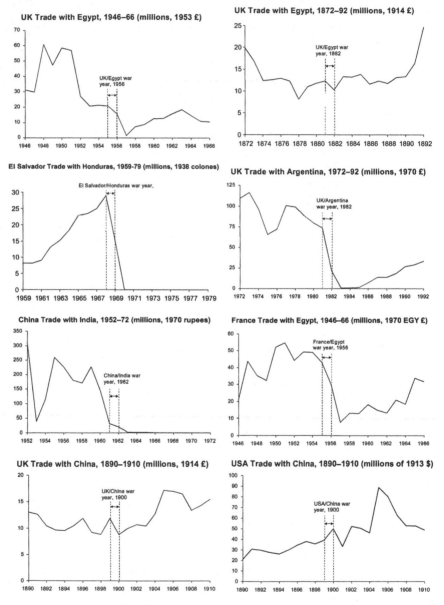

*Note:* Trade is real merchandise trade (imports and exports) in all these graphs.

## Short-War Dyads

Real trade flows are shown in figure 15.3 for each of the 8 short-war dyads. With the exception of USA/China 1890–1910, trade is seen to diminish during each dyad's war year. Regression results are reported in table 15.2, with the dyads again classified according to whether the nations are major or minor powers. Because the wars last less than one year, war trend and peace level drop out of the model. Interest then focuses on whether the $\beta_2$ coefficient on war level is negative, indicating a downdraft in trade volume during the war year. We find that 7 (88 percent) of the $\beta_2$ coefficients are negative, and 4 (50 percent) are significant. Hence, in half of the short-war cases a significant disruption in trade is shown. Note that these results correspond closely to those in the long-war cases, where 84 percent of the $\beta_2$ coefficients are negative and 47 percent are significant. Since most of our long-war dyads show significant evidence of trade disruption at some point in the war (17 of 19 cases), a reasonable conjecture is that more trade disruption would have been attributed to the short wars had they continued into additional calendar years.

## Conclusion

In Anderton and Carter (2001a) we extended Barbieri and Levy's (1999) methodology to test the trade disruption premise for additional war dyads. Using methods that we believe were systematic and reasonable, we identified 27 dyads. Whereas Barbieri and Levy (1999) found little support for the trade disruption premise, we found significant disruption in 21 of our cases. We believe these results constitute reasonably strong evidence that war disrupts trade. Barbieri and Levy (this volume), however, disagree with our assessment. In this final section, we focus on the major source of disagreement between us, namely, what constitutes evidence of significant trade disruption in the interrupted times-series model.

For long-war dyads, the key parameters for assessing war's disruption of trade are b2, which measures the change in the level of trade in the first year of war, and b3, which measures the change in the growth rate of trade during the war. Evidently, Barbieri and Levy acknowledge trade disruption only in cases where b2 is negative and significant. We maintain that if b2 or b3 is significantly negative, then there is evidence of war's disruption of trade. Hence, we believe that Barbieri and Levy's attention to b2 alone causes them to undercount the dyads for which war disrupts trade.

Barbieri and Levy (this volume) summarize our results as follows:

> [Anderton and Carter's] key indicator of the impact of war on trade levels is negative and statistically significant in 3 of 7 cases for major—minor short wars and 1 of 4 cases of major—minor long wars. This leaves 4 of 11 cases of mixed dyads for which war has a significant negative effect on trade. The 2 cases of minor—minor power dyads (1 long and 1 short

war) each show a statistically significant impact of war on trade. Thus, for nonmajor power dyads, 6 of 13 cases show a significant impact of war on trade, basically the same percentage as for major power dyads.

On the contrary, we find that war has a significant negative effect on trade in 9 of 13 nonmajor power dyads (rather than 6 of 13) and in 12 of 14 major power dyads (rather than 7 of 14).

**Table 15.2. Impact of Short Wars on Dyadic Trade**

| Dyads (war years in parentheses) | Constant $(\beta_0)$ | Trend $(\beta_1)$ | War level $(\beta_2)$ | War trend $(\beta_3)$ | Peace level $(\beta_4)$ | Peace trend $(\beta_5)$ | Rho | $R^2$ |
|---|---|---|---|---|---|---|---|---|
| *Major/minor short wars* | | | | | | | | |
| UK/Egypt, 1872–92 (1882) | 2.80* (0.16) | -0.05* (0.03) | -0.14 (0.19) | | 0.12* (0.04) | 0.46* (0.22) | | 0.52 |
| UK/China, 1890–1910 (1900)^ | 2.45* (0.11) | -0.01 (0.02) | -0.18 (0.14) | | 0.07* (0.03) | 0.41* (0.22) | | 0.66 |
| USA/China, 1890–1910 (1900)^ | 3.19* (0.12) | 0.05* (0.02) | 0.18 (0.18) | | -0.03 (0.03) | | | 0.73 |
| France/Egypt, 1946–66 (1956) | 3.45* (0.14) | 0.07 (0.03) | -1.71* (0.21) | | 0.01 (0.03) | -0.43* (0.22) | | 0.75 |
| UK/Egypt, 1946–66 (1956)^ | 3.89* (0.32) | -0.08 (0.06) | -1.39* (0.48) | | 0.17* (0.08) | | | 0.64 |
| China/India, 1952–72 (1962) | 5.70* (1.16) | -0.24 (0.20) | -1.07 (1.32) | | -0.54* (0.30) | 0.52* (0.20) | | 0.94 |
| UK/Argentina, 1972–92 (1982)^ | 4.62* (0.47) | -0.03 (0.09) | -3.93* (0.70) | | 0.32* (0.12) | | | 0.78 |
| *Minor/minor short wars* | | | | | | | | |
| El Salvador/Honduras, 1959–79 (1969) | 2.04* (0.86) | 0.16 (0.16) | -5.40* (1.28) | | -0.49* (0.21) | | | 0.87 |

*Note:* Standard errors are shown in parentheses. An asterisk indicates a two-tailed p-value less than 10 percent. The alternative hypothesis on $\beta_2$ is one-sided. Regressions are estimated using Time Series Processor (TSP) Version 4.4. AR1 results are reported if the absolute value of the t-statistic on rho exceeds 1.3; otherwise OLS results are reported. Dyads marked by a raised caret (^) were also studied by Barbieri and Levy (1999).

In table 15.3 we highlight the three nonmajor power dyads on which we disagree. Barbieri and Levy do not count these three dyads as cases of trade disruption because $\beta_2$ is not negative and significant. Their approach, however, ignores the trade disruption that occurs after the initial year of war. For long wars, the trade disruption premise does not require that $\beta_2$ be significantly negative, only that $\beta_2$ *or* $\beta_3$ be significantly negative. To illustrate the importance of considering both coefficients $\beta_2$ and $\beta_3$, in table 15.3 we show the percentage changes in real trade that occur after one, two, and three years of war. Notice the large percentage drops that occur after the first year of war. To ignore the $\beta_3$ coefficients, as Barbieri and Levy do, is to ignore these drops in trade. Because the $\beta_3$ coefficients are significantly negative, we conclude that war disrupts trade in each of these three mixed dyads. Returning to the Barbieri and Levy quote above, this means that 9 of 13 nonmajor power dyads (rather than just 6 of 13) show significant trade disruption.

Our disagreement with Barbieri and Levy over what constitutes evidence of trade disruption in the interrupted times-series model arises likewise in the major power cases. Barbieri and Levy (this volume) acknowledge evidence of trade disruption in 7 of 14 of our major power dyads, because 7 of the cases show significantly negative $\beta_2$ coefficients. We claim trade is disrupted in 12 of 14 major power dyads, because $\beta_2$ or $\beta_3$ (or both) are negative and significant in 12 of the cases.

Dropping the major versus minor power distinction, we can easily summarize our empirical results. For long wars, the evidence is compelling that war disrupts trade (17 of 19 dyads). For short wars, the evidence for trade disruption is not as strong (4 of 8 dyads). As defined in this chapter, short wars begin and end within a single calendar year. A plausible interpretation of our short-war results is that a period of time counted in months is often too brief for war to significantly disrupt trade. Altogether, the interrupted time-series methodology shows significant trade disruption in 21 of our 27 dyads. We conclude on balance that the trade disruption premise is well supported by our empirical study.

**Table 15.3. Trade Disruption in Selected Nonmajor Power Wars**

| Dyads (war years in parentheses) | War level ($\beta_2$) | War trend ($\beta_3$) | Percentage change in trade after | | |
| --- | --- | --- | --- | --- | --- |
| | | | 1 year | 2 years | 3 years |
| Germany/Canada, 1929–55 (1939–45) | -1.75 (1.30) | -0.54* (0.28) | -39.5 | -98.6 | -98.4 |
| Japan/Australia, 1931–55 (1941–45) | 0.62 (0.96) | -1.78* (0.27) | -26.2 | -89.8 | -100.0 |
| Japan/Canada, 1931–55 (1941–45) | -0.30 (0.72) | -1.59* (0.20) | -79.1 | -95.0 | -97.5 |

*Note:* An asterisk indicates a two-tailed p-value less than 10 percent.

# Notes

1. We continue to differ with Barbieri and Levy (this volume) on whether real trade volume or nominal trade value should be used in studies of conflict and trade. Our view is that a change in nominal trade value by itself cannot be used to determine whether trade has been disrupted. For example, suppose nation X imports 1 million barrels of oil from nation Y at $20 per barrel when a war breaks out between X and Y. Assume that X's oil imports from Y are disrupted and fall to 0.5 million barrels. Moreover, suppose the decline in imports drives the price of oil up to $50 per barrel. Nominal trade value

rises from $20 to $25 million, but this is clearly not a case of enhanced trade. Indeed, it is the decline in real trade volume that leads to the higher nominal trade value. Real trade volume falls from $20 to $10 million, where the latter figure is derived by multiplying the noninflated price of $20 per barrel by the lower import volume of 0.5 million barrels. We define disrupted trade as the reduced flow of goods and services between nations, regardless of the value of that reduced flow. If Barbieri and Levy do not distinguish between nominal trade value and real trade volume in future studies, they risk claiming nondisrupted or even enhanced trade, when in fact real trade volume may have been significantly disrupted.

2. The 27 dyadic data sets are available at www.holycross.edu/departments/ economics/canderto/wartradedata.htm.

3. In some cases our real trade data were slightly elevated during war years for one of two reasons. First, Mitchell (1962, 1998a, b, c) occasionally coded yearly exports or imports with a minus-minus symbol (--) to indicate that the trade value was less than 0.5 of the unit of measure. In these cases we coded the value at 0.5. Second, to accommodate the logarithmic form, we coded real trade as 1 percent of the unit of measure when real trade equaled zero. Note that both approximations err in the direction of underestimating trade disruption.

4. A subtlety of the model worth noting is that a positive $\beta_3$ coefficient on war trend does not necessarily contradict the trade disruption premise. For example, suppose that the trade trend going into the war is downward, so that $\beta_1$ is negative. Suppose further that trade falls to zero in the war's first year. Noting that $\beta_1$ plus $\beta_3$ measures the growth rate during the war, then it follows that $\beta_3$ must be positive, simply because trade volume cannot fall below zero. For further discussion, see Anderton and Carter (2001b).

# CHAPTER 16

# Globalization: Creative Destruction and the Prospect of a Capitalist Peace

*Erich Weede*

## Globalization

In earlier times it was difficult, time consuming, expensive, or even impossible for producers to deliver goods and services to the other end of the globe.[1] Now, Western airlines already buy the services of Indian programmers and back-office workers located in India. Cheap, fast, and reliable communication and transportation enables producers of goods and service-providers in low-wage countries to challenge high-cost producers in rich countries on their home turf. But technological innovation resulting in falling prices and rising speed of inter-continental communication and transportation is not the only determinant of globalization. Political decisions in rich and poor countries alike contributed strongly to globalization, too. It has even been claimed that free markets or free trade result from something like central planning or, at least, unyielding political will and American influence (Gray, 1998: 17). Tariffs and, to a lesser degree, nontariff barriers to trade have been reduced. Many countries try to find and to exploit their comparative advantage, to realize economies of scale and gains from trade by looking for buyers and sellers everywhere. If trade between countries is truly free, then it promises to enrich all nations.

Yet, not even free trade is the proverbial free lunch. It has a cost attached to it. By overcoming borders and distance globalization must reinforce the most important characteristic of capitalist or market economies, that is, competition resulting in 'creative destruction' (Schumpeter, 1942). In capitalist economies competition may start to bite even before it exists. Not only competition itself, but even the mere threat of future competition may generate attempts at innovation and cost-cutting. Where competition and innovation are not stifled by politics, bankruptcies occur and some workers lose their jobs. In principle, no one is safe forever. Many people resent being condemned to an everlasting effort to remain competitive. Moreover, resentment about the need to retain competitiveness grows, the more one lives in material comfort and the more established the welfare state is. This generalization holds across social classes and across countries (Inglehart, 1997).[2]

In principle, globalization permits a global division of labor. Since the days of Adam Smith (1776/1976) we know that the size of the market limits the division of labor and that the division of labor boosts innovation and productivity. In principle, globalization is the logical endpoint of the economic evolution that began when families changed from subsistence farming and household production to production for the market. As long as globalization is not yet completed—and it certainly is not yet—there remain gains from trade to be realized by further market expansion. Since globalization adds to competitive pressure, however, it causes resentment. Since globalization is fed by technological innovation and political decisions promoting free trade, these innovations and decisions attract resentment, too. The world is already globalized enough that nationwide resistance to innovation does little harm from a global perspective; it 'merely' affects the rise and decline of nations. Free trade is more vulnerable. If foreigners are perceived as a cause for the need to adjust—which subjectively may amount to misery—then curtailing free trade becomes politically attractive. After all, *no* politician benefits from the affection of foreigners who cannot vote. Of course, those economists who insist on the benefits of free trade (even if your partner does *not* practice free trade) are right. Benefits include serving customers better at lower prices, but also total factor productivity growth (Edwards, 1998). But the benefits of free trade tend to be dispersed widely, the costs of it (for example, in bankruptcies and job losses) tend to be concentrated and more visible. Therefore, free trade may be politically vulnerable despite the weakness of the economic argument against it. Since people react psychologically more strongly to losses than to gains—even by risk-acceptance in a gamble to avoid the loss altogether (Kahneman and Tversky, 1979)—there is another incentive for politicians to turn protectionist. Although Western societies after World War II mostly avoided outrages of protectionism (except for European agriculture), protectionism remains a permanent temptation.

Who in rich Western societies is most affected by globalization? Although the Stolper-Samuelson or factor price equalization theorem has been derived from unrealistic assumptions, it looks ever more realistic because of globalization (Bluestone, 1994: 336). According to this theorem, free trade reduces the demand for factors that are used intensively in imported goods, that is, low-skilled labor in Western imports. Therefore, the wages of low-skilled Western workers should suffer from downward pressure. Of course, unskilled workers may accept—or they may be forced to accept—low wages. Then globalization should increase income inequality in rich countries. Or, alternatively, unskilled workers may simply not accept declining wages. Then global competition may cost them their jobs.

In continental Europe we observe high unemployment rates. In Germany more than in other big countries, we until recently observed significantly rising unemployment rates (*The Economist*, 1998). In the United States and in Britain, by contrast, we see low and generally falling rates of unemployment, but simultaneously rising income inequality (Atkinson, Rainwater, and Smeeding, 1995: 46, 58, 80). Thus, developed Western societies seem to face a choice between either accepting more income inequality or more unemployment.[3] This is not an appealing choice for politicians who have to face voters in a free election.

According to recent econometric studies (Rodrik, 1999), democracies pay higher wages. Most importantly, this finding persists once income per capita and productivity differentials have been controlled. Conceivably, democracies can afford to do so because they provide secure property rights and political stability and therefore remain attractive to capital in spite of high wages. It is also conceivable, however, that high wages in many democracies become too high to be defensible in a globalized market order. Take South Korea as an example. The process of democratization in Korean society was accompanied by a steep rise in wages. This contributed to low profitability of Korean business and thereby to the Asian crisis of the late 1990s (Cho, 1998: 18; Jung and Kim, 1997; Mazarr and Lewis, 1998: 38, 44–45). Or, take reunited Germany with its high but unevenly spread unemployment with the East being the worst affected region. Some economists (Siebert, 1998: 61–62, 131) argue that German workers should either accept significantly lower wages or a much higher dispersion in earnings if unemployment is to fall. Within a democratic framework it will be difficult to persuade German workers to swallow this type of medicine.[4] The tendency to impose constraints on economic freedom for the sake of equality and justice is a recipe for generating problems.[5]

The trend toward more income inequality in America and some other Western societies has to be put into a wider perspective. Cox and Alm (1999: 70–73) point out that the American poor stand a reasonable chance of overcoming poverty. Out of those who belonged to the poorest quintile in 1975, about 80 percent succeeded to ascend to one of the three richest quintiles, that is, at least to the middle class, until 1991. Thus, poverty need not persist. It is frequently mitigated by mobility. Moreover, even those who remain in the poorest quintile might still benefit from economic growth. In the 1990s the poorest quintile of households was as well equipped with durable household goods as average households were about two decades earlier (Cox and Alm, 1999: 15).

Whatever inequality means to the disadvantaged, it has also been argued that inequality promotes political violence, but undermines political stability or democracy (Kapstein, 1999; Muller, 1985, 1986, 1995). If these effects *were* robust and established beyond reasonable doubt, then there would be considerable reason to worry about the impact of globalization on the political order of Western societies. Fortunately, however, these effects are *not* robust and *not* easily replicable (Weede, 1986; Posner, 1997; Graeff, 2000). Political violence might depend on prospects to prevail in struggles for power instead of depending on relative deprivation. And democracy seems to be as compatible with American-style inequality as with Scandinavian-style equality.

Of course, there is a dispute about the degree to which either trade or techno-logical progress is responsible for the predicament of unskilled labor in the West. While the majority view (e.g., Krugman, 1996) blames most of it on tech-nological progress, this is not entirely satisfying, because technological progress is frequently inferred from residuals rather than directly measured. An outspo-ken minority (e.g., Wood, 1994: 166–167) puts most of the blame on free trade and estimates that about 9 million manufacturing jobs might have been lost in rich countries already by 1990, and many more by now. The complimentary gain of 23 million jobs in poor countries may satisfy humanitarian impulses, but it does not help Western politicians to win elections. Certainly, a cautious and reasonable position is that technology *and* trade matter, that it is premature to close the debate about the relative impact of each.

Forgetting caution, I shall stick out my neck and risk my own interpretation (differing from the author's) of an excellent recent contribution to this debate (Cline, 1997): Human capital formation in rich Western societies should have contributed to some income equalization which we cannot observe because of technological developments requiring ever more qualified labor. Since these two forces might *approximately* neutralize each other, much of the trend toward inequality or unemployment which we actually observe in Western societies is plausibly attributed to free trade.[6] Taking the manufacturing share of employ-ment in OECD countries as the dependent variable, Saeger's (1997) regressions attribute between 25 and 50 percent of the variance to Northern imports from the South.[7] By contrast, according to Barro's (2000: 28) econometric findings, openness might even reduce inequality in rich countries.

So, it is still debatable what the effects of free trade are in rich countries. The mere fact that some reasonable economists explain growing inequality or unem-ployment in rich countries by free trade does increase the political vulnerability of free trade. Whoever loses a job or some part of a wage asks politicians for remedy, preferably immediately. As long as some degree of protection promises some immediate results, it looks attractive, quite independent of the soundness (or even sanity) of the economic reasoning behind protectionist moves.

Currently welfare states find it harder and harder to compete on global mar-kets. After all, the welfare state is expensive and it raises costs. Moreover, it reduces incentives to adjust. In the absence of a social safety net, people have little choice but to accept low pay and bad working conditions in order to avoid starvation. So, reallocation of labor from bankrupt enterprises to new jobs should proceed fairly rapidly. In a welfare state, however, people can afford to wait for better paid and more convenient work that might be offered in future. Moreover, one must not forget that welfare states cannot avoid punishing suc-cess by taxation and rewarding failure by social transfers. If people are subject to such a reinforcement schedule for decades, then the frequency of success must come down and frequency of failure must go up. Nevertheless, the welfare state is here to stay—at least in continental Europe.

In this setting globalization provides reason for hope and reason for fear at the same time. The reason for hope is that globalization ties politicians' hands and prevents them from pursuing politically attractive, but self-defeating policies, like those which got us into the welfare state and its disastrous effects on incentives to produce goods or services for others. Where markets are significantly larger than political units, stifling them by political control becomes difficult. In my view (Weede, 1996, chapter 4; 2000, chapter 7), even the rise of the West and the comparative stagnation of the great Asian civilizations in the last five hundred years is to be explained by political fragmentation and disunity in Europe and by huge centralized empires in China, India, or the Middle East.[8] Capital and to a lesser degree even labor could exit from oppressive rule in the West, thereby mitigating its incidence. By contrast, Asian emperors or sultans were not forced to respect the property rights of merchants and producers.

From a forward- rather than backward-looking perspective the IMF (1996b: 1) pronounces a similar view on the benefits of markets beyond political control: 'When doubt has arisen about the resolve of policy-makers to tackle problems, markets have demonstrated their ability to force the changes at substantial cost'. As this statement points out, the benefits of market forces are somewhat ambiguous because 'substantial cost' may be attached. By and large, postponing essential reforms should raise their cost.

Globalization is linked with increasing tax competition between states. The internet and e-commerce may reinforce these processes. Globalization increases the mobility of capital and high-income earners. By contrast to the earlier wave of globalization before World War I, ordinary labor remains immobile because most rich countries try *not* to let poor migrants come in. So, capital owners and high income earners face a choice about where to live and where to pay taxes. This is unlikely to lead to a race to the bottom, however, where states cut taxes ever more to remain attractive to capital owners and high-income earners. Most people like to stay where they are for reasons of habit or sentimentality. Moreover, wealthy people may actually prefer better services and higher taxes to poorer services and lower taxes. If tax competition forces governments to become more efficient, this effect is as welcome as the benefits of ordinary market competition are. As *The Economist* (2000: 18) recently pointed out, only one type of government activity is likely to be negatively affected by globalization and tax competition: 'using taxes to redistribute wealth from mobile firms and people to the less mobile, and less well off, may become harder'.

The stakes are high because (even in America) the tax burden is very unequally shared. According to *The Economist* (2000: 16), the richest 1 percent of American tax payers contributed more than 30 percent, and the richest 10 percent about 60 percent, and the richest quarter more than 80 percent to the federal income tax revenue actually collected. Moreover, the inequality of the tax burden shouldered actually increased between 1987 and 1997. As yet, tax competition has not effectively limited governmental 'fleecing the rich'. Fears about the impact of globalization and tax competition on the welfare state (for example: Gray, 1998; Kapstein, 1999) are greatly exaggerated or, at the very least, premature. From a libertarian perspective, it is equally exaggerated or premature to place too much hope in globalization and tax competition as instruments to control or roll back government expansion.

## A Downside of Globalization: Power Transitions

Within nations and states globalization reinforces creative destruction. Globalization requires economies and societies to adapt. Since economies almost never succeed equally, some nations will grow faster than others. Because of the potential advantages of backwardness (Gerschenkron, 1962; Maddison, 1969; Olson, 1996) one should even expect that some still poor or underdeveloped powers will catch-up with others and conceivably overtake them.[9] Actually, free trade and foreign direct investment provides them with an opportunity to do so (Dollar, 1992; de Soysa and Oneal, 1999). The purpose of free trade—whether within or between nations—is never to preserve some distributional status quo, nor to achieve distributional goals, but to make participants in it better off than they would be in the absence of free trade. So, one should expect that globalization and free trade undermine any existing hierarchy of power which necessarily is based on economic size and wealth beside other determinants. The leveling effects of free trade as well as the reasons why democracies are under pressure to accept or even to pursue them have been well summarized by Stein (1990: 139): 'A hegemonic power's decision to enrich itself is also a decision to enrich others more than itself. Over time, such policies will come at the expense of the hegemon's relative standing and will bring forth challengers. Yet choosing to sustain its relative standing . . . is a choice to keep others impoverished at the cost of increasing its own absolute wealth. Maintaining its relative position has obvious costs not only to others but to itself'.

While globalization and free trade promise to improve the material quality of life for hundreds of millions of people some of whom are still desperately poor and in visible need of any improvement they can get (Dollar and Kraay, 2002)[10], it simultaneously undermines the pecking order of states. As Waltz (1979: 105) has observed, the distributional effects of the international division of labor and free trade may limit their expansion. In Gowa's (1994: 6) view, distributional considerations are more important with some trade partners than with others; she wrote: 'trade frees economic resources for military uses. Thus, trade enhances the potential military power of any country that engages in it . . . the real income gains that motivate free trade are also the source of the security externalities that can either impede or facilitate trade. Trade with an adversary produces a security diseconomy; trade with an ally produces a positive externality'.

Organski (1958), Organski and Kugler (1980), and Gilpin (1981) argued that the rise and decline of great powers, as well as their satisfaction or dissatisfaction with the status quo, determine the war-proneness of nations and of the global system. If some states rise and others decline, then the hierarchy of states is blurred, some states no longer know their place or role in the system, and an approximation to power parity between a rising and revisionist state and a declining status quo state may result in the hope or illusion on both sides at the same time that they can fight and win a war. By now, there is a number of studies to corroborate the link between parity and war-proneness or between overwhelming superiority and war-avoidance (Geller, 1992; Kim, 1992; Kugler and Lemke, 1996; Lemke and Reed, 1996; Oneal and Russett, 1999b; Russett and Oneal, 2001). So even a globally, but—of course unevenly—successful race for wealth may carry a heavy price tag in international security.

According to Huntington (1996), cultural differences between civilizations are likely to be a major cause of *future* wars. Huntington is specifically concerned with the risks of future rivalry or a clash between the Sinic (or Confucian) and Muslim civilizations on the one hand and Western civilization on the other hand. For a number of reasons I am increasingly skeptical about the 'clash of civilizations' approach. First, it cannot explain why interstate war becomes less frequent and intrastate or civil war more frequent (Carnegie Commission, 1997: 12, 25). In civil wars killers and victims usually belong to the same civilization. Second, a 'clash of civilizations approach' cannot explain why totalitarianism has been even more lethal than war in the twentieth century. Although Hitler perceived most of his civilian victims to be members of an alien civilization[11], neither Stalin nor Mao nor Pol Pot needed this type of rationalization for their campaigns of mass murder. Again, murderers and victims of state terrorism usually belonged to the same civilization. Third, quantitative studies (Henderson, 1997, 1998; Henderson and Tucker, 2001; Russett, Oneal, and Cox, 2000) provide little support for the idea that the risk of war is increased by cultural differences or by belonging to different civilizations.

Nevertheless, it remains conceivable that uneven economic growth rates between civilizations, or power transitions between them, are more dangerous than uneven economic growth or power transitions within the same civilization. It is at least plausible to expect more trouble because of a conceivable future power transition between culturally dissimilar China and the United States than between culturally similar USA and Britain in the past. Moreover, China has been growing significantly faster than the United States in the last two decades. Quite modest optimism about China suffices to expect parity in economic size between the USA and China in the second decade of the twenty-first century (Maddison, 1998). Of course, China would trail the USA for another couple of decades (or even another century) in per capita incomes. Of course, parity in economic size would not suffice to make China's military comparable to American forces. It is almost inconceivable that China will match the U.S. military within the next three decades. If China should remain an autocracy, however, it is useful to remember that such states can allocate a much higher share of their resources for military purposes than democracies can (Payne, 1989).

The purpose of my short discussion of the conceivable rise of China has been to illustrate conceivable costs of globalization and free trade. Although a national security downside of globalization may well exist[12], the ultimate purpose of my chapter is not to provide arguments against it. There is also an upside of globalization to be analyzed now.

## An Upside of Globalization: The Capitalist Peace

Globalization is driven by technological innovation, by the rising speed and falling costs of communication and transportation. Essentially, the role of politics in globalization can consist only of the removal of barriers to free trade, free capital flows and international investment which previous powerholders erected. Globalization implies more competition between enterprises. Competition forces producers to improve quality, cut costs, and innovate, that is, to serve consumers ever better. Efforts to reduce globalization or protectionism would harm consumers. Western consumers would have to pay significantly more if products made by low-cost producers and low-wage labor in poor countries were no longer available. Another benefit of globalization for the rich West concerns labor. Less globalization or protectionism would reduce opportunities for employees to move from worse-paid jobs producing for domestic markets to better-paid jobs producing for foreign markets. Bergsten (1996: 118) summarizes these globalization benefits in the following way: 'Export jobs pay 15 percent more than the average wage. Worker productivity is 20 to 40 percent higher. These firms expand employment 20 percent faster than non-exporting firms and are 10 percent less likely to fail'.

In my view, the economic benefits of globalization and free trade are *much less* important, however, than the international security benefits. The quantitative literature (which is summarized by Weede, 1996: chapter 8, 2000: chapter 11; and by Oneal and Russett, 1997, 1999b; Russett and Oneal, 2001; but entirely neglected by critics of globalization, like Gray, 1998, or Kapstein, 1999) comes fairly close to general agreement on the following four propositions from economics, political sociology, and international relations: First, democracies rarely fight each other. This does not necessarily say that democracies fight fewer wars than other regimes. It is even compatible with the until recently widely shared view that the risk of war between democracies and autocracies might be even higher than the risk of war between autocracies.[13] Second, prosperity or high per capita incomes promote democracy. Third, export orientation in poor countries and open markets in rich countries, that is, trade between rich and poor countries promotes growth and prosperity where it is needed most, in poor countries. Fourth, (bilateral) trade reduces the risk of war between (dyads of) nations. Actually, the pacifying impact of trade *might be* even stronger than the pacifying impact of democracy (Oneal and Russett, 1999b: 29; Gartzke, 2000: 209).[14] Moreover, trade seems to play a pivotal role in the prevention of war because it exerts direct and indirect pacifying effects. In addition to the direct effect, there is the indirect effect of free trade on smaller risks of war mediated by growth, prosperity, and democracy. Since the exploitation of gains from trade is the essence or purpose of capitalism and free markets, I label the sum of the direct and indirect international security benefits 'the capitalist peace', of which 'the democratic peace' merely is a component.[15]

Elsewhere (Weede, 1999b) I have argued that the different long-term effects of the settlements of World Wars I and II derive from failure or success to apply a capitalist peace strategy toward the losers of the war. After World War I, France determined the peace settlement more than anyone else. It failed to promote a capitalist peace. Immiseration and desperation within Germany contributed to Hitler's empowerment and indirectly to World War II in which France had to be saved by its allies. After World War II the United States pursued a capitalist peace strategy toward the vanquished. It succeeded in making allies out of Germany and Japan.

If the West were afraid of the downside of globalization, that is, its inherent tendency to undermine the status quo and Western or American hegemony, if the West turned protectionist, then its policies would look like white racism from the outside. Protectionism in the West would condemn many non-Westerners to avoidable poverty for a long time to come. Protectionism might turn Huntington's (1996) 'clash of civilizations' into a self-fulfilling prophecy.[16]

Protectionism implies not only an ultimately self-defeating security policy. It is morally objectionable because it upholds avoidable poverty and because it is in practice not easily distinguishable from racism. Free trade, however, is based on a cosmopolitan morality, on nondiscrimination (see Giersch 1995; 24). In my view, looking for the best deal one can get irrespective of the skin color of the seller is morally preferable to practicing racial solidarity. Moreover, replacing the discriminatory criterion 'skin color' by the color of the passport or citizenship seems no moral improvement to me, but treating business partners as individuals instead of members or nonmembers of some group is. By and large, the cheaper seller needs the deal more urgently than the more expensive seller. Even from an egalitarian perspective, pure capitalism enjoys some advantages.

Peace by trade seems to be about as strong as peace by democracy. Trade (because of its contribution to prosperity) does underwrite democracy, and thereby the democratic peace where it prevails. Moreover, it does not suffer from a geopolitical complication which affects peace by democratization. According to the best research (e.g., Oneal and Russett, 1997, 1999b), the risk of war between democracies is much lower than elsewhere. The risk of war between a democracy and an autocracy is higher than elsewhere—at least in recent decades.[17] If one attributes causal significance to these observations, as I do, then democratization does *not everywhere* contribute to peace. Imagine the democratization of a nation located in the middle of a deeply autocratic area. Its democratization would generate a number of autocratic-democratic dyads and thereby increase the risk of war. By contrast, the democratization of a nation surrounded by democracies would certainly be desirable. The democratic peace should be extended from its North Atlantic core area to contiguous areas first. Leapfrogging is undesirable. Geographical compactness of the democratic bloc is a prerequisite for the pacifying effects of democracy to apply.[18]

The ambivalence of democratization as a tool of pacification can be illustrated by Israel and Taiwan. Israel is democratic, but has always been surrounded by autocratic regimes. Although an autocratic Israel would not necessarily be safe from autocratic neighbors, a deal on, say, the Golan between two autocracies might be easier than a deal between a democracy and an autocracy. Or, consider Taiwan. Until recently the Mainland and Taiwan considered themselves to be parts of China. Now, Taiwan is a democracy and the Mainland remains an autocracy. The democratization of Taiwan certainly raised obstacles against an elite deal on unification between two ruling classes.[19]

Fortunately, however, the democratization of Taiwan has already refuted the idea that Confucian or Sinic civilization is incompatible with democracy. If the Chinese economy prospers, if China outgrows poverty, then Mainland China may become a democracy in two or three decades. Some promising developments are already observable. At the level of villages there are elections (Rowen, 1996). Some cadres already have been voted out of office. Moreover, China trains more lawyers than before and is starting to perceive the economic benefits of the rule of law (Pei, 1998). Instead of publicly criticizing China's poor human rights performance, it seems more effective to support China in establishing those foundations for a future transition to democracy which China voluntarily pursues for the sake of its economic ambitions (Brzezinski, 2000: 16). After all, post-Soviet Russia provides a vivid illustration of the limited value of electoral democracy without the rule of law.

While the democratic peace component of the capitalist peace is constrained by the geopolitical need of avoiding leapfrogging in the extension of democracy or tiger coat patterns of democracy and autocracy, the peace by trade component of the capitalist peace suffers from no such limitation. It seems to be a rare case of a desirable end which is attainable by a desirable means. By contrast, protectionism promises less wealth and more war. Even if protectionism were required for the sake of equality and domestic stability in rich countries (as argued by Allais, 1994), from the point of view of narrow self-interest *and* from the point of view of cosmopolitan morality it offers an unattractive deal, that is, equality bought by lower average incomes and a higher risk of war.

# Notes

An earlier version of this chapter was presented at one of the geopolitics panels (RC 41.2) of the IPSA Congress, 1–5 August 2000, in Québec, Canada.

1. One should not exaggerate the impact of globalization. Waltz (1999) argued that the world is no more globalized at the end of the twentieth century than at its beginning, and that the more powerful a nation-state is, the more likely it is to succeed in modifying the impact of globalization on itself. Lindert and Williamson (2001: 20) qualify this evaluation by pointing to lower barriers to trade at the end than at the beginning of the twentieth century, but to less foreign investment by the leading economic power now than then, and to much less international migration now than in earlier times. Moreover, Theurl (1999: 72) summarized some facts which demonstrate the limits of globalization:

There remain significant price differences even in internationally traded goods. Domestic savings and investment remain correlated. Even among international investors there is a home bias. Much international investment is not motivated by differences in labor cost, but by hopes of serving foreign markets. Foreign direct investment did not exceed 5 percent in major economies even in the early 1990s. According to Wade (1996: 61), more than 80 percent of production in major economies is for domestic consumption, more than 80 percent of investment is done by domestic investors.

2. Of course, Inglehart should not be blamed for my interpretation of his findings on postmaterialism. In *my* view, postmaterialism is closely related to an unwillingness to compete.

3. See, for example, Kirchgässner (1998: 37). In an econometric study (Weede, 1999a) I find the following pattern. While income equality was positively correlated with employment among Western democracies in the 1990–94 period, the relationship is close to zero for 1997. But about half of the variation in *increases* in unemployment may be accounted for by an unwillingness to accept inequality. Inequality in rich countries might not be as bad as many authors believe. According to Barro (2000), inequality in *rich* countries actually promotes growth.

4. Since the welfare state is largely financed by taxing labor, since trade unions try to shift this burden on to employers or enterprises, it might hurt competitiveness by increasing unit labor costs. A recent article by Alesina and Perotti (1997) demonstrates that an intermediate degree of centralization of the wage setting process (as in Germany) maximizes this effect, and therefore reduces competitiveness more than elsewhere.

5. Of course, trade unionists in the United States also want to impose constraints on economic freedom. Some of them already notice the need for global cooperation in order to do so (Mazur, 2000). In my view, the self-serving character of the demanded constraints becomes obvious once the perspective is shifted from producer to consumer interests. By and large, consumer interests come much closer to being truly public interests than producer interests, which necessarily are quite narrowly focused. Economic freedom serves consumers. All kinds of organized producer interests work to undermine it.

6. Lindert and Williamson (2001: 33) also point out that Cline's (1997) data may be interpreted in this way.

7. In general, the inclusion of time dummies reduces globalization effects, their exclusion enhances them. One interpretation of time dummies is 'that the time dummies are capturing those effects of North-South integration that are common across OECD countries' (Saeger, 1997: 602). Other interpretations are that they might pick up trends in productivity growth or human capital formation. While Iversen and Cusack (2000: 343–345) contradict Saeger's view that deindustrialization is significantly affected by globalization, their analysis does not distinguish between LDC exports to OECD countries and intra-OECD trade. Moreover, they include time dummies that might pick up some of the impact of globalization. Thereby, they twice bias their design against finding globalization effects.

8. At its height, the Ottoman Empire stretched from Algeria to the Arab-Iranian Gulf, from the Crimea to Yemen.

9. There is econometric evidence to corroborate the ideas of 'conditional convergence' or 'advantages of backwardness' (Barro and Sala-i-Martin, 1995; Levine and Renelt, 1992). The most important reasons for it include transfers of technology because imitation is easier and faster than innovation and sectoral reallocation of labor from agriculture to more productive pursuits elsewhere.

10. Although the distributional effects of globalization in poor countries are still debatable, globalization is correlated with equality (Kearney, 2001). Even more important than the impact of globalization on intranational distributions of income is the impact of globalization on income differences between nations. According to Lindert and Williamson (2001: 38), globalization reduces income differences between those who participate in it, but leaves behind those who do not participate. It may even be argued that globalization improves happiness in poor countries more than it does in rich countries (Wright, 2000).

11. Probably, *most* of his victims did not share this evaluation. In World War I most German Jews fought for the German Reich just as Christian and 'Aryan' Germans did.

12. If the United States or the West is afraid of China becoming stronger than the West, there are other and safer strategies than slowing globalization and condemning the Chinese masses and poor people elsewhere to poverty. For example, the West may buy some 'reinsurance' by transatlantic unity or a Euro-American federation or even by ballistic missile defenses. In my view, both policies would be preferable to interfering with free trade and globalization.

13. Russett and Oneal (2001: 116) argue that their most recent research refutes this skepticism about the limits of the democratic peace. In their view, democratization always promotes peace even among nations surrounded by autocracies. I am not yet fully convinced whether this new finding will be robust and replicable. See Gowa's (1999: 107) findings on the democratic peace as well as the autocratic peace which imply that after World War II dyads consisting of a democracy and an autocracy run the highest risk of war.

14. Of course, there are dissenting voices in the literature (Barbieri, 1996a; Beck, Katz, and Tucker, 1998; Beck, 2002). In my view, Barbieri's results are simply overwhelmed by the mass of analyses reported by Oneal and Russett. Beck, Katz, and Tucker as well as Beck raise the serious issue of time dependence in the time-series cross-section data. While fundamental at the methodological level of analysis, the policy conclusions do not necessarily diverge as much from those of Oneal and Russett (1997, 1999b), as a purely method-oriented reading of their objections might suggest. After all, Beck, Katz, and Tucker (1998: 1284) write: 'But while trade may not inhibit conflict, it does appear to shorten spells of conflict.' Moreover, Russett and Oneal (2001) made a major effort to respond to the methodological criticism raised against their earlier work. Barbieri raised an interesting objection against the 'peace by trade' argument in an (unpublished) review of an earlier version of this chapter. If trade within nations runs into fewer obstacles than trade between nations, as it certainly does, and if trade promotes peace, how can we explain the rising tide of rebellions and civil wars? Conceivably, rebels and civil war factions are less easily pacified by economic linkages than governments are, at least as long as they are not challenged by armed opposition at home.

15. Russett and Oneal (2001) refer to a Kantian peace instead which is built upon three components: the democratic peace, peace by trade, and peace by collaboration in international organizations (or IGOs). The IGO element of the Kantian tripod is the weakest and least robust one.

16. Huntington himself is wrong in denying the pacifying impact of trade or the capitalist peace. His excuse is that the pathbreaking work by Oneal and Russett (1997, 1999b) was not yet available when he developed his ideas.

17. As pointed out above, Russett and Oneal (2001: 116) no longer accept this view. I am not fully convinced that they are right. To me, results from a separate analysis of disputes in the Cold War period would look more persuasive than an analysis beginning

in 1885 which collapses results from the multipolar pre–World War II period, the bipolar Cold War period and the beginning of the unipolar period thereafter. Some of the findings reported by Russett and Oneal (2001: 113), namely, the qualitatively different alliance effects on militarized disputes found in the multipolar and bipolar periods of observation, cast doubt on the wisdom of imposing the same causal structure on different periods of world politics. In this respect, I find Gowa's (1999) approach quite reasonable.

18. Promoting democracy in Poland first and in Uzbekistan much later is not only more desirable but also more feasible than the reverse order would be.

19. For more detail, see Weede (1999c).

# References

Aarons, Mark and John Loftus. 1994. *The Secret War against the Jews: How Western Espionage Betrayed the Jewish People*. New York: St. Martin's.

Abegunrin, Olaylwola. 1990. *Economic Dependence and Regional Cooperation in Southern Africa: SADCC and South Africa in Confrontation*. Lewiston, NY: E. Mellen.

Achen, Christopher H. 2000. 'Why Lagged Dependent Variables Can Suppress the Explanatory Power of Other Independent Variables'. Paper presented at the Annual Meeting of the Political Methodology Section of the American Political Science Association, Los Angeles, CA, 14 July.

Achen, Christopher W. 1986. 'Necessary and Sufficient Conditions for Unbiased Aggregation of Cross Sectional Regressions'. Paper presented at the Third Annual Methodology Conference, Cambridge, MA, 7–10 August.

Aghion, Philippe and Jeffrey G. Williamson. 1998. *Growth, Inequality and Globalization. Theory, History and Policy*. Cambridge: Cambridge University Press.

Ahluwalia, Montek S. 1976. 'Income Distribution and Development: Some Stylized Facts', *American Economic Review* 66(2): 128–135.

Alderson Arthur S. and François Nielsen. 1999. 'Income Inequality, Development, and Dependence: A Reconsideration', *American Sociological Review* 64(4): 606–631.

Alesina, Alberto and Roberto Perotti. 1997. 'The Welfare State and Competitiveness', *American Economic Review* 87(5): 921–939.

Alesina, Alberto, Enrico Spolaore, and Romain Wacizarg. 2000. 'Economic Integration and Political Disintegration', *American Economic Review* 90(5): 1276–1296.

Allais, Maurice. 1994. *Combats pour l'Europe 1992–94* [Battles for Europe 1992–94]. Paris: Clément Juglar.

Altfield, Michael. 1984. 'The Decision to Ally: A Theory and Test', *Western Political Quarterly* 37(4): 523–544.

Altfield, Michael and Bruce Bueno de Mesquita, 1979. 'Choosing Sides in Wars', *International Studies Quarterly* 23(1): 87–112.

Amemiya, Takeshi. 1985. *Advanced Econometrics*. Cambridge, MA: Harvard University Press.

Amer, Ramses. 1999. 'Conflict Management and Constructive Engagement in ASEAN's Expansion', *Third World Quarterly* 20(5): 1031–1048.

Amin, Samir. 1976. *Unequal Development*. New York: Monthly Review.

Anderson, James E. 1979. 'A Theoretical Foundation for the Gravity Equation', *American Economic Review* 69(1): 106–116.

Anderton, Charles H. and John R. Carter. 2001a. 'The Impact of War on Trade: An Interrupted Time-Series Study', *Journal of Peace Research* 38(4): 445–457.

Anderton, Charles H. and John R. Carter. 2001b. 'On Disruption of Trade by War: A Reply to Barbieri and Levy', *Journal of Peace Research* 38(5): 625–628.

Andrews, David M. 1994. 'Capital Mobility and State Autonomy: Toward a Structural Theory of International Monetary Relations', *International Studies Quarterly* 38(2): 193–218.

Angell, Norman. 1910. *The Great Illusion. A Study of the Relation of Military Power in Nations to Their Economic and Social Advantages*. London: Heinemann.

Angell, Norman. 1913. *The Great Illusion,* 4th revision and enlarged edition. New York: Putnam's.

Angell, Norman. 1938. *The Great Illusion—Now*. Harmondsworth: Penguin.

Arad, Ruth W. and Seev Hirsch. 1981. 'Peacemaking and Vested Interests: International Economic Transactions', *International Studies Quarterly* 25(3): 439–468.

Arad, Ruth W., Seev Hirsch, and Alfred Tovias. 1983. *The Economics of Peacemaking*. New York: St. Martin's.

Armington, Paul S. 1969. 'A Theory of Demand for Products Distinguished by Place of Production', *IMF Staff Papers* 16: 158–177.

Atkinson, Anthony B., Lee Rainwater, and Timothy B. Smeeding. 1995. *Income Distribution in OECD Countries*. Paris: OECD.

Azar, Edward. 1980. 'The Conflict and Peace Data Bank (COPDAB) Project', *Journal of Conflict Resolution* 24(1): 143–152.

Azar, Edward. 1984. 'The Conflict and Peace Data Bank 1948–1978', International and Domestic Files. ICPSR 7757, Second ICPSR Edition. Ann Arbor, MI: Interuniversity Consortium for Political and Social Research.

Baldwin, David A. 1985. *Economic Statecraft*. Princeton, NJ: Princeton University Press.

Baldwin, Robert E. 1984. *Recent Issues and Initiatives in U.S. Trade Policy: Conference Report*. Cambridge, MA: National Bureau of Economic Research.

Ball, Nicole. 1981. 'The Military in Politics: Who Benefits and How?' *World Development* 9(6): 569–582.

Barber, Benjamin R. 1996. *Jihad vs. McWorld: How Globalism and Tribalism Are Reshaping the World*. New York: Ballantine.

Barbieri, Katherine. 1995. *Economic Interdependence and Militarized Interstate Conflict, 1870–1985*. Ph.D. Dissertation. Binghamton University, Binghamton, NY.

Barbieri, Katherine. 1996a. 'Economic Interdependence: A Path to Peace or Source of Interstate Conflict?' *Journal of Peace Research* 33(1): 29–49.

Barbieri, Katherine. 1996b. 'Explaining Discrepant Findings in the Trade–Conflict Literature'. Presented at the 37th Annual Convention of the International Studies Association, San Diego, CA, 16–20 April.

Barbieri, Katherine. 1997. 'Risky Business: The Impact of Trade Linkages on Interstate Conflict, 1870–1985', in Gerald Schneider and Patricia A. Weitsman, ed., *Enforcing Cooperation: 'Risky' States and the Intergovernmental Management of Conflict*. London: Macmillan, 202–231.

Barbieri, Katherine. 1998a. 'International Trade and Conflict: The Debatable Relationship'. Paper presented at the 39th Annual Convention of the International Studies Association, Minneapolis, MN, 18–21 March.

Barbieri, Katherine. 1998b. Dyadic Trade Data Set. http://pss.la.psu.edu/ TRD Data.htm. December.

Barbieri, Katherine 2002. *The Liberal Illusion: Does Trade Promote Peace?* Ann Arbor, MI: University of Michigan Press.

Barbieri, Katherine 2003. 'Models and Measures in Trade-Conflict Research', in Edward D. Mansfield and Brian M. Pollins, ed., *Economic Interdependence and International Conflict: New Perspectives on an Enduring Debate.* Ann Arbor, MI: University of Michigan Press. [In press.]

Barbieri, Katherine and Jack S. Levy. 1997. 'Sleeping with the Enemy: Trade between Adversaries during Wartime'. Paper presented at the Annual Meeting of the Peace Science Society International, Indianapolis, IN, 21–23 November.

Barbieri, Katherine and Jack S. Levy. 1999. 'Sleeping With the Enemy: The Impact of War on Trade', *Journal of Peace Research* 36(4): 463–479.

Barbieri, Katherine and Jack S. Levy. 2001. 'Does War Impede Trade? A Response to Anderton and Carter', *Journal of Peace Research* 38(5): 619–624.

Barbieri, Katherine and Jack S. Levy. 2003. 'The Trade Disruption Hypothesis and the Liberal Economic Theory of Peace', chapter 12 in this volume.

Barbieri, Katherine and Gerald Schneider. 1999. 'Globalization and Peace: Assessing New Directions in the Study of Trade and Conflict', *Journal of Peace Research* 36(4): 387–404.

Barro, Robert J. 2000. 'Inequality and Growth in a Panel of Countries', *Journal of Economic Growth* 5(1): 5–32.

Barro, Robert J. and Xavier Sala-i-Martin. 1995. *Economic Growth.* New York: McGraw-Hill.

Beck, Nathaniel. 2003. 'Modeling Dynamics in the Study of Conflict: A Comment on Oneal and Russett', chapter 8, this volume.

Beck, Nathaniel and Simon Jackman. 1998. 'Beyond Linearity by Default: Generalized Additive Models', *American Journal of Political Science* 42(2): 596–627.

Beck, Nathaniel and Jonathan N. Katz. 1995. 'What to Do (and Not to Do) with Time-Series Cross-Section Data', *American Political Science Review* 89(3): 634–647.

Beck, Nathaniel and Jonathan N. Katz. 1997. 'The Analysis of Binary Time-Series-Cross-Sectional Data and/or the Democratic Peace'. Paper presented at the Annual Meeting of the Political Methodology Group, Columbus, OH, 23–27 July.

Beck, Nathaniel and Jonathan N. Katz. 2001. 'Throwing Out the Baby with the Bath Water: A Comment on Green, Kim, and Yoon', *International Organization* 55(2): 487–495.

Beck, Nathaniel and Richard Tucker. 1996. 'Conflict in Space and Time: Time-Series-Cross-Section Analysis with a Binary Dependent Variable'. Paper presented at the 92nd Annual Meeting of the American Political Science Association, San Francisco, CA, 29 August–1 September.

Beck, Nathaniel, Jonathan N. Katz, and Richard Tucker. 1998. 'Taking Time Seriously: Time-Series-Cross-Section Analysis with a Binary Dependent Variable', *American Journal of Political Science* 42(4): 1260–1288.

Beck, Nathaniel, David Epstein, Simon Jackman, and Sharyn O'Halloran. 2001. Alternative Models of Dynamics in Binary Time-Series-Cross-Section Models: The Example of State Failure. Paper presented at the Annual Meeting of the Society for Political Methodology, Emory University, Atlanta, GA, 13 July.

Bennett, D. Scott. 1999. 'Parametric Models, Duration Dependence, and Time-Varying Data Revisited', *American Journal of Political Science* 43(1): 256–270.

Bennett, D. Scott and Allan C. Stam. 1996. 'The Duration of Interstate Wars, 1816–1985', *American Political Science Review* 90(2): 239–257.

Bennett, D. Scott and Allan C. Stam. 2000. 'Research Design and Estimator Choices in the Analysis of Interstate Dyads: When Decisions Matter', *Journal of Conflict Resolution* 44(5): 653–685.

Benoit, Kenneth. 1996. 'Democracies Really Are More Pacific (In General)', *Journal of Conflict Resolution* 40(4): 636–657.

Bergeijk, Peter A. G. van. 1994. *Economic Diplomacy, Trade, and Commercial Policy: Positive and Negative Sanctions in a New World Order*. Northampton, MA: Elgar.

Bergsten, C. Fred. 1996. 'Globalizing Free Trade', *Foreign Affairs* 75(3): 105–120.

Bergstrand, Jeffrey H. 1985. 'The Gravity Equation in International Trade: Some Microeconomic Foundations and Empirical Evidence', *Review of Economics and Statistics* 67(3): 472–481.

Bergstrand, Jeffrey H. 1989. 'The Generalized Gravity Equation, Monopolistic Competition, and the Factor Proportions Theory in International Trade', *Review of Economics and Statistics* 71(1): 143–153.

Bhagwati, Jagdish and Marvin H. Kosters. 1994. *Trade and Wages: Leveling Wages Down?* Washington, DC: AEI Press.

Bhagwati, Jagdish N. 1964. 'On the Underinvoicing of Imports', *Oxford Bulletin of Economics and Statistics* 27(4): 389–397.

Bhagwati, Jagdish N. 1967. 'Fiscal Policies, The Faking of Foreign Trade Declarations, and the Balance of Payments', *Oxford Bulletin of Economic and Statistics* 29(1): 61–77.

Bhagwati, Jagdish N., ed. 1987. *International Trade: Selected Readings*, 2nd ed. Cambridge, MA: MIT Press.

Bhagwati, Jagdish. 1998. *A Stream of Windows: Unsettling Reflections on Trade, Immigration, and Democracy*. Boston, MA: MIT Press.

Bhagwati, Jagdish N. and Hugh T. Patrick, ed. 1991. *Aggressive Unilateralism: America's 301 Trade Policy and the World Trading System*. Ann Arbor, MI: University of Michigan Press.

Bhagwati, Jagdish N. and T. N. Srinivasan. 1976. 'Optimal Trade Policy and Compensation under Endogenous Uncertainty: The Phenomenon of Market Disruption', *Journal of International Economics* 6: 317–336.

Blainey, Geoffrey. 1988. *The Causes of War*. Basingstoke: Macmillan.

Bliss, Harry and Bruce Russett. 1998. 'Democratic Trading Partners: The Liberal Connection', *Journal of Politics* 60(4): 1126–1147.

Bluestone, Barry. 1994. 'Old Theories in New Bottles: Toward an Explanation of Growing World-Wide Income Inequality', in Jeffrey H. Bergstrand et al., ed., *The Changing Distribution of Income in an Open US Economy*. Amsterdam: North-Holland, 331–342.

Boehmer, Charles, Erik Gartzke, and Timothy Nordstrom. 2000. 'Do Intergovernmental Organizations Promote Peace?' Paper presented at the Annual Meeting of the Peace Science Society International, New Haven, CT, 26–29 October.

Bornschier, Volker and Christopher Chase-Dunn. 1985. *Transnational Corporations and Underdevelopment*. New York: Praeger.

Boswell, Terry and William Dixon. 1990. 'Dependency and Rebellion: A Cross-National Analysis', *American Sociological Review* 55(4): 540–559.

Boulding, Kenneth E. 1962. *Conflict and Defense: A General Theory*. New York: Harper.

Box-Steffensmeier, Janet M. and Christopher J. W. Zorn. 2001. 'Duration Models and Proportional Hazards in Political Science', *American Journal of Political Science* 45(4): 972–988.

Bremer, Stuart A. 1992. 'Dangerous Dyads: Conditions Affecting the Likelihood of Interstate War, 1816–1965', *Journal of Conflict Resolution* 36(2): 309–341.

Bremer, Stuart A. 1996. Militarized Interstate Disputes Data. http://pss. la.psu.edu/MID_DATA.html.

Brito, Dagobert and Michael Intriligator. 1985. 'Conflict, War, and Redistribution', *American Political Science Review* 79(3): 953–957.

Brooks, Stephen. 1999. 'The Globalization of Production and the Changing Benefits of Conquest', *Journal of Conflict Resolution* 43(5): 646–670.

Brzezinski, Zbigniew. 2000. 'Living with China', *National Interest* (59): 5–21.

Bueno de Mesquita, Bruce. 1981. *The War Trap*. New Haven, CT: Yale University Press.

Bueno de Mesquita, Bruce and David Lalman. 1992. *War and Reason. Domestic and International Imperatives*. New Haven, CT: Yale University Press.

Bueno de Mesquita, Bruce and Randolph M. Siverson. 1997. 'Nasty or Nice? Political Systems, Endogenous Norms, and the Treatment of Adversaries', *Journal of Conflict Resolution* 41(1): 175–199.

Bueno de Mesquita, Bruce, James D. Morrow, and Ethan R. Zorick. 1997. 'Capabilities, Perception, and Escalation', *American Political Science Review* 91(1): 15–27.

Bueno de Mesquita, Bruce, James D. Morrow, Randolph M. Siverson, and Alastair Smith. 1999. 'An Institutional Explanation of the Democratic Peace', *American Political Science Review* 93(4): 791–807.

Bureau of the Census, various years. *Statistical Abstract of the United States*. Washington, DC: U.S. Government Printing Office.

Bureau of the Census. 1976. *Historical Statistics of the United States: Colonial Times to 1970, Parts 1 and 2*. Washington, DC: U.S. Government Printing Office.

Buzan, Barry. 1984. 'Economic Structure and International Security: The Limits of the Liberal Case', *International Organization* 38(4): 597–624.

Cameron, A. Colin and Pravin K. Trivedi. 1998. *Regression Analysis of Count Data*. Cambridge: Cambridge University Press.

Cardoso, Fernando H. and Enzo Felleto. 1969/1979. *Dependency and Development in Latin America*. Berkeley, CA: University of California Press.

Carnegie Commission. 1997. *Preventing Deadly Conflict*. New York: Carnegie Corporation.

Carville, James. 1995. 'Survey of the World Economy: Who's in the Driving Seat?' *The Economist* (7 October): S3–S5.

Cashel-Cordo, Peter and Steven G. Craig. 1997. 'Donor Preferences and Recipient Fiscal Behavior: A Simultaneous Analysis of Foreign Aid', *Economic Inquiry* 35(3): 653–671.

Chang, Yuan-Ching. 1997. *Liberalism and Interdependence: Economic Models and International Relations*. Ph.D. Dissertation. Binghamton, NY: Binghamton University.

Cho, Dong-Sung. 1998. 'For the New Era of the Korean Economy', *Korea and World Affairs* 22(1): 17–22.

Choi, Gyu-Yun. 1994. Trade with the Enemy: Its Welfare Implication. Manuscript, Stanford, CA: Graduate School of Business, Stanford University.

Choucri, Nazli and Robert North. 1975. *Nations in Conflict: National Growth and International Violence*. San Francisco, CA: Freeman.

Cline, William R. 1997. *Trade and Income Distribution*. Washington, DC: Institute for International Economics.

Cohen, Benjamin J. 1973. *The Question of Imperialism*. New York: Basic Books.

Cohen, Benjamin J. 1998. *The Geography of Money*. Ithaca, NY: Cornell University Press.

Collett, Dave. 1994. *Modelling Survival Data in Medical Research*. London: Chapman & Hall.

Collier, Paul. 1999. 'On the Economic Consequences of War', *Oxford Economic Papers* 51: 168–183.

Collier, Paul and Anke Hoeffler. 2001. Greed and Grievance in Civil War. Washington, DC: World Bank. http:// econ.worldbank.org/programs/conflict/library/doc?id=1220 5.

Copeland, Dale C. 1996. 'Economic Interdependence and War: A Theory of Trade Expectations', *International Security* 20(4): 5–41.

Cox, David R. 1972. 'Regression Models and Life Tables', *Journal of the Royal Statistical Society, Series B* 34: 187–220.

Cox, W. Michael and Richard Alm. 1999. *Myths of Rich and Poor*. New York: Basic Books.

Crescenzi, Mark J.C. 2000. Exit Stage Market: Market Structure, Interstate Economic Interdependence and Conflict. Ph.D. Dissertation. Urbana, IL: University of Illinois, Urbana-Champaign.

Crucé, Emeric. 1623. *Le Nouveau Cynée, ou, Discours des Occasions et Moyens d'etablir une Paix Generale et la Liberté du Commerce par tout le Monde* [The New Cynée or the Discourse on the Opportunities and Means of Establishing a General Peace and Free Trade Globally]. Paris: Jacques Villery.

Davies, Graeme A. D. 2001. *Domestic Instability, Trade Expectations and the Initiation of International Conflict, 1950–1992*. Ph.D. dissertation. University of Essex.

de Melo, Jaime and Arvind Panagariya. 1993. 'Introduction', in Jaime de Melo and Arvind Panagariya, ed., *New Dimensions in Regional Integration*. New York: Cambridge University Press, 3–21.

de Soysa, Indra. 2002. 'Paradize is a Bazaar? Greed, Creed and Governance in Civil War, 1989–99', *Journal of Peace Research* 39(4): 395–416.

de Soysa, Indra and Nils Petter Gleditsch. 2002. *Conflict and Development in the Era of Globalization and Fragmentation: The Liberal Globalist Case*. Study for the Swedish Ministry of Foreign Affairs. Oslo: PRIO. [Also as 'The Liberal Globalist Case', in Björn Hettne and Bertil Odén, ed., *Global Governance in the 21st Century: Alternative Perspectives on World Order*. Stockholm: Almkvist & Wicksell, for Expert Group on Development Issues, 26–73].

de Soysa, Indra and John R. Oneal. 1999. 'Boon or Bane? Reassessing the Productivity of Foreign Direct Investment', *American Sociological Review* 64(5): 766–782.

de Soysa, Indra, John R. Oneal, and Yong-Hee Park. 1997. 'Testing Power-Transition Theory Using Alternative Measures of National Capabilities', *Journal of Conflict Resolution* 41(4): 509–528.

de Vries, Michiel S. 1990. 'Interdependence, Cooperation and Conflict: An Empirical Analysis', *Journal of Peace Research* 27(4): 429–444.

de Wilde, Jaap. 1991. *Saved from Oblivion: Interdependence Theory in the First Half of the Twentieth Century. A Study of Causality between War and Complex Interdependence*. Aldershot: Dartmouth.

de Wulf, Luc. 1981. 'Customs Valuation and the Faking of Invoices', *Economia Internazionale* 34(1): 13–33.

Deardorff, Alan V. 1984. 'Testing Trade Theories and Predicting Trade Flows', in Ronald W. Jones and Peter B. Kenen, ed., *Handbook of International Economics*. Amsterdam: North-Holland, 467–517.

Deardorff, Alan V. 1994. *The Stolper–Samuelson Theorem: A Golden Jubilee*. Ann Arbor, MI: University of Michigan Press.

Deardorff, Alan V. 1995. 'Determinants of Bilateral Trade: Does Gravity Work in a Neoclassical World?' *NBER Working Paper*, Cambridge, MA: National Bureau of Economic Research, December.

Deardorff, Alan V. 1998. 'Determinants of Bilateral Trade: Does Gravity Work in a Neoclassical World?' in Jeffrey A. Frankel, ed., *The Regionalization of the World Economy*, Chicago, IL: University of Chicago Press, 7–29.

Deardorff, Alan V. and Robert Stern. 1986. *The Michigan Model of World Trade*. Cambridge, MA: MIT Press.

Deininger, Klaus and Lyn Squire. 1996. 'A New Data Set Measuring Income Inequality', *World Bank Economic Review* 10(3): 565–591.

Deutsch, Karl W., Sidney Burrel, Robert Kann, Maurice Lee, Martin Lichterman, Raymond Lindgren, Francis Loewenheim, and Richard van Wagenen. 1957. *Political Community and the North Atlantic Area*. Princeton, NJ: Princeton University Press.

Diehl, Paul F. 1985. 'Contiguity and Military Escalation in Major Power Rivalries, 1816–1980', *Journal of Politics* 47(4): 1203–1211.

Dixon, William J. 1994. 'Democracy and the Peaceful Settlement of International Conflict', *American Political Science Review* 88(1): 1–17.

Dixon, William J. and Bruce Moon. 1993. 'Political Similarity and American Foreign Trade Patterns', *Political Research Quarterly* 46(1): 5–25.

DOD. 1999. *The Security Situation in the Taiwan Strait: Report to Congress*. Washington, DC: U.S. Department of Defense.

Dollar, David. 1992. 'Outward-oriented Developing Economies Really Do Grow More Rapidly: Evidence from 95 LDCs, 1976–85', *Economic Development and Cultural Change* 40(3): 523–544.

Dollar, David and Aart Kraay. 2001a. 'Trade, Growth, and Poverty'. *Working Paper*. Washington, DC: World Bank, June. http://econ.worldbank.org/files/2207_wps2615.pdf.

Dollar, David and Aart Kraay. 2001b. 'Growth Is Good for the Poor'. *Working Paper*. Washington, DC: World Bank. http://econ.worldbank.org/files/1696_wps2587.pdf.

Dollar, David and Aart Kraay. 2002. 'Spreading the Wealth', *Foreign Affairs* 81(1): 120–133.

Domke, William K. 1988. *War and the Changing Global System*. New Haven. CT: Yale University Press.

Dorussen, Han. 1996. 'Excluding Trade Agreements: Balance of Power and the Governance of Trade'. Ph.D. Dissertation. Austin, TX: University of Texas at Austin.

Dorussen, Han. 1997. 'Trade Coalitions and the Balance of Power'. Paper presented at the ECPR Joint Sessions of Workshops, Bern, 27 February–4 March.

Dorussen, Han. 1999. 'Balance of Power Revisited, Multi-Actor Models of Trade and Conflict', *Journal of Peace Research* 36(4): 443–462.

Dorussen, Han. 2001. 'Trade Coalitions and the Balance of Power', in U. Druwe, T. Plümper, and V. Kunz, ed., *Jahrbuch für Handlungs- und Entscheidungstheorie. Folge 1/2001*. Opladen: Leske und Budrich, 153–180.

Dorussen, Han. 2002. 'Trade and Conflict in Multi-country Models: A Rejoinder', *Journal of Peace Research* 39(1): 115–118.

Dorussen, Han and Jongryn Mo. 1995. Relative versus Absolute Gains: The Politics of Trade between Divided Countries. Manuscript. Austin, TX: University of Texas at Austin.

Doyle, Michael W. 1986. 'Liberalism and World Politics', *American Political Science Review* 80(4): 1151–1169.

Doyle, Michael W. 1997. *Ways of War and Peace: Realism, Liberalism, and Socialism.* New York: Norton.

Drucker, Peter F. 1997. 'The Global Economy and the Nation-State', *Foreign Affairs* 76(5): 159–171.

Edwards, Sebastian. 1998. 'Openness, Productivity and Growth: What Do We Really Know?' *Economic Journal* 108 (March): 383–398.

Ely, J. Edward. 1961. 'Variations between U.S. and Its Trading Partner Import and Export Statistics', *American Statistician* 15(2): 23–26.

Epstein, Martin, ed. 1913. *The Statesman's Yearbook, 1913.* London: Macmillan.

Esty, Daniel C., Jack Goldstone, Ted Robert Gurr, Barbara Harff, Pamela T. Wurko, Alan N. Unger and Robert S. Chen. 1998. *State Failure Task Force Report: Phase II Findings.* McLean, VA: Science Applications International Corporation.

Esty, Daniel et al. 1999. 'Environmental Task Force Report: Phase II Findings', *Environmental Change and Security Project Report* (5): 49–79; http://ecsp.si.edu/Ecsp_pdf.htm.

Ethier, Wilfred. 1988. *Modern International Economics.* New York: Norton. 2nd ed. 1995.

Ethier, Wilfred and Alok Ray. 1979. 'Gains from Trade and the Size of a Country', *Journal of International Economics* 9(1): 127–129.

Evans, Peter. 1997. 'The Eclipse of the State? Reflections on Stateness in an Era of Globalization', *World Politics* 50(1): 62–87.

Faber, Jan and Tom Nierop. 1989. *World Export Data, 1948–83.* ICPSR 9116. Ann Arbor, MI: Inter-university Consortium for Political and Social Research.

Fajnzylber, Pablo, Dainiel Lederman, and Norman Loayza, 2002. 'Inequality and Violent Crime', *Journal of Law and Economics* 45(1): 1–40.

Farber, Henry S. and Joanne Gowa. 1995. 'Polities and Peace', *International Security* 20(2): 123–146.

Fearon, James D. 1994. 'Domestic Political Audiences and the Escalation of International Disputes', *American Political Science Review* 88(3): 577–592.

Fearon, James D. 1995. 'Rationalist Explanations for War', *International Organization* 49(3): 379–414.

Fearon, James D. 1997. 'Bargaining over Objects That Influence Future Bargaining Power'. Paper presented at the 93rd Annual Meeting of the American Political Science Association, Washington, DC, 28–31 August.

Fearon, James D. and David D. Laitin. 2001. 'Ethnicity, Insurgency, and Civil War'. Paper presented to the 97th Annual Meeting of the American Political Science Association, San Francisco, CA, 30 August–2 September.

Feng, Yi. 1994. 'Trade, Conflict, and Alliances', *Defence and Peace Economics* 5(4): 301–313.

Fernández, Raquel and Jonathan Portes. 1998. 'Returns to Regionalism: An Evaluation of Nontraditional Gains from Regional Trade Agreements', *World Bank Economic Review* 12(2): 197–220.

Findlay, Ronald. 2001. 'Trade and Conflict', Paper Presented at the Annual Conference of the American Economic Association, New Orleans, LA.

Finger, J. Michael and Alexander Yeats. 1976. 'Effective Protection by Transportation Costs and Tariffs: A Comparison of Magnitudes', *Quarterly Journal of Economics* 90(1): 169–176.

Firebaugh, Glenn and Frank D. Beck. 1994. 'Does Economic Growth Benefit the Masses? Growth, Dependence, and Welfare in the Third World', *American Sociological Review* 59(5): 631–653.

Firebaugh, Glenn. 1992. 'Growth Effects of Foreign and Domestic Investment', *American Journal of Sociology* 98(1): 105–130.

Frank, A. G. 1994–1997. *EViews User's Guide.* Irvine, CA: Quantitative Micro Software.

Frankel, Jeffrey A. and David Romer. 1996. 'Trade and Growth: An Empirical Investigation', *NBER Working Paper* (5476). Cambridge, MA: National Bureau of Research.

Freeman, John R. 1983. 'Granger Causality and the Time Series Analysis of Political Relationships', *American Journal of Political Science* 27(2): 327–358.

Frey, Bruno S. and Marcel Kucher. 2000. 'History as Reflected in Capital Markets: The Case of World War II', *Journal of Economic History* 60(2): 468–496.

Friedman, Thomas L. 1996. 'Big Mac I', *New York Times*, 8 December.

Friedman, Thomas. 2000. *The Lexus and the Olive Tree.* New York: Farrar, Straus & Giroux.

Friedrich, Robert J. 1982. 'In Defense of Multiplicative Terms in Multiple Regression Equations', *American Journal of Political Science* 26(4): 797–833.

Galtung, Johan. 1971. 'A Structural Theory of Imperialism', *Journal of Peace Research* 8(2): 81–117.

Garrett, Geoffrey. 1999. 'Global Markets and National Politics: Collision Course or Virtuous Circle?' in Peter J. Katzenstein, Robert O. Keohane, and Stephen D. Krasner, ed., *Exploration and Contestation in the Study of World Politics.* Cambridge, MA: MIT Press, 147–184.

Garrett, Geoffrey and Barry R. Weingast. 1993. 'Ideas, Interests, and Institutions: Constructing the European Union's Internal Market', in Judith Goldstein and Robert O. Keohane, ed., *Ideas and Foreign Policy.* Ithaca, NY: Cornell University Press, 173–206.

Gartzke, Erik. 1998. 'Kant We All Just Get Along? Opportunity, Willingness, and the Origins of the Democratic Peace', *American Journal of Political Science* 42(1): 1–27.

Gartzke, Erik. 1999. 'War Is in the Error Term', *International Organization* 53(3): 567–587.

Gartzke, Erik. 2000. 'Preferences and the Democratic Peace', *International Studies Quarterly* 44(2): 191–212.

Gartzke, Erik and Quan Li. 2001. War, Peace, and the Invisible Hand: The Positive Political Externalities of Economic Globalization.' Columbia University and Pennsylvania State University. Typescript.

Gartzke, Erik and Quan Li. 2003. 'How Globalization Can Reduce International Conflict', chapter 6, this volume.

Gartzke, Erik, Quan Li, and Charles Bochmer. 2001. 'Investing in the Peace: Economic Interdependence and International Conflict', *International Organization* 55(2): 391–438.

Garver, John W. 1997. *Face Off: China, the United States, and Taiwan's Democratization.* Seattle, WA: University of Washington Press.

Gasiorowski, Mark. 1986. 'Economic Interdependence and International Conflict: Some Cross-National Evidence', *International Studies Quarterly* 30(1): 23–28.

Gasiorowski, Mark and Solomon W. Polachek. 1982. 'Conflict and Interdependence: East–West Trade and Linkages in the Era of Détente', *Journal of Conflict Resolution* 26(4): 709–729.

Gates, Scott and Sara McLaughlin. 1996. 'Rare Events, Relevant Dyads, and the Democratic Peace'. Paper presented at the 37th Annual Convention of the International Studies Association, San Diego, CA, 17–20 April.

Gates, Scott, Håvard Hegre, Mark Jones, and Håvard Strand. 2001. 'Institutional Inconsistency and Political Instability: Persistence and Change in Political Systems Revisited, 1800–1998'. Paper presented to the 42nd Annual Convention of the International Studies Association, Chicago, IL, 20–24 February.

Geller, Daniel S. 1992. 'Capability Concentration, Power Transition and War', *International Interactions* 17(3): 269–284.

Gelpi, Christopher and Joseph M. Grieco. 2003. 'Economic Interdependence, the Democratic State, and the Liberal Peace', in Edward D. Mansfield and Brian M. Pollins, ed., *Economic Interdependence and International Conflict: New Perspectives on an Enduring Debate*. Ann Arbor, MI: University of Michigan Press. [In press.]

Geraci, Vincent J. and Wilfried Prewo. 1982. 'An Empirical Demand and Supply Model of Multilateral Trade', *Review of Economics and Statistics* 64(3): 432–441.

Gerschenkron, Alexander. 1962. *Economic Backwardness in Historical Perspective.* Cambridge, MA: Harvard University Press.

Giersch, Herbert. 1995. *Wirtschaftsmoral als Standortfaktor.* Jena: Max-Planck-Institut zur Erforschung von Wirtschaftssystemen.

Gilpin, Robert. 1981. *War and Change in World Politics.* New York: Cambridge University Press.

Gilpin, Robert. 1987. *The Political Economy of International Relations.* Princeton, NJ: Princeton University Press.

Giltner, Philip. 1997. 'Trade in "Phoney" Wartime: The Danish–German "Maltese" Agreement of 9 October 1939', *International History Review* 19(2): 333–346.

Gissinger, Ranveig and Nils Petter Gleditsch. 1999. 'Globalization and Conflict. Welfare, Distribution, and Political Unrest', *Journal of World-Systems Research* 5(2): 327–365. http://csf.colorado.edu/jwsr/.

Gleditsch, Kristian S. 2002a. 'Expanded Trade and GDP', *Journal of Conflict Resolution* 46(4): 712–724.

Gleditsch, Kristian S. 2002b. *All International Politics is Local: The Diffusion of Conflict, Integration, and Democratization.* Ann Arbor, MI: University of Michigan Press.

Gleditsch, Kristian S. and Michael D. Ward. 2000. 'Peace and War in Time and Space: The Role of Democratization', *International Studies Quarterly* 44(1): 1–29.

Gleditsch, Nils Petter. 1968. 'The International Airline Network: A Test of the Zipf and Stouffer Hypotheses', *Peace Research Society, Papers* (11): 123–153.

Gleditsch, Nils Petter. 1995. 'Geography, Democracy, and Peace', *International Interactions* 20(4): 297–324.

Gleditsch, Nils Petter and Håvard Hegre. 1997. 'Peace and Democracy: Three Levels of Analysis', *Journal of Conflict Resolution* 41(2): 283–310.

Gochman, Charles S. 1991. 'Interstate Metrics: Conceptualizing, Operationalizing and Measuring the Geographic Proximity of States since the Congress of Vienna', *International Interactions* 17(1): 93–112.

Gochman, Charles S. and Zeev Maoz. 1984. 'Militarized Interstate Disputes, 1816–1976', *Journal of Conflict Resolution* 29(4): 585–615.

Goertz, Gary and Paul F. Diehl. 1992. *Territorial Changes and International Conflict.* London: Routledge.

Goldstein, Joshua S. 1988. *Long Cycles: Prosperity and War in the Modern Age*. New Haven, CT: Yale University Press.

Goldstein, Joshua S. and John R. Freeman. 1990. *Three-Way Street*. Chicago, IL: University of Chicago Press.

Gowa, Joanne. 1989. 'Bipolarity, Multipolarity and Free Trade', *American Political Science Review* 83(4): 1245–1256.

Gowa, Joanne. 1994. *Allies, Adversaries, and International Trade*. Princeton, NJ: Princeton University Press.

Gowa, Joanne. 1999. *Ballots and Bullets: The Elusive Democratic Peace*. Princeton, NJ: Princeton University Press.

Gowa, Joanne and Edward D. Mansfield. 1993. 'Power Politics and International Trade', *American Political Science Review* 87(2): 408–420.

Graeff, Peter. 2000. 'Ökonomische und nicht-ökonomische Gefahren für Demokratien' [Economic and Non-economic Dangers for Democracies], *Kölner Zeitschrift für Soziologie und Sozialpsychologie* 52(2): 226–245.

Gray, John. 1998. *False Dawn: The Delusions of Global Capitalism*. New York: New Press.

Green, Donald, Soo Yoon Kim, and David H. Yoon. 2001. 'Dirty Pool', *International Organization* 55(2): 441–468.

Greene, William H. 1997. *Econometric Analysis*, 3rd ed. Upper Saddle River, NJ: Prentice Hall.

Grieco, Joseph M. 1988. 'Anarchy and the Limits of Cooperation: A Realist Critique of the Newest Liberal Institutionalism', *International Organization* 42(3): 485–508.

Grieco, Joseph M. 1990. *Cooperation among Nations. Europe, America, and Non-tariff Barriers to Trade*. Ithaca, NY: Cornell University Press.

Grossman, Gene M. und Elhanan Helpman. 1994. 'Protection for Sale', *American Economic Review* 84(4): 833–850.

Grossman, Herschel I. and Minseong Kim. 1996. 'Predation and Production', in Michelle R. Garfinkel and Sergios Skaperdas, ed., *The Political Economy of Conflict and Appropriation*. Cambridge: Cambridge University Press, 57–72.

Guedes de Costa, Thomaz. 1998. 'The Role of the Armed Forces in Brazil's Democratization', in David R. Mares, ed., *Civil-Military Relations: Building Democracy and Regional Security in Latin America*. Boulder, CO: Westview, 223–237.

Gurr, Ted Robert. 1974. 'Persistence and Change in Political Systems, 1800–1971', *American Political Science Review* 65(4): 1482–1505.

Gurr, Ted Robert, Keith Jaggers, and Will H. Moore. 1989. *Polity II Codebook*. Boulder, CO: University of Colorado. http://www.icpsr.umich.edu /cgi/file?comp=none& study=9263&ds=1&dsfmt=CARD&filetype=CBPD.

Hamilton, Alexander. 1966. 'Report on Manufactures', reprinted in H. C. Syrett, ed., *The Papers of Alexander Hamilton*. New York: Columbia University Press. [Originally published in 1791.]

Harrison, Ann. 1996. 'Openness and Growth: A Time-Series, Cross-Country Analysis for Developing Countries', *Journal of Development Economics* 48(2): 419–447.

Hartland-Thunberg, Penelope. 1980. *Trading Blocs, U.S. Exports, and World Trade*. Boulder, CO: Westview.

Head, Allen C. 1995. 'Country Size, Aggregate Fluctuations, and International Risk Sharing', *Canadian Journal of Economics* 28(4): 1096–1119.

Heagerty, Patrick, Michael D. Ward, and Kristian S. Gleditsch. 2002. 'Windows of Opportunity: Window Subseries Empirical Variance Estimator in International Relations', *Political Analysis* 10(2): 304–317.

Hegre, Håvard. 1998. 'Does Trade Promote Peace?'. Paper presented at the 32nd Annual Meeting of the Peace Science Society International, East Brunswick, NJ, 16–18 October.

Hegre, Håvard. 1999. *The Limits of the Liberal Peace*. Cand. polit. thesis, Department of Political Science, University of Oslo.

Hegre, Håvard. 2000. 'Development and the Liberal Peace: What Does It Take to Be a Trading State?' *Journal of Peace Research* 37(1): 5–30. Reprinted as chapter 11 in this volume.

Hegre, Håvard. 2001. 'Trade, Size Asymmetry, and Militarized Conflict'. Paper Presented at the Annual Meeting of the American Political Science Association Meeting, San Francisco, CA, 30 August–2 September.

Hegre, Håvard. 2002. 'Trade Decreases Conflict More in Multi-actor Systems. A Comment to Dorussen', *Journal of Peace Research* 39(1): 115–118.

Hegre, Håvard, Tanja Ellingsen, Scott Gates, and Nils Petter Gleditsch. 2001. 'Toward a Democratic Civil Peace? Democracy, Political Change, and Civil War, 1816–1992', *American Political Science Review* 95(1): 33–48.

Held, David, Anthony McGrew, David Goldblatt, and Jonathan Perraton. 1999. *Global Transformation: Politics, Economics and Culture*. Stanford, CA: Stanford University Press.

Henderson, Errol. 1997. 'Culture or Contiguity? Ethnic Conflict, the Similarity of States and the Onset of Interstate War, 1820–1989', *Journal of Conflict Resolution* 41(5): 649–668.

Henderson, Errol. 1998. 'The Democratic Peace through the Lens of Culture, 1820–1989', *International Studies Quarterly* 42(3): 461–484.

Henderson, Errol and Richard Tucker. 2001. 'Clear and Present Strangers: The Clash of Civilizations and International Conflict', *International Studies Quarterly* 45(2): 317–338.

Hibbs, Douglas A. 1973. *Mass Political Violence. A Cross-National Causal Analysis*. New York: Wiley.

Higham, Charles. 1983. *Trading with the Enemy: The Nazi–American Money Plot, 1933–1949*. New York: Barnes & Noble.

Hillman, Arye. 1982. 'Declining Industries and Political-Support Protectionist Motives', *American Economic Review* 72(5): 1180–1187.

Hillman, Arye. 1989. *The Political Economy of Protection*. Chur: Harwood Academic.

Hillman, Arye and Heinrich Ursprung. 1988. 'Domestic Politics, Foreign Interests and International Trade Policy', *American Economic Review* 78(4): 729–745.

Hirschman, Albert O. 1945/1980. *National Power and the Structure of Foreign Trade*. Berkeley, CA: University of California Press.

Hirshleifer, Jack. 1991. 'The Paradox of Power', *Economics and Politics* 3(3): 177–199.

Hirshleifer, Jack. 1996. 'Anarchy and Its Breakdown', in Michelle R. Garfinkel and Sergios Skaperdas, ed., *The Political Economy of Conflict and Appropriation*. Cambridge: Cambridge University Press, 15–40.

Hirshleifer, Jack. 2000. 'The Macrotechnology of Conflict', *Journal of Conflict Resolution* 44(6): 773–792.

Hirst, Monica. 1998. 'Security Policy, Democratization, and Regional Integration in the Southern Cone', in Jorge I. Dominguez, ed., *International Security and Democracy*. Pittsburgh, PA: University of Pittsburgh Press, 102–118.

Hiscox, Michael J. 2001. 'Class versus Industry Cleavages: Inter-industry Factor Mobility and the Politics of Trade', *International Organization* 55(1): 1–46.

Holsti, Kalevi J. 1982. *Why Nations Realign: Foreign Policy Restructuring in the Post War World.* Boston, MA: Allen & Unwin.

Holsti, Ole, Terrence Hopmann, and John Sullivan. 1973. *Unity and Disintegration in International Alliances: Comparative Studies.* New York: Wiley.

Howard, Michael. 1976. *War in European History.* Oxford: Oxford University Press.

Huntington, Samuel P. 1993. 'Why International Primacy Matters', *International Security* 17(4): 52–83.

Huntington, Samuel P. 1996. *The Clash of Civilizations.* New York: Simon & Schuster.

Huxley, Tim. 1996. 'ASEAN's Role in the Emerging East Asian Regional Security Architecture', in Ian G. Cook, Marcus A. Doel, and Rex Li, ed., *Fragmented Asia: Regional Integration and National Disintegration in Pacific Asia.* Aldershot: Avebury, 29–52.

IMF. 1996a. *Direction of Trade.* (ICPSR 7628) Washington, DC: International Monetary Fund [producer]. Ann Arbor, MI: Inter-university Consortium for Political and Social Research [distributor].

IMF. 1996b. *World Economic Outlook.* Washington, DC: International Monetary Fund.

IMF. 1997. *Direction of Trade* (ICPSR 7628). Washington, DC: International Monetary Fund [producer]. Ann Arbor, MI: Inter-university Consortium for Political and Social Research [distributor].

Inglehart, Ronald. 1997. *Modernization and Postmodernization.* Princeton, NJ: Princeton University Press.

Irwin, Douglas A. 1996. *Against the Tide: An Intellectual History of Free Trade.* Princeton, NJ: Princeton University Press.

Italianer, Alexander. 1986. *Theory and Practice of International Trade Linkage Models.* Boston, MA: Kluwer.

Iversen, Torben and Thomas R. Cusack. 2000. 'The Causes of Welfare State Expansion: Deindustrialization or Globalization?' *World Politics* 52(3): 313–349.

Jackman, Simon. 2000. In and Out of War and Peace: Transitional Models of International Conflict. Stanford, CA: Department of Political Science, Stanford University.

Jaggers, Keith and Ted Robert Gurr. 1995. 'Tracking Democracy's Third Wave with the Polity III Data', *Journal of Peace Research* 32(4): 469–482.

Jaggers, Keith and Ted Robert Gurr. 1996. Polity III data. May. http://wizard.ucr.edu/~wm/polity/polity.html.

James, Patrick, Erik Solberg, and Murray Wolfson. 2000. 'Democracy and Peace: A Reply to Oneal and Russett', *Defense and Peace Economics* 11(2): 215–229.

Johnson, Harry G. 1987. 'Optimal Trade Intervention in the Presence of Domestic Distortions', in Jagdish N. Bhagwati, ed., *International Trade: Selected Readings.* Cambridge, MA: MIT Press, 235–263.

Johnson, Harry G. 1953/54. 'Optimum Tariffs and Retaliation', *Review of Economic Studies* 21(2): 142–153.

Jones, Daniel, Stuart A. Bremer, and J. David Singer. 1996. 'Militarized Interstate Disputes, 1816–1992: Rationales, Coding Rules and Empirical Patterns', *Conflict Management and Peace Science* 15(2): 163–213.

Jones, Ronald W. 1971. 'A Three-Factor Model in Theory, Trade, and History', in Jagdish N. Bhagwati et al., ed., *Trade, Balance of Payments, and Growth: Essays in Honor of C. P. Kindleberger.* Amsterdam: North-Holland, 3–21.

Jung, Ku-Hyun and Dong-Jae Kim. 1997. 'Globalization and International Competitiveness in South Korea'. Paper presented at the 17th World Congress of the International Political Science Association, Seoul.

Kaempfer, William H. and Anton D. Lowenberg. 1992. *International Economic Sanctions: A Public Choice Perspective*. Boulder, CO: Westview.

Kahneman, Daniel and Amos Tversky. 1979. 'Prospect Theory: An Analysis of Decisions under Risk', *Econometrica* 47: 263–291.

Kang, Heejoon and Rafael Reuveny. 2001. 'Exploring Multi-country Dynamic Interrelationships between Trade and Conflict', *Defence and Peace Economics* 12(4): 175–196.

Kant, Immanuel. 1795/1957. *Perpetual Peace*. New York: Liberal Arts Press. Also in 'Perpetual Peace: A Philosophical Sketch', in Hans Reiss, ed., *Kant's Political Writings*, translated by H. B. Nisbet. 2nd ed. Cambridge: Cambridge University Press, 1999, 93–130.

Kant, Immanuel. 1914. *Eternal Peace and Other International Essays*, translated by W. Hastie. Boston, MA: World Peace Foundation.

Kapstein, Ethan B. 1994. *Governing the Global Economy: International Finance and the State*. Cambridge, MA: Harvard University Press.

Kapstein, Ethan B. 1999. *Sharing the Wealth: Workers and the World Economy*. New York: Norton.

Kearney, A.T. 2001. 'Measuring Globalization', *Foreign Policy* 122: 56–65.

Keck, Otto. 1993. 'The New Institutionalism and the Relative-Gains-Debate', in Frank R. Pfetsch, ed., *International Relations and Pan-Europe*. Munster: Lit, 35–62.

Keohane, Robert O. 1990. 'Economic Liberalism Reconsidered', in John Dunn, ed., *The Economic Limits to Politics*. Cambridge: Cambridge University Press, 165–194.

Keohane, Robert O. 1993. 'Institutional Theory and the Realist Challenge after the Cold War', in David A. Baldwin, ed., *Neorealism and Neoliberalism: The Contemporary Debate*. New York: Columbia University Press, 269–300.

Keohane, Robert O. and Joseph S. Nye Jr. 1989. *Power and Interdependence: World Politics in Transition*. New York: HarperCollins.

Keynes, John Maynard. 1919. *The Economic Consequences of the Peace*. London: Macmillan.

Kim, Chae-Han. 1991. 'Third-Party Participation in Wars', *Journal of Conflict Resolution* 35(4): 659–677.

Kim, Soo Yeon. 1995. 'Bilateral Conflict and Trade, 1948–86: The Role of Economic Interdependence in Conflict Processes'. Paper Presented at the American Political Science Association Conference, Chicago, IL.

Kim, Soo Yeon. 1998. *Ties That Bind: The Role of Trade in International Conflict Processes, 1950–92*. Ph.D. Dissertation. Yale University. New Haven, CT.

Kim, Soo Yeon. 1999. 'Peace and Conflict among Trading States, 1950–1992'. Paper presented at the 40th Annual Meeting of the International Studies Association, Washington, DC, 16–20 February.

Kim, Woosang. 1992. 'Power Transitions and Great Power War from Westphalia to Waterloo', *World Politics* 45(1): 153–172.

Kindleberger, Charles P. 1969. *American Business Abroad: Six Lectures on Direct Investment*. New Haven, CT: Yale University Press.

King, Gary. 2001. 'Proper Nouns and Methodological Propriety: Pooling Dyads in International Relations Data', *International Organization* 55(2): 497–507.

King, Gary and Langche Zeng. 2001. 'Improving Forecasts of State Failure', *World Politics* 53(4): 623–658.

King, Gary and Langche Zeng. 2002. 'Explaining Rare Events in International Relations', *International Organization* 55(3): 693–715.

King, Gary, James Honaker, Anne Joseph, and Kenneth Scheve. 2001. 'Analyzing Incomplete Political Science Data: An Alternative Algorithm for Multiple Imputation', *American Political Science Review* 95(1): 49–70.

Kinsella, David and Bruce Russett. 2002. 'Conflict Emergence and Escalation in Interactive International Dyads', *Journal of Politics* 64(4): 1045–1068.

Kirchgässner, Gebhard. 1998. 'Globalisierung: Herausforderung für das 21. Jahrhundert' [Globalization: A Challenge for the 21st Century], *Außenwirtschaft* 53(1): 29–50.

Kocs, Stephen. 1995. 'Territorial Disputes and Interstate War, 1945–1987', *Journal of Politics* 57(1): 159–175.

Korzeniewicz, Roberto Patricio and Timothy Patrick Moran. 1997. 'World-Economic Trends in the Distribution of Income, 1965–1992', *American Journal of Sociology* 102(4): 1000–1039.

Krasner, Stephen D. 1999. *Sovereignty: Organized Hypocrisy*. Princeton, NJ: Princeton University Press.

Krugman, Paul R. 1981. 'Trade, Accumulation, and Uneven Development', *Journal of Development Economics* 8(2): 149–161.

Krugman, Paul R. 1995. 'Economic Conflicts among Nations: Perceptions and Reality', Paper presented at the Annual Convention of the American Economic Association, Washington, DC.

Krugman, Paul R. 1996. *Pop Internationalism*. Cambridge, MA: MIT Press.

Kugler, Jacek and Douglas Lemke. 1996. *Parity and War: Evaluations and Extensions of the War Ledger*. Ann Arbor, MI: University of Michigan Press.

Kuznets, Simon. 1955. 'Economic Growth and Income Inequality', *American Economic Review* 45(1): 1–28.

Kydd, Andrew. 1997. 'Game Theory and the Spiral Model', *World Politics* 49(3): 371–400.

Lagazio, Monica and Bruce Russett. 2002. 'A Neural Network Analysis of Militarized International Disputes, 1885–1992: Temporal Stability and Causal Complexity', in Paul F. Diehl, ed., *Toward a Scientific Understanding of War*, in press.

Laveda, Olgu. 1998. Telephone conversation, 24 April.

League of Nations. Various issues. *International Trade Statistics*. Geneva: League of Nations.

Leamer, Edward E. 1988. 'Measures of Openness', in Robert E. Baldwin, ed., *Trade Policy Issues and Empirical Analysis*. Chicago, IL: University of Chicago Press, 147–200.

Lemke, Douglas. 1995. 'The Tyranny of Distance. Redefining Relevant Dyads', *International Interactions* 21(1): 23–38.

Lemke, Douglas and William Reed. 1996. 'Regime Types and Status Quo Evaluations: Power Transition Theory and the Democratic Peace', *International Interactions* 22(2): 143–163.

Lemke, Douglas and William Reed. 2001. 'The Relevance of Politically Relevant Dyads', *Journal of Conflict Resolution* 45(1): 126–144.

Lenin, Vladimir I. 1916/1985. *Imperialism, the Highest State of Capitalism: A Popular Outline*. New York: International Publishers.

Levine, Ross and David Renelt. 1992. 'A Sensitivity Analysis of Cross-Country Growth Regressions', *American Economic Review* 82(4): 942–963.

Levy, Jack S. 1988. 'Domestic Politics and War', *Journal of Interdisciplinary History* 18(4): 653–673.

Levy, Jack S. 1989a. 'The Causes of War: A Review of Theories and Evidence', in Philip E. Tetlock et al., ed., *Behavior, Society, and Nuclear War*, vol. 1. New York: Oxford University Press, 209–313.

Levy, Jack S. 1989b. 'The Diversionary Theory of War: A Critique', in Manus I. Midlarsky, ed. *Handbook of War Studies*. Ann Arbor, MI: University of Michigan Press, 259–288.

Levy, Jack S. 1997. 'Prospect Theory, Rational Choice, and International Relations', *International Studies Quarterly* 41(1): 87–112.

Levy, Jack S. 1998. 'Historical Perspectives on Interdependence and Conflict'. Paper Presented at the 39th Annual Convention of the International Studies Association, Minneapolis, MN, 18–21 March.

Levy, Jack S. 2003. 'Economic Interdependence, Opportunity Costs, and War', in Edward D. Mansfield and Brian M. Pollins, ed., *Economic Interdependence and International Conflict: New Perspectives on an Enduring Debate*. Ann Arbor, MI: University of Michigan Press. [In press.]

Levy, Jack S. and Salvatore Ali. 1998. 'From Commercial Competition to Strategic Rivalry to War: The Evolution of the Anglo–Dutch Rivalry, 1609–1652', in Paul F. Diehl, ed., *The Dynamics of Enduring Rivalries*. Urbana-Champaign, IL: University of Illinois Press, 29–63.

Levy, Jack S. and Katherine Barbieri. 2001. 'Trading with the Enemy during Wartime: Theoretical Explanations and Historical Evidence'. Unpublished manuscript.

Lewis-Beck, Michael S. 1979. 'Some Economic Effects of Revolution: Models, Measurements, and the Cuban Evidence', *American Journal of Sociology* 84(5): 1127–1149.

Lewis-Beck, Michael S. and John R. Alford. 1980. 'Can Government Regulate Safety? The Coal Mine Example', *American Political Science Review* 74(3): 745–756.

Liang, Kung-Yee and Scott L. Zeger. 1986. 'Longitudinal Data Analysis Using Generalized Linear Models', *Biometrika* 73(1): 13–22.

Liberman, Peter. 1993. 'The Spoils of Conquest', *International Security* 18(2): 125–153.

Liberman, Peter. 1996. 'Trading with the Enemy: Security and Relative Economic Gains', *International Security* 21(1): 147–175.

Liberman, Peter. 1996. *Does Conquest Pay? The Exploitation of Occupied Industrial Societies*. Princeton, NJ: Princeton University Press.

Lichbach, Mark Irving. 1989. 'An Evaluation of "Does Economic Inequality Breed Political Conflict?" Studies', *World Politics* 41(4): 431–470.

Lindert, Peter H. and Jeffrey G. Williamson. 2001. 'Does Globalization Make the World More Unequal?' *NBER Working Paper* 8228. Cambridge, MA: National Bureau of Economic Research.

Linneman, Hans. 1966. *An Econometric Study of International Trade Flows. Contributions to Economic Analysis*. Amsterdam: North-Holland.

Lipset, Seymour Martin. 1959. 'Some Social Requisites of Democracy: Economic Development and Political Legitimacy', *American Political Science Review* 53(1): 69–105.

List, Friedrich. 1842. *Das Nationale System der politischen Ökonomie* [The National System of Political Economy], 2nd ed. Stuttgart: Cotta.

Luttwak, Edward. 1993. *The Endangered American Dream*. New York: Simon & Schuster.

McCloskey, Donald. 1993. 'The Insignificance of Statistical Significance', *Scientific American* 272(1): 32–33.

Machlup, Fritz. 1977. *A History of Thought on Economic Integration.* New York: Columbia University Press.

McLaughlin, Sara, Scott Gates, Håvard Hegre, Ranveig Gissinger, and Nils Petter Gleditsch. 1998. 'Timing the Changes in Political Structures: A New Polity Database', *Journal of Conflict Resolution* 42(2): 231–242.

McMillan, Susan M. 1997. 'Interdependence and Conflict', *Mershon International Studies Review* 41(1): 33–58.

Maddison, Angus. 1969. *Economic Growth in Japan and the USSR.* London: George Allen & Unwin.

Maddison, Angus. 1991. *Dynamic Forces in Capitalist Development: A Long-Run Comparative View.* Oxford: Oxford University Press.

Maddison, Angus. 1995. *Monitoring the World Economy: 1820–1992.* Paris: Organization for Economic Cooperation and Development.

Maddison, Angus. 1998. *Chinese Economic Performance in the Long Run.* Paris: OECD.

Magee, Stephen P. 1980. 'Three Simple Tests of the Stolper-Samuelson Theorem', in Peter Oppenheimer, ed., *Issues in International Economics.* London: Oriel, 138–153.

Magee, Stephen P., William A. Brock, and Leslie Young. 1989. *Black Hole Tariffs and Endogenous Policy Theory: Political Economy in General Equilibrium.* Cambridge: Cambridge University Press.

Mansfield, Edward D. 1994. *Power, Trade, and War.* Princeton, NJ: Princeton University Press.

Mansfield, Edward D. 1995. 'International Institutions and Economic Sanctions', *World Politics* 47(3): 575–605.

Mansfield, Edward D. 1998. 'The Proliferation of Preferential Trading Arrangements', *Journal of Conflict Resolution* 42 (5): 523–543.

Mansfield, Edward D. and Rachel Bronson. 1997. 'Alliances, Preferential Trading Arrangements, and International Trade', *American Political Science Review* 91(1): 97–104.

Mansfield, Edward D. and Jon C. Pevehouse. 2000. 'Trade Blocs, Trade Flows, and International Conflict', *International Organization* 54(4): 775–808.

Mansfield, Edward D. and Brian M. Pollins. 2001. 'The Study of Interdependence and Conflict: Recent Advances, Open Questions, and Directions for Future Research', *Journal of Conflict Resolution* 45(6): 834–859.

Mansfield, Edward D. and Brian M. Pollins, ed. 2003. *Economic Interdependence and International Conflict: New Perspectives on an Enduring Debate.* Ann Arbor, MI: University of Michigan Press.

Mansfield, Edward D., Helen V. Milner, and B. Peter Rosendorff. 2002. 'Why Democracies Cooperate More: Electoral Control and International Trade Agreements', *International Organization* 56(3): 477–513.

Mansfield, Edward D., Jon C. Pevehouse, and David H. Bearce. 1999. 'Preferential Trading Arrangements and Military Disputes', *Security Studies* 9(1–2): 92–118.

Manzetti, Luigi. 1993–94. 'The Political Economy of MERCOSUR', *Journal of Interamerican Studies and World Affairs* 35(4): 101–141.

Maoz, Zeev. 1996. *Domestic Sources of Global Change.* Ann Arbor, MI: University of Michigan Press.

Maoz, Zeev. 1999. Dyadic Militarized Interstate Disputes (DYMID1.1) Dataset Version 1.1. ftp://spirit.tau.ac.il/zeevmaos/dyadmid60.xls. August.

Maoz, Zeev and Bruce M. Russett. 1992. 'Alliance, Contiguity, Wealth, and Political Stability: Is the Lack of Conflict among Democracies a Statistical Artifact?' *International Interactions* 18(3): 245–267.

Maoz, Zeev and Bruce Russett. 1993. 'Normative and Structural Causes of Democratic Peace', *American Political Science Review* 87(3): 624–638.

Marquez, Jaime. 1992. 'The Autonomy of Trade Elasticities: Choice and Consequences', *International Finance Discussion Papers* (422). Washington, DC: International Monetary Fund.

Martin, Christian W., Thomas Plümper, and Gerald Schneider. 2001. 'Economic Openness in the Developing Countries: An Empirical Investigation Using CACAO'. Unpublished Manuscript, University of Konstanz.

Martin, Hans-Peter and Harald Schumann. 1998. *The Global Trap: Globalization and the Assault on Democracy and Prosperity*. New York: Zed and St. Martin's. [Originally published in 1996 as *Die Globalisierungsfalle.Der Angriff auf Demokratie und Wohlstand*. Reinbek bei Haimburg: Rowohlt.]

Martin, Lisa. 1992. *Coercive Cooperation: Explaining Multilateral Economic Sanctions*. Princeton, NJ: Princeton University Press.

Mastanduno, Michael. 1991. 'Do Relative Gains Matter? America's Response to Japanese Industrial Policy', *International Security* 16(1): 73–113.

Mastanduno, Michael. 1992. *Economic Containment: COCOM and the Politics of East-West Trade*. Ithaca, NY: Cornell University Press.

Mathews, Jessica. 1997. 'Power Shift', *Foreign Affairs* 76(1): 50–66.

Mazarr, Michael J. and Jeffrey G. Lewis. 1998. 'Global Economic Trends and the RoK Economy', *Korea and World Affairs* 22(1): 23–48.

Mazur, Jay. 2000. 'Labor's New Internationalism', *Foreign Affairs* 79(1): 79–93.

Mearsheimer, John J. 1990a. 'Back to the Future: Instability in Europe after the Cold War', *International Security* 15(1): 5–56.

Mearsheimer, John J. 1990b. 'Why We Will Soon Miss the Cold War', *Atlantic Monthly* 266(2): 35–50.

Mitchell, B. R. 1962. *Abstract of British Historical Statistics*. Cambridge: Cambridge University Press.

Mitchell, B. R. 1998a. *International Historical Statistics: Europe, 1750–1993*, 4th ed. New York: Stockton.

Mitchell, B. R. 1998b. *International Historical Statistics: The Americas, 1750–1993*, 4th ed. New York: Stockton.

Mitchell, B. R. 1998c. *International Historical Statistics: Africa, Asia and Oceania, 1750–1993*, 3rd ed. New York: Stockton.

Modelski, George and William R. Thompson. 1996. *Leading Sectors and World Powers: The Coevolution of Global Economics and Politics*. Columbia, SC: University of South Carolina Press.

Montesquieu, Charles de Secondat, Baron de. 1748/1991. *The Spirit of the Laws*. Cambridge: Cambridge University Press.

Moore, Frank W. 2000. 'China's Military Capabilities', *Institute for Defense and Disarmament Studies*, www.comw.org/cmp/fulltext/iddschina.html

Moravcsik, Andrew. 1997. 'Taking Preferences Seriously: A Liberal Theory of International Politics', *International Organization* 51(4): 513–553.

Morgenstern, Oskar. 1963. *On the Accuracy of Economic Observations*. Princeton, NJ: Princeton University Press.

Morgenthau, Hans J. 1958. *Politics among Nations: The Struggle for Power and Peace*. New York: Knopf.

Morrow, James D. 1991. 'Alliances and Asymmetry: An Alternative to the Capability Aggregation Model of Alliances', *American Journal of Political Science* 35(4): 904–933.

Morrow, James D. 1997. 'When Do "Relative Gains" Impede Trade?' *Journal of Conflict Resolution* 41(1): 147–174. Reprinted as chapter 3 in this volume.

Morrow, James D. 1999. 'How Could Trade Affect Conflict?' *Journal of Peace Research* 36(4): 481–489.

Morrow, James D., Randolph M. Siverson, and Tressa Tabares. 1998. 'The Political Determinants of International Trade: The Major Powers, 1907–1990', *American Political Science Review* 92(3): 649–661.

Morrow, James D., Randolph M. Siverson, and Tressa Tabares. 1999. 'Correction to the Political Determinants of International Trade', *American Political Science Review* 93(4): 931–933.

Mousseau, Michael. 1998. 'Democracy, Development, and Common Interests: An Analysis of UN Voting Patterns'. Paper presented at the Annual Meeting of the Peace Science Society International, East Brunswick, NJ, 16–18 October.

Mousseau, Michael. 2000. 'Market Prosperity, Democratic Consolidation, and Democratic Peace', *Journal of Conflict Resolution* 44(4): 472–507.

Mousseau, Michael, Håvard Hegre, and John R. Oneal. 2003. 'How the Wealth of Nations Conditions the Liberal Peace', *European Journal of International Relations* 9(2). [In press.]

Muller, Edward N. 1985. 'Income Inequality, Regime Repressions and Political Violence', *American Sociological Review* 50(1): 47–67.

Muller, Edward N. 1986. 'Income Inequality and Political Violence', *American Sociological Review* 51(3): 441–445.

Muller, Edward N. 1995. 'Economic Determinants of Democracy', *American Sociological Review* 60(6): 966–982.

Muller, Edward N. and Mitchell A. Seligson. 1987. 'Inequality and Insurgency', *American Political Science Review* 82(2): 425–451.

Murdoch, James C. and Todd Sandler. 1982. 'A Theoretical and Empirical Analysis of NATO', *Journal of Conflict Resolution* 26(2): 237–263.

Murdoch, James C. and Todd Sandler. 2002. 'Economic Growth, Civil Wars, and Spatial Spillovers', *Journal of Conflict Resolution*, 46(1): 91–110.

Myerson, Roger B. and Mark A. Satterthwaite. 1983. 'Efficient Mechanisms for Bilateral Trading', *Journal of Economic Theory* 29: 265–281.

Neff, Stephen C. 1990. *Friends But No Allies: Economic Liberalism and the Law of Nations.* New York: Columbia University Press.

Niehans, Jürg. 1990. *A History of Economic Theory. Classic Contributions, 1720–1980.* Baltimore, MD: Johns Hopkins University Press.

Nielsen, François and Arthur S. Alderson. 1995. 'Income Inequality, Development, and Dualism: Results from an Unbalanced Cross-National Panel', *American Sociological Review* 60(5): 674–710.

Niou, Emerson M. S. and Peter Ordeshook. 1990. 'Stability in Anarchic International Systems', *American Political Science Review* 84(4): 1207–1234.

Niou, Emerson M. S. and Peter Ordeshook. 1994. 'Alliances versus Federations: An Analysis with Military and Economic Capabilities Distinguished'. *Social Science Working Paper* (894). Pasadena, CA: California Institute of Technology, July.

Niskanen, William. 1971. *Bureaucracy and Representative Government.* Chicago, IL: Aldine–Atherton.

Nye, Joseph S. Jr. 1971. *Peace in Parts: Integration and Conflict in Regional Organization.* Boston, MA: Little, Brown.

Nye, Joseph S. Jr. 1988. 'Neorealism and Neoliberalism', *World Politics* 40(2): 235–251.

Obstfeld, Maurice and Kenneth Rogoff. 1996. *Foundations of International Macroeconomics*. Cambridge, MA: MIT Press.

Ohmae, Kenichi. 1996. *The End of the Nation State*. New York: Free Press.

Olson, Mancur. 1996. 'Big Bills Left on the Sidewalk: Why Some Nations Are Rich, and Others Poor', *Journal of Economic Perspectives* 10(2): 3–24.

Oneal, John R. 2003. 'Empirical Support for the Liberal Peace', in Edward D. Mansfield and Brian M. Pollins, ed., *Economic Interdependence and International Conflict: New Perspectives on an Enduring Debate*. Ann Arbor, MI: University of Michigan Press. [In press.]

Oneal, John R. and James Lee Ray. 1997. 'New Tests of the Democratic Peace: Controlling for Economic Interdependence, 1950–85', *Political Research Quarterly* 50(4): 751–775.

Oneal, John R. and Bruce M. Russett. 1997. 'The Classical Liberals Were Right: Democracy, Interdependence, and Conflict, 1950–85', *International Studies Quarterly* 41(2): 267–294.

Oneal, John R. and Bruce M. Russett. 1999a. 'Is the Liberal Peace Just an Artifact of Cold War Interests? Assessing Recent Critiques', *International Interactions* 25(3): 1–29.

Oneal, John R. and Bruce M. Russett. 1999b. 'The Kantian Peace: The Pacific Benefits of Democracy, Interdependence, and International Organizations, 1885–1992', *World Politics* 52(1): 1–37.

Oneal, John R. and Bruce M. Russett. 1999c. 'Assessing the Liberal Peace with Alternative Specifications: Trade Still Reduces Conflict', *Journal of Peace Research* 36(4): 423–442.

Oneal, John R. and Bruce M. Russett. 2001. 'Clear and Clean: The Fixed Effects of the Liberal Peace', *International Organization* 55(2): 469–485.

Oneal, John R., Bruce M. Russett, and Michael Berbaum. 2003. '*Causes* of Peace: Democracy, Interdependence, and International Organizations, 1885–1992', *International Studies Quarterly* 47(1). [In press.]

Oneal, John R., Frances Oneal, Zeev Maoz, and Bruce Russett. 1996. 'The Liberal Peace: Interdependence, Democracy and International Conflict, 1950–1986', *Journal of Peace Research* 33(1): 11–28.

Organski, A. F. K. 1958. *World Politics*. New York: Knopf.

Organski, A. F. K. and Jacek Kugler. 1980. *The War Ledger*. Chicago, IL: University of Chicago Press.

Orr, Robert M. 1989. 'Collaboration or Conflict? Foreign Aid and U.S.-Japan Relations', *Pacific Affairs* 62(6): 476–489.

Papayoanou, Paul A. 1996. 'Interdependence, Institutions, and the Balance of Power: Britain, Germany, and World War I', *International Security* 20(4): 42–76.

Papayoanou, Paul A. 1997. 'Economic Interdependence and the Balance of Power', *International Studies Quarterly* 41(1): 113–140.

Papayoanou, Paul A. 1999. *Power Ties: Economic Interdependence*. Ann Arbor, MI: University of Michigan Press.

Pares, Richard. 1963. *War and Trade in the West Indies*. London: Frank Cass.

Parkinson, C. N., ed. 1948. *The Trade Winds: A Study of British Overseas Trade during the French Wars, 1793–1815*. London: George Allen & Unwin.

Payne, James L. 1989. *Why Nations Arm*. Oxford: Blackwell.

Pei, Minxin. 1998. 'Is China Democratizing?' *Foreign Affairs* 77(1): 68–82.

Peltzman, Sam. 1976. 'Towards a More General Theory of Regulation?' *Journal of Law and Economics* 19: 211–240.

Peña, Felix. 1993. 'Strategies for Macroeconomic Coordination: Reflections on the Case of MERCOSUR', in Peter H. Smith, ed., *The Challenge of Integration: Europe and the Americas*. New Brunswick, NJ: Transaction Publishers, 183–200.

Penubarti, Mohan and Michael D. Ward. 2000. 'Commerce and Democracy'. *Working Paper* (6). Seattle, WA: Center for Statistics and the Social Sciences, University of Washington.

Plümper, Thomas. 2001. *Weltwirtschaft und Wohlfahrt. Die Politischen Determinanten des Wachstumsbeitrages der außenwirtschaftlichen Offenheit* [World Trade and Welfare. The Political Determinants of the Effect of Economic Openness on Growth]. Unpublished Habilitation Thesis, University of Konstanz.

Poirier, Dale J. and Paul A. Ruud. 1988. 'Probit with Dependent Observations', *Review of Economic Studies* 55(4): 593 –614.

Polachek, Solomon W. 1978. 'Dyadic Dispute: An Economic Perspective', *Papers of the Peace Science Society* 28: 67–80.

Polachek, Solomon W. 1980. 'Conflict and Trade', *Journal of Conflict Resolution* 24(1): 57–78.

Polachek, Solomon W. 1992. 'Conflict and Trade: An Economics Approach to Political International Interactions', in Walter Isard and Charles H. Anderton, ed., *Economics of Arms Reduction and the Peace Process*. Amsterdam: North–Holland, 89–120.

Polachek, Solomon W. 1994. 'Cooperation and Conflict among Democracies: Why Do Democracies Cooperate More and Fight Less?' Paper presented at the Annual Meeting of the Peace Science Society International, Urbana-Champaign, IL.

Polachek, Solomon W. 1997. 'Why Do Democracies Cooperate More and Fight Less: The Relationship between International Trade and Cooperation', *Review of International Economics* 5(3): 295–309.

Polachek, Solomon W. 2001. 'Trade Based Interactions: An Interdisciplinary Perspective'. Revised version of the Presidential Address delivered at the Annual Meeting of the Peace Science Society International, October 2000. New Haven, CT. Available at: www.binghamton.edu/econ/wp02/wp0202.pdf

Polachek, Solomon W. and Judith McDonald. 1992. 'Strategic Trade and the Incentive for Cooperation', in Manas Chatterji and Linda Rennie Forcey, ed., *Disarmament, Economic Conversion, and Management of Peace*, New York: Praeger, 273–284.

Polachek, Solomon W. and John Robst. 1998. 'Cooperation and Conflict among Democracies: Why Do Democracies Cooperate More and Fight Less?' in Murray Wolfson, ed., *The Political Economy of War and Peace*. Boston, MA: Kluwer, 127–154.

Polachek, Solomon W., Yuan-Ching Chang, and John Robst. 1997. 'Geographic Proximity and Interdependence: The Relationship between Distance, Trade and International Interactions'. *Working Paper*, Binghamton, NY: Chinese Cultural University and SUNY, Binghamton University.

Polachek, Solomon W., John Robst, and Yuan-Ching Chang. 1999. 'Liberalism and Interdependence: Extending the Trade-Conflict Model', *Journal of Peace Research* 36(4): 405–422

Pollins, Brian M. 1989a. 'Does Trade Still Follow the Flag?' *American Political Science Review* 83(2): 465–480.

Pollins, Brian M. 1989b. 'Conflict, Cooperation, and Commerce: The Effects of International Political Interactions on Bilateral Trade Flows', *American Journal of Political Science* 33(3): 737–761.

Pomfret, Richard. 1997. *The Economics of Regional Trading Arrangements*. New York: Oxford University Press.

Posner, Richard A. 1997. 'Equality, Wealth and Political Stability', *Journal of Law, Economics, and Organization* 13(2): 344–365.

Powell, Robert. 1991. 'Absolute and Relative Gains in International Relations Theory', *American Political Science Review* 85(4): 1303–1320.

Powell, Robert. 1993. 'Guns, Butter, and Anarchy', *American Political Science Review* 87(1): 115–132.

Powell, Robert. 1996. 'Stability and the Distribution of Power', *World Politics* 48(2): 239–267.

Powell, Robert. 1997. 'Bargaining in the Shadow of Shifting Power'. Paper presented at the 93rd Annual Meeting of the American Political Science Association, Washington, DC, 28–31 August.

Powell, Robert. 1999. *In the Shadow of Power*. Princeton, NJ: Princeton University Press.

Przeworski, Adam, Michael E. Alvarez, José Antonio Cheibub, and Fernando Limongi. 2000. *Democracy and Development. Political Institutions and Well-Being in the World, 1950–1990*. Cambridge: Cambridge University Press.

Quinn, Dennis P. 2000. 'Democracy and International Financial Liberalization'. Unpublished paper, Georgetown University.

Raknerud, Arvid and Håvard Hegre. 1997. 'The Hazard of War: Reassessing the Evidence for the Democratic Peace', *Journal of Peace Research* 34(4): 385–404.

Rasler, Karen A. and William R. Thompson. 1989. *War and State Making: The Shaping of the Global Powers*. Boston, MA: Unwin Hyman.

Reed, William. 2000. 'A Unified Statistical Model of Conflict Onset and Escalation', *American Journal of Political Science* 44(1): 84–93.

Reinicke, Wolfgang H. 1998. *Global Public Policy*. Washington, DC: Brookings.

Rengger, N. J., with John Campbell. 1995. *Treaties and Alliances of the World*, 6th ed. New York: Stockton.

Reuveny, Rafael. 1999a. 'The Political Economy of Israeli–Palestinian Interdependence', *Policy Studies Journal* 27(4): 643–664.

Reuveny, Rafael. 1999b. 'Israeli–Palestinian Economic Interdependence Reconsidered', *Policy Studies Journal* 27(4): 668–671.

Reuveny, Rafael. 2000. 'The Trade and Conflict Debate: A Survey of Theory, Evidence and Future Research', *Peace Economics, Peace Science, and Public Policy* 6(1): 23–49.

Reuveny, Rafael. 2001a. 'Bilateral Import, Export and Political Conflict Simultaneity', *International Studies Quarterly* 45(1): 131–158.

Reuveny, Rafael. 2001b. 'Disaggregated Trade and Conflict: Exploring Propositions in a Simultaneous Framework', *International Politics* 38(3): 401–428.

Reuveny, Rafael and Heejoon Kang. 1996a. 'International Trade, Political Conflict/Cooperation, and Granger Causality', *American Journal of Political Science* 40(3): 943–970.

Reuveny, Rafael and Heejoon Kang. 1996b. 'International Conflict and Cooperation: Splicing COPDAB and WEIS Series', *International Studies Quarterly* 40(2): 281–306.

Reuveny, Rafael and Heejoon Kang. 1998. 'Bilateral Trade and Political Conflict/Cooperation: Do Goods Matter?' *Journal of Peace Research* 35(5): 581–602.

Reuveny, Rafael and Heejoon Kang. 2003. 'A Simultaneous Equations Model of Bilateral Trade Value, Conflict, and Cooperation', *Review of International Economics*, forthcoming.

Reuveny, Rafael and John W. Maxwell. 1998. 'Free Trade and Arms Races', *Journal of Conflict Resolution* 42(6): 771–803.

Ricardo, David. 1981/1817. *The Principles of Political Economy and Taxation.* Cambridge: Cambridge University Press.

Richardson, Lewis F. 1960. *Arms and Insecurity.* Chicago, IL: Quadrangle.

Richardson, Neil R. 1978. *Foreign Policy and Economic Dependence.* Austin, TX: University of Texas Press.

Riker, William H. 1962. *The Theory of Political Coalitions.* New Haven, CT: Yale University Press.

Ripsman, Norrin M. and Jean-Marc F. Blanchard. 1996/97. 'Commercial Liberalism under Fire: Evidence from 1914 and 1936', *Security Studies* 6(2): 4–50.

Rodrik, Dani. 1997. *Has Globalization Gone Too Far?* Washington, DC: Institute for International Economics.

Rodrik, Dani. 1999. 'Democracies Pay Higher Wages', *Quarterly Journal of Economics* 14(3): 707–738.

Rogowski, Ronald. 1989. *Commerce and Coalitions.* Princeton, NJ: Princeton University Press.

Rosecrance, Richard. 1986. *The Rise of the Trading State: Commerce and Conquest in the Modern World.* New York: Basic Books.

Rowen, Henry S. 1996. 'China: A Short March to Democracy?' *National Interest* (45): 61–70.

Ruffin, Roy J. and Ronald Jones. 1977. 'Protection and Real Wages: The Neoclassical Ambiguity', *Journal of Economic Theory* 14(2): 237–248.

Ruggie, John G. 1982. 'International Regimes, Transactions and Change: Embedded Liberalism in the Postwar Economic Order', *International Organization* 36(?): 379–416.

Ruggie, John G. 1993. 'Territoriality and Beyond: Problematizing Modernity in International Relations', *International Organization* 47(1): 139–174.

Russett, Bruce M. 1967. *International Regions and the International System: A Study in Political Ecology.* Chicago, IL: Rand McNally.

Russett, Bruce M. 1998. 'A Neo-Kantian Perspective: Democracy, Interdependence, and International Organizations in Building Security Communities', in Emanuel Adler and Michael Barnett, ed., *Security Communities in Comparative Perspective.* Cambridge: Cambridge University Press, 369–394.

Russett, Bruce. 2003. 'Violence and Disease: Trade as Suppressor to Conflict When Suppressors Count', in Edward D. Mansfield and Brian M. Pollins, ed., *Economic Interdependence and International Conflict: New Perspectives on an Enduring Debate.* Ann Arbor, MI: University of Michigan Press.

Russett, Bruce M. and Harry Bliss. 1998. 'Democratic Trading Partners: The Liberal Connection, 1962–1989', *Journal of Politics* 60(4): 1126–1147.

Russett, Bruce M. and John R. Oneal. 2001. *Triangulating Peace. Democracy, Interdependence, and International Organization.* New York: Norton.

Russett, Bruce M., John R. Oneal, and Michaelene Cox. 2000. 'Clash of Civilizations, or Realism and Liberalism Déjà Vu?' *Journal of Peace Research* 37(5): 583–608.

Russett, Bruce M., John R. Oneal, and David R. Davis. 1998. 'The Third Leg of the Kantian Tripod for Peace: International Organizations and Militarized Disputes, 1950–85', *International Organization* 52(3): 441–467.

Sabrosky, Alan. 1980. 'Interstate Alliances: Their Reliability and the Expansion of War', in J. David Singer, ed., *The Correlates of War: II.* New York: Free Press, 161–198.

Sachs, Jeffrey D. 2001. 'The Curse of Natural Resources', *European Economic Review* 45(4–6): 827–838.

Sachs, Jeffrey D. and Andrew M. Warner. 1995. 'Economic Reform and the Process of Global Integration', *Brookings Papers on Economic Activity* (1): 1–118.

Sachs, Jeffrey D. and Andrew Warner. 1999. 'Natural Resource Intensity and Economic Growth', in Jörg Mayer, Brian Chambers and Ayisha Farooq, ed., *Development Policies in Natural Resource Economies*. Cheltenham, MA: Elgar, 13–38.

Saeger, Steven S. 1997. 'Globalization and Deindustrialization: Myth and Reality in the OECD', *Weltwirtschaftliches Archiv* 133(4): 579–607.

Sala-I-Martin, Xavier X. 1997. 'I Just Ran Two Million Regressions', *American Economic Review* 87(2): 178–183.

Sassen, Saskia. 1996. *Losing Control?: Sovereignty in an Age of Globalization.* New York: Columbia University Press.

Saxonhouse, Gary R. 1993. 'Trading Blocs and East Asia', in Jaime de Melo and Arvind Panagariya, ed., *New Dimensions in Regional Integration*, New York: Cambridge University Press, 388–415.

Sayrs, Lois W. 1989. 'Trade and Conflict Revisited: Do Politics Matter?' *International Interaction* 14(2): 155–175.

Sayrs, Lois W. 1990. 'Expected Utility and Peace Science: An Assessment of Trade and Conflict', *Conflict Management and Peace Science* 11(1): 17–44.

Schneider, Gerald and Katherine Barbieri, ed. 1999. 'Trade and Conflict', special issue of *Journal of Peace Research* 36(4).

Schneider, Gerald and Günther G. Schulze. 2002. Trade and Armed Conflict: The Domestic Foundations of Liberal Peace. Unpublished Paper.

Schneider, Gerald and Günther G. Schulze. 2003. 'The Domestic Roots of Commercial Liberalism: A Sector-Specific Approach', chapter 5, this volume.

Schultz, Kenneth A. 1999. 'Do Democratic Institutions Constrain or Inform? Contrasting Two Institutional Perspectives on Democracy and War', *International Organization* 53(2): 233–266.

Schultz, Kenneth A. 2001. *Democracy and Coercive Diplomacy.* Cambridge: Cambridge University Press.

Schulze, Günther G. 2000. *The Political Economy of Capital Controls.* Cambridge: Cambridge University Press.

Schumpeter, Joseph A. 1942. *Capitalism, Socialism and Democracy.* New York: Harper & Brothers.

Seiglie, Carlos. 1998. 'Defence Spending in a Neo-Ricardian World', *Economica* 65 (258): 193–210.

Selfridge, H. Gordon. 1918. *The Romance of Commerce.* London: Bodley Head.

Sheikh, Munir. 1974. 'Underinvoicing of Imports in Pakistan', *Oxford Bulletin of Economics and Statistics* 36(4): 287–296.

Siebert, Horst. 1998. *Arbeitslos ohne Ende?* [No End to Unemployment?]. Frankfurt/Main: FAZ-Verlag.

Simon, Michael and Erik Gartzke. 1996. 'Political System Similarity and the Choice of Allies', *Journal of Conflict Resolution* 40(4): 617–635.

Singer, J. David. 1995. Alliances, 1816–1984. Correlates of War Project, University of Michigan.

Singer, J. David and Melvin Small. 1966a. 'Formal Alliances, 1815–1939: A Qualitative Description', *Journal of Peace Research* 3(1): 1–32.

Singer, J. David and Melvin Small. 1966b. 'National Alliance Commitments and War Involvement, 1815–1945', *Papers, Peace Research Society (International)* 5: 109–140.

Singer, J. David and Melvin Small. 1993. *National Material Capabilities Dataset.* ICPSR 9903. Ann Arbor, MI: Inter-university Consortium for Political and Social Research.

Singer, J. David and Melvin Small. 1994. *Correlates of War Project: International and Civil War Data, 1816–1992.* ICPSR 9905. Ann Arbor, MI: Inter-university Consortium for Political and Social Research.

Singer, J. David and Melvin Small. 1995. National Military Capabilities Data. Correlates of War Project, University of Michigan. Modified 12/28/94.

Singer, J. David, Stuart A. Bremer, and John Stuckey. 1972. 'Capability Distribution, Uncertainty, and Major Power War, 1820–1965', in Bruce M. Russett, ed., *Peace, War, and Numbers.* Beverly Hills, CA: Sage, 19–48.

SIPRI, 1982, 1992. *World Armaments and Disarmament: SIPRI Yearbook.* London/Oxford: Taylor & Francis/Oxford University Press.

Siverson, Randolph and Joel King. 1979. 'Alliances and the Expansion of War', in J. David Singer and Michael D. Wallace, ed., *To Augur Well: Early Warning Indicators in World Politics.* Beverly Hills, CA: Sage, 37–50.

Siverson, Randolph and Joel King. 1980. 'Attributes of National Alliance Membership and War Participation, 1815–1965', *American Journal of Political Science* 24(1): 1–15.

Siverson, Randolph and Harvey Starr. 1991. *Diffusion of War: A Study of Opportunity and Willingness.* Ann Arbor, MI: University of Michigan Press.

Skaperdas, Sergios. 1992. 'Cooperation, Conflict, and Power in the Absence of Property Rights', *American Economic Review* 82(4): 720–739.

Skaperdas, Sergios and Constantinos Syropoulos, 1996. 'Competitive Trade with Conflict', in Michelle R. Garfinkel and Sergios Skaperdas, ed., *The Political Economy of Conflict and Appropriation.* Cambridge: Cambridge University Press, 73–96.

Small, Melvin and J. David Singer. 1969. 'Formal Alliances, 1816–1965: An Extension of the Basic Data', *Journal of Peace Research* 6(3): 257–282.

Small, Melvin and J. David Singer. 1982. *Resort to Arms: International and Civil Wars, 1816–1980.* Beverly Hills, CA: Sage.

Smith, Adam. 1776/1976. *An Inquiry into the Nature and Causes of the Wealth of Nations.* Oxford: Oxford University Press.

Smith, Alastair. 1995. 'Alliance Formation and War', *International Studies Quarterly* 39(4): 405–426.

Smith, Alastair. 1998, 'Fighting Battles, Winning Wars', *Journal of Conflict Resolution* 42(2): 301–320.

Smith, Peter H. 1993. 'The Politics of Integration: Concepts and Themes', in Peter H. Smith, ed., *The Challenges of Integration.* New Brunswick, NJ: Transaction Publishers, 1–14.

Smith, Ron P. 1980. 'Military Expenditure and Investment in OECD Countries 1954–73', *Journal of Comparative Economics* 4(1): 19–32.

Snidal, Duncan. 1991a. 'Relative Gains and the Pattern of International Cooperation', *American Political Science Review* 85(3): 701–726.

Snidal, Duncan. 1991b. 'International Cooperation among Relative Gains Maximizers', *International Studies Quarterly* 35(4): 387–402.

StataCorp. 1997. *Stata Statistical Software, Release 5.0.* College Station, TX: Stata Corporation.

Stein, Arthur A. 1990. *Why Nations Cooperate.* Ithaca, NY: Cornell University Press.

Stein, Arthur A. 1993. 'Governments, Economic Interdependence, and International Cooperation', in Philip E. Tetlock, Jo L. Husbands, Robert Jervis, Paul C. Stern, and Charles Tilly, ed., *Behavior, Society, and Nuclear War*, vol. 3. New York: Oxford University Press, 241–324.

Stigler, George. 1971. 'The Theory of Economic Regulation', *Bell Journal of Economics and Management Science* (2): 137–146.

Strange, Susan. 1996. *The Retreat of the State: The Diffusion of Power in the World Economy*. Cambridge: Cambridge University Press.

Sueyoshi, Glenn T. 1995. A Class of Binary Response Models for Grouped Duration Data', *Journal of Applied Econometrics* 10(4): 411–431.

Summers, Robert and Alan Heston. 1988. 'A New Set of International Comparisons of Real Product and Price Estimates for 130 Countries, 1950–1985', *Review of Income and Wealth* 34(1): 1–26.

Summers, Robert and Alan Heston. 1991. 'The Penn World Table (Mark 5): An Expanded Set of International Comparisons, 1950–1988', *Quarterly Journal of Economics* 106(2): 327–368.

Summers, Robert, Alan Heston, Daniel A. Nuxoll, and Bettina Aten. 1995. *The Penn World Table (Mark 5.6a)*. Cambridge, MA: National Bureau of Economic Research.

*The Economist*. 1998. 'Germany: Is There a Breaking Point?' *The Economist* 346 (8054): 34–35.

*The Economist*. 2000. 'Survey: Globalisation and Tax', *The Economist* 354 (8155): 1–18 (after page 70).

Theis, Wallace J. 1987. 'Alliances and Collective Goods: A Reappraisal', *Journal of Conflict Resolution* 31(2): 298–332.

Theurl, Theresia. 1999. 'Globalisierung als Selektionsprozeß ordnungspolitischer Paradigmen' [Globalization as a Selection Process for Socio-Economic Order Paradigms], in Hartmut Berg, ed., *Globalisierung der Wirtschaft: Ursachen – Formen – Konsequenzen*. Berlin: Duncker & Humblot, 23–49.

Thurston, Charles W. 1995. 'Closer Trade Links Forged with Europe', *Journal of Commerce* (December 4): 6C.

Tinbergen, Jan. 1962. *Shaping the World Economy: Suggestions for an International Economic Policy*. New York: Twentieth Century Fund.

Tullock, Gordon. 1980. 'Efficient Rent-Seeking', in J. M. Buchanan, R. D. Tollison and Gordon Tullock, ed., *Toward a Theory of Rent-Seeking Society*. College Station, TX: Texas A&M University Press, 97–112.

Ursprung, Heinrich. 2000. 'Die Modellierung endogener Handelpolitik: "The Rake's Progress"' [The Modeling of Endogenous Trade Policies], *Aussenwirtschaft* 55(1): 85–119.

U.S. ACDA. 1992. *World Military Expenditures and Arms Trade*. Washington, DC: United States Arms Control and Disarmament Agency. Ann Arbor, MI: Interuniversity Consortium for Political and Social Research.

van den Berg, Hendrik. 1996. 'Trade as the Engine for Growth in Asia: What the Econometric Evidence Reveals', *Journal of Economic Integration* 11(4): 510–538.

Vanhanen, Tatu. 2000. 'A New Dataset for Measuring Democracy, 1810–1998', *Journal of Peace Research* 37(2): 251–265.

Vasquez, John A. 1993. *The War Puzzle*. New York: Cambridge University Press.

Vasquez, John A. 1995. 'Why Do Neighbors Fight? Proximity, Interaction, or Territoriality', *Journal of Peace Research* 32(3): 277–294.

Viner, Jacob. 1937. *Studies in the Theory of International Trade*. New York: Harper & Brothers.

Väyrynen, Raimo. 1997. *Global Transformation. Economics, Politics, and Culture.* Helsinki: Sitra.

Vousden, Neil. 1990. *The Economics of Trade Protection.* Cambridge: Cambridge University Press.

Wade, Robert. 1996. 'Globalization and Its Limits: Reports of the Death of the National Economy Are Greatly Exaggerated', in Suzanne Berger and Ronald Dore, ed., *National Diversity and Global Capitalism.* Ithaca, NY: Cornell University Press, 60–88.

Wagner, Harrison. 2000. 'Bargaining and War', *American Journal of Political Science* 44(3): 469–484.

Wagner, R. Harrison. 1986. 'The Theory of Games and the Balance of Power', *World Politics* 38(4): 546–576.

Wagner, R. Harrison. 1993. 'What Was Bipolarity?' *International Organization* 47(1): 76–106.

Wagner, R. Harrison. 1994a. 'Peace, War, and the Balance of Power', *American Political Science Review* 88(3): 593–607.

Wagner, R. Harrison. 1994b. 'Peace and the Balance of Power in a Three–State World'. Paper presented at the 90th Annual Meeting of the American Political Science Association, New York, 1–4 September.

Wagner, R. Harrison. 2000. 'Bargaining and War', *American Journal of Political Science* 44(3): 469–484.

Wallace, William. 1994. *Regional Integration: The Western European Experience.* Washington, DC: Brookings.

Wallensteen, Peter. 1973. *Structure and War: On International Relations 1920–1968.* Stockholm: Rabén & Sjögren.

Wallensteen, Peter and Margareta Sollenberg. 2001. 'Armed Conflict, 1989–2000', *Journal of Peace Research* 38(5): 629–644.

Waltz, Kenneth. 1970. 'The Myth of National Interdependence', in Charles P. Kindleberger, ed., *The International Corporation.* Cambridge, MA: MIT Press, 205–223.

Waltz, Kenneth. 1979. *Theory of International Politics.* New York: McGraw-Hill.

Waltz, Kenneth N. 1999. 'Globalization and Governance', *PS: Political Science & Politics* 32(4): 693–700.

Waltz, Kenneth N. 2000. 'Globalization and American Power', *National Interest* (59): 46–56.

Ward, Michael D. 1981. 'Seasonality, Reaction, and Conflict in Foreign Policy Behavior', *International Interaction* 8(2): 229–245.

Ward, Michael D. 1987. 'Cargo Cult Science and Eight Fallacies of Comparative Political Research', *International Studies Notes* 13(1): 75–77.

Ward, Michael D. 1995. Review of *Allies, Adversaries and International Trade* by Joanne Gowa, *American Political Science Review* 89(4): 802–803.

Ward, Michael. 2002. 'Green Binders in Cyberspace: A Modest Proposal', *Comparative Political Studies* 35(1): 46–51.

Ward, Michael D. and Sheen Rajmaira. 1992. 'Reciprocity and Norms in US–Soviet Foreign Policy', *Journal of Conflict Resolution* 36(2): 342–368.

Ware, J. H., S. Lipsitz, and F. E. Speizer. 1988. 'Issues in the Analysis of Repeated Categorical Outcomes', *Statistics in Medicine* 7(2): 95–107.

Way, Christopher. 1997. *Manchester Revisited: A Theoretical and Empirical Evaluation of Commercial Liberalism.* PhD dissertation, Stanford University. Stanford, CA.

Weede, Erich. 1986. 'Income Inequality and Violence Reconsidered', *American Sociological Review* 51(3): 438–441.

Weede, Erich. 1995. 'Economic Policy and International Security: Rent-Seeking, Free Trade and Democratic Peace', *European Journal of International Relations* 1(4): 519–537.

Weede, Erich. 1996. *Economic Development, Social Order and World Politics*. Boulder, CO: Lynne Rienner.

Weede, Erich. 1999a. 'Kapitalismus und Solidarität, Arbeit und Wachstum in westlichen Industriegesellschaften: Einfache Berechnungen und widersprüchliche Resultate' [Capitalism and Solidarity, Labour and Growth in Western Industrial Societies: Simple Calculations and Contradictory Results], *Zeitschrift für Politik* 46(1): 30–49.

Weede, Erich. 1999b. 'Capitalism, Democracy and Peace', in Gustaaf Geeraerts and Patrick Stouthuysen, ed., *Democratic Peace for Europe. Myth or Reality?* Brussels: VUB Press, 61–73.

Weede, Erich. 1999c. 'The Political Economy of Asian Reunification Issues. China and Korea', *Korea and World Affairs* 23(4): 558–578.

Weede, Erich. 2000. *Asien und der Westen* [Asia and the West]. Baden-Baden: Nomos.

Werner, Suzanne. 1997. 'In Search of Security: Relative Gains and Losses in Dyadic Relations', *Journal of Peace Research* 34(3): 289–302.

Whalley, John. 1998. 'Why Do Countries Seek Regional Trade Arrangements?' in Jeffrey A. Frankel, ed., *The Regionalization of the World Economy*. Chicago, IL: University of Chicago Press, 63–83.

Wilson, Woodrow. 1918. *Bases of a General Peace: Fourteen Points*. Address to a Joint Session of the United States Congress, 8 January.

Wittman, Donald. 1979. 'How a War Ends: A Rational Model Approach', *Journal of Conflict Resolution* 23(4): 741–761.

Wood, Adrian. 1994. *North–South Trade, Employment and Inequality*. Oxford: Clarendon.

World Bank. 1999. *World Development Indicators*. Washington, DC: World Bank Group.

World Event Interaction Survey (WEIS). 1993. *Coding Manual*, 6th revision, revised by Rodney G. Tomlinson, Department of Political Science, US Naval Academy, MD.

Wright, Robert. 2000. 'Will Globalization Make You Happy?' *Foreign Policy* (120): 55–64.

WTO. 1995. *Regionalism and the World Trading System*. Geneva: World Trade Organization.

Yarbrough, Beth V. and Robert M. Yarbrough. 1992. *Cooperation and Governance in International Trade: The Strategic Organizational Approach*. Princeton, NJ: Princeton University Press.

Yeats, Alexander. 1978. 'On the Accuracy of Partner Country Trade Statistics', *Oxford Bulletin of Economics and Statistics* 40(1): 341–361.

Yeats, Alexander. 1990. 'On the Accuracy of Economic Observations: Do Sub-Saharan Trade Statistics Mean Anything?' *World Bank Economic Review* 4(2): 135–156.

Zorn, Christopher J. W. 2001. 'Generalized Estimating Equation Models for Correlated Data: A Review with Applications', *American Journal of Political Science* 45(2): 470–490.

# Index

# About the Contributors

**Charles H. Anderton** received a Ph.D. in economics from Cornell University and is professor of economics at the College of the Holy Cross. His research interests include theoretical models of trade and conflict and conflict economics.

**Katherine Barbieri** received a Ph.D. in political science from Binghamton University. She is an assistant professor at Vanderbilt University and is the author of *The Liberal Illusion: Does Trade Promote Peace?* (2002). Her research interest lies in international trade and conflict.

**Nathaniel Beck** received a Ph.D. from Yale University. He is a professor at the University of California, San Diego and the editor of *Political Analysis*. His research interests include econometric methods, particularly time-series–cross-section data.

**John R. Carter** received a Ph.D. in economics from Cornell University and is currently professor of economics at the College of the Holy Cross. His research interests include experimental economics and conflict economics.

**Han Dorussen** received a Ph.D. in government from the University of Texas at Austin. He has been a lecturer at the Norwegian University of Science and Technology (NTNU) in Trondheim and is presently a lecturer at the University of Essex. He is associate editor for *Journal of Peace Research*. His research interests include formal theory, international relations, and international political economics.

**Erik Gartzke** received a Ph.D. from the University of Iowa and is an assistant professor at Columbia University. His research interests include formal and quantitative international relations, the liberal peace, and perceptions and international politics.

**Ranveig Gissinger** received an M.A. in political science at the Norwegian University of Science and Technology (NTNU).

**Nils Petter Gleditsch** received an M.A. in sociology from the University of Oslo. He is a research professor at the International Peace Research Institute, Oslo (PRIO) and editor of *Journal of Peace Research*. He is adjunct professor of political science at the Norwegian University of Science and Technology (NTNU). His most recent books in English include *The Peace Dividend* (coeditor, 1996) and *Conflict and the Environment* (editor, 1997).

**Håvard Hegre** is a candidate for a Ph.D. in political science at the University of Oslo. He is presently an economist for The World Bank and is on leave from the University of Oslo and the International Peace Research Institute, Oslo (PRIO).

**Jack S. Levy** received a Ph.D. in political science at the University of Wisconsin. He is a Board of Governors' Professor at Rutgers University. His research interests include balance of power and balancing, preventive war, interdependence and war, prospect theory, political oppositions and war, and evolution and war.

**Quan Li** received a Ph.D. in political science at Florida State University and he is an assistant professor at Pennsylvania State University. His research interests include effects of economic globalization on conflict, democracy and income inequality, causes of capital control liberalization, trade and conflict, and macroeconomic policy coordination.

**Edward D. Mansfield** received a Ph.D. in political science at the University of Pennsylvania. He is Hum Rose Professor of Political Science and director of the Christopher H. Browne Center for International Politics at the University of Pennsylvania. His research interests include the political economy of regionalism and the causes of international conflict.

**James D. Morrow** received a Ph.D. in political science at the University of Rochester. He is professor of political science and senior research scientist at the Center for Political Studies at the University of Michigan, Ann Arbor. He is the author of *Game Theory for Political Scientists* (1994).

**John R. Oneal** received a Ph.D. in political science at Stanford University and is professor of political science at the University of Alabama. He is the coauthor (with Bruce Russett) of *Triangulating Peace* (2001) and has published articles in *American Sociological Review, International Organization, International Studies Quarterly, Journal of Conflict Resolution,* and *World Politics,* among others.

**Jon C. Pevehouse** received a Ph.D. in political science at Ohio State University. He is assistant professor of political science at the University of Wisconsin-Madison and the author of articles appearing in *International Organization, American Political Science Review, American Journal of Political Science,* and *Journal of Conflict Resolution.*

**Solomon W. Polachek** received a Ph.D. in economics at Columbia University. He was assistant and associate professor at the University of North Carolina, Distinguished Professor at the State University of New York at Binghamton/Binghamton University, and Dean of Harpur College of Arts and Sciences at Binghamton University. He is coeditor of *Peace Economics, Peace Science and Public Policy* and associate editor of *Conflict Management and Peace Science.* His research interests include international interactions and economic interdependence.

**Rafael Reuveny** received a Ph.D. in business economics and public policy and a Ph.D. in political science at Indiana University. He is an associate professor at Indiana University and his main interests include international political economy of trade and economic growth, environmental security, sustainable development, and Arab–Israeli conflict and peace.

**Bruce Russett** received a Ph.D. in political science at Yale University. He is Dean Acheson Professor of International Relations at Yale University and editor of *Journal of Conflict Resolution.* His research interests include the Kantian peace, civil war, and other political influences on health.

**Gerald Schneider** received a Ph.D. in political science at the University of Zurich. He is professor of political science in the Department of Politics and Management at the University of Konstanz. He is the executive editor of *European Union Politics.* His research interests include decision making in the European Union, foreign economic liberalization, and civil war.

**Günther G. Schulze** received a Ph.D. and Venia Legendi in economics at the University of Konstanz. He is professor of economics at the University of Freiburg and has made contributions in international economics, environmental economics, and political economy.

**Erich Weede** received a Ph.D. and Venia Legendi in political science at the University of Mannheim. He was professor of sociology at the University of Cologne until 1997 and is presently professor of sociology at the University of Bonn. He is author of *Economic Development, Social Order, and World Politics* (1996) and *Asien und der Westen* (2000).